SYNC OR SWARM

SYNC OR SWARM

IMPROVISING MUSIC IN A COMPLEX AGE

David Borgo

Accompanied by sound disc.
Inquire at the Multimedia Center
Service Desk.

continuum

NEW YORK • LONDON

2005

The Continuum International Publishing Group Inc
15 East 26 Street, New York, NY 10010

The Continuum International Publishing Group Ltd
The Tower Building, 11 York Road, London SE1 7NX

www.continuumbooks.com

Printed in the United States of America

Library of Congress Cataloging-in-Publication Data

Borgo, David.
    Sync or swarm : improvising music in a complex age / David Borgo.
       p.   cm.
    Includes bibliographical references (p.) and index.
    ISBN 0–8264–1729–9 (hardcover : alk. paper)
    1. Free jazz—History and criticism.   2. Free jazz—Analysis,
apperciation.   3. Improvisation (Music)   I. Title.
    ML3506.B67   2005
    781.65'5136—dc22   2005013289

For my wife, Sylvia, and our son, Diego,
whose birth has made the notion of emergence
both more real and more wondrous

CONTENTS

CONTENTS

LIST OF FIGURES

ix

LIST OF FIGURES

LIST OF AUDIO EXAMPLES

Evan Parker

1. *Conic Sections 3* (25:10)
   —Evan Parker, solo soprano saxophone
   ■ Recorded live at Holywell Music Room, Oxford (UK), June 21, 1989
   ■ Released by AhUm Records 015 (CD), 1993
   ■ Courtesy of Evan Parker and AhUm Records

The Sam Rivers Trio with special guest *George Lewis*

2. *Spark/Nightfall/Delve* (10:34)
   —Sam Rivers, tenor saxophone
   —Doug Mathews, electric and acoustic bass
   —Anthony Cole, drums and piano

3. *Sketch* (2:23)
   —Sam Rivers, soprano saxophone
   —Doug Mathews, bass clarinet
   —Anthony Cole, tenor saxophone

4. *Release* (5:49)
   —Doug Mathews, acoustic bass

5. *Glimpse* (7:32)
   —Sam Rivers, piano
   —Doug Mathews, acoustic bass
   —Anthony Cole, drums

6. *Sprout* (2:32)
   —Sam Rivers, tenor saxophone
   —George Lewis, trombone

7. *Source* (4:53)
   —Sam Rivers, piano
   —George Lewis, trombone
   —Doug Mathews, acoustic bass
   —Anthony Cole, drums
   ■ Recorded live at UCSD, March 8, 2004
   ■ Previously Unreleased
   ■ Courtesy of the Sam Rivers Trio, Rivbea Music, and George Lewis

Surrealestate

• Performances feature the following personnel unless otherwise noted:
  —Gustavo Aguilar, percussion
  —David Borgo, tenor and soprano saxophones
  —Roman Cho, percussion and lap steel guitar
  —Andy Connell, clarinet, soprano and alto saxophones
  —Jonathon Grasse, electric guitar
  —Kaye Lubach, tabla and percussion
  —David Martinelli, drums
  —Brana Mijatovic, drums
  —Robert Reigle, tenor saxophone

8. *Contrafactum in the spirit of Weddell Seals* (3:04)

9. *Sync or Swarm* (6:31)
  —David Borgo, alto saxophone
  —Andy Connell, soprano saxophone
  —Robert Reigle, tenor saxophone

10. *FQP* (1:16)

11. *Contrafactum in the spirit of Giacinto Scelsi* (2:34)

12. *Contrafactum in the spirit of John Sheppard* (2:16)
  ▪ Recorded at UCLA, 1999
  ▪ Released by Acoustic Levitation Al-1004 (CD), 2000
  ▪ Courtesy of Surrealestate and Acoustic Levitation

Total Time: 74:38

ACKNOWLEDGMENTS

Although writing a book may at first appear akin to the process of musical composition—both involve relative isolation, the possibility for revision, and a rather drawn out time scale for completion—for me it has felt like an extended improvisation, and in a very real sense, a collective one. As in musical improvisation, one draws on a lifetime of experience and training, but all in service of that elusive and often fleeting moment when an idea or connection is newly forged or a creative direction presents itself for further exploration. From one perspective, the dialogic process of scholarship happens at a far slower pace than that of improvised music, but both involve formative experiences with mentors, considerable time spent exploring and internalizing the work of others, and the lengthy and ongoing process of developing one's own approach or expertise. Like the excitement of a good improvised performance, some of the most fortuitous and mysterious moments during the research process can happen without warning or explanation: when you glimpse the perfect book two shelves up from the one you came to the library to find, or when you encounter a colleague at the coffee shop or on the bandstand who suggests a line of inquiry or makes a pithy remark that leaves a lasting impact on your thinking.

Good improvisation relies on this serendipity. As I worked on different sections of the book, sometimes two or three at a time, new ideas and new collaborations arose that often provoked a conceptual change or expansion, triggered the development of entirely new sections or rewrites of older ones, or just as often ended up going nowhere. Much as in improvisation, great ideas come and go, often without being given their proper due, while others may linger well past their period of usefulness. Still others might initially appear to have little promise, but can, over time, surprise with their nuance or provocative implications. Although the finished product of a book can belie this dynamic process of discovery, in fascinating ways, the process of looking, perceiving, understanding, and describing arise together and shape each other. For me, this book has been about a journey, not about arriving at a final destination. The resoundingly social nature of collectively improvised music means that it has the power to inspire and to infuriate, at times in equal measure; I can hope for no less or no more for my own work.

ACKNOWLEDGMENTS

In addition to the numerous authors and musicians mentioned in the text whose work has left an indelible mark on my own thinking, I would like to thank the following individuals who have graciously offered guidance, feedback, and/or collaboration through the years. As the now-clichéd riff goes, any shortcomings should be viewed as my own rather than inherent in the work of others. Joseph Goguen and Rolf Bader both gave willingly of their time and expertise to produce the collaborative work found in chapters four and five, respectively. Keith Sawyer, David Ake, Pantelis Vasilakis, Robert Reigle, Evan Parker, Bertram Turetzky, and Shlomo Dubnov all read a draft of the manuscript and offered thorough and insightful feedback, for which I am extremely grateful. Timothy Rice, Robert Walser, Katherine Hayles, Roger Savage, Cheryl Keyes, Ali Jihad Racy, Joe DiStefano, Roger Kendall, Steve Loza, and Jacqueline DjeDje provided exceptional guidance during my graduate studies at UCLA. Chuck Dotas and David Pope were outstanding colleagues and good friends at James Madison University. And my colleagues at UCSD, both past and present, have generously offered support and feedback, in particular, George Lewis, Bertram Turetzky, Anthony Davis, and Mark Dresser. Other musicians who have selflessly shared their time and energy with me to discuss this work include: Lisle Ellis, Sam Rivers, Adam Rudolph, Ralph "Buzzy" Jones, and Kevin Eubanks.

The writing of this book was made possible by grants from the Center for Humanities and the Faculty Career Development Center at UCSD. An earlier version of chapter two appeared in *Black Music Research Journal* vol. 22 no. 2 (2004). Portions of chapter three will appear in the edited volume *Playing Changes: New Jazz Studies* (Robert Walser, editor, Duke University Press, 2006). And chapter four appears in a slightly altered form in the IAJE Jazz Research Proceedings Yearbook vol. 25 (2005). I wish to thank these journals and presses for allowing me to include that work here.

Additionally, I would like to thank my musical mentors who, through their shining artistry and example, have profoundly shaped my understanding of, and respect for, the traditions of jazz and improvised music: Larry Aversano, David Baker, Dominic Spera, David Liebman, Kenny Burrell, Gerald Wilson, Garnet Brown, Roberto Miranda, and Billy Higgins. Special thanks go to the many wonderful musicians with whom I have had the good fortune to perform: many are famous, others are not, but all are exemplary in their passion and commitment to the art. To Robert Reigle and all of the musicians who made up the collective Surrealeste I owe a profound debt for their boundless spirits filled with the joy of exploration and the gift of empathy. David Barker, my editor at Continuum, has been a joy to work with, and Gabriella Page-Fort, his assistant, did a superb job of copyediting and preparing the manuscript. Finally, I would like to give special thanks to my parents, Suzi and Peter Borgo, and to the rest of my family, without whose support none of this would have been possible.

PREFACE

I find I do some of my best thinking on airplanes. The romantic in me likes to think that floating above the clouds allows my thinking to become untethered from its normal cycles, habits, and conventions. Perhaps a more down-to-earth explanation, however, is simply that with the complexity and congestion of our daily lives, long flights offer one of the few uninterrupted stretches of time with which to read and contemplate.

It was on an eighteen-hour flight from Los Angeles to Yerevan, Armenia, in the summer of 1995. At the time I was a graduate student studying ethnomusicology at UCLA and I was a teaching assistant and performer in the jazz program. Under the auspices of an exchange program between the university and the Yerevan Symphony, our jazz quartet was invited to travel to Armenia to give a series of concerts at Khatchaturian Philharmonic Hall. The group included myself on saxophones, David Ake on piano, Todd Sickafoose on bass, and David Whitman on drums; friends affectionately knew us as "The Three Daves Plus Todd."

For the flight, I brought along a copy of the book *Complexity*, by Michael M. Waldrop, a Christmas present from my parents that, with all my graduate coursework, I had not gotten around to reading.[1] The book explains for general readers the emerging science of complexity and the internal workings of the Santa Fe Institute. My parents—New Mexicans at heart despite their many years spent on the East Coast—thought Waldrop's descriptions of the institute would be interesting and that these new scientific ideas might rekindle an early love affair of mine with the sciences. They were right.

Back in high school—before I started skipping my calculus classes to practice Charlie Parker solos—I was fascinated by the then-new ideas of artificial intelligence and had been accepted into the program in computer engineering at Carnegie Mellon University. But bebop rather than circuit boards was to be my immediate calling. My first saxophone teacher, Larry Aversano, early in my studies gave me a copy of the *Omnibook*, a well-known collection of Charlie Parker solos transcribed from his Savoy and Dial recordings. I proceeded to practice diligently from the book as if the notes contained within were no different than the other saxophone exercises with which I was familiar, working over examples with odd names like "Ornithology" or "Moose the

Mooche" until my fingers could at least approximate even the most rapid and angular musical passages. I enjoyed the melodic and rhythmic intricacy of the music—its daunting technical challenge—but at that time I could not fathom how these complicated solos were "composed" in the heat of the moment nor how Parker's playing on a given tune could and would differ dramatically from night to night. Since that time the idea of in-the-moment creativity has become an overriding interest in my life.

I declined the offer from Carnegie Mellon and chose instead to pursue a jazz performance degree at Indiana University. After four years of intense "wood shedding" under the tutelage of respected jazz educator David Baker, I embarked on a career as a professional touring saxophonist that took me throughout the United States and to various parts of Europe and Latin America and to the Middle and Far East. Along the way I became fascinated by the variety of cultures I encountered and, in particular, by the diverse musical traditions to which I was being exposed. I returned to school to pursue a Ph.D. in ethnomusicology, by this point my fledgling interest in the sciences a thing of the distant past.

Early in my graduate studies I pursued coursework in the musical traditions of Latin America and Asia and I developed some basic proficiency on the Japanese shakuhachi (flute) and the Indian sitar. My overriding interest in improvisation, however, continued to provide a thread that bound together my disparate pursuits. As my musical horizons were expanding outward, my studies in the discipline of ethnomusicology also provided me with a more nuanced understanding of the complex cultural web that informs all modes of human expression. As a result, I found myself pulled deeper into the vast history of jazz and African-American music and the traditions of improvising with which I felt most at home. Many jazz musicians have historically been very welcoming of non-Western influences. Since the 1960s, these proclivities have only continued to grow in magnitude and scope. I was, of course, already aware of the important work of John Coltrane and others in this regard, but at UCLA I began to investigate in much greater detail the "freer" approaches to improvisation that had emerged in the 1960s and had continued to develop since that time, often well under the radar of the increasingly conservative jazz community.

Through some fortuitous friendships with other interested ethnomusicologists and musicians, I began to play regularly in an improvising collective called Surrealestate, an exciting and eclectic grouping of performers with backgrounds ranging from "new music" composition and modern jazz, to popular, electronic, and various non-Western musics. This diverse yet surprisingly cohesive group met on a weekly basis for nearly six years to explore the practice of improvising music together. These hands-on experiences exploring new musical possibilities, and the particular challenges of doing so within a large and disparate social group, have played an incalculable roll in my understanding of the process of collective improvisation.

My first realization as a performer in this expanded musical realm was that one couldn't rely on the forms, harmonies, and conventions of mainstream jazz, practices that had consumed much of my early apprenticeship years. Yet, as the members of Surrealestate became more comfortable playing with each other, it was equally clear that distinct forms and practices *were* emerging and becoming an important part of our collective identity. Not only did the personnel and instrumentation of the group self-organize to a great degree, as word spread between friends and colleagues about our weekly "sessions," but also the musical terrain and our collective approach to it seemed to congeal with little to no discussion and no strong leadership. With less shared musical experience and agreed-upon musical "vocabulary," the members of Surrealestate began to develop a keen ear for each other's strengths and particular tendencies, an attitude open to unpredictable combinations and experiences, and an outlook filled with collective empathy. I soon realized that the "freedom" inherent in free improvisation is not an "anything goes" type of anarchy, but involves collective discovery in a communal environment and a mode of personal liberation made possible through cooperation and mutual respect.

On that long flight to Armenia, and while Surrealestate was only in its infancy, I read about "The Emerging Science at the Edge of Order and Chaos." Modern science has traditionally sought to take complex systems apart in order to discover their fundamental parts; for instance, to discover the smallest building blocks of matter, or more recently the makeup of the human genome. Reductionism has been enormously successful in helping to explain how complex things are made up of lots of simpler things. But it cannot, by itself, answer important questions regarding how things interact in complex ways to produce striking simplicities; the simplicities of form, function, and behavior. Here I was reading about a new breed of scientist not simply interested in taking things apart, but in understanding how things come together; how diverse systems display collective behaviors that are not predictable in terms of the dynamics of their component parts. As an improvising musician interested in human creativity and collective dynamics, Waldrop's book was striking a chord with me. I read on.

In the book, Waldrop describes scientific work on topics ranging from the origins of life and the workings of the mind, to the unpredictable dynamics of political and social groups and the unnerving disruptions of the stock market. It was not the exact nature of the topics under discussion that caught my attention, but rather the fact that these seemingly unrelated systems might have anything in common at all. I was also intrigued that this wide-ranging and somewhat unconventional approach to science seemed to be gaining momentum. This was the first I had heard of chaos theory.

Chaos, in its everyday usage, is synonymous with disorder or even randomness. I soon learned, however, that chaos in its scientific sense describes an orderly-disorder in which extraordinarily intricate and unpredictable behaviors can arise from extremely simple dynamical rules. Like many, my first glimpse at the fractal diagrams now made famous by chaos theory produced a deeply felt aesthetic response. But it is not their complexity—or not only their complexity—that is fascinating. Rather it is their remarkably ordered and eerily familiar simplicity—or is it simplexity?—that makes them captivating and provocative. Waldrop's descriptions of the science of complexity spoke of systems poised on "the edge of chaos," never quite locking into place nor dissolving into complete turbulence; systems that could self-organize and adapt to a constantly shifting environment. "The edge of chaos," he writes, "is where new ideas . . . are forever nibbling away at the edges of the status quo, and where even the most entrenched old guard will eventually be overthrown. . . . The edge of chaos is the constantly shifting battle zone between stagnation and anarchy, the one place where a complex system can be spontaneous, adaptive, and alive."[2] I can think of no better definition of improvised music.

1

The Sound and Science of Surprise

Surprises play with our expectations, our sense of order and disorder. They are neither predictable nor unpredictable in their entirety. Randomness does not produce a sense of surprise, but rather confusion, dismay, or disinterest. And small departures from an orderly progression, if insufficiently interesting or dramatic, will pass without much notice. Surprises are by definition unexpected, and yet those that most capture our interest or delight have a feeling of sureness about them once experienced.

In 1959, Whitney Balliett, the longtime critic for *The New Yorker* magazine, published a book of essays on jazz that memorably described the music as "the sound of surprise." Balliett heard in jazz the unpredictable and the astonishing: qualities that continue to provide awe and wonder to performers and listeners alike. Some thirty-five years later, mathematician John L. Casti grouped a number of the emerging scientific fields—often with ominous names like catastrophe, chaos, complexity, and criticality—under the general title "The Science of Surprise."

Musicians and audiences tend to be interested in the very human surprises of individual and collective creativity. Scientists, on the other hand, are usually most comfortable investigating the surprising yet presumably manageable workings of the natural world. In the same year that Balliett fixed his memorable phrase into the jazz lexicon, C.P. Snow published a book titled *The Two Cultures*, in which he described a breakdown in communication between the sciences and the humanities, a breakdown that he considered to be a hindrance to solving (or even discussing) many of the most pressing problems the world faces. In the second edition of his work, however, Snow optimistically predicted that a "third culture" would emerge and close the communications gap between the existing two.[1]

Although much does still separate the sciences from the humanities—and some separation may always be important—the emergence of a "third culture" that would improve the communication between the two seems both immanent and eminently desirable. This book takes as its starting point the current historical and cultural moment that has afforded similar self-understandings to emerge in the sciences and in the arts—a moment in which our very ideas of order and disorder are being reconfigured and revalued in dramatic ways. I believe the methods and findings of the new sciences of surprise are useful in illuminating the dynamics and aesthetics of musical improvisation. Conversely, a better understanding of the workings of improvisation,

1

how musical techniques, relationships, and interactions are continually refined and negotiated in performance, can provide insight on how we understand the dynamics of the "natural" world and our place within it.

The idea that cultural threads can organize concurrent scientific and artistic activities is of course not entirely new. From the time of Phythagorus and Aristoxinus, connections between science and art, math and music, have been of considerable interest (although the Ancient Greeks were often more interested in timeless rather than timely connections).[2] In just the past few decades, however, developments in the natural sciences, social sciences, and humanities, all subsumed by a more encompassing change in values and perspectives, now appear poised to produce an unprecedented fusion of ideas across disciplines. In particular, contemporary scientists and artists are beginning to embrace *uncertainty*—a word that tends to evoke doubt, concern, and indecision in the Western worldview—as not only an inherent part of what they do, but more importantly as the fundamental source of novelty and surprise in the world.

During the last century, a "crisis of representation" emerged across many academic and creative disciplines as individuals were forced to abandon the notion that there exists an "absolute" or "privileged" vantage point from which observations, judgments, and analyses can be made. Artists, scholars, and scientists alike gradually shifted their focus from an overriding concern with isolated objects to the changing relationships between those objects: a shift from structures to structuring and from content to context.

In the social sciences, ideas such as history, language, and culture, once thought to have independent meaning and objective status, were repositioned as currents of thought, patterns of behavior, and malleable social and personal constructions. Heady words like post-structuralism and cultural postmodernism were invoked to describe the increasing awareness among scholars of the ethnocentric aspects of static and totalizing investigations.

In the natural and physical sciences, several dramatic new theories questioned and eventually altered the accepted view of reality. In the nineteenth century, Darwinian evolution had the effect of removing man from his privileged position in the universe and placing him firmly in the natural order of things: a natural order seemingly driven by competition and uncertainty. And the laws of thermodynamics showed that the amount of entropy, or disorder, in the universe is always increasing. Then in the early twentieth century, Einstein's relativity theory and pioneering research in subatomic physics appeared to deal a fatal blow to the existing paradigms of Euclidian regularity, Cartesian objectivity, Newtonian reducibility, and Laplacean predictability. The emerging scientific orientation implied that reality does not fundamentally consist of discrete objects in space and there can never be an exterior, objective viewpoint from which to observe.

Musical sounds and artistic sensibilities also underwent a dramatic upheaval around this time. Artists in every culture have always responded to—and have helped to shape—the then-dominant worldview. As scientists and scholars were grappling with ideas of relativity and uncertainty, many artists were questioning the permanence and certainty of their own work, choosing instead to emphasize its inherent polysemy and permeability. And the sounds of surprise provided much of the soundtrack for these turbulent and exciting times.

In the first half of the twentieth century, jazz and other African-American musics dramatically changed the sound (if not always the face) of commercial and creative music in the United States and abroad. These syncopated rhythms and improvisatory sounds prefigured many dramatic changes in both music and society. The emerging modernist (read: pan-European) traditions of composed music also underwent significant changes at this time. While some composers found inspiration in (or sought to "elevate") these exciting new strands of "popular" music, others turned toward a substantial increase in complexity, adopting serialized methods for ordering the various musical dimensions as well as more and more sophisticated ways to notate and control their increasingly complex ideas.

The pendulum, having swung as far as it seemingly could in the direction of explicitly ordered performance, then appeared to shift back toward uncertainty. At approximately the same time that jazz musicians were expanding the role and conception of improvisation in the new styles dubbed "bebop" or later the "avant-garde," "new music" composers began experimenting with less deterministic modes of ordering performance—ranging from chance operations, to graphic or intuitive instructions that afforded the performer a greater degree of musical latitude—and reviving the practice of improvisation—an essential part of earlier pan-European practice which was virtually abandoned (at least in art music circles) around the time of Beethoven.[3] Since these formative years, an eclectic group of artists with diverse backgrounds in modern jazz and classical music—and increasingly in electronic, popular, and world music traditions as well—have pioneered an approach to improvisation that borrows freely from a panoply of musical styles and traditions and at times seems unencumbered by any overt idiomatic constraints. This musical approach, often dubbed "free improvisation," tends to devalue the two dimensions that have traditionally dominated music representation—quantized pitch and metered durations—in favor of the microsubtleties of timbral and temporal modification and the surprising and emergent properties of individual and collective creativity in the moment of performance.

Approaches to free improvisation do differ enormously in their details and aesthetics—and these issues will be teased out in the next chapter—yet it is remarkable that an interest in (or reevaluation of) uncertainty in music emerges at roughly the same historical juncture as similar moves in the natural and social sciences. Katherine Hayles, in her work on the relationship between contemporary science and literature (and perhaps unaware of similar moves made in improvised music) asks the following question: "Why should John Cage become interested in experimenting with stochastic variations in music about the same time that Roland Barthes was extolling the virtues of noisy interpretations of literature and Edward Lorenz was noticing the effect of small uncertainties on the nonlinear equations that described weather formations?" Hayles argues that the work of these and other individuals takes place in a "cultural field within which certain questions or concepts become highly charged."[4] For many researchers and observers, the final decades of the last century brought to light the fact that both scientists and artists engage the world around them through networks of understanding shaped by the current cultural and historical moment.

The Age of Complexity

Ours is a complex age—one in which changes appear to be occurring at an ever-increasing rate, threatening to defy our ability to comprehend and keep pace and exerting immense and unpredictable influence on our personal and shared future. The networks of connections that link individuals, nations, and cultures are becoming more complicated and more complex. And our combined impact on local and global ecosystems is becoming more pronounced and potentially dangerous. Mark C. Taylor, in his book *The Moment of Complexity*, writes: "This is a time of transition betwixt and between a period that seemed more stable and secure and a time when, many people hope, equilibrium will be restored. . . . Stability, security, and equilibrium, however, can be deceptive, for they are but momentary eddies in an endlessly complex and turbulent flux. In the world that is emerging, the condition of complexity is as irreducible as it is inescapable."[5]

With this new age comes an increased need to understand the nature and behavior of complex systems in the physical, social, and humanistic sciences. As opposed to systems that may simply be complicated, complex systems are highly interconnected and through this array of influences and interactions they demonstrate possibilities for adaptation and emergence. In other words, complex systems are those that exhibit neither too much nor too little order. Their dynamics are hard to predict but not entirely random. In short, they offer the possibility of surprise. Complex systems tend to adapt and even self-organize in a decentralized, bottom-up fashion.

Certain aspects of bottom-up organization have been with us since at least Adam Smith's notion of decentralized markets and Charles Darwin's theory of biological evolution, but the dominant metaphor of the Industrial Revolution was undoubtedly that of the machine and of the hierarchy. With the recent development and proliferation of computer technologies, the machine metaphor has continued to hold sway over our collective imaginations. But as these technologies transform from isolated desktop assistants into portals on an increasingly networked world, new metaphors—both justified and overblown—are beginning to creep into common usage. Businesses, governments, the educational community, and artists are all scrambling to understand—and to take advantage of—the power and potential of network culture.

Although the "science of surprise" encompasses diverse work in several disciplines, certain methodological approaches and epistemological notions inform the field as a whole. In general, researchers aim to model spontaneous, self-generating order, not to discover static, reduced, and deterministic laws. Because of the findings of twentieth-century science, contemporary researchers have been forced to accept (often reluctantly) that irreducibility, irreversibility, and unpredictability are essential rather than aberrant behavior in the world. Writing specifically about chaos theory, Steven Kellert identifies three methodological concerns of contemporary science as holism, experimentalism, and diachrony. He explains, "The behavior of the system is not studied by reducing it to its parts; the results are not presented in the form of deductive proofs; and the systems are not treated as if instantaneous descriptions are complete."[6] This systemic, qualitative, and historical approach also resonates well with the methodologies of much social and humanistic research, and with current thinking in musical studies as well.

It is unfortunate that we have but a single English word, music, to describe such a vast array of ways in which to engage with this most human pursuit. We use the word music to describe not only the dynamic sounds themselves, but also the representation of sound as both audio recording and as musical notation. Christopher Small has coined a new verb, "musicking," meant to evoke taking part in any way in musical activity. He intends for it to remind us that music is at heart a dynamic and social form through which we bond with one another and create shared meanings.[7]

The static and symbolic representation of music as notation has provided an invaluable tool to composers and performers (particularly those in the Western tradition). More recently, audio recording has revolutionized the ways in which we can craft and engage with musical sound. But no static representation of music, no matter its detail or fidelity, can purport to capture the whole of musical meaning. With each new hearing or performance, new subtleties and new meanings will emerge. Each listener not only attends to different details and constructs different meanings, but she will bring to bear on her engagement with music a lifetime of personal and cultural experiences and sensibilities. As a temporal art that invokes and plays with memory, identity, and emotion in countless ways, musicking hinges on individual experience and cultural understandings and exploits both our sense of familiarity and surprise.

Our ways of investigating musical behavior and analyzing musical sound in the past have often avoided or downplayed the "sounds of surprise." Much like the way in which our previous scientific models excelled at static and reduced descriptions of physical phenomena, our traditional modes of investigating music have also excelled at illuminating its nondynamic qualities. In an often-quoted passage, Benoit Mandelbrot, the inventor of fractal geometry, eloquently commented on the impossibility of capturing nature's beauty within static Euclidian forms: "Clouds are not spheres, mountains are not cones, coastlines are not circles, bark is not smooth, nor does lightning travel in a straight line."[8] It is also impossible to capture the full beauty and complexity of musical expression in its static, Euclidian form as notation. As David Roberts wryly comments, "The score is no more the music than a recipe book is a meal."[9]

Playing and listening to music together provides a cultural space and a cognitive means through which individuals and social groups can coordinate their actions and behaviors. Improvisation, in particular, focuses special attention on these emergent qualities of performance. By referencing the scientific and cultural paradigm shift that is well underway, I intend to argue for a systems or ecological understanding of music that takes serious account of all of the following:

- Music is an event centered on the real-time production of sound; music is not an abstraction, such as a score, transcription, or recording.
- Music lives when it is heard and understood; the active, human process of listening is the essence of music. Therefore, the physical and cognitive capabilities and limitations of human listeners are crucial for analysis. What cannot be heard and understood is not (human) music.
- Music is always situated in a particular social and historical context. This context includes the location at which music production occurs, the prior musical experiences of both performers and audience, as well as their expectations and prejudices.
- The above cannot be separated from the immediate and further flung networks of performers and audience, up to and including their communities and cultures.

In summary, music is temporal, embodied, enacted, situated, social, cultural, and historical. An important goal of this book is to illuminate these aspects of music in general and, in the process, to demonstrate that the freer forms of musical improvisation, those that have often been dismissed as "chaotic" in the pejorative sense of the word, may actually reveal "chaotic dynamics" that demonstrate turbulence and coherence at the same time. Borrowing poetic language from the new sciences when commenting on a recording of free improvisation, Fred Bouchard writes: "The music's splintered fragmentation implies a new wholeness, its seeming chaos a fresh order, its complexity a ringing simplicity, its turbulence an inner peace."[10]

Surrealestate

On the afternoon of October 19, 1996, I was one of ten musicians who walked into the auditorium at the Armand Hammer Museum of Art in Los Angeles, California, to begin a performance titled "Surrealism in Music." The concert was organized in connection with an exhibit of Rene Magritte's paintings then on display in the museum's corridors. Our group, which had been meeting on a weekly basis to improvise collectively for nearly a year by that point, took on the name Surrealestate that day, a moniker that would stay with us through many more playing sessions, concerts, and an eventual compact disc release.[11] The performance at the Armand Hammer, our first real gig, brought together in nascent form many of the musical strands that the group would continue to explore and develop over the next several years.

For the concert that day we took positions, not on stage, but flanking the audience from both sides and from the back. The group included myself and Robert Reigle on saxophones, Alan Ferber on trombone, Loren Ettinger and Jonathon Grasse on electric guitars, Andrew McLean on North Indian tabla drums, Todd Sickafoose on double bass, and Gustavo Aguilar, Mark Ferber, and David Martinelli on various percussion instruments and drum set.[12] During the performance, the group explored both unscripted improvisation and pieces that were partially structured through the use of compositional schemes developed by various group members. These schemes ranged in style from scores utilizing standard or graphic notations to conceptual pieces that avoided the use of notation entirely. At one point we phoned Steven Keonig, a poet in New York City, and had him read his poem titled "Ants Eating Through Brick" over the house loudspeakers while we improvised a collective and spontaneous accompaniment. And for our finale, the ensemble performed "The Marriage of Heaven and Earth" by group member Robert Reigle, which then segued directly into his arrangement of Movement IV of "Pfhat" by Italian composer Giacinto Scelsi. Although there was no direct influence when the pieces were originally composed, both emphasize a high cluster pitchband that can serve to focus the listener's and player's attention on the sacred and the sublime.[13] To complicate matters even further, during the entire concert that afternoon, a lone boombox sat on the otherwise empty stage, playing Erik Satie's "Vexations" at a volume level only audible during the quietest moments of the performance.[14]

The name Surrealestate brings to mind the bizarre or abstract—the "surreal"—and the grounded and tangible—the "estate" or "real estate." Our musical explorations also tended to draw inspiration from both the mundane and the extraordinary, from the orderly to the disorderly. Perhaps the one thing that unified us as a group was our desire to explore the types of synergy and "orderly disorder"—the sync *and* the swarm—that often go hand in hand with improvising in such a large, diverse, and unpredictable setting. But more than that, we developed a strong bond of friendship, conviviality, and trust through our weekly sessions spent exploring musical possibilities and horizons together. The personnel and the musical direction of the group changed considerably over the five or so years that I actively met with them, and much to everyone's delight, the group has continued on even after many of the original members went separate ways.[15]

From the start, we organized in an egalitarian fashion, although saxophonist Robert Reigle did often serve as a *de facto* leader, not through any brute force, but rather through his infectious spirit and musical convictions. For our weekly sessions, all participants were encouraged to bring in sketches or designs for group improvisations, or to make suggestions as we collectively brainstormed new strategies to implement and explore. Several players, including myself, came to the group from primarily jazz backgrounds, while others had experience with Western classical music, contemporary composition, American popular musics, and various "world" music traditions, including Hindustani, Latin American, East Asian, and Balkan musics. These diverse backgrounds proved to be both an asset and a liability for the group. We reveled in interesting combinations of players, instruments, styles, and techniques, but each musician also had to confront the challenge of reconciling his or her own tradition, tastes, and personal experiences with the ongoing process of musical and community formation.[16]

We often began our weekly playing sessions with a collectively improvised performance; the only instruction, either overt or implied, was to listen first to the silence before beginning to play. After the free improvisation, the group might look over a sketch brought in by a member or establish a group conceptual design on the spot by soliciting individual suggestions. With a membership that could occasionally range in the double digits, we found that these schemes could help us to maintain direction and coherence for our sessions and performances, although many of our most cherished moments were group improvisations without a pre-established framework.

Compositions for the group ranged in scope from a few inspiring words or figures to more lengthy multipage scores employing standard European notation, either borrowed or invented graphic notations, metaphoric or conceptual instructions, or various combinations of all of these.[17] In all cases, however, the group viewed the process of composition as offering a guide or springboard to collective improvisation; and group improvisations could, in turn, lead to new compositional ideas. We also performed interpretations of the work of African-American composers such as Ornette Coleman, John Coltrane, Cecil Taylor, and Albert Ayler, as well as work from pan-European composers ranging from Guillaume de Machaut and Claudio Monteverdi to Alfred Schnittke and Giacinto Scelsi. Yet even when using an explicitly notated score, the group was predisposed to the improvisatory, and, at times, showed a strong propensity for subtle humor.[18]

More often, however, we would establish a few guiding elements prior to beginning a collective improvisation. These could be as simple as a general sense of mood, length, contour, or dynamic that we might want to explore, or they could be of a more specific or conceptual nature, such as exploring difference tones, or "vertical" or "sharp" sounds.[19] Alternately, we might choose to organize ahead of time smaller configurations within the group that could transition from one to the other: for instance, a series of trios, duos, or solos, or various combinations of these.[20] In certain cases, we adopted game-type rules to structure when, how, or how many people might play together, among other things. At other times, we explored ways in which conducted gestures might help to establish interesting ensemble dynamics or transitions. Finally, to make certain our preconceived designs stayed as "fresh" as possible, we frequently incorporated chance elements such as drawing lots just prior to a performance to establish who would perform what aspect of a piece, ensuring that all of the musicians remained on the creative edge.

An alternative to using notation of any form was to look for inspiration in other sounds, other arts, and other media. During several of our live performances we explored intermedia connections with poetry, painting, film, and even television soap operas. And the group's CD release was titled *Contrafactum*, from the plural of the word "contrafact," meaning a newly created artwork that is based in interesting and significant ways on another work.[21] Before the group recorded several of the performances that eventually comprised the CD, we listened to short excerpts from preexisting recordings and then improvised in the spirit of what we had just heard. These source recordings included excerpts of music by Cecil Taylor, John Sheppard, Giacinto Scelsi, and Korean shamans, as well as an environmental recording of Weddell seals in the Antarctic. Several of these contrafactum recorded by Surrealestate, along with a free improvisation by the three saxophonists in the ensemble, can be heard on the compact disc that accompanies this book.

Sync or Swarm

Nothing seems to raise a heated debate among musicians faster than the question of whether improvisation can be taught. In certain respects, the best way to learn about improvisation as a performer is undoubtedly to jump right in and start doing it. When I first joined the faculty at the University of California in San Diego, I was asked to teach a graduate-level performance seminar on free improvisation and was somewhat perplexed by the idea. I had studied jazz improvisation in the university setting early in my career, but many graduate students come to UCSD with a background in composed "new" music and little interest in learning the more mainstream approaches to jazz. For my Ph.D. research I had investigated the cultural and aesthetic dimensions of freer forms of improvisation, but the expectation was that this should be a performance rather than a research-based seminar. My experiences with Surrealestate had provided me with considerable experience improvising in a freer setting, but these meetings had happened outside of the traditional realm of academic coursework. There were no courses on free improvisation at UCLA where I did my Ph.D. in ethnomusicology, and there are few courses of this kind in the university setting anywhere.

Entering into this new pedagogical terrain I had no immediate models on which to draw. So I contacted George Lewis, the noted improviser, researcher, and then professor at UCSD in the Critical Studies and Experimental Practices Program.[22] George gave me a brief description of how he had handled the class in the past and managed to assuage some of my fears that an academic course on free improvisation had to be somehow different from a collective workshop. In fact his own teaching approach, indelibly influenced by his association with the AACM (Association for the Advancement of Creative Musicians) in Chicago, has always focused on this experiential approach to learning.[23]

In his response to my query, George mentioned that he often begins the class in much the same way that they used to teach swimming—throw them in the deep end and work with what naturally happens. The title of this book is a not-so-subtle riff on that idea. Improvising music most definitely has elements of that "sink or swim" attitude. There is the leap into the unknown or the uncharted, the adrenaline rush that can accompany the excitement and danger of an uncertain future, and the mandate to make something happen—to swim—or else that initial excitement may give way to fear and failure. "Sync or swarm" also refers to the delicate and exquisite dynamics that can emerge in complex systems, but only under certain conditions that require intense communication and cooperation and a shared history of interactions. It describes the critical moment at which a complex system either moves toward a state of greater fitness or is extinguished.

Improvising music hinges on one's ability to synchronize intention and action and to maintain a keen awareness of, sensitivity to, and connection with the evolving group dynamics and experiences. The most successful improvisations, to my ears, are those in which the musicians are able to synchronize, not necessarily their sounds—although this too can miraculously happen—but rather their energies, their intentions, and their moments of inspiration. During the most complex and dense passages of collective improvisation, a swarmlike quality also emerges, in which individual parts may be moving in very different directions and yet the musical whole develops with a collective purpose. The health of the community of improvisers also depends on the ability of individuals to synchronize, or come together, for an evening of musicking. Yet at the same time, improvisers must act in swarmlike ways such that new dynamics and configurations can percolate through the community, producing a delicate state in which individuals acting on their "local" information can produce complex global behavior.

I also hope that the subtitle of my book, "improvising music," can be read in multiple ways. Although the more common term "improvised music" does have the advantage of reminding us of the long and important tradition of improvised music, it tends to foreground the more static semantic construction of a "music" that has already been "improvised." I have often been struck by the fact that we describe this dynamic form of musicking-in-the-moment by attaching to it a past tense verb. By adopting the present progressive, "improvising," I hope to highlight the fact that even as I write these words (and as you read them), creative musicians are working in and around established practices and codes, *improvising* music. Although my text will not pretend to touch on all or even most of the creative sonic avenues currently under exploration, I hope that many of the cultural, aesthetic, and scientific issues that I highlight will resonate with those who are actively engaging with contemporary music in all its facets. With a slight shift of emphasis, therefore, my subtitle can also be read as improvising *music*, a play on the fact that the very notion of what we mean by "music" is continually being reshaped as we make our way through a new millennium.

Sync or Swarm looks through the lens of contemporary science to illuminate the process and practice of improvising music, and it explores the contemporary musical domain for its ability to offer a visceral engagement with emerging scientific notions of chaos, complexity, and self-organization. Before introducing the scientific side of the equation, chapter two, "Reverence for Uncertainty," presents a more thorough introduction to contemporary improvised music and the growing body of scholarship on the subject, focusing considerable attention on the cultural values and aesthetic practices that continue to be negotiated within the community of improvisers. In it, I probe important questions about the ways in which artists and involved listeners define, document, perform, experience, and evaluate this music, and I explore the historical, social, economic, political, and even spiritual dimensions of these intriguing issues. Many of the themes that are conveniently sketched out here receive additional treatment in the chapters that follow.

In one sense, the remaining chapters funnel outward in scope, from the perspective of a solo improviser, to that of a group interacting in performance and over time, and finally to the network dynamics that bind together improvisers and groups into a musical community. The final chapter on pedagogy, however, should remind us that network dynamics also affect how individuals learn and perform, completing the hermeneutic circle. From a systems perspective, all of these influences—the individual, collective, and communal—play a role at each level of description.[24] Individuals learn and develop through social experience, groups wax and wane through musical and interpersonal communication, and a community is both formed and shaped by the individuals whom it serves.

The individual chapters also present different aspects of the emerging science of surprise: starting with the cognitive domain and moving through physical, biological, and social perspectives. Yet the way we think is influenced by our biological being and by the fact that we are situated in, and continually engage with, a physical and social world. In other words, although these chapters might be envisioned as investigating separate disciplines, here too we are ultimately led to conclude that these findings and approaches are interrelated.

One of the hallmarks of ecological thinking is to regard systems as "wholes made up of wholes." Each component in a complex dynamical system is, in intriguing ways, not only interconnected but also able to maintain its own internal structure and to evolve over time. To treat the individual as merely a *part* of the improvising group denies not only his or her wholeness, but also his or her connection with, and responsibility to, the musical context and moment. To envision an improvising ensemble as the simple *addition* of individuals also misses the dynamic, interactive, and emergent qualities of performance. Finally, to examine a group or an individual in *isolation* of historical, cultural, and societal contingencies and opportunities ignores the richness of network dynamics.

Chapter three, "The Embodied Mind," focuses on the solo improviser in general and the performance practice of English saxophonist Evan Parker in particular. Describing his approach, I draw on several contemporary ideas in cognitive science that are challenging traditional notions of Cartesian dualism by demonstrating the ways in which mind, body, and environment interact. To highlight these embodied and enactive approaches to cognition, I probe issues of interest to researchers in cognitive linguistics, science studies, and general systems theory. Here, as in most of the later chapters, I aim for a middle way that takes into account the rich details of musical performance, but in so doing does not separate those details from a more comprehensive understanding of the emergent properties of music in general, and the embodied and encultured aspects of musical meaning in particular.

Chapter four, "Rivers of Consciousness," highlights ensemble dynamics in improvised performance, focusing attention on the work of African-American multi-instrumentalist Sam Rivers and his trio. The scientific aspects of this chapter move us from general systems theory to the more specific case of nonlinear dynamical systems. This work emanates from collaborative and coauthored papers with Joseph Goguen, a Professor in Computer Science and Engineering at UCSD, who has wide-ranging interests and expertise in the fields of nonlinear dynamics, cognitive science, consciousness studies, and the philosophy of music. In this chapter we explore the phase space of improvisation, focusing on the delicate group interactions that can occur during transitional moments in this complex dynamical phase space, and we pay particular attention to the ways in which listeners (both audiences and performers) attend to and process the qualitative aspects of musical performance. We illustrate these ideas with a phenomenological analysis of "Hues of Melanin," a collective improvisation by the Sam Rivers Trio featuring Cecil McBee on bass and Barry Altschul on drums.

Chapter five, "The Edge of Chaos," is both more broad and more specialized in its treatment of nonlinear dynamical systems. I investigate certain aspects of the new sciences of chaos and complexity, focusing in particular on the variety of ways in which contemporary music is articulating the emerging cultural framework of "chaotics." And in collaboration with Rolf Bader of the University of Hamburg, I apply some computer analysis of the effective fractal dimension of music to recorded examples by Evan Parker and Sam Rivers, as well as by the Art Ensemble of Chicago, Peter Brötzmann's group, and Derek Bailey. Finally, I offer some general comments in connection with current thinking in the sciences on the promising and problematic aspects of self-organization with regards to collective improvisation, illustrated by a brief discussion of a recent controversial concert event and the variety of listener responses that it provoked.

Chapter six, "Sync *and* Swarm," investigates some very recent ideas in the sciences of sync, swarm intelligence, and network theory, offering some observations about the dynamics of musical performance and community that are just appearing on the horizons of musical research. The discussion moves from instances of physical coupling and biological entrainment, through the decentralized dynamics of swarm behavior, to the complex networks that organize and affect social identity and communication. Along the way I touch on issues ranging from musical groove to human-computer interactions, from generative music making to historiography.

Networks organize and inform many aspects of our physical, biological, and social worlds, from living cells to global ecosystems, and from the dynamics of the human brain to the virtual communities of the World Wide Web. In music, networks organize not only the social world of performance (with whom you play) but also the ideascapes of musical activity (by whom you are influenced and in what directions your creativity flourishes) and the political realities of a musical community (how historical and economic factors often dictate which musicians and musical ideas gain notice and prestige). Networks make communication and community possible, but they can also concentrate power and opportunities in the hands of a few. By looking to our still nascent understandings of "small-world" networks, I explore the complex of factors that establish, maintain, expand, and can even destroy musical communities.

The final chapter, "Harnessing Complexity," highlights the ways in which learning and cognition are situated within and distributed across physical and social settings. Drawing on current research in creativity studies, ethnographic interviews with celebrated improvisers and pedagogues, as well as on my own experiences engaging with

11

improvised music in a collective setting, I propose some strategies for reconceptualizing music pedagogy in general and for harnessing the complexity of improvisation in the classroom.

Within just the last few decades, we have become increasingly aware of the social, cultural, and historical influences that affect the work and perspective of all creative individuals. Researchers and practitioners in both the arts and sciences choose to investigate topics that are deemed interesting, useful, and understandable by the prevailing cultural climate of the times and their "results" necessarily reflect their prior knowledge and their chosen mode of inquiry. Katherine Hayles expresses this sentiment succinctly: "Culture circulates through science no less that science circulates through culture."[25] Philosophers of science now commonly speculate on the broader cultural conditions that authorize or overlook certain scientific fields and modes of investigation. Stephen Kellert, for instance, argues that contemporary science "provides an occasion for investigating the interaction between our methods for gaining knowledge about the world, our notions of what that knowledge should look like, and our conceptions of what kind of world we inhabit"—a descriptive turn-of-phrase that undoubtedly rings true to many artists as well.[26]

In juxtaposing these contemporary developments and understandings, I will show that the method of modeling the natural world emerging from the "science of surprise" is *compatible* with the ways in which musicians are engaging with "the sounds of surprise," not proof of the music's inherent worth. For that, we need look no further than the community of performers and listeners who are passionately committed to this music. My comparison often occurs on the level of metaphor, but this should not be perceived as an inherent shortcoming. In fact, a growing body of scholarship in cognitive studies argues for the notion that the way we think and learn is deeply ensconced in metaphor; new understandings develop by connecting with and by extending previous knowledge and experience. We invoke metaphors when our conventional tools of language and analysis fail to adequately describe a subject or process at hand. Free improvisation confounds most conventional musicological approaches. Like any good metaphor, however, this one can only succeed based on the similarities and on the subtle tensions and new understandings that may be uncovered through the process of comparison. In so doing, we may also find correlations between the two that are more akin to homology than analogy, as well as the possibility for moving beyond metaphorical affinities to distill an explicit method that can be applied in practice.[27] *Sync or Swarm* uses the lens of the new sciences—their shifting methods, goals, and findings—to illuminate the practice and aesthetics of musical improvisation, and it probes the individual, social, and historical aspects of improvisation to illuminate the shared cultural moment in which uncertainty may be revered rather than feared.

2
Reverence for Uncertainty

We regularly face uncertainty in our daily lives. What will the weather be like this afternoon? Will I get to my destination on time with all of this traffic? Has this food been out of the refrigerator too long? And uncertainties operate on larger social and time scales as well. Is our government pursuing the right domestic and foreign policies? Can our planet withstand the environmental impact of X, Y, or Z? Will my health be such that I can still play saxophone when I'm seventy-five? Uncertainties also complicate our understanding of and engagement with the past. How did life evolve on this planet? What provoked the last ice age? What kind of person was my great, great grandmother? I wonder what Buddy Bolden really sounded like.

Out of shear necessity we often plow right through a whole host of daily uncertainties. We can't let the decision of where to go for dinner slow us down to where we get nothing accomplished that day. For other long-term or recurring uncertainties we may take steps to reduce or offset their inherent risk. For example, if the morning traffic is frequently congested and I have an important meeting that day, I may decide to leave twenty minutes ahead of my regular schedule to reduce the chances of arriving late. And I might regularly vote in local and national elections and write to my representatives in government in an attempt to influence public policy. Or I might take out an insurance plan to guard against unforeseen health or natural disasters, or start a savings plan to ensure my family's financial future.

While uncertainties often provoke concern, they also provide hope, surprise, and anticipation. For instance, we can look forward to the uncertainties of visiting new places or meeting new people, or to an unexpected twist or surprise ending in a movie or novel. We may wish the best for our family and friends in the face of an uncertain future. Or, we may simply wonder with anticipation over the sounds that we will hear at a concert that evening.

Musicians are frequently trained to reduce uncertainties. To execute a musical passage, we are told, requires precise timing, intonation, phrasing, and a whole host of expressive qualities under express control of the performer. Uncertainty is also the bane of precise ensemble playing. We need to feel certain that the clarinets will enter with the countermelody four measures after letter B or else the entire composition may be in jeopardy. The string section cannot be uncertain about where to place the pitch or which is the most desirable bowing combination. Missed entrances or imprecisely articulated passages have lost many aspiring classical musicians a spot in their desired orchestra.

But perhaps this is too dismal a picture. Musicians of all types relish certain uncertainties. The joy of making music in a large, orchestral setting comes from those unpredictable moments when the entire ensemble is phrasing perfectly together, the conductor (and perhaps even the audience) all are in sync, sharing and feeling the musical moment. Skilled musicians can continue to find new expressive possibilities in even the most practiced phrases or rehearsed repertoire.

Yet improvising musicians do more than relish the subtle uncertainties that keep a musical composition or performance feeling fresh and vital. Uncertainty is their *raison d'être*. The word "improvisation" is derived from the Latin *in*—"not"—and *provisus*—"forseen." Improvisers not only welcome but they worship the sound of surprise. They revere the uncertainties of new techniques, new conceptions, and new performance occasions, groupings, and venues. During performance, improvisers also must revere the process of exploring and negotiating uncertainties together.

Exploring Uncertainty

> A compromise between order and disorder, improvisation is a negotiation between codes and their pleasurable dismantling.[1]
>
> —John Corbett

> Free improvisation is not an action resulting from freedom; it is an action *directed towards freedom*.[2]
>
> —Davey Williams

Improvisation as an example of human creativity is somehow at the same time both mundane and mysterious. In a musical context this situation is no different. David Cope rightly points out that improvisation "must inherently exist in all music in which exact notation of every detail is not possible: therefore in all music."[3] And Derek Bailey begins his important book on the subject by writing: "Improvisation enjoys the curious distinction of being the most widely practiced of all musical activities and the least acknowledged and understood."[4]

For many (in the contemporary Western world at least), jazz represents the most thorough engagement with improvisation.[5] And for many jazz lovers, improvisation has been *the* defining trait of the music. Louis Armstrong may have been the first to demonstrate fully the individual improvisatory possibilities of jazz, but countless others have followed suit. In a frequently quoted remark when asked about "freedom" music, drummer Philly Joe Jones commented: "Everyone's been playing free. Every time you play a solo you're free to play what you want to play. That's freedom right there."[6]

The unpredictability inherent in jazz improvisation, however, has been diffused at various times in the music's history. For example, Hollywood films and the commercial swing industry of the 1930s and 1940s often severely limited the amount and type of improvisation that could take place. The modern sounds of bebop emerged during the war years at least in part as a reaction to these restrictive and homogenizing influences in the industry.

"Evolution or revolution?" has now become a clichéd question asked by jazz historians regarding the transition from swing to bebop, but the music arguably reflected both continuities with, and radical departures from, earlier jazz practice. The standard instruments of jazz were still favored, even if the preferred ensemble size shrank considerably. Several of the most common song forms (12-bar blues, 32-bar AABA) were still in common usage even if their harmonic structures, melodic phrases, and tempos were dramatically altered. The streamlined bebop combo and compositions did, arguably, represent a dramatic shift toward a more democratic musical setting that could allow for greater portions of improvisation and heightened conversational interactions, and many beboppers sought to integrate the aural, physical, and intellectual aspects of their music in performance. The musical "revolutions" initiated by Charlie Parker, Thelonious Monk, Dizzy Gillespie, Kenny Clarke, Bud Powell, and other bebop pioneers challenged the established practices of the music industry, fought against the stereotyped notions of African-American artists as "entertainers," and often carried with them strong social and political connotations in light of the emerging civil rights movement.[7]

Several revolutionary aspects of bebop jazz were expanded in the "avant-garde" styles of the late 1950s and 1960s, while many of the conventions of jazz dating from the music's earliest days—the use of uniform pulse and cyclic song forms, for instance—were challenged and even dispensed with by proponents of the "new thing." Yet, experimentation with the form and format of jazz could be heard years, if not decades, before this "official" arrival of the avant-garde.[8] In a passage that pokes fun at our desire to pigeonhole history and the emergence of new musical styles, the editors of *Gramophone-Explorations* write: "Quite when the equation of 'tune + improvisation = jazz' somehow got rearranged into 'jazz − tune = improvisation' is one of the more regularly rewritten dates in the history of modern music. . . . Furthermore, it's unlikely that any committed practitioner of free improvised music . . . would subscribe to such a facile, simplistic definition anyway."[9]

When Louis Armstrong liberated the role of the jazz soloist or Papa Jo Jones made swing music truly swing, the reverence for uncertainty in jazz was already evident. When Coleman Hawkins only fleetingly referred to the melody of "Body and Soul" he prepared the way for many more freedoms to follow. And when Charlie Parker began his improvised phrases at unusual points in the chorus structure, or Thelonious Monk used considerable dissonance and rhythmic variety in his performances, the notion that jazz was dominated by conventions was resoundingly laid to waste. Yet when Ornette Coleman offered the jazz community *Something Else* in 1958, his sound and approach did spark the curiosity, creativity, and ire of many performers and listeners. Coleman's words from the album's liner notes seem prophetic:

I think one day music will be a lot freer. The pattern for a tune, for instance, will be forgotten and the tune itself will be the pattern, and won't have to be forced into conventional patterns. The creation of music is just as natural as the air we breathe. I believe music is really a free thing, and any way you can enjoy it you should.

The impact of Coleman's music was not extensively felt until his two-and-a-half-month engagement at the Five Spot in New York City, starting in November of 1959.[10] By this point, his early use of 12-bar blues and 32-bar bop tunes had given way to a mature form of thematic improvisation that, while often still swinging in a more-or-less traditional sense, relied little on preconceived musical harmony and form. According to John Litweiler, Ornette's playing "makes clear that uncertainty is the content of life, and even things that we take for certainties (such as his cell motives) are ever altering shape and character. By turns he fears or embraces this ambiguity; but he constantly faces it, and by his example, he condemns those who seek resolution or finality as timid."[11]

For sympathetic musicians, critics, and audiences, this emphasis on uncertainty allowed for creativity unencumbered by the constricting harmonies, forms, and rigid meters of bebop and swing styles. It evoked a return to the collective practices and ideals evident in the earliest forms of jazz that emanated from New Orleans and pointed the way toward a more inclusive musical stance that could draw on insight and inspiration from the world over. To unsympathetic listeners, these uncertainties resulted only in musical mayhem devoid of the swing, melody, and harmony that made traditional jazz music so vital and technically demanding. John Corbett draws an interesting distinction between people who view free jazz as a failed experiment and those who revel in the constant experimentation of jazz:

> Jazz experiments. . . . Is the second word a noun or a verb? . . . If you see a noun then what we're talking about are discreet events in jazz history, those "experiments" that punctuate the jazz timeline like great exclamation points, or better yet, like giant question marks. . . . On the other hand, perhaps you read the word "experiments" as a verb and "jazz" as its subject. Thus, experimenting is what jazz does.[12]

Coleman's performance approach paved the way for the use of melodic improvisation and open forms not based on strict harmonic associations, but the move to sever completely ties with uniform tempo and to push the envelope of egalitarian ensemble interaction to its furthest extremes may be best witnessed in the work of Cecil Taylor. Taylor studied piano from the age of five, immersing himself in both the work of twentieth-century classical composers (through his studies at the New England Conservatory) and the improvised music tradition of African-American jazz. Litweiler writes that "his very first record [*Jazz Advance* recorded in 1956] placed him unmistakably among the jazz avant-garde, back when John Coltrane was beginning his career with Miles Davis and still discovering himself in bop; when Eric Dolphy was playing bop in Los Angeles and Ornette Coleman's cataclysmic first LP was more than two years in the offing."[13] On that album, bass player Buell Neidlinger and drummer Dennis Charles maintain standard song forms and swing feel throughout, but on the solo piano rendition of "You'd Be So Nice to Come Home To," Taylor anticipates the mature free jazz style of the 1960s and feels no need to maintain a steady pulse or standard song form.[14]

The year 1961 proved to be a pivotal year for Taylor. His father, a loving supporter of his son's activities, died that year and Taylor recalls that it triggered an introspective assessment of his creative direction. While his newly found convictions often led him to menial labor or the welfare office for financial assistance, his musical fortitude would once again set the jazz world on end. The recording *Nefertiti, The Beautiful One Has Come* marks the formation of the Cecil Taylor Unit and the unalterable trajectory of Taylor's music to move without standard song forms and uniform rhythmic pulse. The rhythmic freedom of the Unit was due in great part to the innovative drumming of Sunny Murray. Murray was, along with Milford Graves of the New York Art Quartet, one of the first jazz drummers to abandon completely the long-established timekeeping role for the instrument. His style involved countermelody rather than accompaniment, deliberate contrast instead of overt collusion. Litweiler aptly describes this new rhythmic direction:

> This music has two basic modes: ballad-rubato and whirlwind fast, seemingly as fast as the human physique can stand to play or the human ear can distinguish between notes. Here is the arrival of energy music; such tempo extremes vitiate the possibility of swing, so in the cyclone tempos, continuity is sustained by kinetic force. In fact, Cecil Taylor is introducing an entirely new concept of rhythm to jazz, in which rubato and terrifically fast speeds are not opposites but alternative aspects of a single tempo.[15]

Coleman's "harmolodic" ideas of allowing melody and harmony to share equal organizational footing rattled the jazz establishment, but Taylor's dissolution of jazz pulse and traditional swing pushed the music into vast and uncharted waters.

Centuries before the first strands of jazz music were heard in New Orleans, improvisation had been an integral part of the European art-music tradition. Not only does a tradition of keyboard improvising date to at least the Baroque period, but many of the most respected composers, including Bach, Mozart, and Beethoven, were as well known in their day as improvisers. Instrumentalists were also frequently called upon to improvise the cadenzas to sonatas in performance. According to Alan Durant, only in the nineteenth century did the word improvisation begin to acquire a negative valorization, as in "off-hand" or "spur of the moment," implying the degree of preparation to be insufficient (e.g., an improvised shelter, an improvised solution).[16] During this same period, the improvisational latitude afforded performers of classical music was radically diminished. Durant writes:

> In the development of the new concert forms of the nineteenth century, which were coupled with larger changes in conceptions of art and the artist in society, the participatory possibilities invited by earlier concert forms are displaced by individual compositions whose concern is less to act as a spring-board to creative performance by the musicians playing on any particular occasion than to record individual insights already achieved by the composer.[17]

In the early twentieth century, composed music underwent a substantial increase in complexity, particularly due to the serialization of compositional practice introduced by Arnold Schoenberg and the Second Viennese School. Beginning with a system for ordering and transforming the twelve pitch classes in the Western chromatic scale, these composers eventually designed additional systems for ordering rhythm, texture, timbre, and dynamics that could work in conjunction with the serialization of pitch.

The pendulum, having swung as far as it seemingly could in the direction of explicitly ordered performance, then appeared to shift back toward uncertainty. At approximately the same time that jazz musicians were expanding the role and conception of improvisation in their performances, improvisation appeared to resurface in the pan-European "classical" tradition after a century and a half of neglect. Composers such as John Cage (with his "indeterminate" works) and Karlheinz Stockhausen (with his "intuitive" music) left many musical details of a composition to be decided upon by the performers or through chance operations. These and other modern compositional approaches do vary considerably in their details, and individual composers often express extremely different views on the importance and validity of improvisation, but these new approaches did significantly expand the scope and definition of "composition" as a practice.[18] Some composers at this time even took to exploring the potential of improvisation on their own, in a sense conflating the act of creation and performance by removing the interpretive step from the traditional musical equation.[19]

Not only was the accepted method for musical composition being questioned, but the very nature of music and musical sound was being challenged as well. In a rather prophetic statement, John Cage remarked in a 1937 lecture titled "The Future of Music": "Whereas, in the past, the point of disagreement has been between dissonance and consonance, it will be, in the immediate future, between noise and so-called musical sounds."[20] Midcentury pioneering work with electronics further provoked this "disagreement" and composed work that employed graphical scores began to offer additional avenues for composer-performer interaction. Cornelius Cardew, one of the leading exponents of this practice and an early member of the improvising ensemble AMM, writes:

> Rather than serving as notations, many graphic scores were intended as an "inspiration" to the musicians, or as an aid to improvisation. In this sense graphic music (or musical graphics) represents a reaction *against* notation—though often preserving relics of musical notation—as opposed to graphic notation which represents a *development* of musical notation.[21]

Since these pioneering early years in both the United States and Europe, an approach to improvisation drawing on these and other traditions has emerged in the contemporary music community. A variety of names have circulated at various times and in various locales to describe this musical practice, each with its own group of adherents and each with its own semantic shortcomings.[22] The preferred terms tend to highlight the creative or progressive stance of the performers and the cutting-edge or inclusive nature of the music itself: for example, free or free-form, avant-garde, outside, ecstatic, fire or energy, contemporary or new, creative, collective, spontaneous, and so on. Stylistic references (jazz, classical, rock, world, or electronic) are variously included or excluded, as are cultural or national identity markers (Great Black Music or British Free Improvisation).

The primary musical bond shared between these diverse performers is a fascination with sonic possibilities and surprising musical occurrences and a desire to improvise, to a significant degree, both the content and the form of the performance. In other words, free improvisation moves beyond matters of expressive detail to matters of collective structure; it is not formless music making, but form-making music. Musician Ann Farber explains:

> Our aim is to play together with the greatest possible freedom—which, far from meaning without constraint, actually means to play together with sufficient skill and communication to be able to select proper constraints *in the course of the piece*, rather than being dependent on precisely chosen ones.[23]

Mike Heffley, in a recent book on free improvisation, highlights three kinds of freedom in the music: freedom-from-form, freedom-to-form, and freedom-in-form. Freedom-from-form describes the reactive process of stretching, challenging, and breaking rules and conventions that were once embraced as laws. Freedom-to-form is a proactive step in which rules, patterns, and conventions from other musical traditions, and those of idiosyncratic origin, are embraced as temporary and mutable structures or designs. Freedom-in-form, for Heffley, signifies the consummate stage as well as the point at which the process has gone full circle: "One path is chosen from among all possible, and its route, uncharted from without, has nonetheless imprinted its own order on the improvising body as a law unto itself . . . that will come in its turn to be so challenged and changed."[24]

How exactly this freedom-in-form is achieved by musicians is often a point of extreme contention. As Derek Bailey points out: "Opinions about free music are plentiful and differ widely. They range from the view that free playing is the simplest thing in the world requiring no explanation, to the view that it is complicated beyond discussion. There are those for whom it is an activity requiring no instrumental skill, no musical ability and no musical knowledge of any kind, and others who believe it can only be reached by employing a highly sophisticated, personal technique of virtuosic proportions."[25] Defining free improvisation in strictly musical terms may also potentially miss its most remarkable characteristic—the ability to incorporate and negotiate disparate perspectives and worldviews. Jason Stanyek asserts that free improvisation is above all "a fertile space for the enactment and articulation of the divergent narratives of both individuals and cultures."[26]

Authors interested in free improvisation tend to vary considerably in their approaches to the subject, producing everything from biographical and formalist work to in-depth social, cultural, and political analysis. Arguing that the arts are predominantly autonomous or self-referential discourses, some authors present the "freedom" in the music strictly in terms of varying degrees of liberation from functional harmony, metered time, and traditionally accepted performance roles and playing techniques.[27] Other authors have interpreted free jazz and free improvisation as a social and cultural response to the appropriation and exploitation of African-American music styles.[28] They focus considerable attention on the birth of the practice during the civil rights movement in the United States and on the music's place within the context of an emerging postcolonial world. Still other authors have allied themselves with Marxist or neo-Marxist critiques of hegemonic culture and have focused on free improvisation's implied critique of capitalism and its related market- and property-based economy.[29]

The diverse strands of free improvisation that have emerged since the music's formative years also challenge facile notions of shared identity or idiom. Not only has dissent raged within the jazz community since the early "assault" of Ornette Coleman and others, but the development of a distinctly European approach to free improvisation and the extreme hybridization of the music—incorporating avant-garde, electronic, non-Western, and popular music practices—combine to make generalized discussion of idiomatic qualities or shared cultural aesthetics in the music extremely difficult.[30] John Litweiler believes that, "The precedents of free improvisation . . . are in all kinds of music, and no single kind."[31]

In a special edition of the magazine *Gramaphone-Explorations* dedicated to "Counter-Currents in Modern Music," the editors write, "Music which is entirely improvised, with no overt reference to a predetermined structure, has now been with us for many years. It is often assumed to be derived from jazz. . . . The truth is that there are in fact many improvising musicians who have either worked in the jazz tradition but who see free improvisation as something else entirely, or who have abandoned jazz (often in exasperation) by choice, or who have arrived at free improvisation via avant-garde rock, electro-acoustic music or sound-art."[32]

For some, one's approach to energy, virtuosity, and stylistic inclusion or exclusion can define quite clearly one's idiomatic allegiances. Despite their many differences, the first generation of African-American free jazz musicians all seemed to share an intense approach to energy, momentum, and rhythmic drive; think of Cecil Taylor, Albert Ayler, John Coltrane, Pharoah Sanders, Henry Grimes, Archie Shepp, and Sunny Murray, among many others. The second generation of African-American pioneers, along with many European contemporaries, began to explore other ways—both more and less dense and more and less structured—of creating intensity. For even later generation improvisers, this extreme range of approaches to energy and aesthetics can provide fertile creative ground, but it also presents a point of considerable contention in the community. The spectrum of contemporary improvisation appears to be both strongly linked to the traditions of free jazz and, at the same time, increasingly open to artists with little to no jazz experience. Steve Day argues that, "Jazz always contains improvisation, but improvisation does not always contain jazz."[33] Nick Couldry describes free improvisation as "a hybrid of both classical and jazz traditions."[34] Tom Nunn elaborates on this often-mentioned connection:

> One of the common links that developed between these two traditions was instrumental virtuosity, wherein techniques expanding and extending the sonic possibilities of instruments provided the material of improvisation. The use of atonality, dense textures, asymmetrical or non-metrical rhythm, and open forms or forms derived from the music rather than imposed upon it are other examples of developments common to both jazz and the avant garde leading up to today's free improvisation.[35]

Despite any sonic similarities between the emerging avant-garde traditions, many composers were extremely critical of musical improvisation or reluctant to challenge the implied hierarchy of composer-performer-listener. For example, Luciano Berio dismissed improvisation as "a haven of dilettantes" who "normally act on the level of instrumental praxis rather than musical thought. . . . [B]y musical thought I mean above all the discovery of a coherent discourse that unfolds and develops simultaneously on different levels."[36] John Cage's frequent and well-publicized objections to improvisation also tended to revolve around the notion that it could only produce music based on habit. In conversation with Joan Retallack a month before he died, however, Cage signaled a potential change of heart: "I became interested because I had not been interested. And the reason I had not been interested was because one just goes back to one's habits. But how can we find ways of improvising that *release* us from our habits?"[37] David Toop believes that, "This suggests that Cage had not paid close attention to the kind of improvisation, from the 1960s onward, that either began, or learned through practical experience, to do exactly that."[38]

The denigrating opinions of free improvisation that were frequently expressed by respected twentieth-century composers, particularly during the music's formative years, betray a belief that musical notation is the only means to inventing complex musical structures and, by extension, the only valid measure of musical creativity.[39] This tendency to view all modes of musical expression through the formal and architectonic perspective of resultant structure is deeply entrenched in the music academy and derives in great part from a bias toward the study of pan-European composed-notated works. A story from African-American pianist Cecil Taylor highlights the issue:

> I've had musicologists ask me for a score to see the pedal point in the beginning of that piece ["Nona's Blues"]. They wanted to see it down on paper to figure out its structure, its whole, but at that point I had stopped writing my scores out . . . and the musicologists found that hard to believe, since on that tune one section just flows right into the next. That gives the lie to the idea that the only structured music that is possible is that music which is written. Which is the denial of the whole of human expression.[40]

A pronounced dichotomy between notated and improvised forms of musical creativity appears to be less apparent in the African-American creative music community. Black composers, including Olly Wilson, T. J. Anderson, Hale Smith, William Banfield, and Alvin Singleton, have incorporated improvisation into their work. While many African-American improvisers—particularly those with close ties to the Association for the Advancement of Creative Musicians (AACM)—interact with and incorporate notation in a variety of performance contexts. Trumpeter, composer, and AACM member Wadada Leo Smith, for instance, has devised an open-ended symbolic framework he now calls "Ankhrasmation," the purpose of which is "to create and invent musical ideas simultaneously utilizing the fundamental laws of improvisation and composition."[41] According to George Lewis, the definition of "composition" among African-American creative musicians can be a fluid one, "appropriating and simultaneously challenging and revising various pan-European models, dialoguing with African, Asian, and Pacific music traditions, and employing compositional methods that did not necessarily privilege either conventionally notated scores, or the single, heroic creator figure so beloved by jazz historiography."[42]

Eric Porter, in his recent book titled *What Is This Thing Called Jazz?*, focuses on the frequently neglected ideas of African-American jazz musicians and the self-conscious aspects of black cultural production. Through a close reading of texts by Charles Mingus, Abbey Lincoln, Amiri Baraka, Yusef Lateef, Marion Brown, Wadada Leo Smith, and Anthony Braxton, Porter raises many important issues about the relationship between jazz, classical, and popular musics, the role of improvisation and composition in musical creativity, and the political, economic, and spiritual dimensions of the new jazz. He, along with other recent authors, including Ajay Heble, Sherrie Tucker, and Julie Dawn Smith, also focuses the critical lens of feminist studies on this music, which has traditionally been viewed as a predominantly masculine pursuit.[43] Many jazz musicians are only now beginning to realize these embedded inequities. Anthony Braxton, for one, finds it ironic that many of the politically and spiritually aware musicians of the 1960s could also function as "chauvinist and oppressor."[44]

The frequently touted "openness" or inclusive nature of free improvisation does at times obscure the gender sensibilities and the different cultural aesthetics represented by its practitioners. George Lewis has made a strong case for a clear distinction between an "Afrological" and "Eurological" approach to this music.[45] His terms are not ethnically essential but instead refer to historically emergent social and cultural attitudes. Lewis's study focuses on the work of two towering figures of 1950s American experimental music: Charlie Parker and John Cage. Both artists continually explored spontaneity and uniqueness in their work, and Lewis argues that each musician was fully aware of the social implications of his art. The essential contrast he draws between the two lies in how they arrived at and chose to express the notion of freedom. Cage, informed by his studies of Zen and the *I Ching*, denied the utility of protest. His notion of freedom is devoid of any kind of struggle that might be required to achieve it. Parker, on the other hand, was, paraphrasing LeRoi Jones, a nonconformist in 1950s America simply by virtue of his skin color.[46] Lewis argues that for African-American musicians, "new improvisative and compositional styles are often identified with ideas of race advancement and, more important, as resistive ripostes to perceived opposition to black social expression and economic advancement by the dominant white American culture."[47] An Afrological perspective implies an emphasis on personal narrative and the harmonization of one's musical personality with social environments, both actual and possible. A Eurological perspective, on the other hand, implies either absolute freedom from personal narrative, culture, and conventions—an autonomy of the aesthetic object—or the need for a controlling or structuring force in the person and voice of a "composer."

Contemporary free improvisers often struggle with the issues implied by Lewis's Afrological/Eurological model. English guitarist Derek Bailey betrays a Eurological perspective when he describes his practice of "non-idiomatic improvisation" as a "search for a styleless uncommitted area in which to work."[48] Gavin Bryars, a celebrated English bass player and early improvising partner of Bailey, abandoned improvisation after 1966 to focus exclusively on the "aesthetic autonomy" offered by an Eurological approach to composition. Bryars argued that, "In any improvising position the person creating the music is identified with the music. . . . It's like standing a painter next to his picture so that every time you see the painting you see the painter as well and you can't see it without him."[49]

Not all European improvisers, however, favor a Eurological approach to the practice. English saxophonist Evan Parker clearly sees his approach as part of the African-American jazz tradition:

What's important to me is that my work is seen in a particular context, coming out of a particular tradition. I don't really care what people call it but I would want it to be clear that I was inspired to play by listening to certain people who continue to be talked about mainly in jazz contexts. People like John Coltrane, Eric Dolphy, Cecil Taylor—these were people that played music that excited me to the point where I took music seriously myself. That continues to be the case. That's where what I'm doing has to make sense, if it makes any sense at all.[50]

Contrasting Bailey's and Parker's approaches, British critic Ian Carr writes:

[W]ith monastic vigilance [Bailey] tries to avoid the habitual side of playing. Compared with this religious sense of purity, this sense of keeping an untainted vision, Evan Parker's approach is secular, agnostic, and robust. He is prepared to rub shoulders and get involved with all sorts and conditions of musicians, and seems able to do this without losing his essential identity.[51]

These and other remarks reflect an intriguing tension within the community of free improvisers between Afrological issues of personal and cultural identity and Eurological conceptions of music as an autonomous art. African-American drummer and composer Max Roach stated concisely the issues and his intentions:

Two theories exist, one is that art is for the sake of art, which is true. The other theory, which is also true, is that the artist is like a secretary. . . . He keeps a record of his time so to speak. . . . My music tries to say how I really feel, and I hope it mirrors in some way how black people feel in the United States.[52]

Roach's comments highlight the fact that African-American jazz and improvising musicians have frequently sought to celebrate aspects of black life and culture and, at the same time, cast off the burden of race, especially when that burden of "racial authenticity" infringes on the marketability or the creativity of black musicians and their music. This dilemma has played out since the 1960s most clearly in the tension between Black Nationalism and universalism evident in the commentary of many celebrated African-American improvisers. Despite the helpful and often-illuminating distinctions between Afrological and Eurological perspectives, the continued hybridization in the community of contemporary free improvisation has made discussions of cultural belonging a very prickly topic. As multi-instrumentalist Anthony Braxton wryly comments: "Why is it so natural for Evan Parker, say, to have an appreciation of Coltrane, but for me to have an appreciation of Stockhausen is somehow out of the order of natural human experience? I see it as racist."[53] A growing scene of Asian-American improvisers, centered primarily in the San Francisco Bay Area, also highlights the problematic nature of binary thinking and cultural and aesthetic dyads.[54]

George Lewis, in a more recent article, advances the notion that experimentalism was becoming "creolized." Where the so-called "third-stream" movement (a proposed fusion of jazz and classical styles) had failed, Lewis argues "independent black experimentalism challenged the centrality of pan-Europeanism to the notion of the experimental itself."[55] AACM members, in particular, frequently rejected the prescriptive tenets of cultural nationalism and questioned the idea that black music is a hermetic field. Yet they presented their work as an example of creative black music and as an homage to black people. Weaving together cultural naturalism, pan-Africanism, and universalism offered, to many, the most effective means to negotiate the constraints put upon their creativity by the hegemony of Western economic, discursive, and aesthetic ideals. As saxophonist Marion Brown poetically states, "I'm like a man walking into the future backwards."[56]

Performing Uncertainty

How do individuals and groups negotiate their frequently diverse ideas about and approaches to improvisation in performance? In what ways do culture and creativity, memory and muscle factor into improvisation? And how does context affect the meanings and economics of performing improvised music?

Venues for this music can run the gamut from small, local coffeehouses to well-publicized and well-attended international festivals.[57] And the featured ensembles at these venues cover the full spectrum from one-time meetings between improvisers (the "all-star event") to the many longer-term associations with essentially unchanging personnel (the "working group"). The former can provide a sense of immediacy, excitement, novelty, and risk to participants, whereas the latter may offer an intimacy and depth unavailable in the earliest stages of interaction.[58] Tom Nunn believes that:

> Free improvisation, by virtue of its open and incorporating nature, invites (indeed demands) the development of personal and group styles. As an improviser accumulates experience, a unique style develops naturally. Likewise, as a group develops rapport and players within a group become increasingly familiar with one another's musical tendencies (i.e., personal style traits), a general style peculiar to the group will usually develop.[59]

Free improvisers, in general, share the view that technical and improvisational accomplishments are best arrived at through in-context development and experience rather than through isolated training. The idea of "rehearsing" during playing sessions, however, is less common because, as the term implies, the "re-hearing" of musical details to perfect a musical gesture, formal section, or complete performance runs counter to the aesthetics of improvisation. According to bassist Reggie Workman, he would like to rid our vocabularies of the verb "to try." In improvisation, you do not try, you do![60]

This is not to say that practice techniques are unknown to improvisers. One common device used in both free and idiom-specific improvisation traditions is handicapping. Handicapping refers to a self-imposed challenge designed to limit material or techniques available to the improviser. These may be conceptual or even physical handicaps imposed on the performer. Conceptual handicaps could involve playing only one note or within a specified range or aiming for a uniform mood to an improvisation. Bassist Bertram Turetzky relates that his first instruction to classical musicians who have no previous experience with improvisation is to play a b-flat continuously for several hours in as many ways as possible.[61] Physical handicaps might include using only a particular part of an instrument or only one hand. In a recent clinic, for example, kotoist Miya Masaoka asked a student drummer to improvise using only his elbows.[62]

While from one perspective these devices may appear to limit individual creativity, they can also remind each participant to focus attention on the collective statement and the musical moment rather than to become easily overwhelmed with the enormous scope of individual musical possibilities. Tom Nunn finds that the biggest mistake made among first-time improvisers is to focus exclusively on that for which they, as individuals, are responsible. Or, alternately, participating in simple call-and-response style interactions does not allow for meaningful musical relationships to emerge and be explored.[63]

Many improvisers discuss spiritual, ecstatic, or trancelike performance states.[64] Some cite total mental involvement, while others describe a complete annihilation of all critical and rational faculties. Musicians stress performance goals ranging from complete relaxation or catharsis to a transcendental feeling of ego loss or collective consciousness. The sheer energy and density of sound at times experienced in free and collective improvisation can potentially create a state of hyperstimulation verging on sensory overload. The idea of spirit possession also appears in the improvising community. Saxophonist Jameel Moondoc describes a time when "the music got so intense that spirits came into the room, just hovering around, and in one aspect it was incredibly scary. It was almost like we were calling the ancestors, and they came."[65] Others describe a voluntary, self-induced form of trance—more akin to shamanic practices—as they guide the listener on a spiritual journey.[66] Despite these diverse belief systems, a feeling of spirituality and reverence pervades many improvised performances. William Parker, the celebrated improvising bassist, feels that "free music can be a musical form that is playing without pre-worked structure, without written music or chord changes. However, for free music to succeed, it must grow into free spiritual music, which is not . . . a musical form; it should be based off of a life form. It is not about just picking up an instrument and playing guided by math principles or emotion. It is emptying oneself and being."[67]

While the spiritual concerns of improvisers can be diverse and often difficult to analyze, the economics of performing contemporary improvised music has been a topic of some concern for both performers and scholars of this music. Improvisers have frequently joined together to form artist-run collectives aimed at establishing creative and financial control over the production and dissemination of their work and ensuring the proper respect and remuneration for their efforts.[68] Although the lifetime of these various collectives runs the gamut from months to decades, the impulse to pool resources and to pursue communal approaches to creativity remains strong among improvisers. The tendency to form improvising collectives was and is, in great part, a direct response to the notion that jazz and improvised music most appropriately belong in the underfunded club and cabaret. George Lewis writes:

For the black musicians . . . the "club," rather than the concert hall, had been heavily ideologized as the ideal, even the genetically best-suited place for their music. Early on, however, black experimentalists realized that serious engagement with theater and performance, painting, poetry, electronics, and other interdisciplinary expressions that require extensive infrastructure, would be rendered generally ineffective or even impossible by the jazz club model. In this light, the supposed obligation to perform in clubs began to appear as a kind of unwanted surveillance of the black creative body.[69]

For a time in the 1970s, the "loft" became an "alternative" space for performances of this increasingly multimedia expression, and creative scenes began to flourish, particularly in and around New York City. But just as the term "jazz" had been criticized for decades as a boundary-imposing and financially limiting label, the new loft venues—perceived to require minimal infrastructural investment and therefore undeserving of extensive financial support by established arts-funding agencies—quickly became another obstacle to the recognition-seeking and border-crossing strategies of creative musicians and improvisers. Although the situation has arguably improved since that time, venues and funding for "new music" tend still to be hypersegregated according to racialized categories.[70]

Experiencing Uncertainty

How do listeners and performers of this music engage with the sounds and practices of "uncertainty"? Can improvised performance offer a window into different conceptions of musical structuring and complexity? Improvisation, by virtue of its emphasis on collaboration and in-the-moment creativity, does seems to invite different approaches to performance, listening, and analysis—approaches that focus as much attention on the human and cultural aspects of music making as on the formal structure of the musical work.[71]

Since, on hearing the initial sound in a free improvisation, neither the performers nor the audience know exactly what direction the music will take, open and attentive listening is essential to creating and maintaining the flow of the music and to extracting meaning and enjoyment from the experience. The fact that both the performer and audience perspectives begin at the same point offers, according to Tom Nunn, "a level of excitement, involvement and challenge to the audience listener that is unique, at least in degree, to free improvisation."[72] Derek Bailey writes, "Undeniably, the audience for improvisation, good or bad, active or passive, sympathetic or hostile, has a power that no other audience has. It can effect the creation of that which is being witnessed. And perhaps because of that possibility the audience for improvisation has a degree of intimacy with the music that is not achieved in any other situation."[73]

Writing from the perspective of a devoted fan, Steve Day exclaims: "Improvisation does not end with the musician. The sound is not complete until the sound enters the consciousness of those that hear. Improvised music is unique in that it asks the listener to continue the creative process of interaction. . . . To really listen therefore, is to experiment and experience the spontaneous soundscape that is present in any situation. The listener too must improvise."[74] And Ben Watson, Bailey's recent biographer, playfully argues that, "The audience for Free Improvisation may be small, but it is committed: part of this commitment stems from the way free improvisers respect the specificity of the audience. Deprived of that, you might as well be twiddling your thumbs as some pop act or classical orchestra goes through its well-rehearsed show."[75]

Offering a more pessimistic view of the situation, Jonty Stockdale writes in a recent essay:

> In a freely improvised performance the inconsistent or infrequent use of conventional signposts causes such activity to be challenging and problematic for the musicians involved, but especially so for an audience who are forced to rely on

the accumulated knowledge of prior musical experience and the assimilation of underlying codes embedded within it, to attempt to evaluate and derive meaning from such performance. As prior listening experience and exposure to music of differing practices can vary so dramatically from one listener to another, the likelihood that there is any sense of a shared understanding of what any freely improvised performance might be aiming to convey, is highly speculative.[76]

He concludes that, "The result is a situation where for any performance, each improviser adopts a position from which to start (at the edge of what is already known and what is to be explored) and for the audience (with previous individual experience as a frame of reference) a position from which to start listening."[77]

Like many other commentators, Stockdale finds that experiencing improvisation live affords additional inroads to listeners, including the opportunity to observe body language and visual interaction. He argues that, "Whilst we may not know what represents the current edge of possibility for any one musician, certainly the extent to which physical gestures move from the restrained to the exaggerated, gives us clues as to where this might lay through any given performance."[78] But the notion that audiences would be better at gauging meaning through physical and visual, rather than auditory clues, is also difficult to support, since many musicians may use "exaggerated" physical gestures that have little to do with their "current edge of possibility."

Although Stockdale may be correct in assessing that a shared sense of understanding is difficult if not impossible to come by, other authors have stressed that contemporary music offers the possibility for different approaches to listening, approaches not focused principally on underlying codes. Roland Barthes, for instance, in his essay titled "Listening" in *The Responsibility of Forms,* proposes three types of listening.[79] "Alert" listening, he argues, is one practiced by all beings equipped to hear. In this type of hearing, "a living being orients its hearing (the exercise of its physiological faculty of hearing) to certain *indices* . . . the wolf listens for a (possible) noise of its prey, the hare for a (possible) noise of its hunter, the child and the lover for the approaching footsteps which might be the mother's or the beloved's." With this type of listening, one listens with expectation for specific sounds of disruption in the environment, or in other words, to what one desires to hear.

The second type of listening, "deciphering," takes us further into the realm of the human. "What the ear tries to intercept," Barthes explains, "are certain *signs*. . . . I listen the way I read, i.e., according to certain codes." But Barthes identifies a third approach to listening, which he describes as "entirely modern": an approach that "does not aim at—or await—certain determined, classified signs: not what is said or emitted, but who speaks, who emits: such listening is supposed to develop in an intersubjective space where 'I am listening' also means 'listen to me.'" What is expressed is, perhaps, less important than the fact that it is the production of another human; it carries a sense of identity and holds out the possibility for interaction.

Without conventional codes that might easily guide a listener on a musical journey, many people's first experiences with free improvisation evoke feelings of alienation, confusion, or even hostility. Over time, however, committed listeners may develop new ways with which to approach the music and perhaps even seek their pleasure in the avoidance of conformist practice. A respondent to a survey that I conducted among active audiences members described the qualities of performance to which he attends this way:

> Pulse, texture, use of the instrument's full frequency-range, dynamics, density, timbre, interplay between performers when there is more than one. That's too much to keep in your conscious mind all at once, but after a while one learns how to recognize these elements intuitively and from then on listening attentively becomes easier. I think that's one reason why it is so hard for some listeners to appreciate free improv music—they are used to listening for melody, and not used to listening for density or texture, so they don't know how to decode freely improvised music and as a result it ends up sounding like random noise to them.[80]

In a similar formation to Barthes's, albeit with somewhat different terminology and motivations, composer Barry Truax describes three general modes of engaging with the acoustic soundscape: background listening, listening-in-readiness, and listening-in-search. For Truax, background listening is akin to "distracted listening" while the listener is actively engaged in another activity. Listening-in-readiness involves focused attention, but the attention is on familiar sound associations built up over time that may be readily identified. With listening-in-search, one scans the acoustic soundscape for particular sounds, attempting to extract or create meaning from their production or the environment's response to the sounds produced.[81] A less humanistic vision perhaps than Barthes's, but one that also identifies a type of listening not predominantly focused on identifying familiar sound associations.

Authors concerned exclusively with free improvisation have also remarked on the importance of listening in less directed ways. Borrowing terms from the visual arts, Mark Bradlyn asserts:

> The first step in learning to listen is stopping still and opening our ears, first to figure, next to ground, next to field. The field, the aggregate soundscape is the most difficult to perceive. . . . [T]here must be a constant flux, a never fully focused shifting among figure, ground, and field. . . . One performer's playing may suddenly emerge as a stark figure against the ground of another's only to just as suddenly submerge into the ground or even farther back into the field as another voice emerges.[82]

Bradlyn concludes that collective free improvisation may falter if participants and listeners fail "to hear the texture, the field, in pursuit of the dramatic figure, the gesture."[83] Elsewhere he suggests that improvisation "succeeds as music only to the extent that listening achieves equal status with playing."[84]

Jason Stanyek finds even more at stake in the process of listening than the "musical" success of the improvisation. He asserts that "if free improvisation has anything emancipatory or 'anticipatory' about it, then this kind of proleptic vision is contained within the act of listening, not in the sounds themselves." For Stanyek, "listening is the way identities are narrated and negotiated and the way differences are articulated."[85] He elaborates:

> Indeed, the critical nature of free improvisation, its ability to accommodate the disjunctures which invariably arise out of any intercultural encounter (and perhaps the fact that free improvisation resides outside of many of the economic and

aesthetic strictures of the culture industry), all help to provide a welcome antidote to the music-as-a-universal-language trope which pervades many intercultural collaborations.[86]

Yet the critical commentary on the ability of improvised music to communicate, particularly across cultural divides, seems to agree little. Stanyek describes free improvisation as "a particularly fertile 'communicative arena' in which divergent individual and cultural narratives can be articulated."[87] Wrangling over Derek Bailey's notion of the music as "non-idiomatic," Stanyek finds that, "There's something else going on there, a vital, not reified, connection with idioms and 'markings.'"[88]

Referencing Stanyek's notion of a "communicative arena," however, Ben Watson retorts that "as a way of denoting the particular qualities of the avant-garde extreme plumbed by Free Improvisation, it's useless." Instead, Watson shares a humorous passage from Derek Bailey's book that, as originally intended, was meant to criticize those improvisers who adopt an antivirtuosity attitude, often appropriating "ethnic" instruments for their perceived limited opportunities and, therefore, more direct expressivity. Bailey writes:

> So, in performance, grunts, howls, screams, groans, Tibetan humming, Tunisian chanting, Maori chirping and Mozambique stuttering are combined with the African thumb piano, Chinese temple blocks, Ghanian soft trumpet, Trinidadian steel drum, Scottish soft bagpipe, Australian bull-roarer, Ukranian stone flute and the Canton one-legged monster to provide an aural event about as far removed from the directness and dignity of ethnic music as a thermo-nuclear explosion is from a fart.[89]

This passage, of course, does not address the issues that surround cross-cultural collaborations between improvisers who are themselves cultural insiders. Bailey's passage, in fact, is written as if only Westerners are engaged with (or should be engaged with?) "non-idiomatic" improvisation. With a touch of his own hyperbole, Watson argues that:

> Portraying Free Improvisation as a multicultural, hands-across-the-oceans, United Nations-logoed "communicative arena" (something to be staged in the ghastly Millennium Dome, perhaps?) gives no inkling of either the animosity it encounters or the enthusiasm it inspires. Stanyek's blandishments conceal the way Free Improvisation's dogged pursuit of authentic musical interaction shrieks protest at what capitalist business-as-usual does to music—and what passes for musical communication in official channels, both commercial and "art."[90]

Describing Bailey's annual Company Week gatherings of diverse improvisers, Watson writes: "If you create an oasis for direct communication in a world mediated by commodity glamour and reassuring boredom, it isn't inevitable that everything you hear will be brilliant. But it does *matter*."[91] We must be careful, however, because the uncertainties associated with contemporary improvised music *are*, in important ways, mediated by specific personal, social, economic, and cultural experiences. Since the

1960s, the revolutionary timbres, textures, and approaches of this music have resonated in extremely varied ways, from Black Power or transcendental spirituality to socialism, anarchy, and postmodern angst and confusion, among other things. Yet many artists ascribe to the notion that, in the moment of performance and through the act of listening, our personal, social, and cultural understandings—and interpersonal and intercultural sensibilities—can also be powerfully changed in the rapture and rupture of improvisation.

Documenting Uncertainty

Can and should improvised music be recorded? How do we engage with the sounds of "uncertainty" when they become in some ways fixed, detached from their original context, and replayed at a different time? The many issues surrounding the recording of improvisation have received considerable attention.[92] Tom Nunn argues that "much of the unknown-about-to-be-known is lost in recordings. The image of the musicians playing together, communicating, collectively creating in the moment is impossible to capture on tape."[93] Cornelius Cardew believes that "documents such as tape recordings of improvisation are essentially empty, as they preserve chiefly the form that something took and give at best an indistinct hint as to the feeling and cannot convey any sense of time and place. . . . What you hear on tape or disc is indeed the same playing, but divorced from its natural context."[94] David Roberts finds that "for musics not predicated upon the dissociation of form and performance, recording can, and often does, spell the kiss of death."[95] Vinko Globokar insists that recordings of this music should be listened to once and then discarded.

These artists and authors seem to agree on two central points: (1) an audio recording, no matter its fidelity, necessarily reproduces only a limited spectrum of the performance experience and (2) the act of listening to improvised music away from its initial performance context and on several occasions forever alters its meaning and impact. Their disregard for the simple utility of recordings or of the sense of tradition that they can and do engender also seems to betray a certain Eurological perspective—one focused on the aesthetic autonomy of the artistic experience devoid of its social implications. Martin Davidson, of Eminem Records, expresses a rather different viewpoint. He argues that "recordings and improvisation are entirely symbiotic, as if they were invented for each other. . . . [T]he act of improvising is filling time (either a predetermined or an open-ended amount) with music—something that could be called real-time composition, and something that has more need and more right to be recorded than anything else."[96]

Most improvisers acknowledge the advantages that recordings can offer in establishing and disseminating a tradition, although individual artists may differ widely in their specific views on how the recording process should be approached. Some embrace, while others disavow, the possibilities of editing material or reordering performances that are inherent in the process of producing a recording. There is even little agreement about whether musicians might be more or less conservative in a studio setting or in front of a paying audience.[97] Most improvisers conceive of recordings as important documents or milestones in an evolving career, but there is some disagreement over whether they should be limited to the "best" possible performance of an artist, or if they should simply document one's playing as on any other night. Derek

Bailey remarks that all that is usually claimed for a recording is "that it should provide evidence of musical identity or of changes in identity."[98] From a purely practical standpoint, the exchange of recordings affords an important avenue of social and musical networking, allowing artists and listeners to connect and to build bridges in the dispersed and often marginalized improvised music community. Finally, many performers acknowledge the educational value that recordings can offer through repeated listening.

Scholars of African-American and improvised music have frequently engaged in—and struggled with—the issue of an oral/literate dichotomy in music performance and analysis.[99] The increasingly interconnected and technologically sophisticated context for modern culture challenges us to view contemporary music as a complex site wherein new oral/aural cultural forms and practices are electronically inscribed into society. Tricia Rose, in her study of rap music, adopts (from Walter Ong) the concept of "post-literate orality" to describe hip-hop culture. She writes: "The concept of post-literate orality merges orally influenced traditions that are created and embedded in a post-literate, technologically sophisticated context."[100] Arguing a similar position, Daniel Belgrad states that African-American music offers a model of "secondary orality" in a postliterate culture, "the possibility of asserting the values of an oral culture within a culture already conditioned by writing."[101] Well before these scholars began to tackle the subject, Wadada Leo Smith addressed this same issue:

> In ancient times when all people held improvisation as their art-music form, it was said then that theirs was an oral tradition. . . . In our times now, an oral-electronic tradition is being born, and this signifies the age of a new improvisation-art-music-form. One only needs to think in terms of the media and its proper use to understand how any significant event, and I'm speaking culturally now and particularly of music, can be immediately received anywhere in the world within seconds or minutes depending on the transfer in time lapse through satellite techniques: indeed an oral-electronic tradition.[102]

Improvisers, although centered on collective and spontaneous contribution in performance, are equally aware of developing an individual sound and style and defending a career path within the music industry. Yet their approach confounds many established legal and cultural norms of music ownership and the standard practices of music copyrighting and royalty compensation. For instance, before 1972 it was not possible to register an improvised sound recording with the Library of Congress. In the current era, royalties—an important economic component of countless musicians' careers—are still dispensed almost exclusively to composers (or to the record labels that maintain copyright over the recorded sound), to the detriment of improvising artists.[103] Improvisation also challenges us to rethink ingrained notions of musical value and conventional approaches to musical analysis and discourse.

Evaluating Uncertainty

Can improvisation be criticized? If so, then by whom? What is implied by the word "criticism"? According to Marion Brown, "'Criticism' is by definition a product of the gulf between musicians' ideas and those of the audience. Once a listener determines that his or her interpretation does not match the performer's, one becomes a critic."[104]

Even among performers, a gulf can surface between divergent interpretations. While some artists freely engage in conversations and critical reflection immediately following a group improvisation, others are loath to do so, since each member's immediate impression of the improvisation may differ considerably, and candid discussion can make subsequent improvisations by the group too self-conscious. Listening to recorded playing sessions at a later date, either alone or as a group, is one common means of self-evaluation and group feedback among improvisers.

The jazz critical establishment has historically been harshly divided over the relative merits of freer forms of improvisation. Both journalists and musicians appeared to take sides almost immediately after the arrival of Ornette Coleman's quartet in New York, and the subsequent debate has hardly subsided to this day. Beyond the stylistic quibbling, however, it may be the apparent critical vacuum that has done more harm to the reception and recognition of this music. In 1973, Marion Brown self-published *Views and Reviews* in order to set forth his personal aesthetic philosophy and to challenge the critical status quo of writers who betray a preference for composed music and who, by virtue of their powerful institutional positions, can dramatically affect the lives and livelihoods of black avant-garde artists. Eric Porter, paraphrasing Brown, writes:

> [O]ne is prone to judge a piece of music by its formal, or compositional, elements. Because this presents a problem when analyzing fully improvised music or compositions that include improvisational elements, Brown proposes that a different set of aesthetic principles must be invoked when evaluating such music. "Balance" is achieved in improvised music not through a compositional structure but through musicians' personal expressions and the emotional bond they create with their audience.[105]

In his discussion of the treatment afforded various "downtown" musics by the *Village Voice* in the late 1970s, George Lewis further highlights the issue of how, where, and by whom this music should be criticized. The *Voice,* at that time, separated critical discussion of various musical genres under the headings "Music" (i.e., reviews of work from the high-culture "West") and "Riffs" ("the low-culture, diminutively imagined "Rest"). Lewis concludes that the AACM and other creative artists with similar ideologies were "destined to run roughshod over many conventional assumptions about infrastructure, reference, and place."[106]

The practice of so-called jazz musicians and improvisers engaging with extended notation and graphic scores, electronics and computers, and multimedia approaches to performance directly challenged the binary thought—black/white, jazz/classical, high culture/low culture—that was and is still common in critical discourse. Lewis points out, however, that even African-American critics and activists were not immune from attempting to regulate and restrict African-American creativity. Amiri Baraka, whose important early work strongly supported the then-emerging "avant-garde," later criticized many black creative musicians for being unduly influenced by European modernism.[107]

Several journals and magazines consistently publish reviews of improvised music recordings, performances, and festivals and provide a window into the critical values espoused by the contemporary print media.[108] As with music criticism in more traditional veins, comparisons to previous recordings or similar well-known groups or players factor prominently in these writings. Malcom Barry writes: "[I]nevitably there is difficulty in separating the form from the individuals practicing that form. . . . [T]he anti-composed music becomes identified with particular figures just as composed music does."[109]

Critics of improvised music most often base their evaluations of a performance on the perceived level of ensemble rapport. Did the musicians and music congeal in a meaningful way? Were the ensemble or sectional transitions effective? Did the musicians explore novel and interesting relationships? Reviewers also frequently comment on the presence (or absence) of references to established musical styles (jazz, rock, classical, electronic, or world). Although these comments can be helpful in orienting the reader (and prospective buyer) prior to actually hearing the music, critics variously praise or denounce the use of these "style signs" as ingenious layerings and postmodern juxtapositions or as unfortunate by-products of too heavy a reliance on established techniques and practices.

Even if most overt idiomatic qualities are consciously avoided by the performers, improvisers still incorporate and experiment with the accepted tools of artistic expression: stability, interruption, repetition, contrast, and so on. Improvising music involves a constant balancing act between complexity and comprehensibility, control and non-control, constancy and unpredictability, a balancing act that can invite considerable debate and disagreement. The issue of control verses noncontrol brings to mind an issue touched on earlier in this chapter—the idea of virtuosity in improvisation. Do our standard conservatory conceptions of virtuosity provide an accurate measure of a musician's improvisational skills? A frequently recounted story may serve to illuminate this issue. By his own account, multi-instrumentalist Steve Beresford likes to explore the totally controlled and the totally uncontrolled. His expansive approach to instrumental technique, however, allegedly got him ostracized from a 1977 Company Week (Derek Bailey's annual meeting of improvisers) because his approach to his instruments was deemed "insufficiently serious."[110]

Nick Couldry devotes a rather extensive discussion to the subject of virtuosity in improvised music. He highlights, in addition to conventional notions of instrumental ability or more contemporary notions of so-called extended techniques, the idea of "a virtuosity in finding," or the ability to imagine new sounds and discover an individual voice. He also finds an "intensity of application"—in his view, more virtue than virtuosity—important to the demeanor of improvised performance.[111]

"Extended techniques"—the exploration of unconventional sounds and devices on conventional instruments—have been, and continue to be, an important part of the vocabulary of many improvisers.[112] And critical evaluation is often based on a perceived mastery of these difficult techniques. For example, Tom Johnson wrote in a 1980 *Village Voice* review of an Evan Parker solo performance: "In short, this was not a hit-and-miss affair the way it is with most woodwind players when they turn on their multiphonics. This was a musician who had transformed these new sounds into a vocabulary that was familiar to him as major scales are to most musicians."[113]

"Intensity of application," however, would seem to imply, if not conventional notions of virtuosity, at least a sense of personal conviction and performance energy. Arguably, this intensity can be heard in the full spectrum of sounds explored by contemporary improvisers, ranging from the incredibly dense and loud to the almost unimaginably soft and sparse.

Perhaps what is most often missed, however, in critical discussion of improvised music is its functional quality. In his *Views and Reviews*, Marion Brown seeks to dismantle the Western aesthetic that elevates art as an object of beauty above and beyond its functional purpose. Brown argues not only that improvised music is as "valid" as composed music but also that, even when "arrived at through mutual cooperation at a folk level, [it] may be as successful as any other kind of music."[114]

This may, however, beg the question that many of the music's detractors are quick to level at it: if this music is as social and as liberating as many profess, then why is it not more popular? This question is by no means new. Many politically and socially active black avant-garde artists have faced this continuing question of why black creativity is seemingly so removed from African-American communities. Anthony Braxton, in his *Triaxium* writings, casts blame on a general lack of recognition of artistic creativity in American society and on the market forces that promote popular music to black audiences.[115] George Lewis additionally finds that academic cultural studies have frequently downplayed or even disparaged those indigenously black musics that are not obviously or predominantly based in or represented as mass culture. Lewis argues that in this context, "the entry into classical music by black composers becomes, rather than bourgeois accommodation, an oppositional stance" challenging "fixed notions of high and low, black and white." He summarizes:

> Thus, in the age of globalized megamedia, to the extent that certain oppositional black musical forms have been generally ignored or dismissed by academic theorists, the idea is thereby perpetuated that black culture, as academically defined and studied, is in fact corporate-approved culture, and that there is no necessary non-commercial space for black musical production.[116]

Porter, however, finds historical evidence for a strong connection between creative music making and a vision to make progressive music meaningful to a wide spectrum of people. He expresses that "difficult as it was to implement effectively, [this vision] can be understood as a reflection of the Black Arts movement in the jazz community, where making a living went hand in hand with making music relevant."[117]

Clearly, the diverse personal experiences and opinions of free improvisers and the transcultural and hybrid nature of the musical activity make generalized discussions of critical values within the community somewhat problematic. Yet despite the frequently expressed desire among certain artists for a "styleless" or "nonidiomatic" approach to music, more than four decades of recorded documents and live performances attest to a growing tradition and reveal certain shared traits to the music. Within this dispersed and disparate community, there does appear to be—at the very least—a shared desire to meet together, often for the first time in performance, to negotiate understandings and embark on novel musical and social experiences.

Improvising music, it appears, is best envisioned as an artistic *forum* rather than an artistic *form*; a social and sonic space in which to explore various cooperative and conflicting interactive strategies. It highlights process over product creativity, an engendered sense of uncertainty and discovery, the dialogical nature of real-time interaction, the sensual aspects of performance over abstract intellectual concerns, and a participatory aesthetic over passive reception. Its inherent transience and expressive immediacy even challenge the dominant modes of consumption that have arisen in modern, mass-market economies and the sociopolitical and spiritual efficacy of art in general. Yet improvising music may simply remind us that *all* music takes place within and through social relationships.

Ajay Heble writes that, "From its very inception jazz has been about inventiveness, about the process of change [and] that sense of change and inventiveness is most powerfully registered in its cultural forms that accent dissonance and contingency, in music making that explores the sonic possibilities of traditionally outlawed models of practice."[118] John Gennari also asserts that jazz has served—and continues to serve—"as a progenitor of new forms, an inventor of new languages, a creator of new ways to express meaning."[119] And George Lipsitz argues that jazz and improvised music have offered "cultural, moral, and intellectual guidance to people all over the world."[120] But Jerome Harris reminds us that, "The movement of jazz onto the global stage is a trend that may be judged to hold some dangers."[121] Among other things, Harris identifies "the possibility that jazz may lose benefits that derive from cultural closeness between the makers, mediators, and audience—among them, some easy broad consensus about its aesthetic direction." Slyly referencing Ornette Coleman's seminal work, Harris concludes that, "The shape of jazz to come may differ from that which has come before."[122]

The increasingly transnational and transcultural nature of improvising music does seem to preclude the possibility of a broad consensus. Yet, as musical devices and relationships are negotiated within performances and within the community of improvisers, musicians offer important rhetorical commentary on desirable social organization, the politics of representation, the public function of art, and the possibilities for resistance to embedded cultural and historical constructions. By paying attention to the ways in which artists and involved listeners define, document, perform, experience, and evaluate this music, we may gain insight not only into the process of artistic and cultural innovation but also into the processes by which we engage with and participate in our natural and social worlds. Nearly all societies and artistic communities have an "avant-garde," a cultural space in which new ideas may be expressed and explored. As musicians and musical practices continue to work across and between national, cultural, and stylistic boundaries, improvising music may play a special role in both generating and coping with complexity.

3
The Embodied Mind

One of the challenges I continue to confront in my professional career is how to teach improvisation to aspiring jazz and creative musicians in an effective and appropriate manner. There is, of course, no shortage of pedagogical texts on the subject, most of which focus on the "rules" of theory and appropriate scale and chord choices, or offer "licks" that can quickly make your improvising sound more convincing or "authentic" in a given style. But as many improvisers will attest, it is not the notes you play, but *how* you play them. And how you play them comes at least as much from your physical connection with the instrument as from any mental awareness or intellectual planning. Students frequently wonder what I am "thinking" when I improvise, and I am often led to answer that many of my favorites times spent improvising seem neither entirely mental, nor entirely physical, but rather when these binary divisions seem to dissolve and disappear, if only for a fleeting moment.

In this chapter, I hope to confront—and propose a means through which to by-pass—the Cartesian split between mind and body (or intellect and intuition) that so often plagues the analysis and discussion of jazz and improvised music. Are there more appropriate ways to characterize the nature of the relationship between an improviser's intentions and actions? How does an improviser's physical connection with her/his instrument factor into this relationship? Why has the creative role of the body frequently been neglected in the music academy and conservatory? To address these and other questions, I turn to contemporary approaches in cognitive science that focus on issues of embodiment and I offer a detailed investigation of the performance practice and aesthetics of improvising saxophonist Evan Parker, whose playing and perspective offers a potent example of body-mind integration. Many of the themes developed here will be taken up again in chapter seven with regards to the pedagogy of improvisation.

Taking the Note for a Walk

> The thing I always come back to is Paul Klee's description of drawing—taking a line for a walk. I think of solo saxophone as taking a note for a walk. And we'll see afterwards where we went rather than me leading you round a path I know well.[1]
>
> —Evan Parker

Born in Bristol, England, on April 5, 1944, Evan Parker has emerged as one of the leading saxophone free improvisers. His early musical influences, however, were very much in line with those of other English youth growing up in the fifties. A fascination with pop and skiffle music, especially by the singer Lonnie Donegan, gradually inspired Parker to investigate the roots of these musics in the American blues and jazz traditions. Although only a limited number of records became available in England, Parker began to digest the music of Leadbelly, Sonny Terry, Brownie McGhee, Louis Armstrong, Dave Brubeck, and Paul Desmond.

Parker started his saxophone studies on alto at the age of fourteen, strongly influenced by the velvet sonorities of Desmond's playing on that horn, but soon switched to tenor and soprano after hearing the music of John Coltrane for the first time. Since Parker's father worked for the airline industry, he was able to get free flights to New York City in 1961 and 1962 and had the opportunity to hear and meet many of the great American free jazz musicians, including Cecil Taylor and his newly formed unit with Sonny Murray and Jimmy Lyons. From Cecil Taylor (and saxophonist Eric Dolphy) Parker claims to have inherited a sense of wide interval playing that moves away from clearly ascending and descending phrase structures.[2]

Parker was equally impressed by the explosive saxophone styles being developed by Archie Shepp, Steve Lacy, Albert Ayler, Pharoah Sanders, and John Tchicai.[3] He explains:

In the case of Albert it was to do with his access to the altissimo register, control of the overtones, in the case of Pharoah, it was to do with his articulation, a certain kind of double and triple tonguing. And in Tchicai's case, to do with his way of floating over what was already a non-metric pulse, on those New York Art Quartet records . . . I thought I could achieve . . . not exactly a synthesis, but I could work my way through the gaps that were left between what those people were doing.[4]

Following his truncated undergraduate studies at Birmingham University in Botany, Parker moved to London and, in late 1966, began playing at the Little Theater Club alongside many of England's most capable and celebrated improvisers, including Derek Bailey, Trevor Watts, Dave Holland, John Stevens, Tony Oxley, Kenny Wheeler, Paul Lytton, Barry Guy, Paul Lovens, Louis Moholo, and others.[5] Outside of England, Parker has cultivated longstanding associations with Alexander Von Schlippenbach, Peter Brötzmann, George Lewis, Anthony Braxton, Steve Lacy, Ned Rothenberg, Irène Schweizer, Paul Bley, Sainkho Namtchylak, Philipp Wachsmann, Walter Prati, and Mario Vecchi, among others.

Despite his continuing interest in collective improvisation and his fascinating range of musical collaborators, Parker is perhaps best known for creating a distinctive solo saxophone language. His use of circular breathing, overtone manipulation, multiphonics, polyrhythmic fingerings, and various slap and multiple tonguing techniques (involving an up/down motion rather than the more traditional throat attack) allow him to form complex, overlapping patterns of sound that are both highly virtuosic and serenely beautiful. He states:

My evolution in solo playing has been to exploit technical possibilities and acoustic possibilities unique to the solo situation. When you have all the space to fill,

Evan Parker photographed by Caroline Forbes

you can listen more closely to the specific resonances in the room, to the specific interaction with the acoustic, to the overtone components in the sound—the harmonic components in any one note become more audible. The temptation to fragment individual tones into their harmonic components becomes very attractive because you can hear yourself that much more closely; you can hear the *detail* of what's happening in any one sound.[6]

Evan Parker's solo saxophone recordings now number in the double digits, starting with the album *Saxophone Solos* (1975) and followed by *Monoceros* (1978), *The Snake Decides* (1986), *Conic Sections* (1989), and *Process and Reality* (1991), among others.[7] With *Chicago Solos* (1995), Parker released his first album of solo tenor saxophone playing. And starting in the 1990s, Parker has also released several examples of his solo saxophone playing with live computer processing, including *Hall of Mirrors* (1990) and *Solar Wind* (1997). Since his first foray into the relatively uncharted territory of solo saxophone performance—Coleman Hawkins's "Picasso" (1948) and Anthony Braxton's double-LP *For Alto* (1969) were pioneering examples in this format—Parker's style, technique, and aesthetics have changed considerably, yet a certain fundamental approach remains important, along with a very personal sound and relationship to the instrument.

In describing his solo approach, Parker has spoken of a desire to create the "illusion of polyphony" on a monophonic instrument. He is able to accomplish this by combining circular breathing, a penchant for exploring several layers of musical activity at once, and the specific ability to sustain a low tone while articulating selected overtones (or its reverse, sustaining an overtone while interjecting low notes). He explains: "I try to give [the listener] a sense of dialog with myself anyway, you know the way I move lines around in the overtone structure against lines in the lower register of the instrument. There is still some sense of dialogue in the music but it's just one person speaking to himself."[8]

Parker first explored circular breathing after encountering it in the work of saxophonist Roland Kirk and ethnographic recordings of traditional music from Africa and the Middle East.[9] And he refined this technique in response to the extended duration sounds of amplified strings and controlled feedback being exploited by his colleagues Derek Bailey and Hugh Davies in the Music Improvisation Company in the early 1970s. Parker has commented that his initial decision to play and record solo resulted directly from discovering new instrumental possibilities that the technique of circular breathing made available.[10] Assisted by this uninterrupted flow of sound, he follows his temptation to fragment and his penchant for wide interval leaps—all at phenomenal speeds of execution—to create the illusion of exploring up to three distinct registers of the instrument simultaneously. Parker characteristically explains both the tangible and less tangible influences on his decision to explore these unusual saxophone devices. He recalls:

Listening to the drum music from various African cultures on records, especially the wonderful work published by Ocora and thinking about polyrhythms I started to work on patterns of fingerings in which the left and right hands worked in different superimposed rhythms. To some extent, this overlapped with work on broken air columns (so-called cross-fingerings) and thoughts on how to apply the fundamentals of Bartolozzi's pioneering work *New Sounds for Woodwind* to the saxophone. At a certain point I had a flash of insight the force of which I still find difficult to communicate: that the saxophone can just as well be seen as a closed tube that can be opened in various ways as an open tube that can be closed in various ways. Although this thought may sound obvious I suspect it has been one of the most important keys to my development.[11]

In analyzing Parker's approach to saxophone polyphony, John Corbett offers several parallels between Parker's solo and group playing. Corbet states that:

In a sense, you are like a solo-group, trying to invent or produce a way of playing as a soloist that's like playing as a group: coordinating things in a way that may be controllable, but not predictable . . . something like a group dynamic where you and the relationship between the subset of techniques you might be using at a given time and the instrument are all three interacting in a way that's like different performers.[12]

Parker's own ideas seem to corroborate this solo-group notion when he describes his playing as a "schizophrenic context" in which "it's almost as if there are two people, one of whom is playing the saxophone and one of whom is talking to the guy who plays the saxophone. And when it comes to it, the guy playing the saxophone actually gets the final say, and the one telling him what to do stands there and says, 'I tried, fellas. There he goes again.'"[13] His comments challenge the idea of a singular controlling intellect in improvisation and establish the importance of the body and nonconscious and nonanalytical processes in performance; processes that may be equally important in reception as well (a twenty-five-minute solo improvisation by Evan Parker can be heard on the accompanying compact disc). To probe these ideas further, let us turn to the question of embodiment and its role in expressive communication and cognition.

The Body in the Music

> You get legs dangling down there and arms floating around, so many fingers and one head. . . . Not only can the natural environment carry you beyond your own limitations, but the realization of your own body as part of that environment is an even stronger dissociative factor. . . . What we *do* in the actual event is important— not only what we have in mind. Often what we do is what tells us what we have in mind.[14]
>
> —Cornelius Cardew

Much of the history of Western inquiry has been guided by the principle that the world-out-there and the internal world of mental states are distinct, and analysis can and should proceed by breaking systems into their component parts and by studying their properties and relationships from an observer-independent position. Variously referred to as reductionism, rationalism, objectivism, realism, positivism, or structuralism, this general orientation influenced both philosophical and scientific thinking for centuries.[15] The last half-century has witnessed enormous strides in the study of mind and consciousness and, most recently, a significant shift toward "ecological" or "systems" thinking in the fields of cognitive science and consciousness studies.

Although examples of systems thinking can be found going back centuries if not millennia, its modern origins are often dated to the first Macy Conferences held in New York City in 1946, which brought together pioneering cyberneticists, mathematicians, engineers, and neuroscientists organized by the dynamic leadership of Norbert Weiner and John von Neumann, and humanities and social science researchers clustered around Gregory Bateson and Margaret Mead.[16] Although many of the central ideas of systems thought were adopted from biology, including feedback and homeostasis, the then-nascent field of cognitive science organized instead around a notion of mind that identified cognition with computation, and the brain as the hardware on which it runs. This approach, often called *cognitivism*, has been slowly but steadily replaced by a view of the mind and consciousness that acknowledges the important role that the body, emotions, and social factors play in how we think.

Several assumptions of cognitivism—the idea that we inherit a world outside of ourselves with definite physical properties, that we engage this world through internal representations and information processing, and that "we" do so from a pregiven and undivided sense of self—have been replaced with the notion of cognition as the "bringing forth" of a world and a conception of self that is inseparable from an organism's biology and its history of interactions and lived experience. Summarizing the exciting research in this area, Wayne Bowman explains that, "in contrast to cognitivist theories, *embodied accounts* construe mind as an activity emergent from, structured by, and never wholly separable from the material facts of bodily experience."[17] And because bodies are always both physically and contextually situated, theories of embodiment insist on biological, psychological, and cultural dimensions for all human cognition.

Possibly the most dramatic assault on the cognitivist position came in the form of autopoiesis, a theory first formulated by Chilean neuroscientist Humberto Maturana and his student Francisco Varela.[18] They envisioned reality not as something that was external to and merely reflected or represented in cognitive structures, but as something that was actively *constructed* by organisms as they continuously maintain their structure and self-organize. As a neuroscientist whose primary research was in the field of color vision, Maturana was fascinated by the phenomenon of perception. He was also dissatisfied with the standard definitions of life from biology that offered nothing more than a list of features and functional attributes—descriptions of what living systems do rather than what they are. After a decade or more of struggling with these two fundamental problems in systems thinking, Maturana and Varela proposed the theory or autopoiesis, literally "self-making," as a means of unifying them. By thinking about organization rather than structure, processes rather than properties, they realized that life and cognition share a fundamental circular organization, a network of production processes, in which the function of each component is to participate in the production or transformation of other components in the network. Summarizing this position, Fritjof Capra explains: "The human nervous system does not process any information (in the sense of discrete elements existing ready-made in the outside world, to be picked up by the cognitive system), but interacts with the environment by continually modulating its structure."[19]

In a seminal paper titled "What the Frog's Eye Tells the Frog's Brain," Maturana along with other prominent researchers in the Macy group demonstrated how sensory receptors, far from being passive and objective transmitters of "reality," actually speak to the brain in a way that is already highly processed.[20] Unlike human eyes, which are always moving, scanning, and blinking, a frog fixes its eyes on a scene and leaves them there. Maturana et al. were able to show that a frog's eye perceives small objects in rapid motion well (e.g., flies or other possible prey), but responds far less to larger, slower moving, or stationary objects. In other words, a frog's reality (and by extension our own) is constructed by its sensory apparatus in such a way that there can never be a one-to-one correlation between perception and world. Our ears may even operate much like the frog's eyes, in that we disregard static information over time—a background hum or traffic noises, for instance—and focus our attention instead on changes or discrepancies in the sound around us.[21]

While the early formulation of autopoiesis has been criticized for its marked emphasis on individual autonomy and the "operational closure" of living beings, Francisco Varela, Maturana's student, went on to develop more balanced views on the subject, at times influenced by his study of Buddhism.[22] As Varela and his coauthors in *The Embodied Mind: Cognitive Science and Human Experience* explain, "Cognition is not the representation of a pregiven world by a pregiven mind but is rather the enactment of a world and a mind on the basis of a history of the variety of actions that a being in the world performs."[23] In more simple language, they argue that "knowledge depends on being in a world that is inseparable from our bodies, our language, and our social history."[24] According to this version of embodiment, dubbed *enactive cognition*, human conceptual, sensory, and motor processes have coevolved with each other such that they are inextricably linked. Summarizing this enactive perspective on cognition, Bowman writes, "In this way, the *body is in the mind*. Mind is rendered possible by bodily sensations and actions, from whose patterns it emerges and upon which it relies for whatever intellectual prowess it can claim. At the same time, the *mind is in the body*, in the sense that mind is coextensive with the body's neural pathways and the cognitive templates they comprise."[25]

Contemporary neuroscientific research supports this systems perspective on body and mind. Citing the important work of Valerie Hardcastle, pianist and music cognition researcher Vijay Iyer writes, "We can make more sense of our brains and bodies if we view the nervous system as a system for producing motor output. The cerebellum is connected almost directly to all areas of the brain—sensory transmissions, reticular (arousal/attention) systems, hippocampus (episodic memories), limbic system (emotions, behavior). All areas of our brain seem geared to coping with their functions as they pertain to problems of motor control."[26]

Beyond the realization that mind and body are inextricably intertwined, however, enactive cognition proposes that these neural pathways and cognitive schemata arise from a body's interaction with an experience-shaping environment. As Bowman puts it, "*Mind extends beyond the physical body* into the social and cultural environments that exert major influence on the body and shape all human experience."[27] In this light, embodiment encompasses not only the notion that our ideas, emotions, and actions are all grounded in, and informed by, our bodily selves, but also the perhaps more troubling notion that the boundaries of the human "self" are in fact constructed rather than given. Gregory Bateson, a leading figure at the Macy conferences and a strong proponent of systems thinking, frequently made this point with a koanlike simplicity: "Is a blind man's cane part of him?"[28] The question aimed to spark a mindshift. Although it may be convenient to conceive of human boundaries as defined by their epidermal surfaces, in Bateson's example the cane provides essential information to the man about his environment in a way that makes them, from a systems perspective, inseparable.

For Bateson's koan to work, however, we must envision a blind man *actively engaging* with his environment through his cane as surrogate "eyes." A stoic subject who did not move an inch would not provoke our epiphany that his cane is, in fact, part of his sensorimotor apparatus and therefore his cognitive being. In fact, blind persons have been tested with a video camera that translates images into patterns of skin stimulation. Researchers found that the skin patterns have no "visual" content unless the individual actively directs the video camera using head, hand, or body motions.[29] Like our earlier example of the frog, an organism and its environment are inextricably bound together in a *dynamic* process of reciprocal specification and selection. Not only are sensory modalities evoked by action, they are engaged and re-engaged over time in the individual. For instance, a study of olfaction in rabbits demonstrated that the sense of smell does not objectively map external features but depends instead on the perceiver's engagement and reengagement with external stimuli—in short, on its embodied and enacted history.[30]

In a now classic (albeit rather cruel) study, Richard Held and Alan Hein raised two kittens in total darkness.[31] Periodically, however, they would turn on the lights and place the kittens in separate compartments of a carousel that was specially designed so that only one of the animals was able to reach the ground with its legs. As the active one pulled the passive one along a circular track, both kittens were exposed to near identical visual stimuli. The active one, however, was able to link the act of walking to its own perceptions, while for the other, action and vision did not correlate. After a number of weeks, the kittens were released into the world. The active kitten learned to move and behave normally, but the passive kitten was afflicted with agnosia, a condition of mental blindness brought on by neurological rather than physiological causes. Its eyes could see, but its brain never learned to interpret the sensory input. It continued to stumble and bump into objects, unable to coordinate its movements with what it saw because in its experience, action and perception had never existed in the same continuum, their connection had been severed. Held and Hein's experiment proved that these two faculties were inseparable: perception relied on action and action was only possible through perception. Citing their work, Varela and his coauthors conclude that "this beautiful study supports the enactive view that objects are not seen by visual extraction of features, but rather by the visual guidance of action."[32]

Enactive cognition, therefore, suggests a "middle way" between the traditional view of a world with pregiven qualities that are recovered and represented by the cognitive system—what Varela and his coauthors call the chicken position—and its opposite, an entirely solipsistic cognitive system that projects its own world as a reflection of internal laws of the system—what they call the egg position. Scientific work with color vision offers a basis for this perspective and their explanation is worth quoting at length:

> Our discussion of color suggests a middle way between these two chicken and egg extremes. We have seen that colors are not "out there" independent of our perceptual and cognitive capacities. We have also seen that colors are not "in here" independent of our surrounding biological and cultural world. Contrary to the objectivist view, color categories are experiential; contrary to the subjectivist view, color categories belong to our shared biological and cultural world. Thus color as a case study enables us to appreciate the obvious point that chicken and egg, world and perceiver, specify each other. . . . Our intention is to bypass entirely this logical geography of inner versus outer by studying cognition not as recovery or projection but as embodied action.[33]

This systems view of cognition dramatically highlights that the point for understanding can no longer be a world with pregiven qualities that are passively recovered by the body and represented by an isolated mind. We must instead confront the complexity of the dynamic coupling between an organism, in which its nervous system links sensory and motor surfaces, with its environment. More recent work in cognitive science has supported this systems perspective by demonstrating empirically that many cognitive tasks are greatly simplified by our propensities to (1) anticipate experiences and perceptions (only the differences from expectation need to be processed); (2) use information already in the world (so that mental representations are often not required); and (3) to distribute the demands of real-world cognition among several individuals.[34]

These aspects of the theory of enactive cognition also have significance for the study of music in general and improvisation in particular. Bowman notes: "When we hear a musical performance, we do not just 'think,' nor do we just 'hear': we participate with our whole bodies; we construct and enact it."[35] Music is all too often thought of as an objective and static commodity, whether as a notated score or a recorded performance, rather than as the dynamic individual and social activity that it more accurately represents. Traditional musicological and pedagogical practices have relied heavily on these static representations of music making, to the point that replacing the notion of music as "something-out-there" with a systemic and dynamic perspective may seem as radical as the original formulations of autopoietic theory were to cognitivist-minded researchers. But if music research and applied study is to engage productively with the increasingly systems-centered approach to scientific research, we need to rethink and reconfigure many of our most cherished notions.

For instance, many approaches to improvisation have wrongly separated mind from body. They treat the improviser as an information processing machine that attempts to represent, restructure, and reproduce external musical constructs in real time, often focusing on the unfortunate shortcomings that insufficient time and unreliable memory can create.[36] An embodied and enactive approach to improvisation, however, denies this independent, pregiven world of musical constructs. Just as there is no absolute color "out there" independent of a perceiver's history of coordinated actions with his environment, there is no "swing" eighth note, "bluesy" melody, or even a "lydian dominant scale" independent of an individual's perceptually guided actions operating within a more encompassing biological, psychological, and cultural context. An embodied approach focuses instead on the ways in which improvisers perceptually guide their sensorimotor patterns to engage with local situations, and the ways in which the local situation changes continually as a result of improvisers' perceptions/actions.

Music researchers and educators in general have frequently accepted, either uncritically or unwittingly, a cognitivist explanation of "knowing" and "understanding," such that explanation, analysis, and instruction of music are often conceived of as the simple transmission of "rational," "objective," and therefore "mental" knowledge. Both the notion that music exists primarily as a symbolic rather than incorporated system and the tacitly accepted idea that music "composition" happens away from and prior to music making have contributed to this situation. With an enactive view of music and music cognition, however, not only is the mind embodied in a very real sense (both in performance and in listening), but the body and mind are socially and culturally mediated. In contrast to the detached abstractions of many Eurological musicians, Evan Parker is adamant about the importance of the embodied and enactive aspects of his performance:

> [T]he aim is not to "let sounds be sounds," or however Cage put it, but to acknowledge the fact that producing the sounds means something to you, being in control of the sounds means something to you, interacting with the other players means something to you. And have the outcome, the musical outcome, be at least an expression of those things.[37]

Like Maturana and Varela, philosopher Mark Johnson's work *The Body in the Mind* also challenges the Cartesian split between mind and body and attempts to mediate between extreme objectivism and solipsism.[38] Johnson insists that our reasoning is not rooted in abstract conceptualization but instead in our history of experience with perceptual and physical interactions. For Johnson, much of our verbal and conceptual imagination originates in bodily and kinesthetic experiences that are metaphorically extended to give structure to a wide variety of cognitive domains. Johnson believes that these schemata emerge from certain basic forms of sensorimotor activities and interactions and provide a preconceptual structure to our experience. As an example, consider how our embodied sense of vision, "to see," has come to be used in a variety of ways to mean "to understand." Beyond perhaps its most common usage, "Do you see what I mean," the schemata can be creatively extended to create such sentences as, "Can you shed some light on this subject for me," or even more creatively, "It would take an electron microscope to find the point of this article."

The mental operations that we perform to work through a problem or situation also have analogs to spatial manipulation, orientation, and movement. For example, our physical interaction with a container's interior, boundary, and exterior give structure metaphorically to our conceptualizations of the visual world (things go in and out of sight) and personal relationships (one gets into and out of a relationship) among other things. Container schemata also appear to structure many of our understandings in the musical domain, including our notions of harmony, rhythm, and form. For instance, jazz musicians often talk about staying "inside" the chord changes or traveling "outside" of a tune's precomposed harmony, while a particularly tight rhythmic moment may be described as "in the pocket" or "in the groove."[39] It is interesting to note that container schemata may also affect our tendency to place musical practices into stylistic "boxes," a practice that has often circumscribed African-American creativity in undesirable ways. Many improvisers are increasingly dissatisfied with the notion that musical practices necessarily fall either "inside" or "outside" of conventional thinking.

The general cognitive process through which we structure an unfamiliar or abstract domain in terms of a more familiar or concrete one is referred to as cross-domain mapping. Recent work in cognitive linguistics has offered substantial evidence that cross-domain mappings are not simply manifestations of literary creativity, such as figures of speech, but rather are pervasive in everyday discourse and integral to the very process of cognition and consciousness.[40] Cross-domain mappings do not simply "represent" one domain in terms of another. They are grounded in our bodily experiences and perceptions and create precise, inference-preserving mappings between the structures of both domains.[41]

Because of the rather abstract and transient nature of musical sound, cross-domain mapping plays an important role in musical discourse. Our musical vocabularies are in fact filled with embodied metaphors: pitches are high or low; sounds are close or distant; textures are dense or sparse. We cross modalities with other senses: sounds can be light, bright, clear, or dark; harmonies can be sweet or tart; textures can be sharp, rough, or smooth. Larry Zbikowski, a music theorist whose work draws heavily on cognitive science, writes:

> Although we speak of "musical space" (and locate tones within it), this space does not correspond, in a rational way, to physical space; although we speak of "musical motion," the motion is at best apparent, and not real. The concepts of space and motion are extended to music through metaphorical transference as a way to account for certain aspects of our experience of music. These metaphors are not an addition to musical understanding, but are in fact basic to it.[42]

We should remember, however, that these embodied metaphors are based on human experiences with both the material *and* social worlds. One conceptual metaphor that frequently seems incontrovertible to many is *pitch relationships as relationships in vertical space*. We discuss pitches as moving along a continuum from low to high. From an embodied perspective, this metaphor appears to map clearly onto human anatomy; for all speakers and singers, low tones feel low down in the throat or the chest and high tones feel high up in the head. After a century of ethnomusicological inquiry, however, it is also clear that this metaphor is not valid in every culture or even in every time period in the West. In Ancient Greece, pitches were conceived of as "sharp" or "heavy." The Suya speak of "young" (high) and "old" (low) sounds, based on the changing male voice. Indonesians have "large" and "small" pitches to correspond to the size of their gongs and metallophones.[43] And in Burkina Faso, the notion of "high" and "low" pitches is inverted from that of the West, since the bass notes of the indigenous xylophone are physically higher off the ground to make room for larger calabash resonators.[44] This "inverted" conception also carries over to other instruments in the same music culture as well.[45]

Why, then, has the conceptual metaphor of *pitch relationships as relationships in vertical space* become the dominant one in the contemporary Western world? It does not correspond to the physical layout of all, or even most Western instruments: for example, to go up in pitch on a cello or stand-up bass you must go farther down the neck of the instrument, and even on a piano the "higher" notes simply lie to the right of the performer, not above. But it does correspond well to the Western system of notation that has been in use to preserve and to visualize music for several centuries; "higher" pitches do appear farther up the musical staff.[46] As Zbikowski notes, "The cross-domain mappings employed by any theory of music are thus more than simple curiosities—they are actually key to understanding music as a rich cultural product that both constructs and is constructed by cultural experience."[47]

Robert Walser was one of the first music scholars to champion Johnson's notion of embodied schemata as a useful tool for musical analysis and discussion, because they can describe at the same time general and preconceptual human experiences *and* culturally specific, polysemic signifiers. Paraphrasing Johnson, Walser writes that "metaphor mediates between bodily experience, on the one hand, and discourses of language and music, on the other."[48] In other words, music is mediated by our experiences of our bodies and our interactions with the rest of the material world, just as our bodily experiences are, in turn, mediated by music, language, and other aspects of culture. Remarkably, a similar view to the one emerging in cognitive science can also be found in the field of anthropology. As Jacques Maquet, a proponent of aesthetic anthropology, explains: "A first step is to realize that artifacts, behaviors, ideas are not purely cultural: they are not related only to their traditions of origin. They are also related to what is common to all human beings, and to what is particular to the individual who has created them."[49]

Walser focuses his treatment on Johnson's force schemata and its manifestation in musical timbre, according to Walser, "the least successfully theorized and analyzed of musical parameters."[50] His study focuses on heavy metal guitar and vocal technique as a musical and cultural site where timbre is paramount and images of power and force are continually circulated between musicians, audiences, and the music and marketing industries. The "powerful" sounds of heavy metal can resonate with listeners in both embodied and encultured ways. For instance, people experience distorted sounds and noise on a daily basis, both within their own bodies, as when a scream or yell overexerts the capacity of the human vocal chords (signifying heightened meaning or immediacy of response), and in their interactions with standard technology such as overdriven stereo equipment or poor telephone connections. Improviser/composer Cornelius Cardew also highlighted these forceful interactions: "It is not the exclusive privilege of music to have a history—sound has history too. Industry and modern technology have added machine sounds and electronic sounds to the primeval sounds of thunderstorm, volcanic eruption, avalanche and tidal wave."[51]

Heavy metal and other popular music forms, including rap and techno, have used electronic equipment and effects to exploit these modern industrial sounds and the physical immediacy that can be evoked by musical "noise." In jazz and classical musics, where acoustic instruments and the human voice have remained for many the primary means of expression, extended instrumental and vocal techniques can also reference and impart Johnson's force schemata. But we must remember that although force schemata can communicate certain shared meanings on the basis of human embodiment, their culturally conditioned aspects also signify in a multitude of ways. Just as heavy metal distortion and power chords have been used in differing musical and cultural circles to sanctify the Devil and exalt the glory of God, the forceful extended techniques now commonplace in free jazz and free improvisation have signified in varied ways from the Black Power of the 1960s to transcendental spirituality or postmodern angst and confusion.

Music has the remarkable ability to evoke and reference a whole host of embodied sensitivities and encultured or symbolic qualities. In performance, these work together in extremely complex ways. Combined, they attest to the power of music to influence people and societies, to bring people together and to drive them apart. Wayne Bowman explains:

The list of bodily constituted musical "properties" is an extraordinarily long one, inclusive of such diverse yet central musical features as: tension and release; dissonance and consonance; volume and balance; accent, meter and syncopation; tonal center and modulation; texture and density; line and phrase; height and

depth; advancement and recession; vital drive and groove; movement and gesture—to say nothing of the immense range of so-called expressive attributes like
seriousness, whimsy, playfulness, tenderness, or violence. It is the body's presence
in each of these, and their consequently intimate links to personal *and collective*
identity, that account for music's remarkable capacity to affirm or offend, to confront or console, and that account for the fact that people are seldom diffident
about their musical preferences."[52]

Gilles Fauconnier and Mark Turner, with their notion of conceptual blending, have
built on the idea of cross-domain mapping to provide a more nuanced picture of the
ways in which new meanings and understandings can arise from the blended input
of several conceptual frames.[53] The basic processes of conceptual blending include
composition, completion, and elaboration. Composition projects the content from two
or more inputs into the blended space, completion fills out the pattern in the blend by
referencing information in long-term memory, and elaboration involves extending or
applying the now fully formed blend into new domains or new situations.[54] At each of
these stages of the blend, new content and new meanings may develop that were not
available from either of the input spaces. Blends can be created "on the fly" with only
fleeting significance, or they may become established in conventions of thought and
over time lose their efficacy or allow for other distinct blends to emerge.

While a few scholars have adopted the notion of conceptual blending to analyze the
emergent meanings found in musical settings with text, purely instrumental music
offers a more perplexing challenge.[55] But by engaging with the emerging fields of
embodiment studies, music scholars are beginning to challenge many stereotyped or
tacitly accepted notions about music's relationship with the body. For instance, Su-
zanne Cusick, in her article titled "Feminist Theory, Music Theory, and the Mind/Body
Problem," highlights the ways in which academic discussions of music too often ignore the embodied aspects of performance. She writes, "Music, an art which self-
evidently does not exist until bodies make it and/or receive it, is thought about as if it
were a mind-mind game."[56] By which she means the composer's mind creates patterns
of sounds to which other minds—those of listeners and critics—assign meanings. According to Cusick, these "mind-mind messages" are imagined to be transmitted by
disempowered (and symbolically mechanized) performers between "members of a
metaphorically disembodied class, and, because disembodied, elite."[57]

Embodiment theory has done much to attack the perceived objectivism (and Euro-
centrism) of Cartesian science, but at least in its early incarnation it did not always
take full account of the specific contexts provided by embodiment. While finding
much in Mark Johnson's influential work *The Body in the Mind* to recommend it, Kath-
erin Hayles remarks, "It is ironic that he reinscribes objectivist presuppositions in
positing a universal body unmarked by gender, ethnicity, physical disability, or culture."[58] Other scholars such as Elizabeth Grosz rightly point out that "indeed, there is
no body as such; there are only bodies—male or female, black, brown, white, large or
small—and the gradations in between."[59] And Cusick argues that "when music theorists and musicologists ignore the bodies whose performative acts constitute the thing
called music, we ignore the feminine."[60]

Walser and Susan McClary, in an article titled "Theorizing the Body in African-
American Music," also stress the importance of music scholars engaging with the

complex discursive fields of physicality and sexuality while remaining diligent not to reduce music in general, and black music and its related forms in particular, to the trenchant views that segregate body from mind. Notions of the body have historically been used both to denounce and to celebrate African-American expressive forms, and Walser and McClary highlight the ways in which mind and culture (as "high art") still remain, for many, the exclusive provenance of Eurocentric discourse. They write, "The binary opposition of mind and body that governs the condemnation of black music remains in full force; even when the terms are inverted [by romanticizing the black body], they are always ready to flip back into their more usual positions."[61]

Unlike some in the improvised music community who may wish to distance themselves from the traditions of American jazz, Parker, although English, is adamant about the relationship of his music to the African-American tradition of creative improvisation. In an interview with Graham Lock, Parker was resolute in his convictions:

> What's important to me is that my work is seen in a particular context, coming out of a particular tradition. I don't really care what people call it but I would want it to be clear that I was inspired to play by listening to certain people who continue to be talked about mainly in jazz contexts. People like John Coltrane, Eric Dolphy, Cecil Taylor—these were people that played music that excited me to the point where I took music seriously myself. That continues to be the case. That's where what I'm doing has to make sense, if it makes any sense at all."[62]

Although Parker's playing does bring to mind, to varying degrees, memories of Coltrane, Ayler, Dolphy, Tchicai, Lyons, and Lacy, he has not been content with simple imitation or idolatry. With only a bit of hyperbole, Steve Lake writes: "Coltrane galvanized innumerable saxophonists—to imitation, above all. Parker moved swiftly through this perhaps necessary phase, and grasped the larger challenge implicit in Coltrane's music. To pay appropriate homage, one had to be unsentimental as the master was in affecting radical upheaval in the shape of jazz itself."[63] In the analysis that follows, I hope to illustrate ways in which improvised music in general, and the solo practice of Evan Parker in particular, challenge many of the aforementioned dichotomies by foregrounding the sonic and contextual qualities of an intelligent body and an embodied mind. The social, cultural, and even ethical dimensions of an embodied approach to music and music instruction will also be taken up in the final chapter.

It's a Bit Like Juggling

Evan Parker's saxophone practice has an undeniable physical quality to it. His primary extended saxophone devices include split tones and multiphonics produced by intricate cross-fingerings or "venting" the instrument in different places along the tube; exaggerated articulations, including rapid and multiple tonguing effects and slapping and popping techniques; and polyrhythmic fingering patterns that often produce highly angular and complex linear shapes and subtle microtonal variations of pitch. To develop these extended techniques, Parker has worked to liberate different bodily aspects of his playing—the fingers, the tongue, the larynx, and the breath—so that each physical system may achieve a substantial degree of independence. He then combines these body techniques, most of which are concealed from view, with the acoustic attributes of the instrument and the concert space and with any overriding creative concerns for the performance.

Each of these saxophone techniques exploits sonic textures that in other contexts might be referred to as "noise" in the pejorative sense.[64] Many devotees of Western "classical" music (particularly those with nineteenth-century leanings) idolize a purity of sound, articulation, and pitch, whereas Parker's extended devices seemingly ignore or transcend the normal design and use of the instrument. By expanding the natural range, timbre, and traditional connection between tongue and fingers, Parker may also be able to convey metaphorically a heightened meaning or immediacy to listeners (just as distorting the human voice or overdriving electronic equipment often do). His polyphonic approach also allows him to circumvent obvious ascending and descending phrases in a way that challenges the dominant conceptual mapping (derived from notated music) of pitch relationships as relationships in vertical space. Even Parker's use of circular breathing to set these extended techniques into motion, when examined in isolation, may connote hyperextension on a biological level, appearing as it does to bypass the human need for oxygen. Ethnomusicologist Ali Jihad Racy has noted that in the Arab world, the technique of circular breathing often connotes a certain mystique and may be an important factor in triggering states of elation and psychological transformation among listeners.[65]

Researchers interested in music cognition have proposed a plausible relationship between bodily motions and musical correlates that, to some extent, is bypassed in Parker's solo approach.[66] For example, the standard phrase length in music can be seen to correspond with the dynamic swells associated with breathing or the gradual sway of the body or a limb. The musical beat (particularly of dance-based musics) corresponds not only to the frequency range of our heartbeat (as the musical term implies), but also generally to the rate of walking, sucking, chewing, head nodding, and sexual intercourse. Subdivisions of the pulse, perhaps at the level of the individual note, often correspond to the speed of speech patterns or hand gestures.[67] And on the level of microtiming, small deviations such as grace notes or temporal asynchronies seem to correspond with rapid flams between fingers or limbs, or to the rate of delivery of individual phonemes in speech.

Drawing on considerable neurological and cognitive data, Vijay Iyer suggests that "in the sensoriomotor perspective, a perceived rhythm is literally an imagined movement. . . . Hence the act of listening to rhythmic music involves the same mental processes that generate bodily motion."[68] And Wayne Bowman theorizes a similar position when he writes, "If it is indeed the case that rhythmic/temporal features in music perception/cognition arise from activation of substantial parts of the same neural circuitry involved in bodily movement and action, the bodily dimension so often evident in acts of musical listening (and music making) is not just a function of fortuitous resemblance, representation, or association. If listening and music making activate the same neural circuitry as bodies in motion, we have a material basis for the claim that bodily action is an indelible and fundamental part of what music, *qua* music, is. And if music requires bodily motion as a precondition of its being, so too may music shape and inform other possibilities for embodied being."[69]

As alluded to earlier, however, Evan Parker's solo music seems, in some ways, to deny these first two levels of musical and bodily correlates. His lengthy passages using circular breathing can extend well beyond the natural limits of the breath, and his sense of pulse often avoids any obvious connections to the recurring patterns of walking or of the circulatory system. On closer listening, however, even in the midst of an extended passage made possible by circular breathing Parker tends to introduce a new layer or element at roughly the same interval as a standard phrase. While his repeating-but-not-repetitive patterning frequently seems to cycle at roughly the rate of a medium-tempo pulse or beat, though rarely in such an orderly or predictable fashion. Even on the level of subdivided pulse, Parker's rapid, angular, and "polyphonic" structures seem less akin to the pace and design of regular speech than to glossolalia, or other forms of heightened speech. Expressive microtiming also seems to play a central role in Parker's music, but Iyer's focus on groove-based music and their expressive divergence from a shared pulse offers little help in analyzing the more abstract qualities of Parker's playing. To what might Parker's music be oriented, if not to these standard notions of bodily correlates?[70]

Parker adopts a telling embodied metaphor that captures well the sense of heightened awareness and ability evoked by his music, as well as the seemingly paradoxical way in which his performances are fully embodied and yet seem to point at times to an extension or a denial of the corporeal form:

> It's a bit like juggling. . . . You have to do the easier tricks first: get into the rhythm and suddenly your body is able to do things which you couldn't do cold. The best bits of my solo playing, for me, I can't explain to myself. Certainly I wouldn't know how to go straight to them cold. The circular breathing is a way of starting the engine, but at a certain speed all kinds of things happen which I'm not consciously controlling. They just come out. It's as though the instrument comes alive and starts to have a voice of its own.[71]

This passage is replete with implications for a theory of musical embodiment. Juggling, or more simply balancing objects in gravity, is a physical sensation we are all familiar with. The delicate skills and inherent risk involved with the venture can be appreciated on a biological level. But juggling, as Johnson might point out, has also been metaphorically extended from the biological into the conceptual domain: "juggling" options, careers, or responsibilities. The cross-domain mappings have a cultural dimension as well. For instance, risk taking might be frowned upon in certain societies while in others it is seen as an indispensable tool for survival and success.

In attempting to juggle or balance an object in gravity, there is, in one sense, clear effort and intentionality. Yet a desire for too much conscious control—thinking too hard about the task at hand—can lead to continual corrections that eventually upset the delicate system. When witnessing a juggler at the peak of her of his performance, one can focus on the specific moves and the rhythmic quality of the performer tossing and catching items in succession, but the items in flight and the entire system itself tend to take on a life of their own. At its most basic, juggling represents uncertainty and risk, and audiences are undoubtedly led to empathize with the performer, whose task can seem at times insurmountable, or at least untenable in the long run.

Juggling also highlights that, in order for the system to achieve and maintain its organizational complexity—its constancy—there must be a continual flow of energy and matter and an undercurrent of insecurity. As more items may be added to the "trick," the organizational complexity of the system, and the resulting feelings of both awe and anxiety can be multiplied exponentially. The specific associations and feelings that are evoked in individuals by the embodied qualities of performance will of course be based on personal and encultured sensibilities. Some might wish to turn their head away in fear, unable to watch. Others may revel in the system's remarkable dynamical qualities. Still others may secretly hope for an embarrassing collapse. The performance may also bring to light a whole host of memories or recollections that have less to do with the actual event than with the lived history of the audience members, but which are provoked by the shared and embodied aspects of the performance.

Of course Parker's musical approach involves more than simply repeating a well-worn trick. Unlike some who might wish to envision improvisation, particularly in its freer manifestations, as emerging from nowhere, a *tabula rasa*, Parker does not shy away from certain "fixed" aspects of his performance practice—those things that have been explored and embodied over time. In a more technical description of his solo approach, he remarked:

> In some ways, in some situations, the freedom of the total music, if it has any sense of freedom, is only possible because some parts are very fixed. And by holding those fixed parts in a loop, putting them on hold for a while, then you can look for other regions where variation is possible. But then I might discover a new loop in that new region which immediately loosens up the loop or loops that I've put on hold elsewhere. That's what I'm trying to do: I'm shifting my attention from different parts of the total sound spectrum. . . . That's where the use of repetition, although it appears to be a voluntary loss of freedom, actually opens up regions of the instrument which otherwise I wouldn't be aware of.[72]

Thinking about the Laundry

Parker goes on to describe his playing as a potent means of shifting activity to the creative and intuitive side the brain: "When the music's really going you switch from left-brain activity to right-brain activity—and once you've made that switch the left brain can think about more or less anything it wants. The laundry, anything."[73] Although Parker has worked diligently to establish these extended techniques and to be able to juggle their multiple interactions, he believes the best parts of his playing to be beyond his conscious control and his rational ability to understand.[74] The embodied aspects of his playing have emerged not through conscious or concerted means, but through continually engaging with the musical environment, idea space, and the instrument itself.

Musical complexity may be the first and easiest inroad into Parker's solo improvising style, and the sheer virtuosity of his technique undeniably receives the most comment in print. But this avenue alone can also serve to reify an analytical stance toward his music that denies both its transcendent possibilities and its embodied and contextual nature. Ian Carr, for instance, describes Parker's solo playing this way: "The resultant effect is possibly something like (if it could be done) putting one bar of music under a very powerful microscope or a stethoscope. What we see or experience is still music, but we are aware of the fibers of it, the component parts, the usually concealed physics, in extreme close-up."[75] Although an evocative description of Parker's timbral and textural explorations, Carr's analogy is perhaps too reminiscent of a reductionist brand of science and a structuralist view of music theory. His statement maintains a strong separation between the music being made and the musician making it; "putting one bar of music" under a microscope in the lab.

Despite his command over an extended vocabulary of saxophone devices and sounds, Evan Parker seems to enjoy the inherently unpredictable ways in which they may combine. He allows the intelligent body, the acoustic environment, and a faith in the immediacy of the moment to have a hand in shaping performance. In what could function as a direct rebuttal to Carr, Parker describes his approach this way: "It remains theoretical until it's happened. It's not like somebody doing rigorous scientific research, where you set out to determine, *is this true?* then link together the outcome of those smaller experiments to test the bigger hypothesis. It's not really like that. Could be dressed up like that, but what's really going on is a nonverbal, largely nonconceptual kind of activity, once called 'play.' You know, 'playing' the saxophone."[76] At the end of chapter five we will return to this notion of play to which Parker is referring.

Former *Village Voice* critic Tom Johnson, although also clearly under the spell of Parker's extended techniques, argues instead that it is Parker's seamless integration of the physical and mental aspects of his playing that will continue to impress listeners well after the shock of his technical wizardry has worn off. Johnson writes:

He was never playing "special effects." He was just playing the way he always plays. His circular breathing was so much under control he wouldn't even bother with it some of the time. If a phrase needed to go on and on, he would sneak the extra air into the horn to make it go on and on, sometimes for several minutes. But at other moments, when that wasn't the point, he would quickly revert to normal breathing. When he would go for a particular tonal area, he seemed to know exactly what notes would come out, and he knew just how to wiggle his fingers to make his complex sustained textures ripple or flutter or sputter the way he wanted them to. He heard where the tonic was, when there was one, and how to ease back into it, if he desired. He even had control over the difference tones, which are odd, low tones that vibrate inside your ear when two high pitches, slightly out of tune, vibrate in a certain way. . . . In short, this was not a hit-and-miss affair the way it is with most woodwind players when they turn on their multiphonics. This was a musician who had transformed these new sounds into a vocabulary that was familiar to him as major scales are to most musicians.[77]

Steve Lake agrees that, "A mere combining of 'extended' techniques won't necessarily result in music, much less magic and mystery."[78] And those critics who are even more suspicious of Parker's highly technical approach, or those who fear his aesthetic leans too far toward the transcendent, are often quick to denounce his playing as less interactive, less improvised. Ben Watson, author of a recent book on guitarist Derek Bailey and the development of (primarily British) free improvisation, carps: "In interviews, Evan Parker claimed to be pushing his circular breathing gambit as 'far' as he could—pressing himself up against a brick wall and pressing further—but the totalitarian afflatus of his technique steamrollers specific ambience, turning his music into the kind of dependable commodity required by promoters and applauded by the general public."[79] Watson's comments are undoubtedly sparked, at least in part, by a long-standing and well publicized (although not well understood) professional split between

Derek Bailey and Evan Parker, but he does strike an especially sensitive nerve when he describes the ongoing debate between many free improvisers in general: "To the mainstream, all avant-gardes look the same, but the avant-garde is actually bifurcated by a struggle between transcendental idealists and dialectical materialists."[80]

Parker's approach and aesthetic seems to ask listeners to envision these in dialectical relationship rather than as a simple dichotomy. In response to criticisms such as Watson's, Parker counters that the specific ambience of performance makes all the difference: "Beyond certain preconditions like good physical shape of lower lip and a good reed the most important [factors] are, one, acoustics and, two, a feeling that it means something to some other people in the room."[81] But he is also aware that on certain nights the "magic and mystery" that Lake described remain resolutely out of reach and listeners are forced to settle for, in Lake's words, "interesting/clever/complex music." When pressed Parker responded: "The only hope is that when the magic proves elusive there is still enough in the shell of 'interesting/clever/complex' to have earned my fee."

Although willing to acknowledge the material side of his playing and his livelihood, Parker remains adamant that his music is not principally about its technical features. He has adopted another kinesthetic metaphor that describes well the synergetic impact of his work and makes a strong case against submitting it to a simple reductionist analysis:

There's an analogy with the spokes on a revolving wheel. Everything's in motion, the rim of the wheel is supported by the spokes, but when the whole thing is turning you don't see the spokes any more. If the thing didn't have that speed of rotation, it would make sense to count the spokes and think about them one at a time. But the whole point is to get the thing revolving and the spokes are only there to enable the rim of the wheel to turn. There's some kind of equivalent of that in the music. You could, you can, after the event, slow the thing down and look at how all the pieces fit together. But the whole point is that the pieces fit together that way in order to generate the speed of movement which *is* the music. . . . The music is not what you hear in analysis, it's what is there in the real time of performance.[82]

In his treatment of free improvisation, Watson is determined to champion the physical and material qualities of the music in an effort to reveal "transcendence as a lie," but at times he veers dangerously close to the celebratory primitivism that has plagued discussions of improvisation, and particularly African-American jazz, in the past. For instance, in a passage celebrating Derek Bailey's less referential and reverential approach (by contrast with the "transcendental" work of fellow English guitarist John McGlaughlin), Watson writes: "In comparison to the sweeping virtuosity of the Mahavishnu Orchestra—which evokes traditional virtues from Liszt to Ravi Shankar— the kind of virtuosity proposed by Bailey is so shockingly physical that the listener is forced to think of such acts as armpit-scratching and nose picking. Its return of music to the physical act debunks civilization itself."[83] Elsewhere Watson references Parker's playing in the same light:

When Hugh Davies is pursuing a close-miked scrunch and Bailey is signaling his involvement with a series of rasped pings—or Evan Parker is pushing overblown soprano saxophone into glottal regions of nose-blow anguish—we are witnessing the pursuit of instrumental ability beyond civilized elevation. The unconscious basis of curiosity—the child's interest in the products of the body—is foregrounded in these sounds, refusing the transcendent beauty of staged virtuosity."[84]

Watson seems intent on postulating free improvisation as a "universal human language" with an anthropological basis in "intimations of inhalation and exhalation, of muscular tension and relaxation, of sexual arousal and relief."[85] In so doing, however, he all but ignores the ways in which our relationship to our bodies, and the relationship that others have to them, are constructed within specific cultural settings that can harbor and impart a variety of racial, gender, and sexual constructions.[86]

There is much to be learned from a treatment such as Graham Lock's *Blutopia* that suggests that the music of Duke Ellington, Sun Ra, and Anthony Braxton, but more broadly African-American expressive culture in general, are predicated on two impulses: one impulse to remember (the "blues" impulse of his title) and another impulse to construct through music a vision of the future (the utopic reference).[87] Parker acknowledges the important relationship that his music has to the African-American tradition of creative music in general and to the music of specific individuals as well, and he acknowledges the ways in which his techniques have developed and have become embodied over time. From one perspective, these changes occur at a rather glacial pace. Parker comments: "It's curious how the changes drop into the existing material almost camouflaged. It's only by going back and hearing in blocks of five years that the differences become more obvious."[88] Yet he also acknowledges the ways in which the specific dynamics of performance—its acoustics and ambience—make possible those occasions on which one may enter into the idealized space of music's utopian vision.[89]

As with the wheel in his analogy, Parker's music is firmly grounded in its specifics and yet it is not about them. Rather, the music is about propulsion and momentum and the fact that it can open up an entirely different world of experience, much as the wheel afforded humans a dramatic change in lifestyle and perspective that was unavailable before.[90] The circularity of his metaphor and his playing also bring to mind the "strange loops" that Douglas Hofstadter finds in the ever-rising notes of a Bach canon, in the endlessly rising steps of an Escher staircase, and in Gödel's proof of unprovable mathematical axioms.[91] And these strange loops have much in common with the autocatalytic sets of systems theory that create a circular world in which all causes are results, and all results are causes. Although Parker's earlier comments about scientific research may be on target for the methods and ideologies of reductionism, the emerging scientific paradigm has shifted attention to the importance of qualitative research approaches and of systemic perspectives, taking seriously the notion that, to borrow Heinz von Forester's pun, the act of "observing systems" is inseparable from those "observing systems" who are doing the observing.[92]

A Chameleon on a Mirror

Another koanlike riddle favored by Gregory Bateson, first proposed to him by his student Stuart Brand in the early 1970s, asks, "What color is a chameleon placed on a mirror?" It illustrates well one of the central tenets of systems thinking: reflexivity. Katherine Hayles defines reflexivity as "the movement whereby that which has been used to generate a system is made, through a changed perspective, to become part of the system it generates."[93] As in juggling, the individual parts that generate the system—the performer and his apparatuses—are intrinsically part of the system being generated. Like Bateson's koan provided earlier, in which the blind man's cane becomes part of the observing system, Parker and his horn are involved in generating the music; yet from a changed perspective, they and the reflexive system they define *are* the music. *Wired* editor and futurist Kevin Kelly explains it this way: "The lizard-glass demonstrates an entirely different logic—the circular causality of the Net. In the realm of recursive reflections, an event is not triggered by a chain of being, but by a field of causes reflecting, bending, mirroring each other in a fun-house nonsense. Rather than cause and control being dispensed in a straight line from its origin, it spreads horizontally, like creeping tide, influencing in roundabout, diffuse ways."[94]

The motion of a wheel also highlights rather well another fundamental aspect of systems theory: that experience involves two different but interrelated processes. We can envision these as a linear and circular view. The linear view has more to do with the result of a process, and the circular view animates the feedback loop that shapes its form. For instance, when watching a wheel move, we can focus on either its linear motion, the path it traces out through space, or on its circular motion, the fact that its individual spokes go around and around, maintaining its integrity. You may even have had the experience of watching the wheels on a car go by and, although it is clear that they are moving rapidly, the wheels themselves appear to be frozen in time. In a very real sense, a wheel represents both of these dimensions, its organization as a feedback loop that defines its inherent circularity, and its ability to progress through linear time.

To make our example a bit more illustrative, let's imagine a snowball instead of a wheel. Now we can focus on the path created in the snow as it barrels downhill, the linear view, or we can focus on the circular motion of the snowball itself, which also represents its intimate connection with its environment, its feedback structure. In other words, the snowball emerges from its environment (it is shaped from surrounding snow) and in rolling downhill it takes in new resources from its environment that allow it to grow, leaving a path in its wake. Although we can view each facet of this system as separate—the path and the snowball—and each in turn as separate from its environment—the snowy context—they are coupled together in such a way that they are bound up with one another; they are intrinsically inseparable. No snowball without a path through the snow, no path through the snow without a snowball, and neither of course without the system-wide context of snow.

Although both circular and linear views are tangible in the snowball example, many feedback systems are not as easy to visualize. For instance, instead of a snowball consider a line of dominoes falling. The linear view is clearly embedded in the pattern of pieces that is constructed ahead of time. Once the system gracefully succumbs to the simple touch of a finger, however, we can marvel at the force that both triggers and is fueled by the fall of the dominoes. Sure, we might want to dismiss this as nothing more than gravity, but what is often forgotten about Newton's law is that gravity describes a force between two objects pulling on *one another*. Because our day-to-day experiences with gravity include an extremely large mass, the Earth, we often unconsciously think about it as a one-way relationship. Here we have a nice reminder of the importance of system dynamics. As we watch the dominoes fall, the linear and circular views—the pattern and form of the system—combine to produce an intriguing example of emergence.[95]

The pattern of Parker's musicking—the linear view—can seem impressive on its own, but it is simply the unfolding of the feedback structure, the trace that the musicking leaves behind. The form of Parker's musicking—its circular nature—is enfolded in the relationship between the various physico-cognitive processes of the performer and the tight coupling with the instrument, the sounds that it may produce, and the specific context for performance. Both perspectives are valid alone, but a systems perspective sees them as intimately woven together, fundamentally inseparable. In conversation with David Toop, Parker acknowledged a fondness for thinking in terms of feedback structures:

It's the key notion of the twentieth century. I'm not an expert on cybernetics but bringing an ability to generalise about feedback is a twentieth century phenomenon. Before that there were specific applications but I don't think there was a general awareness of how many control systems can be analysed in terms of the feedback between inputs and outputs. It's certainly high on my list of analytical tools.[96]

This awareness of feedback processes has led to an important shift in Parker's thinking, a move away from dualistic concerns. Speaking of his early solo practice, Parker admitted:

You know I was very keen on the distinction between improvisation and composition at that time, consequently I've come to realize it was a false kind of distinction, but for me the special problem was to distinguish between solo improvising and composing, precisely because it was one mind at work and none of those qualities of group improvisation. But subsequently I've come to think rather differently about the whole thing. I don't think it's accurate to speak about an improvisation as something different from composition. . . . It's more accurate to speak of it as opposed to notated music.[97]

Parker's earlier observation that the saxophone seems to have a life and a voice of its own, although on the surface sounding a bit transcendent, may also be better understood as an example of the circular causality of embodiment and enaction theories; the perceiver and environment determine each other through reciprocal structuring and selection.[98] While it might be hard to envision the saxophone changing as a result of Parker's playing, it must be remembered that the instrument is much more than a tube of brass with keys, pads, corks, springs, and screws. The saxophone takes on a musical identity only in interaction with a performer. Parker's horn is not simply dependent on his playing, nor an extension of it, but in important ways his horn shapes his playing. As he uncovers new sounds, places other layers on hold, new combinations can emerge that were not predictable in their entirety. Just as it is valid from one perspective to say that Parker *plays* the saxophone, it is equally valid from another perspective to say that the saxophone *plays* Parker.

In a rather poetic comment, Parker eloquently expresses the productive tension between pattern and form, permanence and flux, or process and reality that informs his playing and his own brand of systems thinking:

> Every time I start it's the same place and every time I start it's somewhere different. It depends on how you want to look at that place. The same as when you get up in the morning, it's a new day, but it's also got a hell of a lot in common with the day before. It's a question of how you want to incorporate the cyclic repetitive elements into the Heraclitian flux, the river you can never step in twice. Both things are true and both things are absolutely inadequate descriptions of reality.[99]

The contemporary orientation of cognitive science on issues of embodiment points toward a "middle way" between purely objective and purely subjective descriptions of phenomena. This orientation resonates well with contemporary improvisation studies that are attempting to avoid the dichotomy between the objective analysis of improvisation as "product" and the solipsistic description of improvisation as a purely intuitive process. I offer some more technical analysis of Parker's solo improvisations in chapter four, but his performance practice and perspective offer an intriguing subject for this embodied view of improvisation. Parker often provides eloquent and exact descriptions of the technical aspects of his saxophone playing, while at the same time he continually stresses the liberating aspects of improvised performance. According to him, "In the heat of the moment a lot of the stuff you work on and practice is forgotten or takes second role. The impulse to express something through playing becomes more important than the technical procedure. But the more solid the technical understanding is, than the better the basis for expression is."[100]

Parker's very personal and virtuosic solo saxophone style draws attention to the bodily aspects of his performance just as it denatures—at times with the assistance of modern technologies—the very idea of a grounded or objective sense of self. As he eloquently states, "In the end the saxophone has been for me a rather specialized biofeedback instrument for studying and expanding my control over my hearing and the motor mechanics of parts of my skeleto-muscular system and their improved functioning has given me more to think about. Sometimes the body leads the imagination, sometimes the imagination leads the body."[101]

4

Rivers of Consciousness

exploring permuting soundscapes hurtling through dense shifting harmonic clusters, flowing through turbulent fluctuations of
textures
swirling in varying bands of multicolored prisms undulating to
the throbbing pulse bubbling under the myriad of asymmetric polyrhythms weaving through multi-hued atonal variations
punctuated with percussive explosions scattered fragments of
sound eliciting piercing primal screams stimulated by the pyro-
technical display of polyphonic auditory collages generating a constantly mind expanding soundshapes
evolving into a sonic montage of intricate voicings, complex
rhythmic gyrations, tonal aberrations projecting emotion through
sounds
sounds musical
shrieks—howls—cackles
sounds embellished through circular deviations
a simmering mosaic of endless patterns and structures forming
then dissolving into rivers and streams of sound rushing toward
collision only to merge into flowing ethereal harmonies intertwin-
ing like rills, rivulets, brooks
receiving the impetus through the converging tributaries emptying into gulfs, lakes, oceans
blending a cacophonous mélange of colors, shapes, textures into
a unifying essence.[1]

—Sam Rivers

Despite his longstanding dedication to composing challenging music for large jazz
ensemble, and his well respected small-group compositions and recordings, multi-
instrumentalist Sam Rivers may be best know for his dynamic and exploratory trio
work. In this intimate and flexible setting, Rivers has been creating compelling music-
in-the-moment for nearly four decades. Perhaps the most remarkable aspect of Rivers's improvised trio performances, both then and now, is that a delicate yet dynamic

order and balance unfailingly emerges, despite the fact that the musicians do not plan any details of their performance in advance. Rivers describes his trio's approach this way: "The communication is in the music while we are performing. I set a tempo into what we are going into and they're listening to me. We go in and out of tempo by listening, it's an intuitive kind of playing."[2]

In March of 2004, we had the pleasure of hosting Sam Rivers at UCSD under the auspices of the UC Regent's Lecturer Program for a week of performances, workshops, and talks. Sam came from Orlando, Florida, with his current trio, including Doug Mathews on bass and bass clarinet and Anthony Cole on drums, piano, and saxophone. During his visit, Sam shared his wisdom and musicality in a variety of diverse settings. He spoke with our undergraduate music majors about his half-century of professional experience, and he offered a guest lecture to Anthony Davis's jazz history class, ending with an unscripted duo between the two seasoned improvisers that received a standing ovation. He and his trio spent an afternoon providing a performance workshop for my graduate-level improvisation ensemble, and Sam was the guest soloist that evening at the large jazz ensemble concert under the direction of Jimmy Cheatham. For the featured concert with his trio, we invited trombonist George Lewis to "sit in" with the group and reconnect with Sam, who had been something of a mentor to George in New York in the 1970s. Several selections from this performance can be heard on the accompanying compact disc. Throughout the week, Sam's energy, conviction, and passion for his music were continually on display.

During his visit, Sam often described his musical approach with his trio as "spontaneous creativity"—an approach to improvising without preconceived structures in which everything is created "on the spot."[3] But far from implying a music without form, Sam spoke of his preference for music that undulates in an organic manner, foregrounding moments of tension and relaxation, complexity and simplicity. This connection to natural rhythms, frequencies, and processes has been apparent in much of his recorded work, including the albums *Streams, Waves, Contours, Colors, Crosscurrents, Crystals, Sizzle,* and *Hues,* for example. Although Sam feels that "titles come last," he states, "I really try to put a word with the music that will in some way express what the music is all about."[4] In the liner notes to his 1978 album titled *Waves,* Sam admitted to "thinking in terms of forces of nature . . . the motion of waves, changing currents, changing flow."

In the past few decades, several scientific approaches, often grouped under the umbrella of nonlinear dynamical systems theory, have emerged aiming to model the unpredictable behavior of systems in which the whole can be greater than the sum of its parts.[5] Nonlinear dynamical systems theory arose from studying natural processes, such as heartbeats, tides, seasons, and plant growth. The similarity of such processes with the organic qualities of much improvised music, and Sam Rivers's conception in particular, is one indication that the connections we are attempting to build between the two may be warranted. For example, sudden transitions from one stable state to another occur in both and can be interesting, pleasing, or disconcerting. Such behaviors cannot arise in the linear dynamical systems that were the focus of natural systems research until recently.

While the full complexities of musical performance are still beyond the scope of these scientific approaches, their emphasis on systems that involve complex internal

Sam Rivers, photographed by Michael Haynes

dynamics (including both cooperation and competition) along with a pronounced ability to adapt to new circumstances and conditions may offer insight into the complexities of musical production, interaction, and reception, with particular relevance to how
we understand improvisation. This chapter reflects collaborative and coauthored
work done with Joseph Goguen at UCSD.[6] In it we investigate the dynamics of group
improvisation, focusing on the importance of transitional moments in the music.
Many of the most effective collective improvisations, it seems, involve decisive musical
"phase spaces" (in the language of nonlinear dynamics) and transitions between
phases, all negotiated by the group with an awareness of what has occurred and a
conception of what may follow. The exact behavior of the ensemble at transitional
moments appears to be both locally unstable and, in intriguing ways, globally comprehensible. These ideas are illustrated with an analysis of a 1973 performance by
Sam Rivers's trio with Cecil McBee on bass and Barry Altschul on drums ("Hues
of Melanin"). Although we take into account the rich sonic details of the recording,
we do not isolate them from the ways in which listeners (both audience and performers) experience and engage with the qualitative aspects of musical performance, nor

from a more comprehensive understanding of the emergent properties of musical consciousness.[7]

As we saw in the previous chapter, the dynamic complexity that informs, and can be generated by, an individual improviser is immense. Mind and body, moment and place, emotion and intellect, preparation, experience, and spontaneity all collide, collude, and (in the best of moments) cooperate to create a compelling performance. When the complexities of individual improvisation are combined and amplified in a group setting—particularly those settings without an overriding "composition" or a shared harmonic or rhythmic framework—the sheer volume and variety of interactions, influences, intentions, and potential (mis)interpretations that come into play would seem to preclude the possibility for anything meaningful to emerge. Yet these freer settings for group improvisation challenge us to engage with the complexities of collective dynamics and decision-making and with the emergent qualities of ensemble performance.

Complexity and Emergence

> Some of the reasons why free improvisation was a logical development in musical history can be understood retrospectively through relatively recent scientific studies of complexity and emergence. Creating musical coherence, variety and beauty without the instructions of a director was possible through the skills of listening and response that many musicians already possessed.[8]
>
> —David Toop

> The emergent when it appears is always found to follow from the past, but before it appears, it does not, by definition, follow from the past.[9]
>
> —George Herbert Mead

Complex systems are those in which the future emerges out of the interaction of innumerable forces, each leaving its indelible trace on the course of events. As opposed to systems that may simply be complicated, complex systems exhibit the possibility for adaptation and emergence by being open to energy influxes from outside the system and through their own highly interconnected nature. Their dynamics are hard to predict but not entirely random. They can exhibit regularities, but these regularities are difficult to describe briefly and impossible to describe over time with absolute precision.

Within the context of dynamical systems theory, creating the conditions for complexity requires two components: an *irreversible medium* and *nonlinearity*. The irreversible medium of most complex systems is time. Whether one is interested in a physical, biological, social, or artistic phenomenon—a snowflake, an ecosystem, a political movement, or an improvised music performance—it is the notion of time that supports the creation of complexity and the possibility for a sense of surprise that makes these systems both fascinating and fragile. Nonlinearity describes the property of a system whose output is not proportional to its input. The popular adage about the straw that breaks the camel's back or the battle that was lost for want of a horseshoe nail illustrates this principle well; a small quantitative change initiates a dramatic qualitative one.[10]

In the mathematics of dynamical systems theory, iterating nonlinear equations can produce surprising breaks, loops, recursions, and all varieties of turbulence, such that the behavior of the whole is not simply reducible to that of its parts. Many nonlinear systems also display an extreme sensitivity to their initial state and subsequent perturbations, such that a small change in one variable can have a disproportionate, even catastrophic impact on other variables. In these systems, no amount of access to additional detail can alter their inherent unpredictability.

As a result, contemporary work with nonlinear dynamical systems theory often seeks to discover the *qualitative* features of a system. In other words, it tries to predict the possible general shapes of processes, rather than actual numerical values of parameters that may be associated to them. Most "real-world" phenomena exhibit nonlinear behaviors, from the explosive outcome of earthquakes to the spread of ideas in modern society. Mathematician Stanislas Ulam famously described the study of nonlinearity as the "study of non-elephants." But since nonlinear equations can introduce extreme difficulties and uncertainties into the mathematical modeling of natural systems, scientists have focused the bulk of their attention, until recently, on the elephants.

The most common answer to this historical oversight maintains that nonlinear studies needed to wait for the advent of the digital computer to be able to model easily and accurately the long-term behavior of complex equations. Steven Kellert contends that this may be a partial answer, but he finds equally interesting the social and cultural factors that may have influenced this scientific neglect.[11] According to him, the twentieth century's overriding social interest in the exploitation of nature contributed to the institutional disregard of physical systems not readily amenable to analysis and manipulation. This situation is in many ways analogous to the appalling neglect of the study of musical improvisation in the Western academy.[12] Although improvisation may be, following Derek Bailey, "the most widely practiced of all musical activities," music notation (whether in the form of prescriptive "score" or descriptive "transcription") has arguably been the "elephant" of musicology, receiving the bulk of scholarly and pedagogical attention.[13]

To some extent, the relative scarcity of studies on improvised music would also seem to have a technological explanation. Improvisation study, according to this line of reasoning, had to wait for the development of technologies that could "capture" the details and nuances of its ephemeral form.[14] Centuries earlier, musical notation had offered the possibility of a concrete record of musical creativity. It promised (particularly to composers in the Western tradition) a more permanent and unchanging record than oral tradition alone could provide and a medium that could facilitate the creation of complex musical ideas by a single individual over time and facilitate their communication to others when organizing intricate performances.

From its inception, however, notation was devised as a mnemonic aid for performance, neither intended nor expected to capture the full details of the music.[15] Yet by about the mid-nineteenth century, notation began to be viewed by some *as* the actual music rather than a form of musical shorthand.[16] As musical studies matured in the West, the allure of focusing the bulk of attention on this tool that appeared not only to document but also to define musical activity was too hard to resist. Even as early recording technologies were being developed and employed by music researchers, particularly those with an ethnographic bent, notation remained the tool through which these newly recorded music examples were analyzed and shared with other interested researchers, necessarily filtering out many aspects of the sonic and cultural experience.[17] How, one might ask, can the multifaceted and temporal art of music ever be reduced to a static, two-dimensional representation?

Jazz music, for its part, has had an intriguing, if somewhat ambivalent, relationship with recorded sound and musical notation. The development of the music—barring the earliest decades—occurred simultaneously with the burgeoning recording industry so that much recorded jazz has been preserved for archiving and analysis.[18] Recording and disseminating jazz undoubtedly helped the music to spread quickly beyond its geographical origins and facilitated the sharing of improvisational ideas and approaches among players. But from an analytical and pedagogical standpoint, an over-reliance on recorded sound in many academic settings has arguably missed much of the spontaneity and flexibility of jazz, focusing undue attention both on a canon of celebrated recordings and on requiring students to adopt a standard repertoire of "licks" or "clichés."[19] Notation, too, has an ambivalent place in jazz's history, as both an important tool for conveying ideas and organizing performances, but also as something to be feared for its potential, in the absence of a strong commitment to oral and aural methods, to standardize certain aspects of performance practice.[20]

Without a doubt, recording technologies have provided an invaluable tool in the study of improvised music, much as the computer has become the tool *par excellence* for the study of nonlinear dynamics. But it should be clear that a technological explanation to the nontreatment of improvisation in the music academy is insufficient. The undervaluing, in both academic and applied study, of the nonlinear dynamics of musical performance in general and improvisation in particular can also be attributed to the fact that they are much less amenable to formalist analysis and manipulation.

The scientific approaches of reductionism, positivism, and naturalism have relied on breaking down complex systems into their smallest component parts in a search for underlying "natural laws." These approaches have been extremely successful at illuminating the materials and dynamics of nature at a great range of scales. Yet matter, from atoms to organisms and galaxies, appears to have an innate tendency to self-organize, generating complexity and emergent properties that can be described only at higher levels than those of the individual units. Life, for instance, remains one of the great mysteries of modern science. It is not some sort of essence added to a physico-chemical system, but neither can it simply be described in ordinary physico-chemical terms. It is an emergent property that manifests itself when physico-chemical systems are organized and interact in certain ways. Consciousness, too, appears to be neither an epiphenomenon, nor a simple result of neurons firing. After a certain level of complexity, new behaviors emerge that are not fully describable in terms of the behaviors of their parts. On a more mundane level, the qualities of water—its "wetness" and its ability to flow in a variety of controlled and turbulent ways—is not present in the mixture of hydrogen and oxygen; it has a new unity that sacrifices the properties of its parts. Additionally, under the right conditions, water can undergo a "phase transition" into ice or steam, each of which have qualitative aspects that are not present in the original compound.

Music is also best described as an emergent property of humans attending to organized sounds in time. At each level of explanation, qualities emerge that are not describable simply in terms of the dynamics of the previous level. On even the most basic level, a single musical tone, say an A-440 produced by an oboe player, can be analyzed in terms of frequency, intensity, duration, and signal and spectral envelope, among other things. But when perceived and processed by a human listener, it will produce qualitative aspects in her conscious experience that cannot be described completely through physical analysis alone. When asked, she might describe the sound as nasal or buzzing in quality, or it might evoke cultural or geographical references, say to the Middle East, or perhaps a historical reference to the practice of tuning a nineteenth-century symphony orchestra. That single sound also can never exist in temporal isolation; in other words, it might take on different qualitative aspects depending on what came before it or what might reasonably be expected to follow. When that single oboe sound is combined with a second tone, a musical interval is produced that will have emergent properties—with perhaps cognitive, emotional, or cultural connotations—that were not found in the isolated tones. Add a third sound and a chord is produced, the qualitative and emergent aspects of which inspired these lines of poetry from Elizabeth Barrett-Browning:

And I know not if, save in this, such gift be allowed to man
That out of three sounds he frame, not a fourth sound, but a star

In fact nearly all of our common analytical terms for music describe emergent properties. Harmony and rhythm describe qualities that emerge as tones and silences are combined simultaneously and in succession, and melody appears to be an emergent phenomenon that draws on harmony, rhythm, contour, and other musical and cognitive dimensions as well. Our difficulties in approaching the emergent qualities of music in general, and of improvised music in particular, are not dissimilar to those of traditional physicists who tended to steer clear of the complexity that is readily apparent in daily life. Quantum theory and cosmology may have much to say about the behavior of matter at the smallest and largest spacio-temporal scales, but clearly many interesting things emerge at a human scale—including life, intelligence, and consciousness—whose qualities are not simply explainable in terms of interacting particles or unfolding galaxies. As we will see more in the chapters that follow, many emergent properties only reveal themselves in the dynamics of collective groupings, not only as a superstructure of culture, but also in the symbiotic relationships that develop between individuals, and in the ways in which knowledge and learning can be distributed across groups. Adopting a musical analogy, science writers John Briggs and F. David Peat highlight the interdependent and emergent qualities of complex systems this way:

In the sense that parts seem autonomous, they are only "relatively autonomous." They are like a music lover's favorite passage in a Beethoven symphony. Take the passage out of the piece and it's possible to analyze the notes. But in the long run, the passage is meaningless without the symphony as a whole."[21]

Time and the Qualia of Experience

One of the most fundamental and also most mysterious features of music (and of experience generally) is the way in which what is essentially a continuous flow gets divided unconsciously and nearly instantaneously into "chunks," each of which has a distinct qualitative character.[22] In philosophy, the phenomenological units of experience, including their qualitative "feel," are called *qualia* (the singular form of this Latin word is "quale"). But qualia are often treated by reductionist science as a "residual category": that which is left unexplained or which remains after all objective features have been subtracted. Even philosophers often give simplistic examples of qualia, such as the "redness" of the color red. Our notion of qualia differs from that of philosophers in that qualia are not atomic, nor are they discrete. Rather, they have complex internal structure, consisting of other qualia. For instance, the qualia that appear in music can range from whole performances, through sections and phrases, down to fragments of tones and sounds. Following are some of our conclusions about the nature of musical qualia:[23]

- Qualia are created as part of the process of perception; they do not exist independently.
- Qualia are associated with segments of experience, but not all such segments are qualia, only those that are considered significant.
- Qualia are hierarchically organized; some qualia appear as parts of other qualia.
- Each quale has as its context the larger grain qualia in which it is embedded, and most qualia have an internal structure consisting of subqualia. Foreground and background are determined by the structural organization of qualia; they are not predetermined.
- Qualia have different *saliencies*, which indicate their relative significance; these can change over time.[24]
- If left alone, the saliency of a quale will gradually decay, but when it or something related to it is heard, then its saliency increases, since it becomes more likely to be relevant to future musical events.
- A quale can also be retroactively "swallowed up" by other qualia, ceasing itself to be a quale; this can be considered an instance of what is sometimes called "downward" or "backward" causation.
- There is no direct relationship between the saliencies of qualia and their sizes; very salient qualia can be any size.
- Consciousness consists of qualia, and the degree to which we are conscious of a quale is proportional to its saliency.
- Our perceptions of time are also linked to qualia; the qualitative character of the flow of time is that of the largest grain salient qualia (for example, it may be smooth, bumpy, fast, slow, etc.); our sense of time may even appear to disappear at moments of great intensity (as in Mihaly Csikszentmihalyi's sense of "flow").[25]

Unlike the usual scientific analysis of time that envisions it as a point moving along a line at a constant rate, our phenomenological experience of time is considerably more complex. In music, for instance, both performers and listeners continually look into the future and the past in order to engage with sounds and their meanings as they unfold.[26] Although actual experience necessarily occurs in the present, according to phenomenologist Edmund Husserl we experience the flow of time as a continual "sinking away" of present events into the past.

Husserl named this mode of experience *retention*. With retention, the immediate past can be experienced in the present, but in a different "mode" from that in which it was originally experienced. For instance, in music we can "hear" an "echo" of a phrase just played for about ten seconds after, but beyond that most details are lost. Husserl named this short-term buffer "fresh memory," and it has recently been experimentally verified and given a neurological basis in what is called "sensory memory." This form of memory differs from the more familiar short-term and long-term memories that have been much studied in psychology in that it is not conscious, that is, it works whether we are aware of it or not (though conscious attention may make it work better).

Humans also continually anticipate what might come next, greatly reducing our cognitive processing needs and allowing us to experience the sensation of surprise. Husserl adopted the term "protention" to describe this mode, and, like the related concept of retention, it appears to be "hardwired" into the brain, although there have, as yet, been few neurological studies of protention.

For Husserl, "objective moments" of time are not predetermined, but rather, *objects-in-time* arise through the processes of retention and protention. Unlike moments in physics, these objects-in-time are "temporally thick," since they relate to real events that take time to process. Based on considerable experimental research, it appears that qualia, or at least "emotional" qualia, function as "indices" for the retrieval of these temporally thick memories and they play important roles in many other mental processes as well.[27]

In light of these phenomenological and experimental findings, we argue that musical meanings are best located in the act of listening rather than at the structural level of notation or even sound. Just as a painting becomes more than simple brushstrokes when viewed as a whole, music lives when it is heard and understood. The active, human process of listening is the essence of music, making the physical and cognitive capabilities and limitations of human listeners crucial for analysis. Therefore, we will construct models of musical experts (either performers or listeners) rather than models of disembodied pure music, a vacuous abstraction that cannot ever really exist.

Our primary goal here is to define two functions that describe the dynamic qualities of *music* and *listening*.[28] By *music*, we mean music making, the process of sound unfolding in time from instruments in response to the control exercised by musicians and to any predetermined instructions that may exist (the "score" in a generalized sense), plus of course any applicable fixed acoustic properties of instruments, microphones, halls, etc. By *listening*, we mean the active, dynamic process of understanding music, which includes the hierarchical segmentation of what has been heard into qualia, the anticipation of what may come in the future, the saliencies associated with these, as well as the current state of relevant memories, including sensory, short- and long-term memories, and transpersonal cultural memories.

Music and listening, as we define them here, are *tightly coupled*, in that the current state of each acts as the control of the other. For example, musicians are continually listening to the combined sound of the performance (and to their own sounds when actively playing) in ways that directly affect what they do next. Listeners are also continually engaging with the acoustic soundscape and the activities of the perform-ance in ways that affect their perceptions and understandings of what is occurring, what has occurred, and what might reasonably be expected to occur next. In other words, our evolving understanding of music (as performer or audience member) and the future directions it may take are determined by what sounds are heard now and our expectations based on what has been understood about what was heard before, taking into account as well long-term cultural patterns and personal predispositions.

Nonlinearity can arise in this tightly coupled system due to both the great complex-ity of factors involved and the fact that the state of each function, music and listening, acts as the control of the other.[29] In improvised performances in particular, small de-tails in sound production or perception can, when attended to or acknowledged by participants and listeners at appropriate moments, trigger transformations in the music or its reception, such that the eventual outcome is disproportionate to any initial causes. This includes the possibility that current activity in the performance or its reception can force a reinterpretation of previous moments. In other words, the qualia of musical experience remain dynamic; they can be altered, incorporated into, or even supplanted by more recent qualia.

We conjecture that active listeners try to construct a *minimum complexity description* of what they hear now by combining and transforming fragments of what they heard before and what they expected to hear now.[30] These stored fragments are not simply unprocessed sonic details; rather, they include the qualia of musical experience. The various transformation possibilities that may be anticipated by listeners are also asso-ciated with cognitive weights that reflect the perceived difficulty of their application. By anticipating what might come next and comparing that with what does come next, listeners can greatly reduce the complexity of understanding.

The level of surprise at a given moment of listening, therefore, is determined by the difference between what is heard and what is expected. Despite Whitney Balliett's memorable description of jazz as "the sound of surprise," music that is maximally surprising would not, in fact, be maximally "interesting" or good. Jazz and improvised musics do, however, place great importance on engendering a sense of freedom by surprising listeners in ways that involve manipulating expectation through the trans-formation of both large- and fine-grain structure.[31] More technically, the level of sur-prise can be described by a *conditional complexity measure*.[32] Intuitively, this measures how difficult it is to understand the current musical moment in relation to those moments that directly preceded it, assuming as well some given knowledge about the types of musical moments of which this is a particular instance. The conditional complexity measure does not measure aesthetic preference, rather it is an "under-standing" of the music based on psychologically and culturally appropriate compo-nents and weights. Because our model takes into account memory hierarchy—with sensory, short- and long-term, and transpersonal components—such an analysis will reveal not only small-grain, but also large-grain structures, as well as how all these structures are interrelated.

It is important to note, however, that human listeners are not capable of doing arbitrarily complex computations in real time. As a result, this process can fail badly for unfamiliar forms of music, resulting in a sense of confusion and displeasure. On the other hand, it seems to work remarkably well for familiar forms of music, and it provides us with a sense of pleasure when approximate understandings are readjusted.

Humans evolved a general capacity for anticipation in order to enhance survival both in the wild and in highly social communities. We continually predict the physical actions of others and their complex thoughts and behaviors by attributing intention and planning to them. This natural mechanism rewards correct anticipation with pleasure, arouses curiosity when anticipation fails mildly, arouses doubt and uncertainty for greater failures, and arouses fear in case of significant failure in a dangerous situation. To invoke our previous discussion of Husserl, emotion arises from relations in the temporally thick "now" among retention, protention, and perception. When comparing anticipation with reality in the relatively safe environment of music listening, these same instinctive responses appear to provide the origin of musical emotion (these ideas will be taken up again at the conclusion of the next chapter).[33] Music pleasure, it seems, arrives not from exact matching of expectation with reality, but rather from slight readjustments to our future anticipations following surprise. This also helps to explain the ongoing pleasure that musicians encounter when transforming familiar materials in subtle ways.

The Phase Space of Improvisation

> This kind of thing happens in improvisation. Two things running concurrently in haphazard fashion suddenly synchronize autonomously and sling you *forcibly* into a new phase.[34]
>
> —Cornelius Cardew

An important goal of this chapter is to study the structure of the phase space of improvisation, with a particular focus on the transitions between phases. Our emphasis will be on a space of possible *understandings* within that phase space. The *phase space* of a system is a multidimensional "map," sometimes referred to as its "geometry of possibilities," which allows investigators to describe and analyze a system's dynamics. The number of dimensions of a given phase space is based on the *degrees of freedom*. For instance, the motion of a standard pendulum can be mapped into a two-dimensional phase space charting its relative position and momentum. The motion of a car driving in open terrain could be mapped into a four-dimensional phase space corresponding to the two dimensions of direction available and the relative momentum of the vehicle moving in each of those two directions. A rocket ship moving freely in space has available an extra dimension of direction and momentum, increasing its phase space dimensions to six. Phase space diagrams, just like more conventional forms of mapping, bring into focus aspects of reality that might otherwise be overlooked.[35] In more technical language, phase spaces are lower dimensional subspaces of *state space*, since only certain variables are given a key role.

Conventional music notation, whether used as a prescriptive score or as a descriptive transcription, details a linear dimension of time (running steadily from past to future), a pitch dimension (lower to higher) for each available voice, as well as additional markings that can describe changes in tempo, dynamics, timbre, articulations, etc. As notated, these dimensions are discrete, not continuous. Pitches come in twelve chromatic varieties within octave intervals, time markings (rhythms) are available in a limited number of divisions, primarily of twos and threes, and markings for dynamics, timbre, articulation, etc. also come in a limited array of options. Without a doubt, contemporary composers and skilled transcribers have expanded and elaborated on these available options, but the representation of music on notation paper, by necessity, limits a more complete description.

The frequent reliance on notation as a compositional, performance, and analytical tool in the traditional academy has also tended to shape our perceptions and evaluations of music in subtle ways. In other words, notation is never value neutral. It involves choices of what to notate, that is, of what is important. Even the choice to notate involves the value of exercising certain kinds of control over performers. The situation is similar for transcription and analysis, since an analyst must make value-laden choices of what to analyze, how to analyze it, and how to report the results, among other things.

Music performance, in its vast cultural and historical diversity, is of course not limited to the prescribed or described dimensions of notation, nor is it discrete in this fashion. Musicians from all genres and backgrounds explore in performance the continuous features of those musical dimensions that can be represented by notation, as well as others, such as timbre and the subtleties of phrasing, that are even more difficult to notate conventionally. In addition, musics that hinge on a high degree of improvisation in performance often foreground the dynamic qualities of sound and style that are only hinted at in notated form.

Jazz history, for instance, is littered with stories of performers from Pee Wee Russell to John Coltrane who, when given a detailed transcription of their improvisations, could not perform them, highlighting the ways in which many important musical qualities remain implicit rather than explicit for performers. The freer forms of improvisation, those without a strong allegiance to notation and with an often more flexible approach to temporal, tonal, and timbral dimensions, would seem to imply a huge number of degrees of freedom and an enormously complex phase space.[36] For our purposes, musical "phases" refer to phenomenologically distinct sound worlds. These might be articulated by a pronounced textural, harmonic, temporal, or timbral quality, or they may involve complex arrangements of these and other factors. During an improvisation, each musician explores her or his own phase space, while the group phase space is defined by the combination of all of these.

Researchers have adopted the notion of *attractors* in phase space to help understand and simplify the behavior of a wide variety of dynamical systems. An attractor is a region of phase space that seems to "pull" the behavior of the system toward it, as if magnetically. A small number of attractor types can describe the behavior of a wide variety of dynamical systems. For instance, a simple pendulum operating with friction will eventually settle on its lowest gravitational point; this final resting point "attracts" the behavior of the system. But many other dynamical systems, say a rock rolling down a hill into a valley, can be described with this same notion of a *fixed-point* (or *static*) attractor. In fact, a simplified way of conceiving phase space is to consider the hills and valleys of a real landscape to be hills and valleys of energy.

A second type of basic attractor, a *limit cycle* (or *periodic*) attractor, describes the behavior of systems that forever oscillate within a fixed or limited range. Take the pendulum discussed above and place it in a vacuum to eliminate the effects of friction, and its continual swing is describable by a limit-cycle attractor.[37] Limit cycles, particularly when coupled together in interesting ways, have proven effective in modeling the behavior of many natural systems, including some simple ecological systems and stable predator-prey relationships. With the introduction of notions such as quasi-periodicity and the sophisticated geometry of torus attractors, scientists had hoped to be able to model accurately the behavior of all complex systems.

The Newtonian vision of a regular and predictable universe, however, was placed under stress as early as the late nineteenth century when the French mathematician, physicist, and philosopher Henri Poincaré wondered about the long-term stability of the solar system. He found that, although Newton's equations work perfectly well for any idealized two-body system (e.g., the moon orbiting the earth), the small effects of adding a third body to the system (e.g., the influence of the sun on the earth and moon) requires a series of approximations, precluding the possibility of a closed form solution. Initially, Poincaré's warning shot across the bow of reductionism went unheeded; only a few short years later, physicist were immersed in the emerging fields of relativity and quantum mechanics.

In the 1960s, as the story goes, Edward Lorenz rediscovered a fundamental limit to the predictability of complex systems while attempting to model the dynamics of weather formations.[38] When restarting his computer simulation that involved three nonlinear equations, Lorenz entered a slightly truncated version of the initial values from a previous run only to be shocked at the rapid and pronounced divergence from his previous results. He realized then that the complex and nonlinear dynamics of weather formations would preclude the possibility of accurate predictions in the long run. His most picturesque analogy for this postulates that the flapping wings of a butterfly can significantly alter weather conditions halfway across the globe, the famed "butterfly effect" of chaos theory. Lorenz's 1963 paper published in *The Journal of Atmospheric Sciences*, however, garnered little attention outside of the field of meteorology until the 1970s, at which time it helped to reinvigorate work on the theory of nonlinear dynamical systems.

A third type of attractor in nonlinear dynamical systems has been given the evocative title "strange." Mathematical physicist David Ruelle first coined the term, but the Lorenz attractor and the Mandelbrot set—named after Benoit Mandelbrot who discovered fractal geometry—may be the most familiar strange attractors. Both have appeared on thousands of T-shirts and computer screens around the world. Yet even a simple system of two pendulums linked in a way that the behavior of each affects the other will produce chaotic results that can be described by a strange attractor.[39]

For another example, imagine a rotating water wheel that allows for a controlled drainage in the buckets. When the speed of water supplying the buckets reaches a critical value, the wheel will begin to slow down, reverse directions, and speed up, all with a strange unpredictability. Despite the seemingly controlled nature of this example, even the slightest change in the rate of water flow after the critical point can cause the system to exhibit strikingly different behaviors, highlighting its *extreme sensitivity to initial conditions*. To conceptualize this principle you might also imagine shooting two balls into a pinball machine with an extremely small difference in their initial force and then charting their respective trajectories. Although the second ball approaches the first obstacle with only a minor difference in trajectory, that small difference will quickly be amplified by the complexity of the layout and the positive feedback of the bumpers until the second ball's path diverges radically from that of the first. Or you might envision dropping two snowboards from near identical positions at the top of a ski slope filled with moguls. Here too, due to the complexity of the system and its extreme sensitivity to initial conditions, the path of the objects will diverge significantly.[40]

One of the hallmarks of the dynamics of nonlinear systems is *iteration*, which involves a continual re-absorption or enfolding of what has come before through the process of feedback. Negative feedback is well known as a common way to regulate mechanical and social systems; the thermostat in a house, for instance, uses negative feedback to achieve but not exceed a desired temperature. Piloting a boat, an analogy adopted by Norbert Weiner when founding the field of cybernetics, involves a constant cycle of steering, assessing deviation from the desired course, and counter-steering.[41] Judicial and punitive systems also provide negative feedback in society so that individuals or businesses operate within acceptable bounds.

The feedback found in nonlinear systems, however, is positive. If negative feedback regulates, positive feedback amplifies. Despite its cheery sounding name, positive feedback, according to Mitchel Resnick, has an image problem: "People tend to see positive feedback as destructive, making things spiral out of control."[42] The standard examples offered of positive feedback include the screeching sound that results when a microphone is placed near a speaker or the folk notion of "the bandwagon effect," which tends to evoke a mindless mob latching on to a new idea unthinkingly. But positive feedback plays a crucial role in creating and extending new structures, particularly in nonlinear environments. For instance, a howling PA system is due to the linear effects of positive feedback, but when driven into a nonlinear range, we hear the tools of the trade of Jimi Hendrix and countless other creative electric guitarists. In nonlinear dynamical systems, positive feedback can become a generative or organizing force.

Like all forms of human activity, music relies heavily on feedback. But at least in its more conventional forms, music often seems to rely more heavily on the regulatory or negative variety. Musicians not only use regulatory feedback when practicing to improve specific techniques on their instrument, but this type of feedback is a crucial part of the way musicians tune and balance their sounds in an ensemble setting: attempting in the former case to minimize the "beating" between tones and, in the latter case, to "phase lock" in order to maximize the resonance of the combined group sound. Within the pan-European concert traditions, the score and any rehearsed interpretive decisions also provide a strong source of negative feedback in performance. Although seasoned performers make countless important expressive decisions in the moment, the score (at least in its more traditional forms) ensures that many of the musical details of the performance will remain intact and predictable (at least for those already familiar with the piece). Historically speaking, in the pan-European concert traditions the surprising but also potentially disrupting qualities of positive feedback in performance have been downplayed.

In an improvising situation without a preconceived musical score or any formally agreed-upon performance attributes, this balance of feedback appears to be rather different. Each gesture can conceivably produce rather sudden and dramatic shifts in the ensemble sound and approach; in other words, radically divergent and nonlinear effects. Admittedly this is an abstraction that stereotypes both notated and improvised music performance. No score can prescribe all of the variables, nor predict all of the vagaries of a musical performance, and equally, no improvised performance begins from a *tabula rasa*, devoid of individual, social, and cultural traditions and expectations. In addition, positive feedback undoubtedly plays a role in musical creativity of all types; on both the macro level, as artistic ideas can spread rapidly within a community, and on the micro level, as a minute performance gesture or a compositional germ may blossom into an important creative moment or full-blown work. But free improvisation, at least in its idealized form, would seem to display a far greater sensitivity to its initial state. The musical iterations in performance are allowed to feedback into the system, the content of the music, to a far greater extent than with performances that use traditionally and even most unconventionally notated scores. Even a small change in the first performance gesture—a shift in dynamic level, attack, or articulation, etc.—can lead to a sudden divergence from the evolution of a system started with nearly identical initial conditions. In more poetic language, the slightest musical disturbance—the metaphorical flapping of a butterfly's wings—can potentially lead to surprising and divergent performance outcomes. Unpredictable sonic combinations, unintended "noise," and the intentional process of interpolation and dissociation all introduce additional complexities into the evolving system.

None of this, of course, negates the possibility of theorizing, which is arguably an innate aspect of the way in which all human beings engage with their environment. Music scholarship has always relied on modeling techniques, from formal transcription and/or score analysis to historically and culturally sensitive contextual readings of a performance. As was shown in the previous chapter, our musical terminology is also filled with analogies, many if not most of which relate to our own sense of embodiment. Recent scholarship has drawn insight from literary, linguistic, semiotic, cognitive, and philosophical paradigms, to name only a few. A fundamental mistake is made only when a given model is seen to supplant the actual experiences it describes.[43]

Our increasing sensitivity to the nonlinear behavior found in many natural and social systems is already beginning to provoke a shift from quantitative reductionism to a more qualitative and holistic appreciation of complex dynamics. Briggs and Peat explain:

> Nonlinear models differ from linear ones in a number of ways. Rather than trying to figure out all of the chains of causality, the modeler looks for nodes where feedback loops join and tries to capture as many of the important loops as possible in the system's "picture." Rather than shaping the model to make a forecast about future events or to exercise some central control, the nonlinear modeler is content to perturb the model, trying out different variables in order to learn about the system's critical points and its homeostasis (resistance to change). The modeler is not seeking to control the complex system by quantifying it and mastering its causality; (s)he wants to increase her "intuitions" about how the system works so (s)he can interact with it more harmoniously.[44]

We are still in the earliest stages of extending these modeling techniques into the domain of human and social dynamics to the point where they can help explain *why* and *how* these forms and dynamics can be aesthetically and emotionally powerful. But models need not be complex to be useful. For example, a sequence of chord symbols and cadence markings provide a very useful model for classic forms of jazz. Nonlinear dynamical systems theory, in its current form, does not offer a full explanation of the structure or beauty of improvised music, but it may offer fresh insight to our discussions of the complex dynamics that are involved in all musical performance and, in particular, to our discussions of contemporary forms of group improvisation.

Like other complex dynamical systems, the exact development and structure of an ensemble improvisation is inherently unpredictable, and yet through certain shared understandings, nuanced interactions and interconnections, and a shared cognitive ability to attend to and parse musical sound, dynamical orderings can emerge that are both surprising and comprehensible. Without predetermined arrangements or techniques for managing the flow of the music (such as a Butch Morris-style "conduction" or a John Zorn-style game piece), the ability to transition as a group from one musical "phase space" to another becomes critical. Many improvisations display a sectional nature in which distinct phase spaces may be explored and then surprisingly discarded. Small-scale interactions and individual phase transitions may continuously occur within the ensemble as relationships and ideas are dynamically articulated, but larger-scale group "phase transitions" occur less frequently, often at moments of unexpected synchrony when the ensemble's combined explorations seem to coalesce around a common set of ideas, or at moments when a need for new complexities (or more comprehensibility) is felt by one or all of the members. From a phenomenological perspective, these transitions may appear to happen either on their own or to be directed by certain individuals or by the group as a whole, but in most cases their appearance is acknowledged by the group and necessarily influences the ongoing formation and reception of the music.

Although it may be tempting to imagine locating the initial gesture of an improvisation as a point in phase space and starting an analysis from there, in truth, that initial point is already implicated by feedback processes in a complex network dynamic (in the case of improvised music, to the encultured and embodied techniques and sensibilities of all of the performers, to the specific context for performance, etc.) such that an immense uncertainty is already built in. As the system iterates (as the improvisations continues) and its parts feed back into each other, the complexity and uncertainty begin to reveal themselves.

This immense and innate complexity makes improvised music locally unpredictable, but the dynamics of group improvisation can also reveal more stable global behaviors. In the theory of nonlinear dynamics, systems can *bifurcate* (or *multifurcate*) by branching off into entirely new states and demonstrating novel behaviors and emergent order in ways that are intrinsically unpredictable.[45] Yet the behavior of the system at these moments is profoundly influenced by the previous history of the system. Depending on which path it has taken to reach instability, the system will follow one of many available branches. By way of analogy, all of the factors that contribute to the development of an improvisation up to the point of transition—including each individual's personal history and cultural understandings and the ensemble's collective experience improvising with each other—can affect which subsequent musical path the group pursues.

To continue our analogy, contemporary improvisers tend to favor "strange" musical attractors to those that rely on periodic cycles or predictable interactions. They avoid low complexity regions (called "basins of attraction") while constantly creating new patterns, or patterns of patterns, in order to keep the energy going, all the while working to maintain the coherence of the performance. They metaphorically surf the "edge of chaos"—an evocative phrase that has technical implications that we will explore further in the next chapter—to ensure continual development and excitement without exceeding the cognitive abilities and aesthetic interests of listeners. Although from the perspective of an uninitiated listener, contemporary improvisation may seem to veer in the direction of confusion and displeasure, it, like all music, engenders an emotional and aesthetic response by playing with familiarity and expectation.

For example, if too many references to traditional musical idioms creep into a performance or an underlying harmonic character or tempo lingers for too long, many improvisers will immediately begin to search for more uncharted and uncertain musical terrain. The exact aesthetic approach and tolerance of idiomatic components will vary considerably from individual to individual, ensemble to ensemble, and even from performance to performance, as will the speed at which the group transitions into new dynamics, from mere seconds to several minutes or more. Some improvisations, in fact, may not "bifurcate" at all, offering instead a detailed and focused investigation of a single attractor. Improvised performances on the whole, however, tend to contain moments in which apparent order—stable states and limit cycles—can quickly dissolve into "chaos" (in the everyday sense of the word), and sections in which "chaotic" (in the mathematical sense) dynamics can produce surprising periods of emergent order and structure.

Like this general description of the music, there is something of an inherent tension or paradox in the dynamics of strange attractors. Even though they can involve an infinite number of loops and spirals, they are also contained within a finite region of phase space. They are seemingly able to reconcile contrary effects; as attractors, nearby trajectories converge on them, but their extreme sensitivity to initial conditions means that initially close trajectories diverge rapidly. Jack Cohen and Ian Stewart ask us to think of ping-pong balls in the ocean. If you release two balls from near identical locations below or above the surface of the water, they will both be attracted to the surface.[46] But once there, they will continue to bob freely and unpredictably, perhaps quickly diverging from one another only to possibly cross paths at some unlikely future moment. To push this analogy further, even as an improvising group may have temporarily settled into a musical attractor, like our bobbing ping-pong balls each musician will still continue to explore micro details and personalized variations so that the improvised section remains highly surprising and unpredictable. Additionally, moments of "attraction" in which players seem to be working together toward a shared musical end may be interrupted or compounded by intentionally disruptive or dissociative behavior from others, which may or may not lead to a dramatic transition in the music.

"Hues of Melanin"

To illustrate these ideas in a specific musical context we will focus on a few transitional moments in the work of Sam Rivers's trio (with Cecil McBee on bass and Barry Altschul on drums) from their 1973 concert at Yale University, released as "Hues of Melanin." The complete improvisation lasted just over forty-four minutes and was broken into three distinct sections on both the original and re-release of the performance.[47] We will focus on the first section, before Rivers switches to piano, which comprises the first thirty-four minutes of improvisation. In the next chapter, the same performance is given a computer analysis that provides a means to link the perceptual and phenomenological frame of the listener, discussed here, with a more technical look at the musical sound stimulus itself.

During the performance, a pronounced change in the flow of the improvisation tends to occur every two or three minutes as the trio transitions between moments of rapid propulsion and phlegmatic rubato. The group also moves between more and less dense textures and frequently switches between periods of polytonal exploration, extended harmonic drones, and more open sections exploring chromatic and timbral variation. Table 1 provides a phenomenological reading of the various transitions between sections and subsections that occur in "Hues of Melanin." For it, we borrowed terminology about transition types from Tom Nunn's book *The Wisdom of the Impulse,* although many of the trio's dynamics do not fall neatly into one of his seven categories.[48]

The large-scale sectional transitions—or, in our terminology, bifurcations—are most easily recognized by a shift from shared tempo to more open rhythmic realms, or vise versa. We designated subsections for moments of minor cadences or moments at which the group's synchrony or dialog is most pronounced. The catalysts for these phase transitions vary, but a few common ones include trill-like figures, repeated tones, or a gradual descent that can signal a slowing of pulse and energy.[49] A quick, tossed-off melodic fragment or rhythmic impetus is often used to jumpstart the group's up-tempo explorations.

For example, at approximately two minutes into the trio's improvisation, Rivers begins a trill figure on soprano that triggers Cecil McBee and Barry Altschul to relax their dense and intense development, in favor of more sparse musical territory (*A3* in Table 1). And at approximately seven-and-a-half minutes into the performance, Rivers plays another trill that eases the group's energy, then follows it with a quick melodic fragment that triggers Altschul and McBee to shift into up-tempo exploration (*D*). While signals frequently come from Rivers's horn, the other two members also can and do initiate bifurcations. For instance, Cecil McBee often adopts a similar trill figure on his bass to function as a sectional cue, or he improvises a figure that gradually descends into the lowest register of the instrument to signal a slowing of pulse or lessening of energy to the other musicians. Withdrawing and re-entering into the trio texture, as Barry Altschul often does, or shifting instruments (and adding voice), as Sam Rivers is prone to do, provide other opportune moments for musical bifurcations and nonlinear dynamics in the performance.

Although these catalysts can be effective in triggering sectional transitions, their use and influence never become predictable, but frequently produce dramatically different results over the course of an extended performance. For example, ten-and-a-half minutes into "Hues of Melanin" Rivers interjects a melodic catalyst that does not provoke a complete shift to shared tempo, but rather a gradual collapse into a drone-filled melodic and rhythmic space. Soon a powerful moment of sync arrives when Rivers and McBee land on the same pitch during a gradual scalar ascent, provoking a moment of heightened intensity and spurring increased collective exploration. Finally, a fresh melodic fragment by Rivers launches the trio into an up-tempo improvisation full of gentle tug-and-pull between the three members (*E2 to F*).

Perhaps the most difficult aspect of highlighting the subtleties of the structural transformations and transitions that take place in much improvised music is providing

Table 1: Sam Rivers Trio—"Hues of Melanin"—Phenomenological Analysis

T1 *sudden/unexpected segue*—an unprepared, immediate change with unexpected continuation

T2 *pseudo-cadential segue*—an implied cadence with sudden and unexpected continuation

T3 *climactic segue*—a peak moment that stimulates unexpected change and continuation

T4 *feature overlap*—one feature of the antecedent section is sustained and becomes part of the consequent section

T5 *feature change*—a gradual change of one feature that redirects the flow (usually subtly)

T6 *fragmentation*—a gradual breaking up, or fragmenting, of the general texture and/or rhythm

T7 *internal cadence*—a prepared cadence followed by a short silence then continuation with new material. (In addition to presenting a moment of resolution, an internal cadence can signal a moment of extreme unpredictability in the performance because there is always the possibility that it will become the final cadence of the improvisation.)

Letter	Time	Transition Type (salient detail)	Texture/Tempo
A	0:00		FREE—introductory call
A2	0:46	T5 (bass repeated tones-Ab)	repetition/density
A3	1:57	T2 (soprano trill D-Eb)	relaxation/intensify
A4	2:33	T2/T4 (cadence on C)	layered complexity
B	3:02	T1 (soprano descending phrase)	FAST tempo
B2	4:06	T5 (soprano and bass dialog/ glissando)	
B3	4:26	T5 (bass drone)	
B4	4:55	T5 (soprano pedal tones)	
C	5:29	T2 (soprano trill on D)	FREE
C2	5:48	T7 (drum cadence)	
C3	6:43	T2 (soprano high note)	
C4	7:05	T2/T4/T6 (soprano and bass low A)	
D	7:35	T7 (trill/melodic trigger)	MEDIUM tempo
D2	9:20	T6 (drums fall out of time)	begins to fragment
E	9:54	T7 (cadence to B/unison trill on E)	FREE—intensifies
E2	10:29	T1/T6 (melodic trigger leads to fragmentation)	
E3	11:04	T2 (C- tonality, unison G, drum cadence)	
F	12:02	T1 (melodic trigger)	FAST tempo
G	13:10	T2 (trill on D) followed by T5 (bass groove)	GROOVE

RIVERS OF CONSCIOUSNESS

Letter	Time	Transition Type (salient detail)	Texture/Tempo
G2	14:04	metric sync	
G3	14:52	T6 (bass triggers descent)	FREE
H	15:17	T7 (trill, drum cadence)	*bass solo w/ voice&perc*
H2	16:45	T6/T5 (flute and voice hollers)	FREE—intensifies
I	17:55	T7 (drums drop out, bowed bass)	*flute solo*
I2	18:18	T5 (bass overtone bowing, voice and flute)	more activity
I3	18:50	T2 (flute cadenza, bass drone)	
I4	19:25	T2/T5 (flute, bass, drums, activity, voice)	intensifies
J	20:00	T7 (brief *flute solo*, drums bring in time)	FAST tempo—very complex
J2	21:24	T5 (bass rises, interaction, flute&voice)	FREE—interactive
J3	22:00	T2/T4 (drums briefly relax)	
K	22:36	T6/T1 (flute descending phrase, drums time)	FAST—bass drone
K2	23:47	T5/T6 (melodic fragment)	FREE
K3	24:30	T2 (trill)	FREE—voice
L	25:25	T7 (voice and bowed bass sync—unison)	sparse drums
L2	26:30	T5 (flute reenters, bass bowed harmonics)	
L3	27:15	T2	*flute solo*
M	28:23	T1 (flute trigger, bass figure, G mixolydian)	MEDIUM tempo
M	229:10	T5/T6 (bass alternates whole step)	begins to fragment (esp. bass)
N	29:56	T2/T6 (vocal scream, drums drop down)	FREE
N2	30:50	T2/T5 (bass drone, speed drums and flute)	intensity (screams!)
N3	31:41	T6/T7 (flute chromatic descent, ritardando)	
O	32:00	T1 (flute melodic trigger) now expected	MEDIUM/fractured tempo
O2	32:40	T5 (flute fast runs, bass drones)	
P	33:30	T6 (voice, bass drone, drums)	*drum solo* *(transition to piano section)*

a sense of their hierarchical complexity. The linear aspects of cause-and-effect style playing and analysis can be interesting, but the nonlinear, part-whole relationships that emerge in performance frequently convey more subtle meanings to listeners and performers. For instance, the transitional devices used early in the trio's perform-ance—the trills and melodic and tempo triggers—diminish in cognitive "weight" when they reappear at subsequent moments, necessitating altered formulations and responses and highlighting new strategies of collective expression and interaction in order to maintain the overall complexity of the performance.

On close analysis, certain subsections of the performance also have enough similari-ties to give the listener the impression that the "phase spaces" of the improvisation are warping in on themselves. Attractors in the phase space of nonlinear, chaotic sys-tems are often described as analogous to pulling taffy. Points that may at first be close together can quickly diverge only to nearly reconnect at surprising moments in the future. For one example, an intense group development begins to bifurcate at five-and-a-half minutes into the performance (*C1*) when Sam Rivers lands on a trill, fol-lowed by a medium-tempo melodic trigger that initiates a Latin-esque groove from Barry Altschul. The group, however, soon aborts this groove to explore a rubato, modal area, followed by a decisive climax (*C3*).[50] And at thirteen minutes into the perform-ance, a similarly intense development is again subdued by a soprano sax trill. This time, however, the groove that was prematurely halted earlier appears to resurface (with slight alterations) from a strong, flowing, funk-type bass line provided by Cecil McBee. A similar modal exploration is still there, but this time layered on top of the reformulated groove in such a way that the earlier moment is both remembered and reconfigured.

Although moments of sync and similarity are clearly cultivated and enjoyed by the musicians, the trio rarely lingers in these basins of attraction for long. For instance, shortly after the climax of the first section discussed above (at *C3*), the soprano and bass briefly synchronize on a pedal tone on concert A (*C4*). Both musicians are aware of the connection, and yet rather than linger on its implied togetherness, they quickly, and with apparent conviction, move into more distant, chromatic areas in search of new sonic orderings.

This tendency for the group to flirt with the known while surfing the edge of the unknown is apparent as well in the rhythmic domain. At just after the fourteen-min-ute mark, the trio arrives at a shared pulse and meter—perhaps provoked by the strong "add-of-four-into-one" figure by Altschul that seems to lift the energy of the entire group (*G2*). Though the moment of synchrony is clearly felt by all, the players also quickly begin to work against the groove and any strong sense of tonality so that the nonlinear dynamics of the improvisation can continue to evolve (*G*).[51]

Our final example—one we have dubbed "coupled oscillators"—is drawn from near the end of this thirty-five-minute improvisation and illustrates how even the sectional structure and transitional nature of this trio's music can evolve into a complex layering or coupling of multiple tempos and textures (*N2*). Rivers is by now on flute and voice and the trio seems able to successfully articulate not a unified sense of pulse or texture as in many of the previous examples, but the coexistence of conflicting and comple-mentary expressions and motivations. We hear a sort of speed pulse in the drums, a type of sheets-of-sound playing in the flute, and a powerfully articulated and varied drone in the bass. Even as Rivers improvises a final melodic fragment to signal a collective transition back to a shared sense of tempo for the trio (O), the saliency of this type of transitional gesture, which has been used several times by this point in the performance, has increased to the point at which new strategies for responding are required to maintain the complexity and interest of the performance. We hear a new sense of tempo referenced by the group, but in rather loose and playful ways that immediately deconstructs this more traditional performance practice.

The notion of *signifyin(g)* refers to a mediating strategy for discourse, rooted in pan-African discursive mythologies, involving aspects of repetition and revision to create double meaning, indirectedness, and subtle humor.[52] To signify is to replace the static concepts of signifiers and signifieds (objects—persons, places, things) with a dynamic in which dialog informs all modes of communication and meanings become malleable and, at times, intentionally ambiguous.[53] In a general sense, our approach may provide some cognitive basis to phenomenological explanation on how this process of signifying, which is deeply entrenched in African-American arts, language, and music, invokes a subtle and continual play of reference and revision, of complexity and comprehensibility. We conjecture that these occur, at least sometimes in music, after the saliency of a quale has become so large that it is incapable of sustaining surprise, and can therefore be used as a riposte, a goad, or even a rebuke. Complexity then arises from the failure of the quale to conform to its previously established role. Another way to put this is that the system becomes increasingly unpredictable and hence chaotic as the saliencies of cadences rise to a critical level.

With regards to the general practice of Sam Rivers's trios and the specific dynamics evidenced on "Hues of Melanin," we find that:

- The improvisation as a whole can be segmented into sections, each a region of phase space, on which intersubjective agreement by expert listeners can be obtained.
- Within each segment, performers shift among a number of "voices," each of which is also a certain region of phase space, again with transitions that are intersubjectively stable.
- Thus, the phase space is hierarchically structured. However, different performers may have different subspaces for their own particular set of voices.
- Transitions among segments are often prefigured by certain figures, which have quite different saliencies for performers: some are quite subtle, while others are rather obvious; all can be considered cadences, in a broad sense of that term. A short trill to signal a lessening of intensity and a quick melodic fragment to establish a sense of tempo appear to be the strongest transition triggers in this performance. Weaker markers include figures that descend to a strong low note, and hints (of varying strength) of V/I chord sequences.
- The presence of a transition-prefiguring cadence may not actually produce a transition, and even when it does, there may be a period of reorganization that precedes it. These figures may at times be repeated, which increases their saliency as transition triggers, but also increases the expectation that they will produce novel, and therefore more complex results on each reoccurrence. At certain levels of complexity, obvious cadence points may even be intentionally ignored or subverted.

A Delicate Balance

An important goal of improvised music appears to be ensemble self-organization so that critical levels of complexity, responsiveness, and surprise can be reached and maintained over the course of an extended performance. While each new gesture could conceivably trigger a structural transition in the music, players must not allow themselves to be overwhelmed by the speed of interaction and availability of options in order to avoid potentially crippling states of oversaturation and indecision. In a workshop setting with our graduate student improvisation ensemble, Sam Rivers, with his current trio, stressed the importance of interactions and awareness, but he also made it clear that certain levels of complexity would emerge only if individuals stay true to their own creativity.

Both inexperienced and overbearing improvisers tend to focus too much attention on what they, as individuals, are responsible for. The inexperienced improviser can, through indecision or a reliance on overly simple cat-and-mouse-type interactions, offer too much "inertia" and not enough "momentum" to the situation. While the overbearing improviser can offer too much "momentum"—in the overpowering strength of his or her ideas and convictions—and not enough "inertia" in the form of measured interactions so that a critical level of complexity and coherence is never achieved. To return to our earlier model, in one case the coupling between listening to and producing music is too tight, and in the other it is too loose. A story recounted by Steve Lacy about his time spent playing with Thelonious Monk highlights the issue well. Lacy said of Monk, "He mostly told me what not to do." Monk would remind Lacy to "play your part, I'm accompanying you. Don't pick up on my things." In other words, offer some "momentum" to the improvising situation. But Monk also told Lacy to "make the drummer sound good. . . . Don't play everything. Just play certain things, let other things go by."[54] In other words, allow some space (or inertia) for the collective improvisation to develop.

Although dramatic transitions can conceivably occur at any moment in the freer forms of jazz, in practice, experienced improvisers tend to explore ideas, identities, and relationships for considerable stretches of time. If distantly related ideas were circulating at every moment, the desired balance between complexity and coherence might never be achieved. In other words, a complete lack of coherence would eliminate the possibility for surprise by not supporting predictions or expectations.

Improvising music certainly requires focused listening, quick reflexes, and extreme sensitivity to the group flow, but it equally demands individual fortitude and tenacity not to be overwhelmed by the speed of interaction and the availability of musical options. Sam Rivers expressed it this way:

> I want to keep moving and experimenting and not be repetitive. I mean when you're reading *The Iliad* and *The Odyssey*, you don't repeat! You just keep going and going! But how do you do that? Because you have experience with so many different types of melody, so many different kinds of music. So that's how you become creative and prolific in improvising.[55]

Improvising music, then, can demonstrate turbulence and coherence at the same time. The findings of nonlinear dynamical systems theory require that we confront and rethink ingrained notions of order and disorder, simplicity and complexity. Jazz music has, for its brief century or so of development, challenged many of the same notions in the artistic community. Swing and improvisation, hallmarks of even the most conservative definitions of jazz, both rely on nonlinear dynamics to create the sense of momentum and surprise. Since roughly the 1960s, freer styles of improvising have pushed the ideas of nonlinear musical dynamics even further, challenging the adequacy of older musicologies and highlighting the need for innovative approaches to studying the emergent properties of musical performance and musical consciousness. These performances often have a sense of coherence like that of a natural process, rather than an artificial symmetry like that of a classical sonata or a 32-bar AABA song form.[56]

We have focused on the hierarchical complexity of the phase space of improvised music and the pronounced moments of phase transition, in which improvisers give listeners the subjective experience of being delicately poised between evolving along two or more quite different paths. Not only is science evolving, as nonlinear, qualitative models and computation intensive analyses overtake older linear models that demand explicit solutions, but also music and the arts are evolving, as representational, individual-centered works are being overtaken by interactive, socially oriented, nonlinear forms. By drawing on aspects of these contemporary sciences, we offer a way of looking at music that takes account of its inherently dynamical nature and focuses attention on the act of listening, since music only lives when it is heard and understood.

5
The Edge of Chaos

The emerging notion of chaos as a creative force, a dynamic form of orderly-disorder, has resonated with countless artists in the past several decades. Two heavy metal groups adopted names taken directly from the new sciences—Chaos Theory and Order from Chaos—while references in song and album titles have cropped up in the work of artists as diverse as the Sex Pistols, Steve Coleman, Alanis Morisette, Ozomatli, and Yusef Lateef. Improvising turntablists Otomo Yoshihide and Martin Tétreault make reference to chaos in their work, as does the improvising "supergroup" Organized Chaos, featuring saxophonist Peter Brötzmann, guitarist Nicky Skopelitis, and drummer Shoji Hano. The appeal of chaos as a type of orderly-disorder seems unbounded by notions of musical style or genre.[1] Most recently, the electronic music composer/improviser/live computer processor Lawrence Casserly titled one of his recent compact disc recordings *The Edge of Chaos*

Although chaos may the best-known term connected to the new scientific paradigm, there have been others. Before "chaos" became the rallying cry of interdisciplinary science, "catastrophe theory," inspired by the pioneering work of French mathematician René Thom in the 1950s and 1960s, demonstrated the ways in which abrupt, qualitative changes in a system may be caused by sudden dislocations or disruptions rather than quantitative and continuous developments. Thom examined a broad range of natural, social, and cultural phenomena to support his conclusions.[2] And more recently, the label "complexity theory" has emerged to describe a related, but in many ways different, approach to the study of nonlinear dynamical systems.

John Briggs and F. David Peat, in their very readable introduction to chaos theory, present the differing aspects of the new sciences as two sides of the same turbulent mirror: a portal through which order and chaos dynamically and mysteriously intertwine.[3] Their treatment is informed by the mythic idea, shared by many ancient cultures, that cosmic creativity depends on reciprocity between order and disorder.[4] Artists, in particular, have felt similar connections to this dynamic interplay of forces. "To be a creator," Briggs and Peat write, "requires operating in a shadowy boundary line between order and chaos."[5] But the world of science has traditionally been one of regularity and predictability—from planets to atoms to the genetic code, the world has been divided into its parts and, until recently, held up to a mirror of platonic purity. Scientists have long admitted that the world outside of the laboratory seldom behaves as orderly as the mirror of those laws we hold up to nature, but chaos was thought to be the result of a complexity that in theory could be stripped down to its orderly underpinnings.

Contemporary scientists, however, are beginning to construct a new mirror to hold up to nature: a turbulent one. On one side of this mirror, researchers have been most interested in the orderly decent into chaos: how mathematically simple systems can demonstrate complex behaviors. In intriguing ways these systems are *deterministic*, in that every step is determined by the state immediately preceding it, yet *unpredictable*, because one cannot predict a distant future state without going through every intermediate state.

On the other side of the turbulent mirror, more recently referred to as complexity theory, researchers are attempting to understand how order can emerge out of chaos: how extremely complex systems can spontaneously give birth to delicate forms and structures. Put another way, chaos theory deals with systems that rapidly become highly disordered and unmanageable, while complexity theory deals with highly interconnected systems that may, at certain times and under certain conditions, self-organize in a way that produces emergent forms of order.[6] These emergent forms cannot be deduced from the equations describing a dynamical system but can describe the patterns arriving from the evolution of such systems in time.

Scientists on both sides of this turbulent mirror share a fascination with the "edge of chaos," the balance point between stability and extreme turbulence. The edge of chaos is a technical term (often associated with the Santa Fe Institute) that describes when a dynamical system is in a critical region between order and disorder.[7] You might envision water boiling or evaporating on the boundaries of its phase space. This critical state only occurs in dynamical systems that are dissipating internal energy, are open to continual energy influxes from outside the system, and are operating under what are known as "far-from-equilibrium" conditions.

Because we now have better probes for collecting data in turbulent situations, and we have powerful computers for analyzing that data, chaos researchers have begun to make some limited progress on the various routes that *lead to chaos*.[8] Many of these discoveries have directly influenced musical practice, but these direct applications have been most easily integrated into a compositional approach that values not only complexity, but also control. This branch of chaos theory focuses on the process by which relatively simple equations can, when iterated, produce extreme complexity in an entirely deterministic fashion.

Understanding how order can *emerge from chaos* has remained somewhat more elusive, and the very question is forcing many scientists and artists to rethink their methodologies and epistemological assumptions. The interactive and improvisational dimensions of musical performance may best articulate this other side of the same turbulent mirror. Like the word "chaos," "free" improvisation has produced its fair share of semantic confusion. But although it may imply randomness to some, it too can be about relatively simple iterative and interactive processes that create a complex musical tapestry and a type of emergent order.

On both sides of this turbulent mirror and at the center, musicians, like their scientific counterparts, are beginning to cross the boundaries that have traditionally separated disciplines, practices, and genres. As old ways of doing things begin to dissolve, however, new tensions can arise, and old ones can persevere. In this chapter, we will investigate practices on both sides of the mirror and in the middle, and we will probe further into the fascinating qualities of self-organization that have been identified by chaos and complexity researchers, finding some analogies with qualities of improvised music. With the assistance of Rolf Bader at the University of Hamburg, I also employ some of the tools of chaos theory to analyze examples of improvised music, including performances by Evan Parker and the Sam Rivers Trio that connect with the previous two chapters, as well as improvisations by the Art Ensemble of Chicago, Peter Brötzmann's group, and Derek Bailey. Although these new analytical tools provide a window into the orderly-disorder of music that was unavailable only a few short years ago, like earlier methods that investigated music in the physical or symbolic domains alone, they must be integrated into a systemic perspective that recognizes the nature of music as inextricable from its personal, social, and cultural particulars.

The Turbulent Mirror

> Chaos does not mean disorder. . . . It represents an abstract cosmic principle referring to the source of all creation.[9]
>
> —Ralph Abraham

> Somewhere underneath, very deeply, there's a common place in our spirit where the beauty of mathematics and the beauty of music meet. But they don't meet on the level of algorithm or making music by calculation. It's much lower, much deeper—or much higher, you could say.[10]
>
> —Györgi Ligeti

> I accept chaos. I'm not sure whether it accepts me.[11]
>
> —Bob Dylan

Chaos theory, according to many, has changed not only the findings of science, but also its presiding methodology and epistemology. While much has been written in the fields of science studies and even literature on the broader cultural conditions that set the stage for, and have been altered by, chaos theory, surprisingly little has been written on the role that contemporary music has played in articulating or responding to this new cultural paradigm.[12] The term "chaotics" has been used to describe not the specific mathematics of chaos theory, but rather the emerging cultural framework that is authorizing new visions of order and disorder in society. According to Katherine Hayles, chaotics is a new cultural paradigm "affecting not simply scientific practices but social and intellectual ones as well."[13] Chaotics, it seems, affects not only the answer, but also the thought that provokes the question.

The mathematics of chaos theory is already beginning to have a pronounced effect on music and music studies. For composers, chaos theory offers a set of tools that can transform relatively simple operations into extremely complex material in order to generate musical ideas for compositions.[14] Among many in the newest generation of composers, fractals and iterated algorithms are as familiar as tonic and dominant chords were to their distant and not-so-distant predecessors. For music theorists, the new sciences hold out the appealing promise of a precise method for analyzing the seemingly insurmountable complexities of much contemporary music.[15] But as Judy Lochhead points out in her provocative article titled "Hearing Chaos," within the interpretive domain "scant work has been devoted in either music or cultural studies to the role that musicians played in disclosing the new cultural paradigm of 'chaotics.'"[16]

For her treatment, Lochhead focuses on mid-twentieth-century musical practices and the work of chaotics, focusing on a disparate group of composer/creators, including John Cage, Pierre Boulez, Steve Reich, György Ligeti, Iannis Xenakis, and Elliot Carter, as well as Ornette Coleman, Roscoe Mitchell, Jimi Hendrix, and the Grateful Dead. She finds in the creative work of these artists "multiple construals of chaotics through musical manifestations of disorder, order, probability, randomness, freedom, and indeterminacy."[17] In order to frame these diverse approaches within a descriptive scheme, Lochhead articulates four categories of musical chaotics: *ordering to create unpredictability; ordering to create an aural analogue to chaos; chaos as creative potential;* and *liberatory chaos*.

Within the first mode, ordering to create unpredictability, Lochhead locates the integral serialism of Boulez, the process-oriented minimalism of Reich, and the complex micropolyphony of Ligeti. Although these methods are not identical to the mathematical formulations of chaos, she argues that, like the current mathematical theory, they demonstrate how relatively simple deterministic operations can, when iterated, produce extremely complex and unstable results. In other words, Boulez's notion of the "ambiguity of a surfeit of order being equivalent to disorder" is, in Lochhead's formulation, analogous to the way in which science writer James Gleick describes chaos as "order *masquerading* as randomness."[18]

Lochhead finds aural analogs to chaos in work by Carter and Xenakis. In Carter's *Double Concerto for Harpsichord and Piano with Two Chamber Orchestras*, for instance, the five seamless movements can be heard to evolve from the spontaneous creation of order out of a seemingly random or entropic state, to a coda section that recounts the entropic flow into disorder. And Xenakis used mathematical formulae, including gas laws that describe probabilistic behaviors, to create aural imagery of such seemingly chaotic natural events as the collision of hail or rain with hard surfaces and the songs of cicadas in a summer field. Despite their compositional differences, however, Lochhead argues that Carter and Xenakis shared an advocacy for control and precision in order to create sound worlds that evoke chance and unpredictability, and they both, in varying ways, strongly denounced improvisation-based compositional practices as inherently limited by the conditioning of the performer or the real-time constraints of performance.[19] John Cage espoused similar ideas at various times, and it is with his work and philosophy that Lochhead locates her only example of chaos as creative potential.

Lochhead reserves the category of liberatory chaos for comments about the music of Ornette Coleman and the AACM, Hendrix's burning guitars, and the Grateful Dead's use of feedback. She locates these musics within the African-American and counterculture rebellions of the 1960s, and she offers a (now standard) definition of free jazz in terms of its negative features: liberated from "such things as tonal harmonic structure, hierarchical textures, metrical rhythmic structures, sectional form, and timbres traditionally construed as 'musical.'"[20] "For the performer/creator of free jazz," Lochhead concludes, "the execution of music liberated from traditional modes of organization enacted a negation of the status quo—musically and socially—while aligning new modes of organization sometimes with chaos as creative force and sometimes with randomness and unpredictability as emancipation."

Throughout, Lochhead argues compellingly that music gave shape to the new paradigm of chaotics in ways distinct from literature and science, allowing "a unique visceral engagement with concepts of chaos."[21] But by segregating the improvised examples into the category of liberatory chaos and by effectively reducing them to an "oppositional stance to musical order," I fear that Lochhead misses the opportunity to highlight the interactive, adaptive, and constructive qualities of improvisation that make it, in the best of instances, a system continually on the "edge of chaos." In a footnote, she informs the reader that Cage's work would be equally at home in the philosophical category of liberatory or expressive chaos, but she does not seem to afford this same latitude for the improvisers to "cross over" (or is it to "move up"?) into the "ontological" and "denotative" modes of chaos.[22] They are left simply to offer "alternatives" to the status quo.

I would not want to downplay the importance of liberatory tropes in the performance practice of free jazz and progressive rock, especially during the 1960s in the United States. People as diverse as George Lewis and Jerry Garcia have highlighted the "anti-authoritarian" impulse in improvisation.[23] Even in Europe, the early years of free improvisation were often inspired by a rebellious attitude toward the "accepted" forms of modern music, as well as a fear of spreading fascism. One need only listen to the album, *Machine Gun* (1968), by the Peter Brötzmann Octet, perhaps the first recording to bring together many of the first generation European free improvisers, to glimpse the general desire at the time to demolish as many barriers to musical expression as possible. Albums such as Paul Rutherford's *Iskra 1903*, the title of which references the birth of Bolshevism in Russia, also made explicit that the musical revolution went hand-in-hand with revolutionary political leanings for many. Or for a subtler example, an often-told story in the annals of free improvisation describes a 1974 concert by Rutherford who, while performing Luciano Berio's explicitly notated work *Sequenza V for Trombone*, offered a healthy dose of his own improvised extended techniques, all of which evaded the notice of the critics and intelligentsia in attendance.[24]

This example, however, may also highlight the different sides of our turbulent mirror. Without a doubt, a significant number of composers have produced work that discloses or resonates with the emerging paradigm of chaotics. But in many of these cases, once the various compositional strategies have been employed, resulting in a finished "work," the relationship between the performers, audience, and music remains unchanged from standard practice. In other instances, the latitude that performers can expect is still markedly less than that commonly assumed by improvisers. When discussing Cage's use of chance operations in *Music of Changes,* Lochhead herself points out that, "Once a score is fixed, however, a predictable relationship exists between composer, score, and performed sound."[25] And referencing Cage's indeterminate pieces, Lochhead explains: "While the relation between composer and work is indeterminate in such pieces, the relation between performer and work or listener and work remains much the same as in pieces employing chance procedures."[26]

Musical performance based on notation, in both its traditional and more unconventional manifestations, preserves what theorist Jacques Attali called the mode of "Representation," in which music is seen as an object of exchange.[27] Improvisation and other highly interactive art forms, however, can foreshorten or even eliminate the distance between artist, audience, and work. They may herald Attali's final stage, confusingly called "Composition" since it actually describes something more akin to improvisation, in which musicians are inventing the message at the same time as the language. Attali specifically locates this mode in the transgressive aspects of African-American free jazz and he proposes that music might again emerge as the harbinger for a new social order.

Unlike similar treatments of chaotics that highlight the emerging paradigm's connection to cultural markers of postmodernism (the work of Katherine Hayles, for instance), Lochhead argues that midcentury "chaotic" music was most directly linked to practices of high modernism. She contends that composers, such as Cage, Boulez, and Carter, "aspired toward an 'objective,' less culturally determined music."[28] But this aspiration certainly does not pertain to the music and improvisational approaches of many African-American musicians, including Ornette Coleman and the members of the AACM, both subjects of Lochhead's analysis. One need only consider the slogan adopted by the Art Ensemble of Chicago, "Great Black Music Ancient to Future," to put this rather Eurocentric notion to rest.

George Lewis argues that the "power of whiteness" has served to mask the important role that improvisation played in establishing the contemporary music paradigm and, in particular, to denigrate the important contributions of African-American jazz musicians in this regard.[29] According to Lewis, words like "indeterminacy" and "intuition," or even "happening" and "action," are used to hide the presence of improvisation in contemporary music discourse. Also referencing Cage's musical and philosophical stance, Lewis writes:

> After three hundred years of the very real silence of violence and terror, rather than a freely chosen conceptual silence of four minutes or so, one can well imagine the newly freed African-American slaves developing a music in which each person is encouraged to speak, without conflict between individual expression and collective consciousness. In contrast to this notion of improvisation as a human birthright, a simple response to conditions, an embodied practice central to existence and being in the world, Cage's Puritanical description of improvisation contrasted the image of a heroic, mystically ego-driven Romantic improvisor, imprisoned by his own will, with the detached, disengaged, purely ego-transcending artist who simply lets sounds be themselves.[30]

Many pan-European composers disavowed improvisation simply because the post-WWII forms of jazz were becoming widely recognized as art forms that could compete for the mantle of high art music. But as Lewis's comments highlight, this battle was often waged on philosophical terrain that downplayed issues of race and class in favor of the more solipsistic and community-denying isolationism of Eurocentric discourse.

Lochhead includes a frequently quoted passage of Cage in which he described his desire to create music "free of individual taste and memory (psychology) and also of the literature and traditions of the art."[31] Although Cage could control the compositional process, he could not control listening. It is in listening that music is created, and listening is never free of memory. Cage did arguably play an important role in urging listeners to hear more fully their natural environment, but he did so by attempting to displace the human from its integral role within that environment.[32] Free improvisers advocate similar qualities of active and engaged listening, but they implicitly acknowledge that the infinite variety of sound around us requires a human social space for interaction and selection.

Chaotics is an exciting avenue of exploration that draws on many sympathetic and synergetic connections between science, culture, and art. Far from simply responding to scientific discoveries, musicians have played an active role in disclosing and exploring the paradigm of chaotics. But as we highlight this important role, we must also be careful not to reify existing notions or re-inscribe old hegemonies. As Lochhead's treatment and the burgeoning literature for composers and theorists on the subject suggest, the tools and orientations of "chaos" are not always equally applied.

As I have argued in the earlier chapters, improvisation, like all music, should most appropriately be situated in the embodied, phenomenological, and social realms. But many of the tools of chaos can be usefully applied to this music as well to shed light on its structural complexities and to help us avoid the Eurocentric notion that only those musics that are conceived of prior to performance (and represent the singular and controlling vision of a composer, I am tempted to add) can manifest themselves through ontological and denotative modes of chaos. Improvisation, particularly in its freest manifestations, may in fact afford a better avenue for investigations into the visceral qualities of chaotics because it encourages musical creations that involve the paradoxical link between determinism and unpredictability characteristic of chaotic systems. In order to pursue this further, I had to enlist the assistance of Rolf Bader, an expert on measuring the fractal dimension of music.

Fractal Worlds

> Paradoxically, complex systems, whether in music or physics, produce turbulence and coherence at the same time. . . . As mathematicians topple the tyranny of the straight line of Euclidian geometry, one is reminded of that ecstatic sense of discovery with which twentieth-century composers proclaimed their liberation from the bar line.[33]
>
> —Richard Steinitz

> [Fractals] provide our first glimpse into a new realization spreading across science—that randomness is interleaved with order, that simplicity enfolds complexity and complexity harbors simplicity, and that orders and chaos can be repeated at smaller and smaller scales.[34]
>
> —John Briggs and F. David Peat

> [T]o some extent all sounds are fractal in nature, for example an organ pipe can be thought of as making sound which begins with air hitting an edge, which creates turbulence, a fractal sound, which is then resonated by the pipe. So by symbolising a sound as a note, one not only loses most of the data, but also replaces fractal properties with the linear ones of a note.[35]
>
> —Chris Melchior

Fractals are the poster child of chaos theory. These strange yet strangely familiar plots have by now been seen on computer screens around the world. Countless people have been fascinated by their intrinsic complexity and by their ability to unfold new levels of pattern and structure on all scales. Fractal geometry was the brainchild of Benoit Mandelbrot, a Polish-born French mathematical physicist, who has been a tireless missionary for spreading the word about their usefulness in contemplating the complexities of the world around us.

Mandelbrot coined the term "fractal" from the Latin *fractus*, which means broken or irregularly shaped. He explains that "fractals are geometrical shapes that, contrary to those of Euclid, are not regular at all. First, they are irregular all over. Secondly, they have the same degree of irregularity on all scales. A fractal object looks the same when examined from far away or nearby—it is self-similar."[36] Mandelbrot is fond of demonstrating the notion of self-similarity by breaking off successive pieces of cauliflower; each smaller piece maintains the distinctive characteristics of the whole yet exhibits novelty and subtle difference.

In his now classic paper that introduced the notion of fractal dimensions, Mandelbrot asked: how long is the coastline of Great Britain? This may at first seem a silly question, since humans have been mapping out continents and national borders for centuries. But all maps will smooth out a certain amount of detail. At what level should we be content to take our measurements? Every hundred meters? Every ten meters? How about at the level of individual pebbles or sand along the shore? Mandelbrot reasoned that the length of a coastline would always vary depending on what quantity we chose as the measurement unit.[37] As Briggs and Peat explain: "If in the end quantity is a relative concept—it always involves some smearing out of details—then it is considerably less precise than we believed. In place of quantity, such as length, Mandelbrot puts the qualitative measure of effective fractal dimensions, a measure of the relative degree of complexity of an object."[38]

A similar difficulty exists for measuring musical sounds. Like our conventional maps, notational approaches by necessity reduce the immense sonic detail of music to discreet and linear representations in the form of notes, rhythms, dynamic and articulation markings, etc. By applying the analytical tools of fractal dimensions to the sonic aspects of recorded music, however, we may be able to arrive at a useful measure of the relative degrees of complexity of a given performance. An important disclaimer is needed here. Although computers can process the digital information contained in a musical recording in rather involved ways, they will never replace the need for analysis to be informed by a contextually rich and culturally sensitive understanding of the performance. Combined with a phenomenological perspective, however, an analysis of the fractal dimension of recorded sound may be able to offer some helpful insight into the music. At the very least, it offers a visual representation of the evolving sonic complexity (not perceptual complexity, as we will see) of a musical passage or an entire performance that is unavailable through any other existing analytical means. With this representation, it is often possible to see significant structural changes within a single performance, and to compare various performances in terms of their dynamic properties.

One of my motivations for pursuing this line of inquiry is that transcribing music like that produced by Evan Parker in a solo situation would not only be near-impossible, but also arguably a fruitless task as well. Fellow improviser Steve Beresford once remarked: "At its most multi-layered, Parker's solo playing would drive the best human transcriber round the bend, let alone a machine."[39] But modern computers are able to crunch the sonic details of Parker's recorded output in ways that may be help-ful, even if they too could not possibly hope to notate those same sounds in any con-ventional way. Another motivating factor for this direction was simply the fact that many musicians, including Parker himself, have noted connections between the emerging sciences and the process of improvising music:

> Nowadays we all know about fractals in nature and all of that . . . the idea that there is detail at every level. So you could look at the landscape, or then you could look at the tree, or then you could look at the leaf, and then you can take a microscope out. . . . And at every level there is detail that's just beyond what you can focus clearly on. That's it. I mean to try to have that, in improvisation, to have that quality as well—this is quite a challenge.[40]

Reflecting on his approach to solo improvisation in particular, Parker finds several intriguing comparisons with the iterative dynamics of chaotic processes, although they must have been intuitively felt at first:

> Through the repetition of simple phrases which evolve by slow mutations (a note lost here, a note added there, a shift of accent, dynamic or tone color) their appar-ent "polyphonic" character can be manipulated to show the same material in different perspectives. The heard sound is monitored carefully and the small in-crements of change introduced to maintain or shift interest and the listeners' attention. Recent popularization of the ideas of chaos theory means that most people are now familiar with fractal patterns and Mandelbrot figures. Without wishing to jump on a band wagon, the process involved in the evolution of a phrase in this way of improvising has something in common with the equations that generate these patterns and figures where the output from one basically sim-ple calculation is used as the input for the next calculation in an iterative process which by many repetitions finally generates a pattern or figure whose complexity is not foreseeable from the starting point.[41]

Well before the notion of fractal patterns became commonplace, Parker was think-ing about audible processes in music, and he was also concerned with the ways in which the emerging discourse about them was being dictated by composers. In a 1968 essay titled "Music as a Gradual Process," composer Steve Reich wrote: "What I'm interested in is a compositional process and a sounding music that arc one and the same thing."[42] In the essay, Reich compared performing and listening to a gradual music process to "placing your feet in the sand by the ocean's edge and watching, feeling, and listening to the waves gradually bury them." To conclude, however, Reich writes of a "particular liberating and impersonal kind of ritual," arguing that, "The distinctive thing about musical processes is that they determine all the note-to-note details and the over all form simultaneously. One can't improvise in a musical proc-ess—the concepts are mutually exclusive." Parker took issue with this at the time, writing a formal response to Reich's dehumanizing notion of process, and more re-cently he communicated to me that he "objected to the notion that the process needed to be mathematically rigorous in order to be perceived or to function as 'process.'"[43]

Fractal patterns in nature tend to be the result of growth processes or near-repetitive, continuous, and cumulative dynamics. As examples, you might envision the crack in a rock ledge or the dendritic web in a river system formed through earthquakes and tectonic shift. But complex fractal patterns are also found in the human body, in the way that our respiratory, nervous, and circulatory systems branch out in self-similar ways to maintain a high level of complexity even at the smallest scales. For instance, our blood supply is transported through the body via veins and arteries at the largest scale, but the same characteristic branching structure is repeated with smaller blood vessels right down to the capillaries, allowing for all parts of the body, from organs down to the smallest tissues, to be as close as possible to both the supply and exhaust systems. Even our brain activity appears to have low-level chaos as its default state, allowing for a spontaneity and flexibility that would be impossible with more regular forms of order.

The most common method for measuring the fractal dimension of a visual pattern involves a box-counting algorithm. Researchers mathematically employ progressively smaller and smaller "boxes" to measure the density of a pattern at various levels of magnification in order to calculate an overall fractal dimension to the object. For instance, in a fascinating article devoted to analyzing the fractal dimensions of Jackson Pollock's drip paintings, Taylor, Micoloch, and Jonas employed a box-counting algorithm to computer scans of Pollock's work. They discovered that Pollock was not only able to produce remarkably consistent fractal properties and dimensions, but also to increase the complexity of his work gradually over the span of his career, from roughly $D = 1.45$ to $D = 1.72$.[44] These numbers can be intuitively understood if we remember that a line has a dimension of $D = 1$ and a plane has a dimension of $D = 2$. The scans of Pollock's paintings are two-dimensional representations, but his designs do not cover the entire surface of those two dimensions. To be clear, however, D refers to more than simple coverage density. Rather, it indicates "depth" of development and self-similarity (and it also reflects the fineness of measurement units). For a point of comparison, values for natural fractal patterns such as coastlines and lightning range between about $D = 1.25$ and $D = 1.30$.

The fractal qualities of Pollock's work can also be intuitively appreciated with the notion of scaling. The visual consequence of fractal scaling is that it is not always easy to determine the magnification and hence the size of what is being viewed. For examples in nature, you might envision snow-covered rocky terrain or a moss-covered wall, both of which may display similar patterns up close and from far away such that a photograph of either may not easily convey a sense of scale. By extracting color detail from their computer scans of Pollock's work, Taylor et al. also found that each individual layer of his paintings consist of a uniform fractal pattern, and when they are layered to build up the complete pattern, the fractal dimension of the overall painting rises. Finding fractal properties in the work of Jackson Pollock does not imply, however, that he was attempting to represent the forms of nature. Rather, it demonstrates that his painting techniques and sensibilities intuitively emulated the patterns of growth found in nature. It may be interesting to note here as well that Ornette Coleman's 1960 album *Free Jazz*, which launched the movement for many, prominently featured a Jackson Pollock painting on its cover.

Analyzing the fractal dimension of patterns in time has proven to be considerably more difficult. Time series are, at least in one sense, only one-dimensional, since they simply move through the time axis; they do not have an immediately apparent independent physical reality in our three-dimensional world. Many of our conceptual metaphors for music make connections to the physical world of motion, space, distance, and texture, but as we saw in chapter three, these dimensions are not inherent in the musical sounds themselves. So any higher dimensionality for music is always, in some senses, artificial.

Despite these challenges, researchers have developed mathematics designed to analyze transient signals in terms of a fractal correlation dimension. In brief, these techniques calculate how many simple dynamical subsystems would be needed to achieve the complexity of the initial time series. An example may help to clarify this. For instance, C. Nicolis and G. Nicolis calculated from time series data of the Earth's ice volume record that there may be a global climatic attractor of approximately $D = 3.1$. This means that models involving only four variables could provide a description of the salient features of global climate change.[45] The challenge is that we do not know exactly to what subsystems these variables might refer. For musical examples, the fractal correlation dimension measures the recorded sound in terms of the number of vibrating subsystems that would be needed to produce its complexity at a given moment. Far from a simple frequency analysis, this method provides a means to describe the richness of musical sound in a manageable yet abstract way to facilitate analytical and comparative work.

In the procedure used by Rolf Bader, there are three main subsystems taken into account: the harmonic overtone components of the sound; the inharmonic frequencies that are part of the sound; and any large amplitude modulations, all measured by correlating successive moments in time.[46] The harmonic and inharmonic components of a sound describe in more technical ways the sonic dimensions we normally associate with pitch, timbre, and noise, among other things. And amplitude modulations take account of traditional parameters such as dynamics, articulations, and phrasing.

The exact calculations that Rolf's system performs are incredibly complicated. A single twenty-minute example of music can require upward of a week of number crunching from even a top-of-the-line personal computer system. The analysis starts by embedding the time series in a multidimensional space called pseudo-phase space. A space of up to eighty dimensions is necessary to get correct results.[47] These dimensions, I should note, are completely different from the final fractal correlation dimension reported by the system. The system arrives at a final plot by embedding the eighty or so pseudo-phase space dimensions into a two-dimension space, using the Takens embedding theorem among other things.[48]

This process of embedding the multidimensional pseudo-phase space into a format that can more easily be comprehended by humans is a delicate one. Therefore, the final results sometimes visualize the data very well, but not always. Additionally, the computer integrates over a minimum time interval of 50ms, arriving at twenty distinct readings per second of music—a rather large data set.[49] In order to display an entire performance or large sections of one in graphic form, however, only a few hundred distinct points can be easily represented. To avoid taking a random sampling of moments for the plots (which would have little meaning), the computer calculates mean values. This limits the level of detail we are visualizing through the plots, though it has the benefit of reducing analysis "noise" and the irregularities that arc artificially imposed by the analysis process, as well as the effect of "smoothing" the contour of the plot in ways that reveal broad trends in the musical signal. Only when we look at the smallest time scales, in the range of a few seconds, can the computer display the exact values it calculates for each time interval.

Consequently, this method should not be relied on as a starting point for analysis. We should also keep in mind that these plots offer one measure of the complexity of the recorded sound itself, and do not encompass all of the aspects of a phenomenological hearing of the music. They can, however, provide visualizations of the evolving sonic complexity of a musical signal in a way that, when compared against the perceptions of human listeners, can be particularly useful.

Before discussing any individual results, it may be helpful to gain a slightly better sense of the general range of fractal dimensions in music. A pure sine wave has a fractal dimension of one, as does the steady state of a pure harmonic overtone spectrum produced on an instrument. But when attack transients, intensity increases, and decay are taken into account, all musical sounds produce higher fractal dimensions, including all complex sounds produced by a computer. The attractor of a chaotic system has a fractal dimension typically exceeding $D = 2$. For instance, John Argyris, one of Rolf's mentors, calculated the fractal correlation dimension of the Lorentz attractor, one of the best known strange attractors of chaos theory, as $D = 2.08$.[50] In contrast, white noise, which has no correlation between subsequent sounds, has infinite degrees of freedom and a fractal correlation dimension of infinity. This is why the final moment of a plot often produces a rapid rise because as the final tones fade, noise briefly dominates, and the fractal dimension rises quickly toward infinity. Pure silence would also produce a fractal dimension of infinity; however, the slight background noise of recordings prevents this from happening in our analyses.

Different instruments also have inherently different fractal characteristics because they incorporate very different approaches to producing sound. For instance, Rolf found that violins have the most complex attack transient, with dimensions up to $D = 8$. The saxophone and other reed instruments, however, hover around $D = 3$ for a standard tongued attack. The drum set and various percussion instruments also have the potential to produce rather large dimensional readings due to their many inharmonic components of sound and their possibilities for rapid and significant amplitude modulations. Changes in pitch alone can, in many cases, have little effect on the fractal dimension plot. But variation in the density of sound events, in the range of amplitude modulations, and in the sonic qualities of timbre and attack will produce more dramatic results.

It is critical to note here that perceptually salient moments are not always accompanied by an increase in the fractal correlation dimension. In fact, the perception of complexity by listeners happens on several levels and should not be thought of as a property of the stimulus alone. Rather, it is a property of the *relationship* between stimulus and listener. This relationship reflects not only the complexity of material at each time point, but also the change in complexity through time as well as the previous experience and implicit rules that determine what is complex to a listener. In other words, significant changes in the relative complexity of sound over time, and the experiences one has with listening to similar or related stimuli, will also affect which moments are deemed most salient or most interesting. For instance, although a complex sound stimulus may provoke listeners' immediate attention, a sudden diminution in the complexity of the overall sound can also correspond to arresting or intriguing moments for listeners. It is possible to represent by a temporal derivation plot the relative changes in the fractal correlation dimension—rather than the moment-by-moment figures presented here—but this also represents only the change in the stimulus rather than the evolving and complex relationship between stimulus and listener.

In all cases, therefore, it is important to correlate the fractal dimension plots with the perception of "tension" or "complexity" by listeners. For now, this is left for the reader to experience by following the plots while listening to the music.[51] A follow-up study could correlate the fractal dimension plots with a significant sampling of individuals of various backgrounds and experience reporting on the "tension" or "complexity" of the music as they listen. These results could in turn be correlated to the responses of the artist(s) listening back to their own recording(s). Even here, however, the researcher must be content with the fact that much of our cognitive processing while listening happens unconsciously, so listeners may not always be aware of their own judgments, nor of their own inherent biases.

Since we have already investigated music by Evan Parker and Sam Rivers in some detail, I asked Rolf to do some computer analysis of their work, along with a few interesting examples from the Art Ensemble of Chicago, Peter Brötzmann, and Derek Bailey to provide general points of comparison. As in the investigation of Pollock's drip paintings, the fractal correlation dimension may also provide an interesting measurement for comparing a single artist's work over a longer span of time, so for this reason I included several representative improvisations by Evan Parker spanning over twenty-five years of his recording career. Table 2 lists information about the various performances along with the mean fractal dimension calculated and the standard deviation.

For many of the examples I have also included a correlogram that maps time in the horizontal axis (aligned to the fractal dimension plots) and the presence of any overtone structures (from 100Hz at the bottom left to 20kHz at the top left) in the vertical axis. This is not simply a spectrogram, but rather a plot of any periodicity in the spectrogram, such that the white points in the plots correspond to the overall amplitudes of the harmonic structure at a given frequency. In many instances, these correlograms provide a helpful overview of any subsections within a performance (although certain recordings by Evan Parker produced nearly black correlograms due to the presence of many inharmonic frequencies in his sound and articulations).

The first three Evan Parker performances that Rolf and I analyzed are considered by most listeners to be not only representative of different phases in his development, but also exemplary in their own right. They are all rather lengthy improvisations (between sixteen and twenty-five minutes each), which allows for the exploration of multiple textures and techniques and the possibility for large-scale formal developments to emerge.

Figures 1a and 1b provide plots of the fractal correlation dimension and a correlogram of Parker's solo titled "Aerobatics 1," recorded at his very first solo saxophone concert given in 1975. The title is a nice allusion to the juggling metaphor that we encountered in chapter three, but in many ways Parker had not yet developed the ability to seamlessly keep three or more distinct musical layers "in the air" at the same time. The improvisations on *Saxophone Solos* tend to be more segmented than his later work, moving between sections that explore a single dominant extended technique on

Table 2: Analyzed Performances with Mean Fractal Dimension and Standard Deviation

Performer(s)	Performance	Album	Date	Mean	Standard Deviation
Evan Parker (soprano sax)	Areobatics 1	Saxophone Solos	1975	3.882	1.609
Evan Parker (soprano sax)	Monoceros 1	Monoceros	1978	3.514	0.622
Evan Parker (soprano sax)	Conic Sections 3	Conic Sections	1989	4.779	0.624
Evan Parker (soprano sax)	Broken Wing	Process and Reality	1991	3.917	0.556
Derek Bailey	Improvisation 5	Solo Guitar Volume One	1971	3.029	0.412
Evan Parker (tenor sax)	Chicago Solos 9	Chicago Solos	1995	3.482	0.521
Evan Parker (tenor sax)	Chicago Solos 10	Chicago Solos	1995	3.279	0.624
Evan Parker Electro-Acoustic Ensemble	Turbulent Mirror	Toward the Margins	1997	4.847	1.095
Peter Brötzmann Group	Machine Gun	Machine Gun	1968	8.797	3.492
Art Ensemble of Chicago	Ancestral Meditation	Urban Bushmen	1980	2.956	0.443
Art Ensemble of Chicago	People In Sorrow Parts I and II	The Pathe Sessions	1969	2.886-I 4.491-II	0.814-I 1.535-II
Sam Rivers Trio	Hues of Melanin	Trio Live	1973	4.060	1.121

the instrument. Both the fractal dimension plot and the correlogram clearly show five primary sections of development, each roughly three minutes in length.

In the first section, Parker starts in the extreme overtone range and gradually intersperses tonguing devices, rapid figuring techniques, multiphonic sounds (split tones), and occasional humming into the instrument (a technique that he would later abandon) to increase the complexity of the performance. The peak in fractal dimension for this section, $D = 8 +$, comes at approximately 1:38 into the improvisation, when Parker emphasizes a very rich and powerful multiphonic.[52] This is followed by a section of rapid "chattering" that maintains the fractal dimension near $D = 5$.

The second section begins with the sudden drop in fractal dimension, a result of a dramatic decrease in the density of sounds. After a few isolated gestures with pregnant pauses, Parker begins an extended exploration of the extreme overtone range at 2:45 into the performance. While sustaining these high sounds, Parker employs slight fluctuations in pitch and surprising leaps to the normal range of the horn that produce variations in complexity. The long tones that Parker uses prominently in many of the performances on *Saxophone Solos* gradually disappear in his later solo soprano work,

Figure 1a: Evan Parker—"Aerobatics 1"—Fractal Correlation Dimension

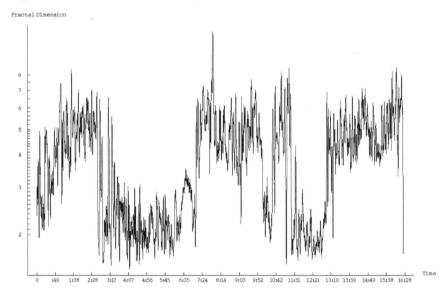

Figure 1b: Evan Parker—"Aerobatics 1"—Correlogram

although as we will see they have reentered his solo vocabulary by way of the tenor saxophone. Although these extreme overtones can produce a perceptual feeling of tension or hyperextension for the listener, their sonic components are relatively non-complex (and therefore have a lower fractal correlation dimension). In the extreme upper range of the instrument, sounds have few additional harmonic partials above them to enrich their character. For instance, listeners often have difficulty differentiating saxophone and clarinet sounds when the instruments are played in their extreme altissimo registers because many of the identifying timbral qualities of the instruments are absent

At approximately 6:30 into the improvisation, Parker increases his fluttering with these extreme overtones, eventually cadencing at 7:10. The third section begins with high-amplitude multiphonics, the most pronounced of which leaps off the fractal dimension plot at just before 8:00. More rapid chattering takes us to the 9:00 mark. Here Parker produces a type of reverse sound envelope by muting the bell of the horn with his left leg, effectively closing off the tube.[53] A return to extreme overtones at 10:10 produces another drop in the fractal dimension, but it is followed by multiphonic exploration at 10:45.

A forth section begins in earnest with a more pronounced and lengthy drop in the fractal correlation dimension, around 11:30. Parker is again in the whistle tone region of the instrument, exploring long tones with fluctuations. His circular breathing technique is often audible at these points, an aspect of his playing that he more effectively hides in his later solo work.

The fifth section begins at the 13:00 mark and leads us to the end of the performance. The techniques that were formerly explored independently are now crossing paths in rapid and unpredictable ways. Parker seems to be accelerating toward an ending, all the while increasing the overall density of his sound and patterning. Here we begin to glimpse the "polyphonic" nature of his solo playing that emerges more prominently in subsequent years. The brief dips in the fractal dimension plot during this final section correspond to times when Parker ceases vocalizing along with his playing. Although the final ending follows an intensification of the performance, it still seems to arrive rather suddenly, with little preparation.

In the following years, Parker was able to integrate the extended techniques that are already prominently displayed in his first recordings into a more seamless developmental practice. The shock value of these new instrumental sounds gave way to a more concerted exploration of the evolving complexity of an improvisation. Figures 2 and 3 present the fractal dimension plots for "Monoceros 1" (1978) and "Conic Sections 3" (1989), two lengthy improvisations that highlight well this shift in Parker's approach. The significant decrease in the standard deviation for these two performances as compared with "Aerobatics" (from 1.61 to .62 for both Monoceros and Conic Sections) underlines their more unwavering composition. I have not included the correlograms for these two performances, as they are both almost completely black from the density of inharmonic sounds.

The plot of "Monoceros 1" shows the outlines of a strong fractal arc: the performance gradually increases in complexity, only to give way in the final minutes. The one prominent drop in dimension, just after the 8:10 mark, corresponds to another extended development of extreme overtones, which provides a brief respite in the development. The shorter drops in the complexity arc also correspond to moments of

Figure 2: Evan Parker—"Monoceros 1"

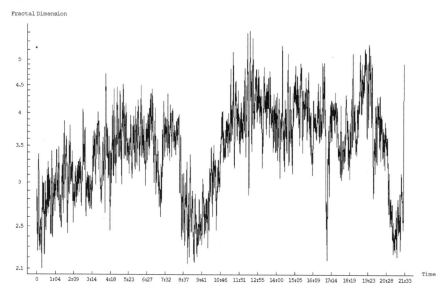

Figure 3: Evan Parker—"Conic Sections 3"

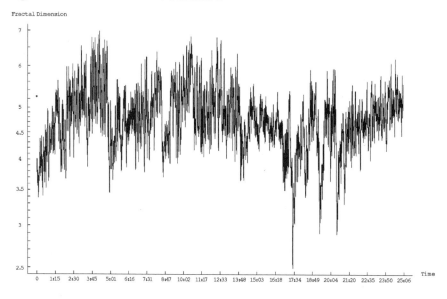

overtone exploration. During these moments, however, Parker is often employing much more variation than in similar sections of the "Aerobatics" example from three years prior. In general, he sounds more comfortable sustaining and controlling the extended sonic properties of the instrument.

The fractal dimension plots also show quite well moments when Parker is achieving his full "polyphony"—with three or more distinct registers of the instrument being explored near simultaneously—and moments when he slips (both intentionally and perhaps at times unintentionally) into a reduced texture or into the regular range, timbre, and monophonic qualities of the instrument. For one example, at 12:30 into "Monoceros 1," following a minute or more of polyphonic exploration, we hear Parker briefly drop the top voice from the texture only to regain it almost as quickly. The plot here shows a drop from the $D = 4$ range to approximately $D = 2.8$. In the final minutes of the performance Parker's dense, polyphonic exploration seems to be approaching a ceiling of physical possibility. Starting around 19:30, he begins to ease the density of patterning until he is left exploring only the extreme overtone range. With a final graceful decrescendo, he concludes the improvisation.

"Conic Sections 3" (Figure 3 and Audio Example 1), recorded eleven years after "Monoceros," demonstrates even more ability and flexibility in improvising dense and overlapping patterns. The mean fractal dimension for this twenty-five-minute improvisation is $D = 4.78$, considerably higher than the other two examples we have already encountered. Some of the increase, it should be noted, may be due to the higher degree of reverberation present on the recording. Parker recorded *Conic Sections* in the Hollywell Music Rooms in Oxford. In the accompanying notes, Parker comments that, "The acoustics of the Rooms are so distinctive that I was pushed away from the kind of playing I'd had in mind; it seemed as though the room itself had something in mind too." Reverberation, according to Rolf, can add chaoticity since if a sound is prolonged as a reverberated event while another event is played, both our perception and the computer's calculation will take note of the additional complexity. But the performance on "Conic Sections 3," one of Parker's most celebrated, does seem to bear out a higher plateau of complexity in general.

The first half of the plot shows Parker developing an arc of increasing complexity that at times drops briefly only to continue its climb. He begins the improvisation already deeply entrenched in interlocked patterns. The first small dip arrives at approximately 1:40 when the already dense polyphony seems to reach a moment of temporary gridlock, slowing down but not halting the overall patterning. At 3:35, one of the polyphonic voices disappears briefly, only to be followed by some dramatic register leaps that create even more complexity. At nearly the 5:00 mark, the dense sonic traffic comes to a sudden halt, with only one voice surviving to carry on the development.

Parker has spoken of his use of "interruptions"—pauses, immediate segues to simpler textures, or the held tones of his earlier work—to regain the listener's awareness and to allow him the chance to begin combinations anew:

When you've been playing complex music for longer than a certain amount of time, you're in danger of losing the audience's attention. They just oversaturate with the detail, the information. After a while, it's like there's new information but it's the same *kind* of new information. So the change is no longer a change. It's like looking at new ways to make changes that are really changes.[54]

His comments bring to mind Gregory Bateson's definition of information as "a difference that makes a difference."[55] Parker calls these "interruptions on a bigger scale than the usual interruptions." For him, "the usual interruptions are the substance of the music—the interference between the two patterns or the compatibility or lack of compatibility between two patterns. That's the usual stuff of the detailed music, so to impose a break on that you need to do something different, with long notes or whatever."[56]

Another interruption occurs at 7:40, followed by one a minute later (8:36) that has more of a gradual rallentando quality to it. But perhaps the most dramatic shift in musical materials occurs at the 14:00 mark. Here, Parker switches from his three-part polyphony to a development centered in the middle range of the instrument focused on a more linear contour with occasional bursts of rapid tonguing. Because of the highly reverberant room, this section, lasting until 17:30, has an uncanny "swarmlike" quality to it. Starting around 16:50, Parker begins to relax this insistent texture, adding some high register bursts and eventually slowing the pulse and reducing the dynamic. He resolves to a microtonal figure at 17:30, the lowest fractal dimension reading in the performance.

The final section of development is interrupted by a few additional brief respites—at 19:18 with a chromatic figure using alternate fingerings, at 20:30 with a flurry of high notes, and at 21:02 with a return to the chromatic figure of 19:18—before building with articulation and fingering cascades to a dramatic conclusion. Parker has discussed in some detail the two ways in which his solo improvisations often conclude:

One is where the thing unravels. If you think about the music as the pattern in a carpet—you know how the fringe of a carpet is made out of the weft, you can see the component threads? Sometimes it's interesting for me to let the thing unravel so the pattern is gradually pulled apart and you're left with only the threads, the strands. Or another way—and again this is me observing what tends to happen rather than me describing a plan of action—is the complexities reach such a pitch that they cancel one another out and you get a blur of . . . almost like white noise. Not white noise but an impenetrable kind of thickness. The whole thing *locks.* It's a gridlock. Everything locks solid and—it stops![57]

In order to take full advantage of the computer's ability to analyze recorded sounds in minute detail, I selected a particularly dense passage of Parker's solo "polyphony" for a closer analysis. Figure 4a shows the section from 4:00 to 5:00 in "Conic Sections 3," a passage in which Parker's acoustic "juggling" is fully engaged. Only near the very end of the plot do we see a quick drop in overall complexity that corresponds well with Parker's transition to less dense materials. On this scale we can clearly see regular waves of complexity occurring approximately every six seconds or so—roughly the length of a standard musical phrase or human breath. But there are also microstructures along the peaks and valleys that are just barely in view.

Figure 4b brings out the detail from 4:00–4:20. Here we can see more clearly the shorter waves of complexity that occur in Parker's playing, usually with one or more

Figure 4a: Evan Parker—"Conic Sections 3"—Detail of Fractal Correlation Dimension

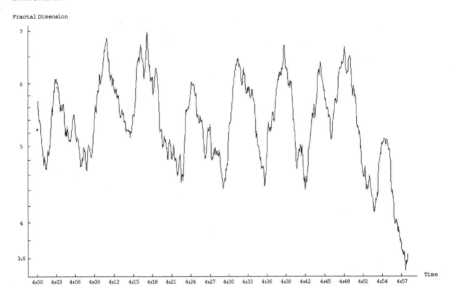

Figure 4b: Evan Parker—"Conic Sections 3"—Detail of Fractal Correlation Dimension

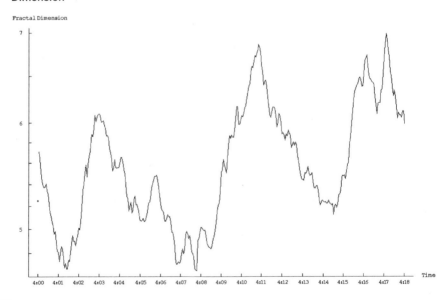

Figure 4c: Evan Parker—"Conic Sections 3"—Detail of Fractal Correlation
Dimension

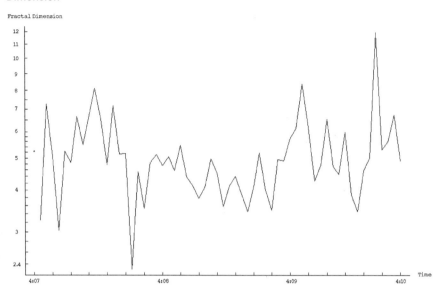

cycles occurring within a single second. Like Mandelbrot's cauliflower, this additional
detail uncovers self-similar structures to the whole. In fact, the similarity of these
fractal dimension plots to a mountain range that demonstrates scaling properties is
uncanny.

In Figure 4c, Rolf and I looked at the detail of Parker's playing over the span of only
three seconds, from 4:07–4:10. At this scale, we are able to see the exact results calculated for each time interval. This level of detail highlights some additional qualities of
Parker's playing but also some limitations to this type of computer analysis. The plot
displays pronounced cycles of complexity that have a certain similarity to those that
we saw on the level of musical gesture and phrasing. Parker appears to be dealing
with waves of complex sound from the smallest to the largest scales. But on listening
at a greatly reduced speed, it is also clear that there is much more detail in Parker's
playing than the computer is able to take account of. Here we are forced to confront
the intersection between "signal," "signal noise," and "analytical noise" that plagues
this, or any other, analysis method.

Figures 5a and 5b offer the fractal dimension plot and correlogram for Parker's
performance on "Broken Wing," from the album *Process and Reality*. This considerably
shorter performance provides an excellent example of a developmental arc. The only
significant interruptions occur at 1:07, when Parker slows briefly to a sustained tone
before continuing, and at 1:19, 1:30, and 1:46, when he offers dramatic breath-length
pauses, all of which are easily seen on the correlogram.

As a point of comparison, Figures 6a and 6b present the fractal dimension plot and
correlogram for Derek Bailey's guitar improvisation titled "Improvisation 5," originally
released on the Incus LP *Solo Guitar Volume One* from 1971.[58] Bailey's improvisation

Figure 5a: Evan Parker—"Broken Wing"—Fractal Correlation Dimension

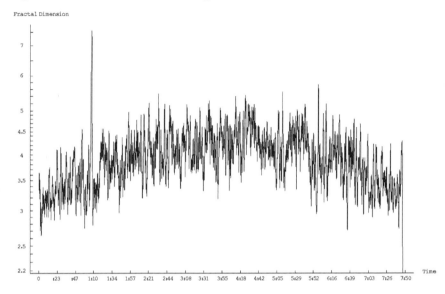

Figure 5b: Evan Parker—"Broken Wing"—Correlogram

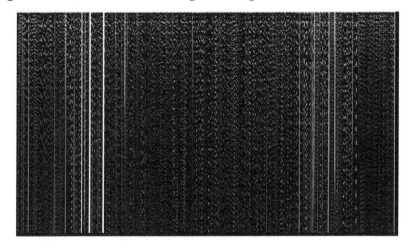

Figure 6a: Derek Bailey—"Improvisation 5"—Fractal Correlation Dimension

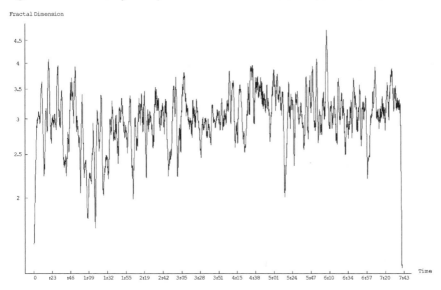

Figure 6b: Derek Bailey—"Improvisation 5"—Correlogram

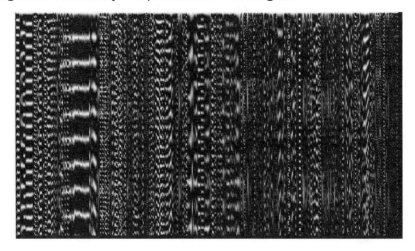

105

here is roughly the same length as "Broken Wing," but he tends to avoid any clear developmental strategies in favor of a more sectionalized approach. Within each section, Bailey often explores in detail only a few specific techniques. Due to the more stately pace of the improvisation, the correlogram here nicely shows the sectionalized nature of his work. One of the more visible moments on the correlogram, from 1:00 to 1:30, highlights Bailey exploring some subtle timbral shadings of a sustained sound.

Figures 7a/7b and 8a/8b detail two tenor saxophone solos by Evan Parker from his first solo release on that instrument, titled *Chicago Solos* (1995). Although many connections can be made between his solo styles on soprano and tenor, the sheer size of the larger horn, and the additional air that it requires, make some things less possible. These are two of the more dense solos from the album, yet they still do not reach the mean fractal dimension of most of his soprano work. But because Parker can rely less on the mesmerizing effects of his soprano polyphony, much of his tenor work explores quite a few more musical directions and options. As Stuart Bloomer noted in a *Cadence* review at the time, Parker's tenor approach has some connections to the first soprano recordings. For instance, he focuses on much shorter pieces, but with nothing of the feeling of a technical exercise that tended to pervade *Saxophone Solos*.[59] Although Parker is quite capable of circular breathing for considerable stretches of time on tenor as well (as "Chicago Solo 9" demonstrates), he tends to use standard phrase lengths to greater effect (as in "Chicago Solo 10").

The fractal plots of "Chicago Solo 9" demonstrate well the contour of Parker's improvisation: entering at a relatively high degree of density and complexity, working toward a calmer plateau, only to build up again to a final burst and then subside: a rather different technique than much of his solo soprano playing. While in "Chicago Solo 10," Parker employs dramatic pauses and unpredictable phrases. Starting from pianissimo, he gradually builds to a dramatic height that offers a hint of his complexity on soprano, but never abandons the more capricious quality of his tenor.

Finally, figures 9a and 9b highlight a recording by Evan Parker's Electro-Acoustic Ensemble titled "Turbulent Mirror" from their first ECM release, *Toward the Margins*. The ensemble is comprised of Evan Parker's working trio of many years, with Barry Guy on bass and Paul Lytton on drums and percussion, along with live electronics and signal processing by Walter Prati, Marco Vecchi, and Philipp Wachsmann, who also adds violin and viola. Even in this larger, denser, and more convoluted musical setting, the ensemble is able to create a nice developmental arc to the performance. The mean fractal dimension is considerably higher, no doubt due in part to the additional electronic processing that not only keeps certain sounds alive in the ear as reverberations, but also re-interjects transformed versions of the live sound into the ensemble.

Because of the size and the "regenerative" possibilities of the ensemble, each individual tends to play less than he might otherwise, allowing space for comment and transformation and producing something of an undulating quality to the work. When Parker does launch into a circular breathing passage at 1:48, the overall dimension elevates, while the final decrease in fractal dimension is dominated by the sustained sounds of Wachsmann's viola, a transition that is clearly visible in the accompanying correlogram as well.

Deciding what feature or set of features may have provoked a certain shift in the fractal dimension of ensemble music is not always easy. It is interesting to note, however, that the softer passage—from about the 3:30 mark when the sound processors

Figure 7a: Evan Parker—"Chicago Solos 9"—Fractal Correlation Dimension

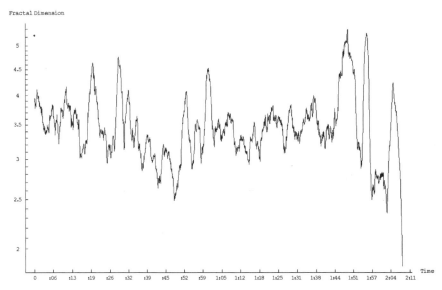

Figure 7b: Evan Parker—"Chicago Solos 9"—Correlogram

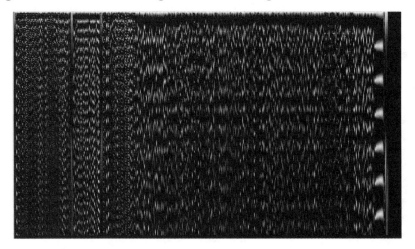

Figure 8a: Evan Parker—"Chicago Solos 10"—Fractal Correlation Dimension

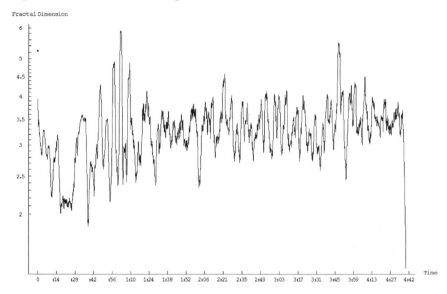

Figure 8b: Evan Parker—"Chicago Solos 10"—Correlogram

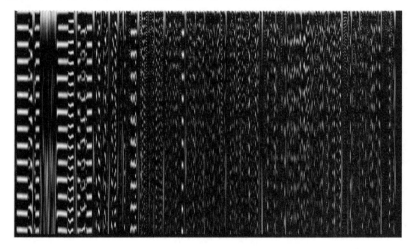

Figure 9a: Evan Parker Electro Acoustic Ensemble—"Turbulent Mirror"—Fractal Correlation Dimension

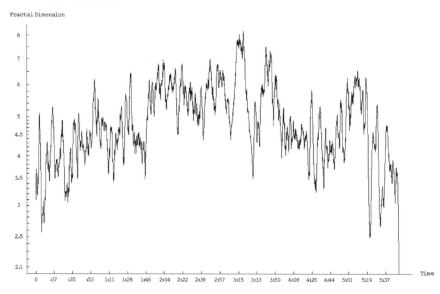

Figure 9b: Evan Parker Electro Acoustic Ensemble—"Turbulent Mirror"—Correlogram

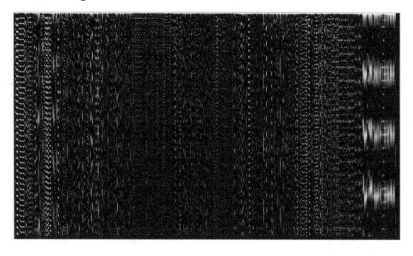

are more clearly heard—drops in dimension only briefly, as all of the acoustic instruments fall silent—before maintaining a rather high fractal dimension. The computer's calculations seem to be able to take notice of very subtle and soft sound transformations as well.

After Rolf had run many of the Evan Parker examples for me, I was still grappling with the computer's ability to arrive at these results and my own ability to understand them. So I asked if he could analyze a few examples as test cases that, to me, seem to represent the sonic extremes plumbed by improvisers. We ran plots of Peter Brötzmann's "Machine Gun" (Figures 10a/10b) from the 1968 album of the same name, and the Art Ensemble of Chicago's "Ancestral Meditation" (Figures 11a/11b) from the 1980 live album *Urban Bushmen*. The Brötzmann example is one of the most famous (or is it notorious?) examples of early European free improvisation. It brought together Brötzmann, Evan Parker, and Willem Breuker on saxophones, Fred Van Hove on piano, Peter Kowald and Buschi Niebergall on basses, and Han Bennink and Sven-Ake Johanson on drums. The title track includes, after some sonic "machine gun" fire, some extremely high-volume and high-energy playing from everyone involved. The Art Ensemble piece is, by contrast, one of their most delicate and sublime. It involves, after a powerful stroke on a gong, a timbral meditation on a single pitch.[60] I have included the plots and correlograms as Figures 15 through 18, because they demonstrate that the computer is able to take account of both obvious and more subtle sonic variations.

In his email forwarding the results of the "Machine Gun" analysis, Rolf excitedly wrote, "The Brötzmann piece is noise! We never had such high fractal numers up to $D = 18$, which is unbelievable!" The mean fractal dimension for the entire performance is $D = 8.8$, nearly twice as high as even the Electro-Acoustic ensemble performance. The plot does reach some impressive heights during the background "screams" behind Parker's solo, but it also shows well the drop in sonic complexity during the improvised call-and-response of the two bass players (starting at 6:00) and the gradual buildup with the reentry of the horns. Further dips correspond to moments when Willem Breuker is playing entirely alone on bass clarinet (8:40), and when the group uses a brief second of silence (at 11:25). The rather odd big-band-style riff (13:15) also reduces the fractal dimension, as does the brief moment of Han Bennink providing military style drums behind Breuker (at 9:40). Musical devices that follow a strong rule-based system will tend to reduce fractality because the computer detects things happening on a more regular basis.

Even more encouraging, however, was the computer analysis of The Art Ensemble of Chicago performance, which captured many of the group's subtle timbral variations. The correlogram displays nicely the fundamental overtone series of the piece and its subtle variations, while the peaks of the fractal dimension plot highlight well the moments when the sound intensifies or when a new timbral layer is introduced, including the evocative breath sounds and instrumental gurgles of the wind players near the end. The valleys in the plot match moments when the drone sound seems to simplify or purify for a moment, before new complexities are added to enrich the composite texture. The lower mean value of $D = 2.97$ and a standard deviation of only .44 reflects the meditative quality of the piece, and yet the dramatic contour shows nicely how very small changes can make a world of difference in focusing our ears and minds.

Figure 10a: Peter Brötzmann—"Machine Gun"—Fractal Correlation Dimension

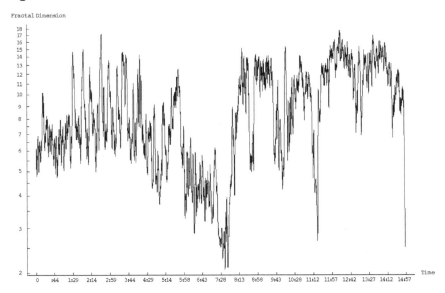

Figure 10b: Peter Brötzmann—"Machine Gun"—Correlogram

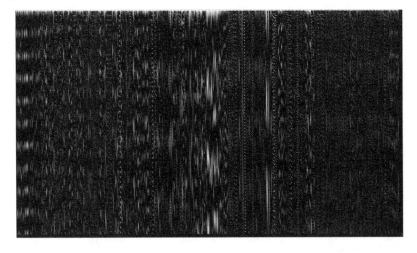

Figure 11a: The Art Ensemble of Chicago—"Ancestral Meditation"—Fractal Correlation Dimension

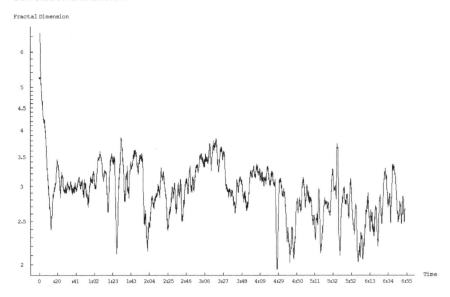

Figure 11b: The Art Ensemble of Chicago—"Ancestral Meditation"—Correlogram

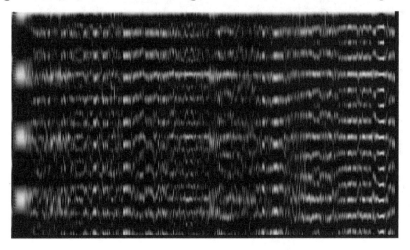

To offer another snapshot of The Art Ensemble's sonic breadth, Rolf and I also did an analysis of their performance titled "People in Sorrow," which was recorded in 1969 during their time spent in Paris. The complete performance is over forty minutes in length, although it was originally released in two parts to fit the sides of a long-playing record. This division was maintained on the CD re-release and for our analysis, although the two figures represent one complete performance. Some background noise is still present—the CD appears to have been mastered from a vinyl source—so the absolute readings for fractal dimensions should not be trusted in their entirety, but the relative changes in dimension provide an excellent example of the group's uncanny ability to develop complexity over long stretches of time.

Starting at fractal dimension readings of $D<2$, the performance builds very gradually, eventually reaching heights of approximately $D=14$ three-quarters of the way through the performance, and finally returning to relative calm. The piece is loosely structured around a minor-key melody that returns throughout the work, in various guises, but always, as one Amazon.com reviewer put it, "just under the surface of things, just slightly out of reach." The members of the group improvise with, over, and around these subtle appearances of the theme, producing several prominent subsections that build and subside in complexity as the overall development of the performance continues.

Part I (Figures 12a/12b) begins with the Art Ensemble's characteristic percussion and "small instruments" that only obliquely hint at the melody to come. Eventually Lester Bowie's trumpet, Roscoe Mitchell's flute, and Malachi Favors's bass playing begin to take more prominent roles. After a brief bass solo, a more intense percussion section creates the most sustained plateau of complexity. This is followed by a very soft section, filled with small percussion and breathe sounds, and in which one of the members can be heard to say, "Mommie, there's a rat scratchin' in the walls," bringing to mind the difficulties of growing up in a housing tenement. A final unison statement of the theme produces a temporary cadence.

Part B (Figures 12c/12d) begins with all three horns playing the melody, leading into a poignant bassoon solo by Joseph Jarman. The ensemble gradually intensifies, and with the addition of drums, percussion, and vocalized screams, reaches several more brief climaxes. A sudden and unexpected moment of silence (15:16) is followed by an intense section that features an insistent, sirenlike drone, rapid walking figures by Favors, and all three horn players variously improvising angular phrases and unhurried fragments of the melody together. The final statement of the theme is interspersed with brief moments of dissonance until the ensemble texture finally dissolves to whence it came.

The most lengthy and involved computer analysis that Rolf and I did concerned the Sam Rivers Trio improvisation "Hues of Melanin." The fractal correlation dimension plot and correlogram are provided in Figures 13a and 13b. The overall contour can broadly be attributed to instrumentation and intensity changes, but a closer analysis also reveals many interesting developments in the performance. For this reason, I have included a few more detailed plots of subsections of the piece that correspond to some moments that were highlighted in the phenomenological analysis provided in chapter four (see Table 1).

The first fifteen minutes are a collective improvisation by the entire trio, with Rivers on soprano saxophone. The fractal dimension hovers around $D=5$, with several prominent peaks and a few valleys. The first prominent dip, at 5:45, follows a strong cadence

Figure 12a: The Art Ensemble of Chicago—"People in Sorrow (Part I)"—Fractal Correlation Dimension

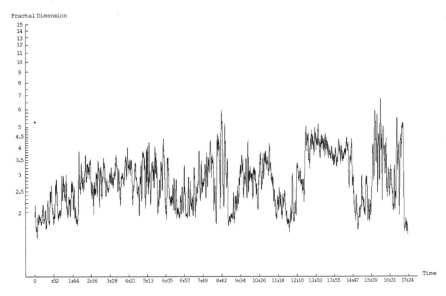

Figure 12b: The Art Ensemble of Chicago—"People in Sorrow (Part I)"—Correlogram

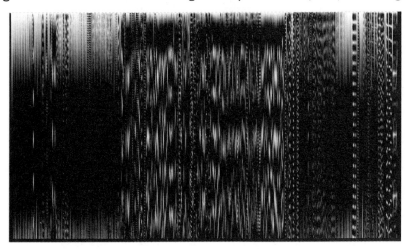

Figure 12c: The Art Ensemble of Chicago—"People in Sorrow (Part II)"—Fractal
Correlation Dimension

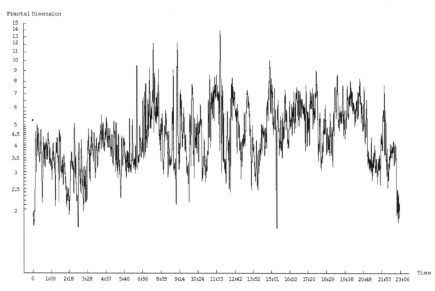

Figure 12d: The Art Ensemble of Chicago—"People in Sorrow (Part II)"—Correlogram

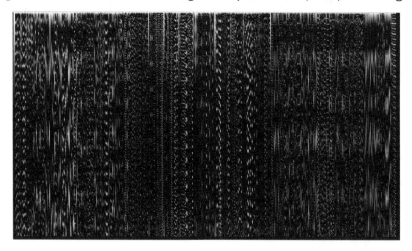

Figure 13a: Sam Rivers Trio—"Hues of Melanin"—Fractal Correlation Dimension

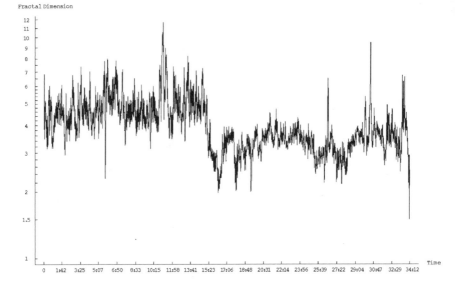

Figure 13b: Sam Rivers Trio—"Hues of Melanin"—Correlogram

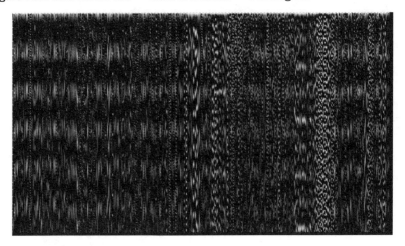

by the trio as Barry Altschul, the drummer, drops out for a time to allow for a soprano and bass duet. The prominent peak at 11:07 also involves a strong cadence accented by Altschul, and the subsequent unison moment of sync makes for one of the most dramatic shifts from $D = 11+$ to $D = 4.3$ within the span of a few seconds.

In the second half of the performance, Rivers switches to flute (with occasional vocal interjections) and the trio explores several more extended moments in which various solo and duo opportunities arise. Combined, these reduce the overall fractal dimension of the performance but the trio builds through several fractal arches with many prominent peaks and valleys. For instance, starting at 15:20, the trio relaxes into a bass solo by Cecil McBee. At 16:15, McBee hits on a repeated note figure and is left to play almost entirely by himself for a short time, producing the lowest fractality reading. But the complexity builds again as Rivers and Altschul add commentary and supportive textures behind McBee's continuing solo. Rivers slowly usurps the spotlight until, near the 18:00 mark, he is suddenly left to perform briefly unaccompanied, producing another prominent valley. McBee soon joins him, now performing *arco* and, with Altschul creating percussion colors, the three musicians undulate together. At 19:20, McBee drops out entirely, and by 20:00 Rivers is again by himself on flute. But he does not let the intensity subside, and the bass and drums reenter and build to a frenetic up-tempo emsemble section. At 25:30, Altschul drops out briefly again leaving an arco bass and vocal duet. For a full minute, from 27:15 to 28:23, Rivers is alone on flute until he signals with an in-tempo melodic fragment for the others to reenter. From here they build together with the most prominent peaks corresponding to Rivers's ecstatic hollers. With another melodic fragment, the trio shifts to a playful, shared tempo, and a drum solo provides a segue during which Rivers switches to piano for the continuation of the performance (not analyzed). The moments of bass and flute solos can be seen easily on the correlogram (since this is when the spectrum of the sound is harmonic and can be interpreted by the correlogram).

For a more detailed analysis, we need to look at some finer grain structures. Here, it can be especially illuminating to explore the ways in which a phenomenological analysis, like the one offered in chapter four, relates to the computer analysis of fractal correlation dimension.[61] Figure 14a corresponds with the section from letters A to B in my original phenomenological analysis. Here, as elsewhere in the performance, most of the structural points that I identified correspond extremely well with significant shifts in the fractal correlation dimension. The moments of cadence and transition line up with sudden changes in the calculated complexity of the recording, or often precede the shift in complexity by a few seconds as the players respond to or affect changes in the group sound.

For instance, the repeated tone in the bass that triggers a shift to more dense and intense exploration at letter *A2* appears as a prominent valley in the computer reading, followed by a strong developmental arch. Additionally, the trill figure at *A3* that signals a temporary cadence corresponds with the lowest dip in fractal dimension. Even the pseudo-cadence that I identified as *A4* mirrors a relative drop in the plot. And the tempo trigger that launches the trio into a fast-pulsed exploration also lines up extremely well with letter B. Some of the most prominent peaks in the plot correspond to powerful cymbal crashes that, because of their inharmonic frequencies, can produce relatively high fractality (e.g., at 3:32).

Figure 14a: Sam Rivers Trio—"Hues of Melanin"—Detail of Fractal Correlation Dimension

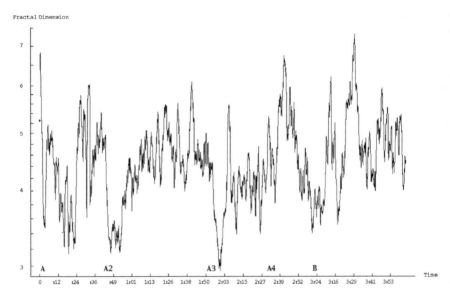

Figure 14b: Sam Rivers Trio—"Hues of Melanin"—Detail of Fractal Correlation Dimension

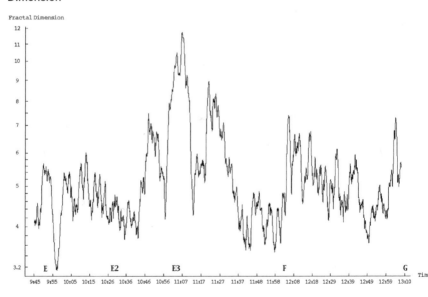

The more detailed plots can also remind us that, as listeners, the moments in the music that are most compelling from a phenomenological perspective are often those in which a dramatic shift in perceived complexity takes place, or when a given expectation is either confirmed or denied by the musicians. In other words, increasing musical complexity can attract the attention of listeners, but, as Evan Parker noted, too much complexity can overwhelm. Listeners are often most provoked by well-timed and dramatic shifts in the relative complexity of a performance. For instance, at 3:15, Rivers ends his improvised line with a short, bluesy call that the others acknowledge through their reduced intensity, rather than by a more direct response. The fractal dimension here drops significantly, but for the listeners this exchange signals a moment of heightened attention, as an expectation has been created and resolved in a surprising way.[62]

Figures 14b and 14c highlight the section between letters E and H of my original analysis. There is so much going on here in the music that an even closer level of detail could provide additional insight. Broadly speaking, E to E3 acts as an extended cadence, E3 to F is organized around the bass drone, and F results from a melodic trigger that launches the trio into shared tempo. G highlights another temporary cadence brought about by a trill figure, and the trio slowly works into a groove section that eventually synchronizes at G2 and climaxes at G3. H signals the shift to the bass solo as Altschul reduces his complexity on the drums and Rivers partakes in some playful mimicry.

Although the drone section at E3 may sound rather relaxed, the fractal dimension is quite high, most likely a result of Barry Altschul using some auxiliary percussion that adds inharmonic components to the combined sound. But here again, the dramatic rise and sudden drop in complexity (provoked by the unison figure) attracts listeners' attention. The fast-pulsed section at letter F is sprinkled with drum crashes that produce peaks in the fractal dimension, while the trill at letter G triggers a reduction in the overall complexity until a groove slowly emerges. On close listening, the moments when the bass and drums synchronize or when Rivers and McBee land on a unison pitch produce the small dips in the fractal dimension. These moments may, however, be perceived by listeners as structurally important or of increased interest.

The final detailed plot that I have included highlights the section from letter N to O2 (Figure 14d). During this section Rivers begins vocalizing to provoke even more complexity from the group (and perhaps to add a bit of humor as well: "Just do it," "Do it tonight," "Save me!"). His most pronounced scream is accompanied by heavy crashes by Altschul and a rising figure from McBee, resulting in a fractal dimension of $D = 9+$. The drone section following N2 is also perceptually rich with detail and tension, but sonically it remains in the area of $D = 3.5$: another nice reminder that perceptual and sonic complexity do not always go hand in hand. Rivers cues a lessening of intensity with a chromatic descending line at N3, and a cadence by the trio follows shortly thereafter at letter O. His final melodic trigger launches the group into a shared tempo full of playful fluctuations, discussed in chapter four in the context of *signifyin(g)*.

Many of the properties of mathematical fractals have captured the interest of artists and laypeople alike. The characteristic quality of fractal organization, in which branching structures continue to elaborate themselves in order to allow for maximum

119

Figure 14c: Sam Rivers Trio—"Hues of Melanin"—Detail of Fractal Correlation Dimension

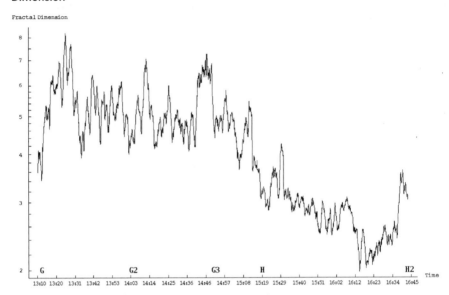

Figure 14d: Sam Rivers Trio—"Hues of Melanin"—Detail of Fractal Correlation Dimension

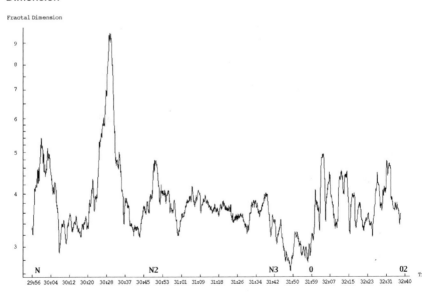

efficiency in exchanges, provides an interesting metaphor for some group improvisation that focuses on this delicate sonic filigree yet still maintains a certain clarity of presentation, speed of communication, and flexibility for quick shifts and transitions. Noticing this connection, Todd Jenkins writes in his recent encyclopedia of free jazz and free improvisation:

> The best free performances are often those in which the players do not seem to clash. Even without set boundaries, musicians build structures based upon intuition, anticipation, and logic. The mathematical discipline of chaos theory states that even supposedly random events can have a basis in logical action and reaction. Good free performances reflect this idea of controlled chaos, and players who work together long enough develop an uncanny intuitiveness as to their next moves.[63]

Next to the rich complexity and subtle self-similarity of fractals, Euclidian geometry seems horribly dull.[64] Mandelbrot has shown that irregularity is exciting and that it is not just noise distorting Euclidian forms. According to Briggs and Peat, this "noise" is "the bold signature of nature's creative forces."[65]

In some ways, conventional European music notation may be akin to conventional Euclidian geometry. The regular and static forms that are at the heart of both approaches have led researchers to ignore many subtle properties of nature and sound, lumping together and dismissing those qualities that do not easily fit the model as "chaos" and "disorder" on the one hand (geometry), or "performance practice" and "improvisation" on the other.[66] But one of the most exciting things about our emerging understanding of fractal organization is that it demonstrates that similar principles of growth and form are operating at vastly different scales. Briggs and Peat ask, "How could something that measures thousands of light years across have anything in common with objects that can be encompassed in the hand or on the head of a pin?"[67] Rather poetically they muse:

> Strange attractors and fractals evoke a deep recognition, something akin to the haunting recognition afforded by the convoluted and interwoven figures of Bronze Age Celtic art, the complex designs of a Shang ritual vessel, visual motifs from the West Coast American Indians, myths of mazes and labyrinths, the iterative language games of children or the chant patterns of so-called "primitive" peoples. The regular harmonies of classical Western art become almost an aberration set beside these forms. Yet as we look at the greatest art we realize that even in classical forms there is always a dynamism of chaos within the serenity of order. All great art explores this tension between order and chaos, between growth and stasis. In confronting the orders of chaos, of growth and stability, it appears we are now coming to face with something that is buried at the foundations of human existence.[68]

Self-Organization

We tend to imagine chaos as the inevitable outcome of a system that exhibits no central control. Primary-school educators are intimately familiar with the all-too-real notion of chaos that can ensue in a classroom when students are losing focus or not following the prescribed rules for work or social conduct, or when the teacher steps out of the room for a moment, leaving the students unattended. In many other social, biological, and physical systems, we are also predisposed to think of order in terms of hierarchies and control. Our governments are often structured around the notion of leaders, from kings to councilmen. Even our own bodies and our sense of self, as the story goes, are operated by command centers: the heart provides the pulse and pace for our body, and the brain controls our thoughts and movements and provides an undivided sense of self in the process (a notion that we of course challenged in chapter three).

Yet, the deeper we probe, we are often led to conclude that systems do not always (or even inherently) organize in this way. The natural world is filled with examples of species that operate in a collective fashion that defies a top-down or centralized chain of command (we will explore this idea more in the next chapter). In the physical domain, a stream of water can create a vortex that remains stable despite the fact that its exact components are rapidly changing. And our own bodies maintain their form despite the fact that our individual cells are fully replenished every seven years or so.[69]

The Great Red Spot on Jupiter is a fascinating example of a self-organizing system that can even make our all-too-easy distinctions between the living and nonliving worlds rather complicated. Essentially a storm system in the upper atmosphere of the planet, it has been present for at least several centuries, substantially exceeding the lifetime of the average gas molecule contained within it. Biologist Stuart Kauffman of the Santa Fe Institute writes of the Great Red Spot that, "The similarity to a human organism, whose molecular constituents change many times during a lifetime, is intriguing. One can have a remarkably complex discussion about whether the Great Red Spot might be considered to be living—and if not, why not. After all, the Great Red Spot in some sense persists and adapts to its environment, shedding baby vortices as it does so."[70]

The work of the Russian-born, Belgian chemist Ilya Prigogine is most often referenced in relation to the increasing attention being paid to self-organizing systems. In particular, his work focuses on the ways in which open systems operating in far-from-equilibrium conditions can spontaneously self-organize. To envision what this might mean, let's look at the famous "butterfly effect" of Edward Lorenz. First, imagine a balloon filed with air. The molecules of air inside the balloon are either paralyzed or moving around at random, the definition of a system at equilibrium. Now place a butterfly inside of the balloon. The butterfly will surely flap it wings and stir the air molecules, but since the system is self-contained, no large-scale patterns can emerge and it will remain at a near-to-equilibrium state. Few "real world" physical, biological, or social systems, however, are self-contained in this way. If instead we place that same butterfly in the earth's atmosphere—where the weather is continually stirred, agitated, and energized from rotation, gravity, and solar radiation, among other things—even the slight disturbance created by its flapping wings could amplify through positive feedback to produce a severe thunderstorm in another part of the world weeks later.

Although reasonable predictions of local weather patterns over the span of a few days can be reliable, when viewed as a whole, the global weather system is in a state of nonequilibrium. Temporary storm systems can form and even maintain themselves for days or weeks, but they can also suddenly disappear without warning. These storms systems, like the relatively long-lived Great Red Spot on Jupiter, must continually take in energy, leaving disorder in their wake.

Prigogine has named these types of emergent phenomena *dissipative structures*, to highlight their near paradoxical qualities of ordering and dissipation. As Briggs and Peat explain, "Dissipative structures are systems capable of maintaining their identity only by remaining continually open to the flux and flow of the environment . . . arising out of a far-from-equilibrium flux and riding upon it . . . organizing space and giving an inexorable direction to time."[71]

Prigogine began his Nobel Prize winning work by contemplating the question of time. He was struck by the fact that time reversibility—a rather counterintuitive notion—was deeply entrenched not only in Newtonian physics, but also in quantum theory. According to both sets of equations, systems can run both forwards and backwards; time has no preferred direction.

Yet two nineteenth-century theories, evolution and thermodynamics, proposed a world that was governed by an arrow of time, albeit with radically different connotations. The second law of thermodynamics, first formulated by German scientist Rudolf Clausius, states that the universe is heading toward a state of maximum entropy or disorder: a thermodynamic equilibrium. But to biologists, like Darwin, life appeared to represent not only stable order, but an order that could reproduce itself and increase its own fitness over time. Prigogine wondered in what way these discrepant visions of time's arrow—one negative and the other positive—could be reconciled. And how might they, in turn, reconcile with the notion of reversible time that was commonly accepted in physics? Rather ambitiously, Prigogine hoped to unify the microscopic and macroscopic worlds and the fields of dynamics and thermodynamics. One of his earliest books on the subject urged researchers to shift their perspective *From Being to Becoming*.[72]

One of Prigogine's favorite examples of dissipative structuring is Bénard instability. In general, as a pan of liquid is gradually heated from below, the heat begins to travel from the lower surface to the upper one through convection. At first, while the system is still near equilibrium, this flow proceeds in an orderly fashion. But as the difference in temperature between the layers grows and the system moves farther from equilibrium, it undergoes the rapid onset of chaos. Under laboratory conditions, researchers have shown that this path to chaos proceeds through an orderly process known as a period doubling cascade. A similar orderly decent into chaos has been found in many other systems and provides one of the first great discoveries from the order-into-chaos branch of nonlinear dynamics.

Prigogine focuses on the system's ability to undergo another bifurcation point as the liquid continues to be heated and the heat can't disperse quickly enough. At this point, the system shifts out of its chaotic state and transforms into an orderly lattice of hexagonal currents known as Bénard cells. These rotating convection cells represent patterns that are millions of times larger than the range of the intermolecular forces that cause them. They provide a textbook example of order out of chaos, a defining quality of emergent and self-organizing systems. Certain chemical reactions, such as the Belousov-Zhabotinsky reaction, also produce remarkable self-organizing patterns, such as evolving spirals and changing colors that highlight qualities of dissipative structuring. Similar processes are at work in the flicker of a candle flame, in the traffic patterns at rush hour, and perhaps in the growth of cities and social movements.

Increasingly, cities and societies are being envisioned as complex, self-organizing, and adaptive systems that operate through an intertwined network of flows, from money, food, and energy to people and information. As with the scaling properties we saw in fractal geometry, these flows, patterns, and functions often appear self-similar across many scales, from neighborhoods and districts to nations and international conglomerates. To some extent, increasing economic interdependence between the local, the regional, and the global is provoking this scaling property, but changes in society and the arts may also have a profound impact.

Prigogine's work does not violate the second law of thermodynamics, but it relies on a formulation of entropy that contextualizes its negative *and* positive powers. Briggs and Peat write of dissipative structures:

> They are open systems, taking in energy from the outside and producing entropy (waste, randomized energy) which they dissipate into the surrounding environment. Of course one system's entropy may be another system's food; consider the dung beetle, for example, or the mitochondria in our own cells which transform wastes from fermented food molecules into ATP, a molecule that in fact stores energy. The second law (that entropy overall always increases) is not violated by the appearance of these systems, any more than gravity is violated by an orbiting moon. As a moon takes advantage of gravity to stay in orbit, so dissipative structures take advantage of entropy.[73]

In what ways might these ideas of self-organization and dissipative structuring reflect on the musical process? The notion of an "arrow of time" is of course crucial to all music, but it is particularly pronounced in improvised forms. My favorite illustration comes from a chance meeting between composer/improviser Frederic Rzewski and improviser/composer Steve Lacy. Rzewski asked Lacy to describe in fifteen seconds the difference between composition and improvisation and Lacy replied: "In fifteen seconds, the difference between composition and improvisation is that in composition you have all the time you want to decide what to say in fifteen seconds, while in improvisation you have fifteen seconds."[74] Lacy's formulation of the answer lasted exactly fifteen seconds.

An improvising ensemble can also be described as an "open" system. In a very general sense, the ensemble takes in energy gradually from the enculturation, education, training, and experience of its members, and more immediately in the form of interactions between members and influences from the physical and psychological context of the performance (i.e., the acoustic space, the potential sonic materials, the performers' state of mind, the audience's reaction, etc.). More technically, because active listening plays such a central role in shaping the dynamics of improvised performance, the control and feedback parameters are tightly coupled and the system remains open to continual energy influxes from its environment. Improvised music is also "dissipative" in the literal sense that if no external energy is applied to the system, the complexity of the music will decrease, tending toward zero as listeners get bored.

Improvisation requires a constant influx of energy to offset these dissipative qualities. (These qualities are discussed in more detail in chapter four.)

The "equilibrium" of an improvised music performance is disturbed, in a general sense, through the expectation by all present that music will be made. Free improvisation, in particular, often carries with it the specific mandate to deconstruct or re-contextualize known or familiar musical properties. But more technically, the freer forms of improvisation can be said to be "far-from-equilibrium" because (in good performances, at least) the musicians are supplying a great deal of external energy. Similar to the dual nature of entropy in dissipative systems, one person's "waste" in an improvised performance—perhaps an unintended gesture or "noise"—may also become grist for the improvising mill of others in the ensemble.

Over time, an improvising ensemble will often establish its own sense of identity or coherence. Although the system remains open to environmental fluctuations, in the language of dissipative structures it is "operationally closed." Audience engagement is certainly crucial to a successful improvised performance, but the musicians tend to focus their direct attention on one another rather than on the audience explicitly. The boundary that develops naturally within an ensemble is not necessarily one of personal affinity or exclusion, or one of aesthetic mandate, but rather one of trust and conviviality. Like the boundary of a storm or the membrane of a human cell, this boundary is both permeable and permanent. It defines the identity of the system but also allows for the ongoing dynamics of exchange that are necessary to maintain its existence. Of course, a certain danger may lurk for both physical and musical systems if this boundary becomes either too porous or too impermeable. If too much exchange is fostered with outside forces, the identity of a system may be put in jeopardy. Likewise, if too little exchange is allowed or encouraged, a system may decline either from reduced internal dynamics, or from its inability to continue to adapt to the changing dynamics of its environment.

Acknowledging what many reluctant, first-time, or even veteran listeners to free improvisation may at times feel, saxophonist Steve Lacy recounted that after a year of playing in this manner with the same group he felt that they were playing "freely" but it didn't sound free anymore: "What is this? I couldn't believe it—it sounds the same every night. What are we going to do? That's what we were trying to get away from."[75] In describing his preferred working method, Evan Parker offers another perspective on this delicate balance of permanence and permeability, trust and freedom:

> Things that are established as known between yourselves probably form as useful a context for the evolution of something new as anything. But the inter-personal relationships should only form the basis for working, they shouldn't actually define the music too clearly, which they very often do. In practice, the closest I would get to a laboratory situation is working with the people I know best. It can make a useful change to be dropped into a slightly shocking situation that you've never been in before. It can produce a different kind of response, a different kind of reaction. But the people I've played with longer actually offer me the freest situation to work in.[76]

Individual musicians can differ widely in their specific preferences for maintaining a creative balance in their work, but most seem to acknowledge the defining qualities *and* the inherent dynamism of one's own identity and the ways in which it may be shaped through immediate interaction with others *and* over time. For another point of comparison, consider these positions espoused by Eliott Carter and Derek Bailey. Carter argues that, "You could say that a musical score is written to keep the performer from playing what he already knows and leads him to explore other new techniques and ideas. It is like a map leading a hiker through unknown country to new vistas and new terrain, revealing to him new possibilities of experience that he did not know he could have."[77] Employing the same analogy to hiking, Bailey writes, "One could approach the unknown with a compass and a method but to take a map makes it pointless to go there at all."[78]

Carter's comments are more allied with a top-down model of organization that involves a hierarchy and the execution of sequential operations. Bailey appears more connected to the notion of a bottom-up, self-organizing system that involves decentralized or overlapping authority and typically a patchwork of parallel operations. The former might best be described as complicated, while the latter is truly complex. Nearly all systems in real life appear to involve aspects of both of these approaches, but many of the things that we find most interesting in nature hover near the complex end of this spectrum.

Complexity, however, is a surprisingly difficult concept to define well. The Latin root of the word "complex," *complexus*, means different elements interlaced together to form a single fabric, a type of unity in diversity.[79] Physicist Murray Gell-Mann offers a definition of complexity focused on its structural qualities. He argues that a system should be called complex when it is hard to predict, not because it is random but rather because the regularities it does have cannot be briefly described.[80] Robert Axelrod and Michael D. Cohen stress the interconnectivity of complexity, arguing that "a system is complex when there are strong interactions among its elements, so that current events heavily influence the possibility of many kinds of later events."[81]

Self-organizing systems (SOS) is a general term that describes a diverse range of systems that exhibit both complex and adaptive dynamics. SOS, by definition, operate without imposed centralized control. They are most often comprised of numerous individual agents that are autonomous but also exhibit a high degree of interconnectivity. In other words, SOS rely on the nonlinear causality that comes from peers influencing peers. As a result, the dynamics of SOS can be both promising and problematic. To borrow terminology from Kevin Kelly, SOS are *adaptable, resilient,* and *boundless,* but they are also *nonoptimal, noncontrollable,* and *nonunderstandable* in their entirety.[82]

Due to their nonlinear dynamics, SOS are able to adapt to new stimuli and to internal changes. Although clockwork systems can be built to adjust to predetermined stimuli, only nonlinear systems can evolve (in the biological sense) over time. SOS actively respond to changing circumstances in order to transform whatever happens to their advantage.

SOS are also resilient, in the sense that the whole can be maintained while individual parts change or even disappear. In fact, moments of change or failure create the possibility for new forms of order to emerge and for the system as a whole to reorganize at higher levels of complexity. Think of a flock of birds. With only the slightest motion to flight from one individual, the entire flock can spontaneously take flight. And since the activity of the flock is based on individual birds adjusting and adapting to their neighbors, if one bird disappears, the flock simply rearranges itself and continues unabated.

Finally, SOS are boundless, in the sense that positive feedback can lead to ever-increasing order. SOS are able to build on their own scaffolding by extending new structure beyond the bounds of its original state.

Decentralized systems, however, do not always work well, just as those based on top-down organization can fail. For instance, SOS are inherently nonoptimal, since without centralized control they can foster inefficiencies and redundancies. Although their emergent properties can dampen some of these effects, much as a free market can establish a generally agreed-upon price for goods, SOS can never eliminate inefficiencies as a well-designed linear system could. But by accepting rather than avoiding error, SOS offer fertile conditions for learning, adaptation, and evolution.

SOS are also inherently noncontrollable. They can be guided at "leverage points" or tweaked from within, but without centralized control or an explicit hierarchy, it can be impossible to initiate system-wide changes quickly and efficiently. But noncontrollability can also be an asset. For instance, our dreams are noncontrollable in their entirety yet often produce rather exciting and unexpected results.

Even when working well, the dynamics of SOS are, in their entirety, nonunderstandable. Without clear lines of causality, SOS can quickly become tangled swarms of intersecting influence and logic until it becomes impossible to arrive at an objective or complete understanding of the system's dynamics.

Finally, SOS are often slow to emerge; they are nonimmediate. The more complex they are, the longer it may take them to warm up: hierarchical layers have to settle down; lateral causes have to slosh around a while; individual agents have to acquaint themselves with one another. Summarizing the differences between top-down and self-organizing systems, Kelly writes: "For jobs where supreme control is demanded, good old clockwork is the way to go. Where supreme adaptability is required, out-of-control swarmware is what you want."[83] Most tasks, of course, will forsake some control for adaptability or vise versa.

Several relevant analogies can be drawn from music. The freer forms of improvisation lie perhaps closest to the ideal of a self-organizing system. Their bottom-up style emphasizes the possibilities for adaptation and emergence; they accentuate creativity-in-time and the dynamics of internal change. The structures of improvisation can also continue to be extended in boundless ways (although the system may be circumscribed, at least in part, by the abilities, materials, and experiences of those who are participating). Improvised music is, from one perspective, resilient to individual "mistakes" because sounds can be recontextualized after the fact by either the original performer or others in the group. And if one musician drops out or is unable to make a performance, the system can often continue to function without major interruption, perhaps even organizing in ways that are both novel and more complex.

From another perspective, however, group improvisation may be less resilient to personality conflicts or pronounced aesthetic differences between individuals. With traditional musical practices that are organized in a predominantly hierarchical manner, personality differences can often be managed in deference to the group leader, the authority of the musical score, or the professionalism of "getting the job done." Free improvisation ensembles tend to aim for a more egalitarian organization that makes them particularly susceptible to the full spectrum of both musical and so-called "extra-musical" influences.

Despite its many promising qualities, improvisation is also rarely, if ever, the "optimal" means to achieve a specific musical end (although it may in fact be both a quicker and easier route to certain types of chaotic dynamics). The internal dynamics of an improvising ensemble (particularly larger groupings of musicians) can be slow to respond to change and are, for the most part, beyond the control of any one individual. Even when things do appear to work well, it will be impossible to analyze the system's dynamics during or after the fact with absolute precision. As with other emergent forms of order, the collective dynamics of improvisation will, by definition, always transcend the full awareness of individuals. For these and other reasons, many ensembles choose to adopt certain compositional schemes or devices in order to offer some additional degrees of control over the situation. In general, however, SOS and improvisation have the remarkable ability to absorb the new and the diverse without disruption.

There is no guarantee, particularly in individual performances, that divergent components will find ways to self-organize effectively. Similar to mechanical systems, we may learn as much or even more by examining occasions on which improvised performance appears to falter.[84] But because this hinges on issues of intention, reception, and interpretation, even locating these moments can provide a distinct challenge.

A recent event that occurred at the eleventh annual Guelph Jazz Festival highlights these issues well. The festival's slogan, "Sounds Provocative," got a particular workout this year.[85] Sainkho Namtchylak, a Tuvan singer noted for her extended vocal techniques, was invited to participate in an improvised concert with African-American musicians William Parker and Hamid Drake, on bass and drums, respectively.[86] Namtchylak began her performance with a short, undulating melody and proceeded to repeat this phrase, with only subtle alteration for half an hour while the bass and drums duo developed an improvised discourse that complemented, or by some accounts simply worked in tandem to, her irresponsive performance. Namtchylak sang with arms folded tightly across her chest, checking her watch in the first moments of the performance and at occasional intervals thereafter, as if to say, in the words of Toronto *Globe* critic Mark Miller, "How much longer?"[87]

She appeared visibly irritated, and it was clear that she only intended on performing as long as contractually required.[88] Much of the subsequent controversy that surrounded the event centered on her treatment by the festival staff and the heavy-handed decision by festival organizers to interrupt the group's performance. (The musicians later resumed and finished the performance after a collective uproar from the audience.) Without weighing in on this aspect of the controversy, but rather by surveying the variety of reactions to the performance from an Internet discussion, we can get a sense of the polysemic nature of improvised music and the challenging questions of reception and meaning that it raises.[89]

Initial reactions in the audience were mixed, as some left visibly irritated and others began to have conversations among themselves (often at full volume) as if to imply, in the words of a contributor to a subsequent Internet discussion, "Nobody could possibly be listening to this." Others later remarked that the layered tensions produced by this approach struck them as "conceptual" in the ears of one, and "remarkable" in the ears of another. One simply chose to envision what he was witnessing on stage as a type of live theater or reality television. Another listener didn't hear repetition in Ms. Namtchylak's performance at all, but rather "a fairly interesting display of microtonal pitch shifting." Some felt that Parker and Drake were "smoking" or that they at least "valiantly tried to get things going," while at least one remarked that it was they who were "playing on another planet . . . not very improvisational." Some wondered about the motivations behind grouping these musicians together to begin with, while others felt that improvisational pairings with Asians in general often aim for this "enormous tension" in which "musicians don't sound like they are playing together in the conventional sense." Another questioned whether Parker and Drake should have in fact wound things down on their own to confer with Namtchylak and "try to get on the same page."

When the musicians resumed after the interruption from festival staff, Ms. Namtchilak abandoned her repetitive melody and offered a performance that was praised to varying degrees as "her trademark if a touch lackluster throat singing" by one; or "more tuneful but still with some apparent distraction" by another; to "transspendid," "unbelievable," "furious, virtuosic, and encyclopedic," and, perhaps most poetically, as "a textbook case of kicking ass and taking names, Tuvan-shaman style." At one point Namtchylak shifted into an "incantory stream of hyperspeed syllables" described by one listener as a "Pentecostal fire of labial and glottal cascades." That same listener felt that most in the audience agreed that she was "putting one mother of a curse on us all."

Several respondents argued that the success of a given collective improvisation ultimately rests on the degree of communication between the players, and in this light Ms. Namthcylak's performance for the first half-hour would seem to have failed miserably. A particularly adamant Internet contributor remarked, "I really do wish . . . that alongside the feel-good PC nonsense served up as rationale for the value of the music, someone at the festival would take an aesthetic stance and defend the decision to shut Namtchylak down on the grounds that she was not performing the improvisational music she had been hired to perform." Yet another expressed, just as steadfastly, "I will maintain to all corners, that first section was worth hearing for the bizarre contrast of her inertia and their dynamism—a supremely interesting combination if you closed your eyes to her scowling and just listened to the sound."

So was this particular meeting of improvisers a successful musical interaction, or was it a disaster that would have been best avoided altogether? Were the individual musicians communicating, albeit in perhaps unconventional ways? Parker and Drake's gradual and tandem build-up of energy and intensity seems to clearly fall into the accepted realms of musical communication, but what of Ms. Namtchylak's performance? Perhaps Parker and Drake had grounds on which to decry foul play. And yet they didn't. They, in fact, seemed most disturbed when the proceedings were prematurely brought to a sudden halt.

In halting her performance, was the festival acting under preconceived notions of the types of material and interactions that Ms. Namtchylak would be expected, and therefore allowed, to perform? Acknowledging this slippery slope in free improvisation, Steve Day, a self-pronounced avid fan and author of the book *Two Full Ears,* writes:

> In a live concert, both musicians and audience have, to some extent or other, predetermined the expectation of their ears. If I go to hear Evan Parker I would

not expect to hear Charles Lloyd's "Forest Flower," nor when I go traveling to some foreign field for a Charles Lloyd concert, would I expect Mr. Parker's multi-harmonic circular breathing solo patterns. However inventive and spontaneous, the areas of interest have been drawn. . . . Not only do I expect the great improvisers to improvise, I also expect them to be "true" to their own agendas. As soon as I voice these statements, I am back in a land of rules and regulations. Egg shells to be trod on.[90]

In some respects the various listener responses appear to be shaped by the issue of whether intense personal emotions, such as anger, should be given voice in the collective arena of improvised music. One listener chastised many of the other respondents for thinking that Namtchylak "should be allowed to continue expressing her very personal anger at the expense of the 3 or 4 hundred people who'd paid to see her in good faith." Others commented that a decision to pull Ms. Namtchylak off stage provoked by contractual violations or the possibility of sponsor discontent was not only distasteful but also potentially dangerous for the continued health of improvised music on the whole. One even remarked that removing an improviser for "contractual reasons" was analogous to handing out speeding tickets at a Formula-One car race. Finally, one listener took his hat off to her for "having the courage to scream and vent in front of us all, exposing herself as vulnerable, hurt, frustrated, furious, and steadfast in her belief that people need to listen."

Ironically, the festival director Ajay Heble's own book titled *Landing on the Wrong Note* has a chapter devoted to the ethico-political authority of jazz, titled "Up for Grabs," in which he discusses his difficulty in reconciling his admiration for saxophonists Charles Gayle's music with his distaste for Gayle's oppressive onstage pronouncements about the sins of abortion and homosexuality. As Heble works through this "peculiar problem," he attempts to find a balance between a respect for postmodernism and its recognition of the value of difference and multiplicity and a certain accountability that he finds is missing in Gayle's own brand of free jazz. Heble struggles with the very questions that I am foregrounding here: "Whether meaning is best understood as a function of intent or effect." In a telling remark he asks, "Do we arrive at judgment on the basis of the artist or of the offended audience? And what if only half of the audience is offended, and the other half is moved to applaud or shout praises?" Heble reluctantly concludes that "music's complex and multiple ways of inhabiting the social landscape necessarily complicate our understanding of any determinate ethicopolitical allegiances."[91] At least for that one recent September evening in Guleph, a majority of listeners were willing to counteract the decision of the festival organizers and to allow a space for Ms. Namtchylak's fierce and frustrated outpourings.

The Rage for Chaos

The music represents our disillusionment with the fundamental impulse of other modern, Western musics to organize nature, as represented in sound. We have a different way of dealing with so-called "chaos": it is not our enemy, not even a matter to be fashioned into durable, self-validating human objects. We are "at play" with sound.[92]

—Jack Wright

I'm attracted to improvisation because of something that I value. That is a freshness, a certain quality that can only be obtained by improvisation, something you cannot possibly get by writing. It is something to do with the "edge." Always being on the brink of the unknown and being prepared for the leap. And when you do go out there you have all your years of preparation and all your sensibilities and your prepared means, but it is a leap into the unknown.[93]

—Steve Lacy

Chaos has become a metaphor, but far too often the wrong metaphor. Not only is the metaphor being extended to areas where there is no reason to expect a dynamical system, but the very implications of the metaphor are being misrepresented. Chaos is used as an excuse for the absence of order or control, rather than as a technique for establishing the existence of hidden order, or a method for controlling a system that at first sight seems uncontrollable.[94]

—Ian Stewart

Morse Peckham, in his 1965 book *Man's Rage for Chaos*, considers artistic behavior not as some special kind of activity cut off from the rest of human behavior, but rather as much an adaptation to the environment as any other human activity. Peckham was most concerned with finding a way to reconcile all of the various arts with the notion of a physiological basis for artistic behavior. In brief, he theorizes that a primary drive of human beings is toward order: to perceive the environment as comprehensible and to make successful predictions about the future. In a statement that anticipates much of the current thinking in cognitive science, Peckham argued: "I am convinced that to every situation a human being brings an orientation which is not derived from that situation but already exists in his perceptual powers before he comes to that situation. Such an orientation works only because it filters out any data which is not relevant to the needs of the moment."[95] But he also felt that, because such an orientation does not prepare an individual to deal with a *particular* situation but only with a *category*, or *kind*, or *class* of situations, much of the suppressed data may very well be relevant.

The arts, according to Peckham's hypothesis, serve the function of breaking up entrenched orientations, weakening and frustrating the "tyrannous drive to order," so that humans may be better able to deal with change, complexity, and chaos. Artists present the unpredicted; they offer the experience of disorientation. "The artist's primary function," according to Peckham, "is executed by offering a problem, but not a problem to be solved."[96] If art were simply about a search for unity and order, then, as Peckham sees it, the job of art would have ended long ago, since our esteemed aestheticians have claimed the ultimate in unity and order for so many past works. Instead, Peckham views art as the continual presentation of discontinuities, and he locates art not in the "work" itself, but in the perceiver's role of maintaining a search-behavior focused on awareness of discontinuities. With interesting similarities to the phenomenological model that we proposed in chapter four, Pekham posits the emotional quality of art as the result of a discrepancy between expectation and actuality. For him, and for us, the emotional affect is not inherent in the work, but rather in a successful performance of the perceiver's role.[97]

Pekham distinguishes between four types of discontinuities: implicit discontinuities, internal discontinuities, modal discontinuities, and external discontinuities. In short, they are produced when an art perceiver experiences discontinuities with cultural expectations of a perceptual field, expectations established with the work of art itself, expectations established by a tradition of art activity or style signs, and expectations established by learning to anticipate or predict art activity from engaging with predecessors in the same category. For Peckham, art helps us to envision and to cope with chaos.

Recent work in the cognitive neuroscience of music concerned with the role that music plays in human evolution and development supports Pekham's views rather well. Summarizing work in the field, Ian Cross argues that music is especially well suited to testing out aspects of social interaction by virtue of its nonefficaciousness (from a strict biological perspective), while its polysemic nature—its multiple potential meanings—provides a vehicle for integrating our domain-specific competences so as to endow us with the multipurpose and adaptive cognitive capacities that make us human. Cross writes: "[M]usic can be both a consequence free means of exploring social interaction and a 'play space' for rehearsing processes that may be necessary to achieve cognitive flexibility."[98]

"Play" is one of those marked words in the contemporary English language. For most, the word evokes pleasant emotions or memories (perhaps of childhood), but it also brings to mind the Puritan-influenced notion of play as nonserious and unproductive action of a frivolous or even ethically suspect nature. While this view of play as a marginal, even subversive activity may be prominent in the West, other cultures frequently view play as something that is both embedded within cosmology and integral to the daily social activities of individuals.[99] Trumpeter Don Cherry was fond of saying, "There is nothing more serious than fun."[100] And philosopher Hans Georg Gadamer appears to echo his words when he writes: "Seriousness is not merely something that calls us away from play; rather, seriousness in playing is necessary to make the play wholly play."[101]

To speak of "play" in relation to the sciences, however, may strike some readers as an oxymoron.[102] Yet Jay Mechling argues that, by altering our usual patterns and deconstructing our notions of common sense, play can provide a source of creativity in both the arts and the sciences. According to him, the ability to bi-sociate, or to perceive self-consistent but habitually incomparable frames of reference together, allows both the scientist to "solve the problem" in an experiment and the audience member to "see the joke" or "get the point" of a story or performance.[103]

Anthropologist Edward T. Hall agrees that, "Play is serious business." In an article on improvisation in music, Hall discusses the biological origins of play, asserting that play originates in the limbic system of mammals, a region that is also the center of emotions, parenting, and social organization and is distinct from the word- and number-based learning of the neocortex. In a statement that supports a similar position to those of Pekham and Cross, Hall writes: "Play is the device which not only permits mammals to have fun, but gives them a means of mastering the skills needed for survival."[104] For humans in particular, Hall argues that, "Without this variety—the sheer joy of being able to 'play' with the system—life would gradually lose its meaning."[105]

People cooperating in a musical activity, like the concert event described above, need not find the same meaning in what they do in order for the musical event to assist them in acquiring and maintaining the skill of being a member of a culture. As Cross sees it, "The singularity of the collective musical activity is not threatened by the existence of multiple simultaneous and potentially conflicting meanings."[106]

To reference my own subtitle, the activity of "improvising music in a complex age" allows participants and listeners to experience and explore complex, decentralized, interconnected, and emergent dynamics without an immediate concern for their own survival. Congestion or confusion in improvised music, while perhaps momentarily unfortunate, does not carry with it the immediate dangers of biological survival (such as confusion or congestion on the highways can). Yet through continual engagement with art, viewed as the successful performance of the perceiver's role, we may in fact be better prepared to survive and flourish in our increasingly interconnected, and therefore interdependent, world.

There is of course some danger that these new scientific theories could become nothing more than hosts to rather mindless syllogisms. As in the past, the most egregious examples of interdisciplinary euphoria often trumpet this new work as the final "theory of everything." In his advanced introduction to the field of science studies, David Hess argues that the new sciences of chaos and complexity mark a postmodern shift in emphasis toward open systems and patterns of self-organization. But he also worries that applications of chaos and complexity theories to social phenomena "may obfuscate as much as they clarify." He continues:

In a sense, we are back to the key concept of reification: changing social processes are projected onto nature in new scientific models (that may also be "true" in the sense that they represent part of the world that had not been seen previously), and in turn these new models are fed back into theories of society. These theories of society may point to new aspects of the social world that had not been seen previously, but at the same time they may deflect attention from a more critical inspection of the fundamental continuities of modernity and capitalism.[107]

Encouragingly, however, chaos and complexity studies frequently predict what anthropologists and researchers interested in culture have always known, that several answers may be equally valid: in other words, that alternative styles of social life are possible. Chaos and complexity theories tell us not only that diversity and adaptability are desirable traits, but also that irregularity and unpredictability are essential qualities for the health of a system.[108] Complex dynamical systems are best able to function adaptively since their network dynamics allow for both enduring patterns of organization and spontaneous responses to unexpected occurrences; they are poised at the edge of chaos. The complex dynamics of human societies also appear to illustrate the idea that the more complex a system, the more robust it may become, but also the more numerous the fluctuations that can threaten its stability. In this light, improvising music together may offer a consequence-free space in which to explore the complex dynamics created by a continual tension between stabilization through communication and instability through fluctuations and surprise.

6
Sync *and* Swarm

Sync makes life possible: from the cascade of biochemical reactions that allow for the operation of a single cell, to the circadian rhythms that control sleep and allow for proper functioning of our organs, to the firing of neurons whose synchronized symphony leads to human consciousness. Our growing understanding of sync in the physical world has also made countless technologies possible: from the lasers that allow us to listen to CDs, check out at the supermarket, and improve our eyesight; the clock circuitry that allows radio and television signals to be decoded and computer chips to function properly; to the satellite signals that make possible global communication and positioning technologies that can locate and direct everything from cell phones and cars to missiles.

A new science of sync is just now on the horizon, as biologists, physicists, mathematicians, astronomers, engineers, sociologists, and artists are beginning to notice connections with the work of others and to find compelling reasons to begin working together. Steve Strogatz, in his book *Sync: The Emerging Science of Spontaneous Order*, offers a primer on much of the work that has been done to date and a reminder of just how far we are from understanding sync in its more complex forms. He writes: "For reasons we don't yet understand, the tendency to synchronize is one of the most pervasive drives in the universe, extending from atoms to animals, from people to planets."[1] Despite the increasing resources being dedicated to the subject, however, only in a few instances do we have a clear idea of how order can emerge on its own. And these tend to be examples of sync in physical space, such as when water molecules crystallize into ice just below the freezing point. As Strogatz laments, "Explaining order in time, however, has proved to be more problematic."[2]

Music offers an excellent site for the study of sync in performance and in the dynamics that shape a musical community. In his book *Keeping Together in Time*, historian William H. McNeill's makes the argument that coordinated rhythmic activity is fundamental to life in society. Although he focuses his treatment on group activities such as military drill and certain forms of religious ritual and social dancing that produce a type of "muscular unison," there is no reason to believe that similar forms of collective bonding are not at play in all forms of musicking, including those that do not rely, at least overtly, on a shared or steady sense of pulse. In fact, there is increasing neurological evidence that the perception/cognition of music's temporal features arises from activation of substantial parts of the same neural circuitry involved in bodily movement and action.[3] So as listeners and performers share in the same sonic experience they are, in effect, moving together.

William Benzon, in his book *Beethoven's Anvil,* envisions a type of coupling and entrainment that takes place during musicking, both within the minds and bodies of individuals, and also with the minds and bodies of others. According to him, music requires that our symbol-processing capacities, motor skills, and emotional and communicative skills all work in close coordination such that, under ideal circumstances, it can produce a type of group interactional synchrony. Avoiding many of the "information processing" and "conduit" metaphors that tend to dominate conventional scholarship on music cognition and communication, Benzon envisions ways in which the sonic flow of music correlates with the flow of neurophysiological substrates, supporting the possibility for tight coupling among individuals who share a common musical culture.[4]

The notion of tight coupling may bring to mind simple imitative behavior. Albert Einstein famously remarked: "He who joyfully marches to music rank and file has already earned my contempt. He has been given a large brain by mistake, since for him the spinal chord would surely suffice."[5] Yet in musicking, we also experience far more subtle and supple forms of sync. According to Strogatz, these supple forms of sync "embody the qualities that we like to think of as uniquely human—intelligence, sensitivity, and the togetherness that comes only through the highest kind of sympathy."[6]

These types of human sync, however, may turn out to be different from other animals' sync in degree rather than kind. Social insects, for instance, frequently display intricately woven group behaviors through a type of swarm intelligence. Colonies of bees have fascinated observers for millennia with their ability to move around with apparent abandon yet at the same time to display a collective sense of purpose. Watching bees in flight, one can even sense the underlying undulation between sync and swarm, order and chaos, which appears to inform many qualities of life.

If, as I have argued in the previous chapters, group improvisation may be heard in its best moments to demonstrate complex and emergent properties that are somehow greater than the sum of its parts, then investigating individuals and ensembles in isolation of the network of surrounding influences will not suffice. We need to reorient our analytical framework to take account of the dynamics that occur in ensembles as they musick together over days, weeks, months, and even years. And we need to acknowledge the ways in which influences in musical communities circulate through more than the sounds of performances and recordings; meaning is everywhere, not simply in the "sounds themselves." The networks involved include a host of social conventions and material artifacts that affect the ways in which music is made and heard: from the funding sources or media attention that a performer may receive to the casual conversations or critical reviews that a performance may provoke. While it may be fairly common to acknowledge the subtle influence that specific audiences and venues can have on performance, especially in relation to improvisation, the network of material, economic, technological, educational, and social factors at play, and the complex meanings that they generate through their interactions, are far more involved than that. In fascinating ways, this network-style organization both shapes and is shaped by the activity of all of its participants; everyone changes the state of everyone else. Although the spontaneous and surprising occurrences in improvised performance can attract our immediate attention, it is through the dynamic interplay of social, material, and sonic culture that we begin to sense the true lifeblood of the music.

Coupling and Entrainment

> The picture that is emerging suggests that we are like wheels within wheels, hierarchies of living oscillators. Or to put it more vividly, the human body is like an enormous orchestra. The musicians are individual cells. . . . The players are grouped into various sections. Instead of strings and woodwinds, we have kidneys and livers, each composed of thousands of cellular oscillators. . . . The conductor for this symphony is the circadian pacemaker, a neural cluster of thousands of clock cells in the brain, themselves synchronized into a coherent unit.[7]
>
> —Steve Strogatz

The phenomenon of sync can appear to be both mundane and miraculous. When all is working well, we rarely notice its precision. But on closer investigation, our internal dance of time—the way we synchronize with the twenty-four-hour day and regulate our various body processes accordingly—is actually rather challenging and complex. (Parents with newborns and many blind people know all too well the debilitating aspects of not being able to synchronize with regular sleep patterns.) The ways in which we can synchronize with the outside world, through social bonding, language, and music, however, are truly remarkable.

Steve Strogatz describes three levels at which sync operates. At the lowest, microscopic level, cells within a particular organ vary their chemical and electrical rhythms in lockstep with one another. At the next level, the body's internal synchronization keeps all of the various systems and organs synched to the same twenty-four-hour cycle, yet engaged at different intervals in order to maximize efficiency while conserving energy. At this level of self-synchrony we are also able to synchronize our speech with our gesturing, among other things. The third level of synchrony happens between our bodies and the world around us. At this level we synchronize to the environment and have the ability to entrain with others.

Entrainment describes a shared tendency of a wide range of physical and biological systems to coordinate temporally structured events through interaction. Dutch physicists Christiaan Huygens first identified entrainment in 1665 when he realized that two pendulum clocks in his room were synchronizing on their own. Huygens deduced that vibrations were being transmitted through the wall that physically linked the clocks thereby minimizing their collective energy expenditures. A well-known biological example of entrainment involves the ability for women who live or work together to synchronize their menstrual cycles (here the interaction happens through pheromones), but we also entrain with others when we enter into conversation, timing our phrases and pauses and synchronizing our body postures and movements to facilitate close communication.[8]

For over three decades, William Condon and his colleagues have been studying this type of interactive synchrony through close analysis of videotapes. Their research demonstrates that, in conversation, listeners can synchronize their body movements to the speech patterns of others with a lag of only forty-three milliseconds (roughly one frame of film at twenty-four frames per second).[9] Not only are human infants able to demonstrate this type of synchrony twenty minutes after birth (and perhaps they are learning to synchronize to voices in utero during the last months of pregnancy), so far as we know our closest primate relatives can neither synchronize with one another nor hold a steady beat.[10]

Timothy Perper's work on human courtship found that, during dating, a couple moves from standard forms of conversational synchrony to full-body synchrony where they are looking at each other continuously and touching each other regularly.[11] R. C. Schmidt studied the dynamics of two people given the task of coordinating the swinging motions of a leg to a metronome while sitting within sight of one another. He found that, below a certain tempo, people are able to synchronize either in phase (with parallel swinging motions) or out of phase (moving in opposite directions). When the tempo reaches a critical point, however, only in-phase coordination is possible. Surprisingly, these results are the same if a single person is asked to coordinate the movement of their own fingers, suggesting that interactional synchrony and self-synchrony have the same structure, exhibit the same dynamics. Based on this and other research, William Benzon hypothesizes that "human beings create a uniquely human social space when their nervous systems are coupled through interactional synchrony."[12]

This type of entrainment is a much noticed although sadly understudied aspect of musical performance. Outside of isolated studies of musical meter, and some research in the fields of music therapy and biomusicology, little work has been done on the subject.[13] Martin Clayton, Rebecca Sager, and Udo Will are publishing a useful resource on the topic of entrainment for music scholars that might be especially helpful to ethnomusicologists:

> An entrainment model suggest we look at engagement with music not simply as a process of encoding and decoding information, but of embodied interaction and "tuning-in" to musical stimuli. . . . Entrainment in musicking implies a profound association between different humans at a physiological level and a shared propensity at a biological level. The implications of this view for studies of socialization and identification are obvious, and so too is the link to questions of enculturation: someone's ability to respond appropriately to a given musical stimulus can, since it is a learned application of a basic biological tendency, be a marker of the degree to which an individual "belongs" in a particular social group.[14]

Studies on groove, many of which emanate from the fields of ethnomusicology and jazz and improvised music studies, are relevant here as well.[15] For instance, Charles Keil's notion of participatory discrepancies, although a cumbersome phrase, reminds us that music involves participation and that it is founded on appropriate degrees of being "out-of-time." Steve Feld's discussion of "lift-up-over-sounding," an aesthetic principle of the Kaluli of Papua New Guinea, also evokes a musical relationship that is synchronized but out-of-phase. In fact, Clayton et al. offer what seems to me a compelling definition of groove as "the socio-musical process of being entrained at the preferred degree of synchronicity."[16] This allows room not only for marches, but also for free improvisation to groove.

To return to Strogatz's three levels of sync, the first two occur in music within the individual performer, as his or her mental and physical concentration synchronize. Ethnomusicologist Paul Berliner describes this as the moment when "the gap between intention and realization disappears."[17] More poetically, pianist and phenomenologist David Sudnow describes this in his book *Ways of the Hand* as "singing with the fingers."[18] The third level of sync, that with the outside world, occurs as performers listen to each other and respond to ongoing events, the audience, and the context of performance in order to make music together.

While it might be tempting to argue, as Bruce Johnson does, that jazz and improvised music offer an especially fertile space for this type of synchronization—"an ear-site in an epistemology dominated by eyesight"—all musical performance involves, in its own way, the process of synchronizing actions, intentions, and sounds in order to make for a compelling experience.[19] The process of listening to music together can also bring audiences and performers into a type of neural synchrony as cognitive, perceptual, and motor constructs all may be engaged together. Clayton et al. believe that, "If entrainment is a factor in any interpersonal interaction and communication, we should expect that it is a factor in any variety of musicking."[20]

To counterbalance the "jazz and its others" orientation of much improvisation research, musicologist Nicholas Cook highlights the interactive format of a classical chamber group and argues that musicians of all types must make continual, detailed, and spontaneous decisions in order to perform music together well. Rather than make a strong distinction between ear and eye music, as Johnson does, Cook argues that a more helpful distinction can be made between music as text and music as performance. He argues that in a chamber group the score "choreographs a series of ongoing social engagements between players, setting up a shared framework or goal."[21] While discussing orchestral music, however, Cook concedes: "We *hear* the music of large groups as embodying social interaction even when that is not literally the case; music, in short, symbolizes social interaction even when it doesn't actually represent it." Although I am sympathetic to Cook's main points, I will be most concerned here with the ways in which collective improvisation challenges players and listeners to establish and maintain a very immediate and visceral type of social synchrony.

At its most basic, collective improvisation requires synchronizing starting and ending gestures. These brief initial and concluding moments, however, can take on heightened meanings. Evan Parker once commented, "The starts of pieces are very good often because they are impossible to theorize about."[22] They occur without immediate sonic materials on which to base the ensemble's development and without explicit expectations from listeners (although there may be many implicit ones from both audiences and performers). If an earlier piece has just concluded, a new beginning may of course be heard in relationship to it. And the history that improvisers share together can also provide a strong point of reference for subsequent meetings. But in principle, beginnings can emerge from nowhere and quickly move in unexpected ways. Endings, too, can be one of the most challenging and satisfying moments of improvised performance, as the entire ensemble must collectively agree on what will then become the final gesture (and the final mood) of a given performance.

At times, improvisers can also synchronize their simultaneous gestures without warning: perhaps landing on a unison pitch together, implying a similar rhythmic pattern, or producing a particularly compatible timbral quality during an improvisation. These moments of *transient* sync can arrive by chance or through a heightened sensitivity brought on by interactional synchrony: a skill that may be developed over time as well.[23] Bassist Bertram Turetzky told me in a recent interview, "Sometimes you play with people who have E.S.P. [extra-sensory perception]. You'll hit a high E and all of a sudden someone else hits the high E. And sometimes they'll tell you after, 'I had no idea what you were playing, my hand just went there.'" Turetzky recalled, "It has happened to me many times."[24]

While these moments of transient sync can be both surprising and pleasing, an even more durable type of sync is involved when performers are able to develop their energy levels and emotions together over long stretches of time. Steve Strogatz points out that "when the bells of two different churches happen to ring for a time together on Sunday morning, or for a moment the blinker in your car flashes in perfect time with the car ahead of you at a stop light, such sync is pure coincidence, and hardly worth noting."[25] Of course moments of musical sync are already far more complicated than this. Spontaneously landing on a unison pitch or near-identical gesture, for instance, is much less likely to occur than car blinkers temporarily synchronizing, since the range of choices available to improvisers is far greater and there is no specific mandate that individual musicians follow repetitive patterns that might naturally overlap. But Strogatz's point is well taken. *Persistent* forms of sync, those that could not possibly happen by accident or those that occur far more frequently than would otherwise be predicted, are even more interesting and more challenging to explore. Strogatz observes:

> Such persistent sync comes easily to us human beings, and, for some reason, it often gives us pleasure. We like to dance together, sing in a choir, play in a band. In its most refined form, persistent sync can be spectacular, as in the kickline of the Rockettes or the matched movements of synchronized swimmers. The feeling of artistry is heightened when the audience has no idea where the music is going next, or what the next dance move will be. We interpret persistent sync as a sign of intelligence, planning, and choreography.[26]

The (perhaps unique) challenge of freer improvised music, then, is to provide this heightened sense of expectation and surprise to both audience members and to other performers *collectively*, in a more or less bottom-up fashion.

One of Strogatz's main research areas has been the remarkable synchronized flashing of fireflies. In parts of Southeast Asia, Africa, and isolated pockets in the United States, large groupings of fireflies can synchronize their flashing without warning and seemingly without design. For at least three hundred years, Westerners traveling to these regions have mused in print about their fascinating encounters with this natural light show, but few offered an explanation, and those who did assumed some sort of central firefly must be cueing all the rest. George Hudson wrote in 1918, "If it is desired to get a body of men to sing or play together in perfect rhythm they not only must have a leader but must be trained to follow such a leader. . . . Do these insects inherit a sense of rhythm more perfect than our own?"[27] We now know that each firefly contains an oscillator, a little metronome, whose timing adjusts automatically in response to the flashes of others. Through the use of computer modeling techniques,

Strogatz and his colleague Rennie Mirollo showed that under the right conditions a perfect synchrony could emerge. Strogatz describes this and other recent work in the area of sync as "a crucial step in the development of a science that could finally contend with the mysteries of spontaneous order in time as well as in space."[28]

The models that Strogatz describes for understanding sync among coupled oscillators, despite their rather simplified design, demonstrate some fascinating connections to improvised music. To help visualize this work, Strogatz describes the oscillators as runners doing laps on a circular track. Each runner is influenced by his own internal dynamics and by his interactions with other runners. In the simplest case, if the runners completely ignore one another they diffuse all over the track, each running at his own preferred speed, unaffected by the others. But by giving each runner an influence and sensitivity function, in addition to a preferred speed, interesting orderings begin to emerge. The influence function might be analogous to a musician's ability to recruit support or at least attention from others in the group. The sensitivity function measures that same musician's willingness and ability to pay attention to and connect with the musical developments of others in the ensemble. The preferred speed can also be seen as roughly analogous to a preferred aesthetic, including expectations of such things as musical density or dynamic. For the purpose of analogy, we may wish to think of the coupled sync explored by these models in the broader sense of groove described above.

Even these rather simplified models showed a remarkable range of behaviors. For certain combinations of influence and sensitivity, the group actively opposed synchronization, even if everyone started together. In other instances, certain combinations of influence and sensitivity produced a type of runaway positive feedback that led everyone to synchronize quickly, to rush to an emerging consensus. These dynamics, when transposed into the musical realm, could offer some interesting sonic results. Layering highly intentional sounds that avoid any sense of collusion can produce a very complex texture. And the rapid dovetailing effect of all of the musicians coalescing around a shared idea, theme, or gesture can also be intriguing to hear. But without additional dynamic tensions available for exploration, or a coupled and evolving sense of entrainment, both of these formats would arguably lose our interest over time.

One of the nice things about envisioning these models is that they represent a type of cooperative sync in which there are no leaders, no ultimate boss, and yet remarkably coordinated behaviors can arise. More complex versions of the models showed that, although group synchronization is not hierarchical, it is not purely democratic either. Runners did not necessarily synchronize at the speed of the fastest member. Rather, by varying the influence and sensitivity functions, runners might synchronize near the speed of the average runner, or the pack might actually go faster or slower than the preferred speed of any of its members. Strogatz remarks that, "It was all wonderfully counterintuitive."[29] While under ideal circumstances, musical entrainment in improvised performance can and should produce an emergent whole that is greater than the sum of its parts, sync does not always work that way. At times it may simply maintain the status quo or even bring down the overall energy and interest of the group.

By controlling the diversity of the initial population of runners in the models, some additional dynamics emerged as well. When starting with groups comprised of extremely diverse members, the models showed that a pack would never form, even if their influence and sensitivity functions predisposed them to do so. In musical situations involving a group comprised of individuals of extremely diverse experience and ability levels, improvising together will often fail to produce much interest without some sort of preconceived scheme or strategy to assist the development. Although one might think that a homogenous group would stand a better chance of synchronizing, the models of runners actually showed that only beyond a certain threshold of diversity could a phase transition to mutual synchronization occur. In situations where musicians share too much in common to begin with—say they emanate from near identical backgrounds or idiomatic traditions—it may be equally challenging for the group to collectively discover new musical territory. Finally, regardless of the relative homogeneity of the group to begin with, the models showed that a final state of incoherence was always possible, perhaps offering another analogy to the challenges inherent in freer forms of group improvisation.

These and similar models have proven useful in understanding many situations in which order can emerge in complex systems, but it remains difficult to verify them experimentally since it would require exact measurements that can be extremely difficult to come by. Even in the case of fireflies, taking measurements at the level of the individual insect and their individual cells and at the level of the entire system is a daunting thought. But these models have helped us to envision ways in which complex systems can organize themselves. As Strogatz remarks, "No maestro is required. . . . Sync occurs through mutual cuing, in the same way that an orchestra can keep perfect time without a conductor."[30]

Insect Music

> At one level, improvisation can be compared with the ultimate otherness of an ant colony or hive of bees. Perhaps it was no coincidence that in the wake of drummer John Stevens and the Spontaneous Music Ensemble, certain strands of English improvised music were known, half-disparagingly as insect music.[31]
>
> —David Toop

> Improvisation is not a revolution that pits itself against codification; it is diffuse. Like ants stripping a carcass, it works from the inside and outside of codes.[32]
>
> —John Corbett

> In Euro-American art-music culture this binary [between composition and improvisation] is routinely and simplistically framed as involving the "effortless spontaneity" of improvisation, versus the careful deliberation of composition—the composer as ant, the improviser as grasshopper.[33]
>
> —George Lewis

Scientists, artists, and laypeople alike have for centuries watched in wonder as a flock of birds spontaneously takes flight and navigates in perfect harmony, or as a hive of bees throws off a collective swarm into the air. The ancient Greeks and Romans were famous beekeepers and harvested respectable yields of honey from homemade hives, yet they got almost every fact about bees wrong. As Kevin Kelly points out in a chapter of his book *Out of Control* provocatively titled "Hive Mind," the idea of the hive as an emergent, decentralized system was late in coming.[34] It was not until the modern era that the hive was found to be a radical matriarchy and sisterhood (with only a smattering of male drones) and that the notion of the Queen bee as supreme supervisor was discounted. When a swarm pours itself out through the front slot of a hive, the queen bee can only follow.

At the dawn of the twentieth century, the Belgian poet Maurice Maeterlinck wondered, "Where is 'this spirit of the hive' . . . where does it reside? What is it that governs here, that issues orders, foresees the future?"[35] We now know that within the swarm a half dozen or so anonymous workers scout ahead to check for possible hive locations. When they report back to the swarm, they perform an informative dance, the intensity of which corresponds to the desirability of the site they scouted. Deputy bees follow up on the more promising reports and return to either confirm or disconfirm the desirability of the new location. Although it is rare for a single bee to visit more than one potential site, through the process of compounding emphasis, the more desirable sites end up getting the most visitors. In other words, the hive chooses: the biggest crowd eventually provokes the entire swarm to dance off to its new location.

We can sense in this and other examples of decentralized decision-making a quality that appears to inform all life: emergence. William Morton Wheeler, the founder of the field of social insects, argued as early as 1911 that an insect colony operates as a type of *superorganism*: "Like a cell or the person, it behaves as a unitary whole, maintaining its identity in space, resisting dissolution . . . neither a thing nor a concept, but a continual flux or process."[36] Other terms have been proposed as well. Kelly adopts the notion of a "vivisystem" since, like superorganism, it extends certain qualities and dynamics of living systems into the social realm without the more problematic claim of extending life to them. Both terms leave open the idea that "multiorganism organisms" may take a very different form than multicellular ones.[37]

Even the sound of the swarm can fascinate human ears. For her aptly titled "Bee Project," kotoist and multimedia artist Miya Masaoka's positioned a glass-enclosed bee hive of 3,000 bees in the center of the stage and amplified, manipulated, and blended its sounds with those from a trio of improvisers, all according to the instructions in her score. Later versions of the same work have used spatialization software to twist and tilt the sound of the hive so that listeners can be sonically located within the swarm.

As the three quotes offered at the beginning of this section illustrate, there are several ways in which we might wish to locate musical connections to the swarm. Some improvised music provokes such quick reactions from players and evokes such complicated and dense soundscapes for listeners that a literal analogy to a swarm of insects may seem rather appropriate. And the ways in which individual improvisers can be heard to be "picking at" a shared body of modern techniques and sensibilities but in resolutely individualistic ways, or to be following their own creative spark while also being sensitive to and dependent on the evolving group dynamic, may bring to mind the behavior of social insects that seem to have their own agenda while also working in ways that organize the group without supervision. Finally, as we will see more in the next section, the notion of "insect music" has perhaps become most associated with a type of generative compositional scheme, and often with the power of computers to create complex patterns from relatively simple materials, such that questions about the ways in which creativity may be facilitated or constrained and the ways in which cultural understandings may be reflected, reshaped, or remain concealed in this type of work become particularly important.

In addition to being an extremely skilled improviser, the English drummer John Stevens will always be remembered for his instrumental role in developing the scene at the Little Theater Club in London that nurtured many in the first generation of English free improvisers and for his commitment to passing on this music in general. One of his early pedagogical approaches was titled *Click Piece*, and it included little more that the instruction to play the shortest sounds on your instrument.[38] In the collective setting, however, one would gradually become aware of an emergent group sound. As David Toop explains, "The piece seemed to develop with a mind of its own and almost as a by-product, the basic lessons of improvisation—how to listen and how to respond—could be learned through a careful enactment of the instructions."[39] Stevens's *Click Piece* highlights one of the central aspects of swarm intelligence: that relatively simple decentralized activities can produce dramatic, self-organizing behaviors.

In the scientific community, a growing number of researchers are exploring new ways of applying swarm intelligence (or SI) to diverse situations.[40] For instance, the foraging of ants has led to improved methods for routing telecommunications traffic in a busy network. The way in which insects cluster their dead can aid in analyzing bank data. The distributed and cooperative approach used by many social insects to transport goods and to solve navigational problems has led to new insights in the fields of robotics and artificial intelligence. And the evolving division of labor in honeybees has helped to improve the organization of factory assembly-line workers and equipment. As Eric Bonabeau and Guy Théraulaz see it: "The potential of swarm intelligence is enormous. It offers an alternative way of designing systems that have traditionally required centralized control and extensive preprogramming."[41]

But beyond these business and technological applications, one of the main lessons of contemplating SI is that organized behaviors can develop in decentralized ways. Can exploring and thinking about SI affect the way we make and think about music? It remains difficult for many people to envision complex systems organizing without a leader since we are often predisposed to think in terms of central control and hierarchical command. The notion that music can be organized in complex ways without a composer or conductor still leaves many scratching their heads in doubt. Scientists have also been predisposed in the past to look for chains of command, instances of clear cause and effect. But the emerging field of SI demonstrates that complex behaviors and efficient solutions can be arrived at without a leader, organized without an organizer, coordinated without a coordinator.

The secret of the swarm lies in the intercommunication of its members. Through direct and indirect interactions among autonomous agents and between agents and their environment, swarm systems are able to self-organize in decentralized, robust, and flexible ways. Bonabeau, Théraulaz, and Marco Dorigo, a physicist, biologist, and engineer, respectively, working together at the Santa Fe Institute, offer a list of four basic ingredients that through their interplay can manifest in swarm intelligence: 1) forms of positive feedback, 2) forms of negative feedback, 3) a degree of randomness or error, and finally 4) multiple interactions of multiple entities.[42]

Positive feedback in SI can be usefully summarized as simple "rules of thumb" that promote the creation of structures: activities such as recruitment and reinforcement. Negative feedback counterbalances positive feedback and helps to stabilize the system: it may take the form of saturation, exhaustion, or competition. A certain degree of randomness or error is also crucial, because it enables the discovery of new solutions and produces fluctuations that can act as seeds from which new structures develop. Finally, SI generally requires a minimum density of mutually tolerant individuals, because individuals should be able to make use of the results of their own activities and the activities of others.

While something of a general and descriptive list, these ingredients do play important roles in collective improvisation. Through positive feedback musicians not only develop their own ideas from a kernel of inspiration, but they also work together to support the ideas of others and the evolving ensemble sound. They "recruit" others to support or sustain their own developments, or they may choose to "reinforce" the creative direction of others instead. Similar to the ways in which information about the best food source or the shortest path can be compounded among a swarm of bees or a colony of ants, positive feedback increases the ability of an improvising group to follow the more "promising" of many concurrent ideas being pursued by various members.

Negative feedback in improvisation helps to keep things interesting. By intentionally looking elsewhere for new ideas or new musical areas to explore, individuals can either signal transitions away from ensemble moments that have lingered too long or seem to be going nowhere (the feelings of saturation and exhaustion), or they can productively layer divergent sonic qualities and musical ideas together or provoke others to boost their own creativity (through a competitive element). Negative feedback helps to maintain a balance in the evolving improvisation so that one idea does not continue to amplify indefinitely (although a more static approach can produce interesting results as well).

Unexpected occurrences, in the form of randomness or error, often provide both source material and inspiration for individuals and groups to explore new sonic territory, musical techniques, and interactive strategies. Noticing and capitalizing on unexpected fluctuations as an improvisation unfolds can produce important structural cues, developments, and transitions, and it represents a particular joy of improvised music making in general. Without this third ingredient, groups of improvisers who work together over a longer period of time might become too familiar with one another's musical language and approach or might fall into regular strategies of support and counterbalance (and this of course does happen). Finally, the notion that individuals and the group as a whole benefit from multiple interactions and perspectives is something of an axiom in ensemble forms of improvisation. One of the particular challenges of much contemporary improvisation, for both players and listeners, is to remain aware of and sensitive to the many musical gestures and processes circulating within the playing of each individual (including one's own playing) and between members of the group.[43]

Systems demonstrating swarm intelligence do differ widely in the amount and types of intercommunication between members. Without a doubt there are important differences in the degrees of freedom allowed in a swarm of bees and in the sonic swarm of collective improvisation. But if interesting complexities can emerge from groupings of individuals with a limited array of communication possibilities, how much more can we expect from experienced and creative artists? J. Stephen Lansing, an anthropologist who also serves as external faculty at the Santa Fe Institute, wonders about complex adaptive systems in general: "What if the elements are not cells or light bulbs but agents capable of reacting with new strategies or foresight to the patterns they have helped to create?"[44] Much of the current research by social scientists on complex adaptive systems is concerned with precisely this question.

Even within the field of improvised music, the range of allowable or expected participation can vary greatly. To return to our earlier example of John Stevens's *Click Piece*, although this generative approach to collective improvisation offered an effective way to make "quite ravishing" music with a large ensemble comprising players of mixed ability and experience to more skillful and confident musicians—such as Evan Parker, an early duo partner with Stevens—it quickly became an unproductive limitation. Simplifying the parameters for improvisation can be useful and even necessary for making large ensembles swarm effectively, but in the more intimate setting of a small group, arguably the preferred arrangement for the majority of free improv enthusiasts, a less restrictive framework is usually desired.[45]

In much freer improvisation, the collective pattern of the group is more important than any of the individual actions heard in isolation. But this does not deny freedom to individual musicians. In an interview with *Monastery Bulletin*, an online magazine with the subheading "Timeless Periodical for the Liberation of Music and Literature," Evan Parker highlighted ways in which freedom works within the collective unfolding of what might easily be termed swarm dynamics:

> The freedom is of course that since you and your response are part of the context for other people, and they have that function for you, it's very hard to unravel the knots of why anybody is doing what they do in a given context. I think it's pretty clear that you could sort of go with the flow, or you could go against the flow. And sometimes what the music really needs is for you to go with the flow, and sometimes what it really needs is for you to do something different. Or anybody, somebody, to do something different. So that's why people improvise, presumably, because they want the freedom to behave in accordance with their response to the situations. But since their response then becomes part of the new situation for the other players, it's very hard to say why a particular sequence of events unfolds in the way it does. But we get used to following the narrative of improvisational discourse.

Parker's notion that "the music" *needs* for things to happen, *needs* for musicians to do things, is a fairy common way in which improvisers speak about the process of performance. In his liner notes to the album *In Order to Survive*, bassist William Parker expresses that, "Creative Music is any music that procreates itself as it is being played to ignite into a living entity that is bigger than the composer and player." While his comments certainly resonate with the notion of a vivisystem or superorganism touched on earlier, they may also highlight an additional dimension of SI research: interactions within a swarm can be both direct and indirect. The direct interactions are the obvious ones: with ants this can involve antennation or mandibular contact,

food or liquid exchange, chemical contact, etc. But indirect interactions are more subtle. In SI they are referred to by the rather cumbersome term "stigmergy" (from the
Greek *stigma*: sting, and *ergon*: work).[46] Stigmergy describes the indirect interaction
between individuals when one of them modifies the environment and the other responds to the new environment rather than directly to the actions of the first individual. This helps to describe the process of "incremental construction" that many social
insects use to build extremely complex structures or to arrange items in ways that
might at first seem arbitrary or random. And because positive feedback can produce
nonlinear effects, indirect interaction can result in dramatic bifurcations when a critical point is reached: for example, some species of termites alternate between noncoor-
dinated and coordinated building to produce neatly arranged pillars or strips of soil
pellets.

But swarm intelligence has its limits and its drawbacks. Social insects can adapt to
changes in their environment, but only within a certain degree of tolerance. For instance, many social insects are able to seek out and find new food sources when an
existing one is exhausted, or some species are able to reallocate labor roles if the number of required workers for a specific task dwindles, all without explicit instruction.
But the "army ant syndrome" offers a compelling example of the limits to this adaptability and of swarm intelligence in general. Among army ants, when a group of forag-
ers accidentally gets separated from the main colony, the separated workers run in a
densely packed "circular mill" until they all eventually die from exhaustion. Although
able to function well within the group under normal circumstances, an unpredictable
perturbation of a large enough degree can destroy the colony's cohesiveness and make
it impossible for the group to recover.

For a musical analogy, while sensitivity to the group is an essential component of
improvised performance, to blindly base one's own playing on what others do or to
simply follow the group as an overriding strategy can lead to rather inflexible and
ineffective results, producing a musical "circular mill." And many improvisers, if they
sense that all of the participants are following each other too carefully, will "go against
the grain" or "forge out on their own" into new sonic territory; in other words, they
will defy the logic of the hive mind.

The cohesion of small groups can also be jeopardized by imbalances that lead to
polarization. Drawing on research with decision-making among corporate boards and
committees, James Surowiecki identifies a few qualities that appear to factor into all
intimate social settings: earlier comments are more influential; higher status people
talk more and more often; status is not always derived from knowledge/experience.[47]
Since constantly making comparisons and adjustments to others can result in an unproductive "group think," it is important for individuals to champion their own ideas
in small group settings. But too much vehemence in this can lead to a completely
polarized setting or to an "information cascade" when others are subsumed by a singular view or opinion. In short, deference to the ideas of others is important, but so is
dissent when required.

The field of SI is still very much in its infancy. It is often extremely difficult for
researchers to understand the inner workings of insect swarms and the variety of rules
by which individuals in a swarm interact. Even in those cases when we can understand the behaviors of individuals, we may still be unable to predict or understand the
dynamics of the overall system because countless other environmental factors come

into play. When transposed into the realm of humans, these uncertainties only compound themselves. Discussing the business and technological applications of SI, Bonabeau and Théraulaz confess that: "Although swarm-intelligence approaches have been effective at performing a number of optimization and control tasks, the systems developed have been inherently reactive and lack the necessary overview to solve problems that require in-depth reasoning techniques."[48] We still don't know enough about social insects, much less social humans, to be able to understand how certain group behaviors emerge and evolve.

Nevertheless, the notion that a group can have capacities and capabilities that extend beyond the scope of any of its participating members is a powerful one. As Kevin Kelly points out, the hive does possess much that none of its parts possesses. Not only does swarm intelligence represent a type of distributed perception for the hive, but the hive also possesses a type of distributed memory; the average honeybee operates with a memory of six days, but the hive as a whole operates with a distributed memory of up to three months, twice as long as the lifetime of the average bee.[49] Bonabeau et al. write:

> We suggest that the social insect metaphor may go beyond superficial considerations. At a time when the world is becoming so complex that no single human being can really understand it, when information (and not the lack of it) is threatening our lives, when software systems become so intractable that they can no longer be controlled, perhaps the scientific and engineering world will be more willing to consider another way of designing "intelligent" systems where autonomy, emergence and distributed functioning replace control, preprogramming, and centralization.[50]

We might also hope that the music world will continue to explore ways of organizing sonic and social experiences that do not hinge on centralized notions of control.

By Lead or by Seed

> People seem to have a strong preference for centralization in almost everything they think and do. People tend to look for *the* cause, *the* reason, *the* driving force, *the* deciding factor. When people observe patterns in the world (for example the flocking of birds or the foraging of ants), they often assume centralized causes where none exist. And when people try to create patterns and structures in the world (for example, new organizations or new machines), they often impose centralized control where none is needed.[51]
>
> —Mitchel Resnick

> The evolution of a complex dynamical system is not ruled by a Platonic king, constructed by a Cartesian architect, or forecast by a LaPlacean spirit, but grows much like a living organism.[52]
>
> —Klaus Mainzer

> If the practice of free improvisation continues and grows, control over music will tend to decentralize toward a communal expression

and experience—not the work of a single composer, not at the direction of any controlling individual or style, not an expression of one ego, and not the separations between player and instrument, musicians and audience, amateur and professional, art and life.[53]

—Tom Nunn

The behavior of the slime mold *Dictyostelium discoideum* confounded scientists for centuries. Under hospitable conditions, when the weather is cool and the food supply abundant, the mold operates as thousands of distinct single-celled units, moving and feeding separately from one another. But when those conditions shift for the worse, the distinct life forms coalesce into a single, larger organism that can withstand a higher level of ecological adversity and can move en masse to find new sources of food. The question that confounded scientist for centuries was simply, how do these individual slime molds synchronize their behaviors in order to coalesce into an aggregate swarm, a collective whole? The conventional wisdom was that this display of group solidarity must come at the behest of a smaller group of "pacemaker" cells that send out chemical messages in the form of cyclic AMP. But despite years of working on the problem, no one was able to locate these "pacemaker" cells. None of the individuals possessed any distinguishing characteristics that set them apart from the others.

The problem, it turned out, was not that scientists were unable to locate these pacemaker cells but rather that they presumed their existence to begin with. Until just recently, scientists were often heavily conditioned to look for centralized rather than decentralized systems: instances of control rather than cooperation. The story of slime molds offers an example of just how recalcitrant these conditioned views can be. In 1970, Evelyn Fox Keller, a Harvard Ph.D. in physics who was interested in applying mathematical insight to biology, proposed an alternate view.[54] She demonstrated that slime molds could self-organize into a community without a centralized command, without any specialized cells initiating the aggregation. Despite the appearance of corroborating research, it took more than a decade for the scientific establishment to accept her view and it remains difficult for many to think in terms of decentralized, emergent phenomena.[55]

Mitchel Resnick, author of *Turtles, Termites, and Traffic Jams* and the creator of the StarLogo agent-based modeling program, finds that people tend to assume that patterns are created either by lead or by seed.[56] By which he means that when people observe patterns in the world they either assume a leader orchestrated it or some preexisting or pregiven inhomogeneity in the environment gave rise to the pattern. For instance, while Resnick was working in his office one afternoon on a StarLogo simulation of emergent slime mold behavior, Marvin Minsky walked in. Minsky, who is perhaps most famous for his decentralized notion of a "society of mind," watched the computer-generated slime molds moving around and inside of little green blobs on Resnick's screen for some time. Then he remarked, "But those creatures aren't self-organizing. They're just moving toward the green food." Even Minsky, who has thought long and hard about self-organizing behaviors, jumped to the conclusion that the green blobs were pieces of food placed throughout the virtual world to act as seeds that would attract the slime molds. But in fact the green blobs were pheromone trails that each slime mold dropped behind itself while also "sniffing" ahead to follow the scent others had already left behind. When he introduces his modeling techniques to students, Resnick finds similar tendencies to want to impose a leader or at least a collective goal on these computer agents.

Why do people have such a strong commitment to centralized approaches?[57] Why, for example, did scientists believe that bird flocks and bee hives must have leaders, or that slime molds required pacemaker cells in order to aggregate successfully? Resnick asserts that, "Our intuitions about systems in the world are deeply influenced by our conceptions of ourselves."[58] Although modern theories of cognition are increasingly demonstrating that our minds are composed of thousands of interacting entities and that we function in social settings by distributing cognitive demands and resources among the group, we tend to experience ourselves as singular. In his work using Star-Logo as an educational tool, Resnick found an inherent tension: "[P]eople felt a gut attraction to decentralized phenomena, even as they clung tightly to centralized preconceptions."[59]

This situation appears to be the same in many musical circles as well. I can remember well walking the halls of UCLA's Ethnomusicology Department after I had published my first scholarly article, titled "Emergent Qualities of Collectively Improvised Performance," and one particular fellow graduate student always asked me when she saw me, "What is an emergent quality?" Despite my many earnest (and at times horribly confused) attempts to answer her well-meaning question, she still found it difficult to envision ways that any system—and in particular a musical one—could produce emergent qualities. But for most people this sense of emergence is a very real yet notoriously hard to pin down aspect of all good music.

Steve Johnson, in his book *Emergence*, offers a compelling romp through "the connected lives of ants, brains, cities, and software," and identifies three general historical phases to our fascination with emergence. The first phase involved innovative but often isolated thinkers who sensed forces of self-organization without knowing exactly what they were up against. For not-too-distant examples of this phase we might look to the school of organismic biology or the Romantic movement in art, literature, and philosophy. During the second phase, since roughly the middle of the twentieth century, scientists began to see the benefits of working across disciplinary lines to identify qualities of self-organization. Johnson writes, "By watching the slime mold cells next to ant colonies, you could see the shared behavior in ways that would have been unimaginable watching either on its own."[60] Here we can locate work from the early Macy conferences and the beginnings of cybernetics and systems theory, as well as the formation of the Santa Fe Institute and similar interdisciplinary research centers that make the study of self-organization and complexity their primary focus.[61] In the most recent phase, according to Johnson, only in the past few decades or so, we stopped analyzing emergence and started creating it.

In this third phase we can locate software simulations of cellular automata such as John Conway's deceptively simple yet brazenly titled computer program the "Game of Life." Conway's simulation captures some remarkably complex and lifelike behaviors by modeling the birth, survival, and death of individual cellular automata based solely on their local conditions and a small set of operational rules. On an even grander scale, James Lovelock's computer simulation titled "Daisyworld" models global temperature regulation to support his Gaia theory, which envisions the planetary ecosystem as a type of superorganism. We may also wish to locate in this most recent phase the ways in which our day-to-day life is now swarming with systems designed to exploit the properties of emergence: from network, communication, and global positioning technologies of all types, to the ways in which they are increasingly being combined to harness and increase their collective synergy.

The musical world has witnessed a similar proliferation in the ideas and technologies of emergence. Music making, regardless of cultural or historical particulars, is arguably about emergence, not only in the sonic domain as vibrations coalesce and combine, but more important, in the cognitive and social realms. As Christopher Waterman puts it, "Good music is good consociation."[62] The first phase has been in place since the earliest musical gestures aligned people into emergent groups through the process of shared musicking. Johnson's second phase corresponds roughly to the mid-twentieth-century shift when ideas of improvisation and open and emergent form began to circulate more freely across stylistic and cultural divides, although not without difficulty, as we have seen in previous chapters and will see more in this one. The most recent phase of musical emergence has seen these ideas continue to flourish in disparate corners of the music world, perhaps most dramatically when supported by the convergence of acoustic and electronic music technologies. But although new technologies have frequently made these approaches possible, generative music, as some have dubbed this approach, has strong foundations in the experimental music from earlier phases as well.

In conversation with David Toop, electronic composer Brian Eno discussed how he was attracted to the early minimalist works of Steve Reich and Terry Riley for their economy of compositional materials: "There's so little there. The complexity of the piece appears from nowhere." Reflecting on these experiences and the current shift underway, Eno remarks: "I think one of the changes of our consciousness of how things come into being, of how things are made and how they work, is the change from an engineering paradigm, which is to say a design paradigm, to a biological paradigm, which is an evolutionary one." Favoring these organic metaphors, Eno likens generative music making to gardening. In gardening, you have some degree of control, but you never know precisely what will emerge, since living things respond to changing conditions during their growth. "Generative music," according to Eno, "is like trying to create a seed, as opposed to classical composition, which is like trying to engineer a tree."[63]

Modern biology has done much to shape our thinking about the dynamics of complex systems that can emerge without a grand overseer, but it has been only relatively recently that the collective, cooperative, and bottom-up aspects of biological development have begun to receive their proper due. Darwin's influential theory of evolution described the increased fitness of biological species through natural selection based on random mutations. While his theory has remained a pillar of much modern science, its emphasis on strictly random mutations and the highly competitive aspects of nature (frequently described as "red in tooth and claw") has been challenged by many for its inability to take account of the self-organizing, interconnected, and cooperative aspects of life.

The current orthodox paradigm in biology is Neo-Darwinism, a synthesis of Darwin's theory of evolution by natural selection, Mendel's laws of inheritance, and modern genetic findings from molecular biology. Although considerable new scientific insight has been added to Darwin's original evolutionary ideas, Neo-Darwinism still hinges on the notion that small, undirected, essentially random changes allow for reproductive success and produce evolutionary change. There are, however, an increasing number of dissenting voices that are highlighting the important role that self-organization can play in the evolution of life forms and in the regulatory aspects of life on a planetary scale.[64] As Fritjof Capra explains in *The Web of Life*:

> The driving force of evolution, according to the emerging new theory, is to be found not in the chance events of random mutation, but in life's inherent tendency to create novelty, in the spontaneous emergence of increasing complexity and order. . . . Our focus is shifting from evolution to coevolution—an ongoing dance that proceeds through a subtle interplay of competition and cooperation, creation and mutual adaptation.[65]

"Symbiosis," a term first coined by German botanist Anton DeBary in 1873 to describe the process through which members of different species live in physical contact, has tended to be relegated to specialized biological status. If we learned of the term at all in our high school biology classes, it was most likely illustrated with an example of a parasite: perhaps a tapeworm that can live within the stomach of a dog. But symbiosis is far more prevalent than we were originally led to believe. Lynn Margulis, one of the preeminent researchers dedicated to refocusing contemporary evolutionary theory on the cooperative aspects of life, writes in her book *Symbiotic Planet*: "We are symbionts on a symbiotic planet, and if we care to, we can find symbiosis everywhere."[66]

Microbes are Margulis's true passion. Because they are often construed as primarily agents of disease, their role in regulating the global ecology as well as the health of humans, animals, and plants is often ignored. Additionally, since the microbial world is downplayed in conventional evolutionary theory, so too is the important role that cooperation, sharing, and symbiosis play as sources of innovation in evolution. She writes: "From the level of microorganisms on up to the so-called higher organisms, including multi-cellular plants, animals, and even human beings, sharing is as essential to survival as struggle."[67] According to Margulis and her son Dorion Sagan, "Life did not take over the globe by combat, but by networking."[68]

This belief has led Margulis to the much stronger claim that in certain cases long-term cohabitation results in *symbiogenesis*, the appearance of new tissues, organs, organisms, even new species. Although it has taken some time, her work finally convinced the scientific establishment that cells organized through the permanent incorporation of bacteria as plastids and mitochondria. Margulis believes, however, that *most* evolutionary novelty arose, and still arises, directly from symbiosis.[69] Although gradual changes within a species due to environmental pressures can be well demonstrated by the current theory, the biological community has yet to produce compelling evidence of the formation of even a single new species due solely to natural selection and the gradual accumulation of gene mutations. Unfortunately, as Margulis laments, "the idea that new species arise from symbiotic mergers among members of old ones is still not even discussed in polite scientific society."[70]

Despite the inherently social nature of music performance, the notion of creative cooperation in music composition circles still remains something of a taboo subject as well. Pauline Oliveros's work developed at approximately the same time as Reich's and Reiley's and in great part as a reaction to the dominant "engineering" paradigm that was prevalent in mid-twentieth-century "new music" composition (and to some extent still is today). Her fascination with improvisation, "deep listening," and the integrated body-mind of the performer also positions her strongly within this emerging biological paradigm. Some of her early tape delay pieces were reportedly inspired by hearing the sounds of frogs living in the pond outside of her window at Mills College. When large groups of frogs are calling, an observer can hear startling moments of perfect synchronization, moments in which groups and individuals are slowly moving out of phase with one another, and moments when the calling suddenly stops, all for reasons that are difficult for humans to discern. More than two decades after Oliveros's work, David Dunn made her amphibian inspiration even more tangible in his "Chaos & the Emergent Mind of the Pond," a sound installation that incorporates both ambient field recordings and computer-generated sounds and effects.

Some of Evan Parker's recent projects also reflect a generative or biological perspective in both overt and subtle ways. On perhaps the most overt level, he recently released a recording dedicated to fellow soprano saxophonist Steve Lacy, titled *Evan Parker with Birds*, in which he improvises to bird sounds that were recorded and processed by John Coxon and Ashley Wales of Spring Heel Jack. More subtly, certain aspects of Margulis's sybiogenesis research inspired and shaped his third ECM album with the Electro-Acoustic Ensemble. And for his sixtieth birthday, Parker soloed with the London Symphonietta, improvising to a work that he heard for the very first time during performance. Django Bates had arranged the piece "Premature Celebration" from individual bars of music that had been supplied by composers from around the world though a type of "open source" design. David Toop finds that Parker's improvising can give the impression to listeners that "something is alive and growing, like a timelapse photograph of plant growth, one of the creatures grown in the 'garden of unearthly delights' by William Latham's computational breeding program or the volatile communities generated in Conway's Game of Life."[71]

The English group Morphogenesis demonstrates their connections to the emerging biological paradigm in name as well as in sound and approach. Morphogenesis is a biological term that describes the capacity of all life forms to develop ever more complex and baroque bodies out of impossibly simple beginnings. The group Morphogenesis integrates instrumental, electronic, and environmental sounds into "a kind of hinterland between composition, improvisation, and process/generative music."[72] In concert, they often use remote microphones situated outside the performance venue to add the sounds of wind, rain, or traffic to their evolving improvisations. [73] And group member Michael Prime has created a "bioactivity translator" which he uses on humans and trees among other things in order to incorporate patterns produced by living things into the group's music.

In addition to her Bee Hive project already discussed, Miya Masaoka has created interactive installations that translate a plant's real-time responses to its physical environment into sound. Plants can exhibit a surprisingly complex relationship to their environment, including demonstrating a level of self-recognition, sensing the presence of friends, foes, and food, and challenging and exerting power over other species. Scientists believe that not only can plants communicate with each other and with insects by coded gas exhalations, they can perform cellular computations and remember even the tiniest transgression for months. A testament to the growing notion of "plant smarts," the first-ever conference on plant neurobiology was held in 2005.[74] Masaoka has also explored related projects in the human domain that use medical equipment, such as EEG, EKG, and heart monitors, to make audible the processes of the brain and body. Challenging audiences' cultural as well as sonic perceptions, her most recent version of this work asks, "What Is the Sound of 10 Naked Asian Men?"[75]

The tendency for generative musicians to find inspiration and sound sources outside of the human realm (or directly wired to it!) does raise some particularly hairy questions. Perhaps most controversial of these is the issue of abdicating control of the creative process. David Rothenberg, the author of *Hand's End: Technology and the Limits of Nature* and *Sudden Music: Improvisation, Sound, and Nature*, asks simply: "My main question on generative music is: can we trust machines to create for us?"[76]

One might wish to dismiss this question with the quick answer that computer's don't create, people do. Or better still, if we accept that listeners "create" music, then the question becomes unimportant, since humans will do the "creating" regardless of who or what generated the stimulus. But the notion that computers are simply the tool with which people do their creating deserves some scrutiny. This line of reasoning implies that, just as writing can be used to quite different effects by different authors, computers simply provide a platform and a means for human creativity. This just-a-tool answer, however, fails to distinguish between those tools whose main role is to improve a user's ability to do a pre-existing job and those tools that can in fact create a job that nobody thought to do, or nobody could have done, before.

Although computers are extremely good at storing and retrieving large amounts of data, this is an example of their ability to improve on a pre-existing job: humans were already able to store and retrieve data. It often takes considerable time before the possibilities inherent in a new technology become apparent.[77] Early film was described as "photographed theater." And when Edison invented the phonograph he envisioned an automatic Dictaphone, not a technology that would go on to shape dramatically our relationship with music: not only where and how we hear it but also how we create, manipulate, and define it, and how we define ourselves in relationship to it.

Applications like Conway's Game of Life and Resnick's StarLogo simulations demonstrate that computers may be best suited to modeling emergent and decentralized forms of order: those qualities that tend to be difficult for humans to conceptualize easily. Mitchel Resnick finds that when students work with computers in this way it helps them to internalize a sense of emergent behavior, making intuitive something that may at first seem rather counterintuitive. Along these same lines, Brian Eno recounts his early experiences with Conway's Game of Life at the San Francisco Exploratorium:

> *Life* was the first thing I ever saw on a computer that interested me: almost the last actually, as well. For many, many years I didn't see anything else. I saw all sorts of work being done on computers that I thought was basically a reiteration of things that had been better done in other ways. Or that were pointlessly elaborate. I didn't see many things that had this degree of class to them. A very simple beginnings and a very complex endings [*sic*].[78]

Computers can and do assist composers in hearing and notating their ideas, improving on their ability to do a pre-existing job. But their generative possibilities offer a window into musical orderings and possibilities that were, for the most part, unimaginable beforehand. Yet we must be careful, since even these "decentralized" approaches to generative music making can mask certain cultural assumptions. Perhaps the more insidious concern raised by ongoing human-machine interactions is in what ways do they reflect notions about the nature and functions of music that may already be deeply embedded in their construction and use?

Writing about human-computer interactions in general and his *Voyager* system in particular, George Lewis finds that, "Interactions with these systems tend to reveal characteristics of the community of thought and culture that produced them." Many have commented on the problematic and biased language often adopted by computer engineers in general. For instance, it has become commonplace to talk about machine intelligence, memory, or languages in ways that not only encourage the dangerous metaphor of humans as machines but ignores the fact that these terms are full of rich, subtle, and not always well-understood meanings in the human realm. And the language of computer use is filled with military and masculine metaphors of control—enter, escape, command, target, master, slave, etc.

New technologies can also, if implemented uncritically, mask the ways in which decisions about the integrity, usefulness, and by connection the funding of public art are culturally sanctioned. The dangers of evoking a biological paradigm without also being alert to this unquestioned cultural dimension have played out many times before as well, perhaps most notoriously in Social Darwinism. Social Darwinism saw only competition in nature, and in its application it was very much allied with the notion of systems organized "by lead." The emerging symbiotic outlook that emphasizes the continual cooperation and codependence of all living things may make us less fearful of these metaphorical forays from biology into the social sphere.

But care must always be taken not to accept current scientific wisdom at face value when the concerns of people are involved. In his book *Silicon Second Nature*, anthropologist Stefan Helmreich offers an ethnography of the Santa Fe Institute and argues that the artificial-life models being explored there reflect the unconscious cultural assumptions and social prejudices of their creators: "Because Artificial Life scientists tend to see themselves as masculine gods of their cyberspace creations, as digital Darwins exploring frontiers filled with primitive creatures, their programs reflect prevalent representations of gender, kinship, and race and repeat origin stories most familiar from mythical and religious narratives."[79] Simulation models, just like their generative counterparts, may serve as a type of Rorschach test, revealing the researcher/creator's cultural background and psychological idiosyncracies. Lewis, well aware of these types of criticisms, argues that his *Voyager* program explores a type of multidominance that is central to African-American aesthetics and musical practices.

Composers such as John Cage, however, seem to propose with pieces like *The Music of Changes* (1951) an inverted formulation of Rothenberg's question: "Can we trust humans to create music?"[80] And Eno, although often characterizing generative music as a polar opposite of most "classical" music, talks of "removing personality" from his music and of giving the music no more prominence than a painting hanging on the wall, preferably a landscape without a foreground figure. The newest forms of generative composition demonstrate that music can now easily be made that is inherently unpredictable, unrepeatable, and unfinished: a situation for which our notions of "composer" as leader do not comfortably apply. But these systems, as currently conceived, rely on an initial "seed" planted by an individual who is external to the system and who then stands back and observes the result from a distance. To this person, whether "engineer" or "gardener," we still attribute the usual benefits and baggage that accompany the notion of "composer." At a lecture on his concept of generative music making, Eno remarked:

> If you move away from the idea of the composer as someone who creates a complete image and then step back from it, there's a different way of composing. It's putting in motion something and letting it make the thing for you. . . . This is music for free in a sense. The considerations that are important, then, become questions of how the system works and most important of all what you feed into the system.[81]

Eno's words may bring to mind, for some, biologist Stuart Kauffman's notion of emergence as "order for free." But in the biological world, as in our social one, this order can and does come at a cost: species die out and cultures are diminished or extinguished.

For now at least, there does appear to be a split between those most interested in exploring emergent properties on computers and those most interested in doing so in the human social realm. Acknowledging perhaps a growing divide in the new and improvised music communities, Evan Parker remarked: "If the more instrumental approach, the more expressive approach is gradually succeeded by the PowerBook players and the very quiet players, you'd have to say it has evolved into something else or it simply died out depending on the way those successors choose to represent their activities."[82]

Music making has always had an intimate relationship with technologies. And perhaps that relationship has always been perceived, in varying and overlapping ways, as able to facilitate, constrain, and even coopt aspects of human creativity. But for improvisers, a human element of risk and empathy does often remain paramount. Pianist Denman Maroney, in a recent presentation at UCSD, demonstrated how he uses various bars, bowls, and sticks made of copper, rubber, and plastic inside of a standard grand piano to produce an enormous vocabulary of "hyperpiano" sounds. These tools, at times remnants of new technologies (CD jewel boxes, for instance), allow him to unlock timbres and textures inside the piano in both well and not-so-well-understood ways. Early in his career, Maroney spent several years sampling these hyperpiano sounds to be used in performance in order to avoid the stares of worried club owners who imagined that their instruments were being damaged. But he was never satisfied with the results. The samples always reproduced the exact same sounds, denying him the joy, as he put it, of wallowing in the tension between determinate and indeterminate outcomes. (Of course current generative and processing techniques might allow for a more interactive approach with digital technology.)

Even when he plays on the instrument in the conventional manner, Maroney has devised extremely complex ways of composing and improvising using up to three layered rhythmic cycles at a time. For example, he might play a pulse of seven beats atop one of six beats atop one of five beats, using various registral and articulation decisions to differentiate the voices. And he often takes advantage of the rare points of coincidence (210 beats in this example) to affect formal changes in the music. Inspired as a child by the chirping of crickets and the sawing of his woodworking father, he set out to capture the sounds of chaos but paradoxically arrived there through a very deterministic solution. Even though he has used computers to hear these and other more complicated rhythmic layerings, Maroney insisted that he is interested in the human aspect of performance: the opportunity to make difficult things sound easy and easy things sound difficult that can only come from human intentionality and action. He also hopes to maintain those childhood feelings that led him to explore these complexities in the first place.

One of the challenges of continuing to incorporate computers into musical performance will be to create this sense of empathy for human listeners. This obstacle may not be insurmountable, and the simple fact the people often become very attached to their computers is an encouraging first sign. But computer "musicians" do not (yet) have a body as such, and it will remain difficult for listeners to empathize with them in the same way that they can with human performers.[83] Yet generative and decentralized behaviors already seem to have an inherent pull on our psyches: the unexpected success of screen saver programs that exhibit unending processes of transformation would seem to offer some indication of this as well.

Mitchel Resnick found that his StarLogo slime-mold program tended to evoke very different interpretations from different observers: an economist was reminded of the development of cities; an educational researcher saw instead the interaction of children in classrooms as they form learning communities; a business student envisioned information flowing through an organization; and finally a Zen student saw people in search of religion. When people constructed their own multiagent simulations, Resnick also found that they frequently became deeply invested in the fate of their "turtles" and the outcome of their virtual worlds. One student compared the experience to visiting a relative in the hospital and watching the heart monitor alongside the bed continually fluctuating.[84]

To return to the question that began this section, why do people assume that systems are organized either by lead or by seed? In part, this is undoubtedly due to the fact that many if not most of our social institutions and artistic creations *are* organized in this way. Our schools, businesses, and even families often carry with them a strong notion of hierarchy and control (perhaps too much at times, although certainly some of it is needed). When people hear music they tend to assume a composer, a leader. And in many cases this intuition is also right. But one of the more encouraging aspects of much contemporary music is that it is not always easy or even possible to know if a particular instance of music was or was not composed ahead of time.[85] And the generative power of computers is blurring these lines even further. Perhaps most encouraging of all, however, is the fact that creativity is increasingly being viewed as a web of network interactions operating on all scales, reflecting individual, social, cultural, and historical dimensions. An extreme reliance on centralized organization and centralized metaphors in the past has led to a situation in which many people are unwilling or unable to imagine systems organizing in a decentralized fashion. Decentralization may be biologically coded for ants and other social insects, but it does not seem to be as natural or automatic for humans. Or it may simply be that, because we are within the system, we remain unaware of its emergent properties, just as individual bees and ants may be unaware of their group's emergent social organization (although this hypothesis is difficult if not impossible to test).[86] At any rate, we appear to be living in an age of increasing complexity and increasing decentralization. Yet when confronted with complex situations that negate the possibility of a clear leader, most people will assume that an external seed is responsible for a given pattern. For instance, when people are stuck in a traffic jam they invariably want to find *the* reason that their trip is being delayed. Is there an accident? Are they doing construction? Did the police pull someone over or set up a radar trap?[87]

In general these can be useful intuitions and in many cases they may even be correct. As Resnick sees it, "The problem is that people have too narrow a conception of seeds. They think of only preexisiting inhomogeneities in the environment. . . . In self-organizing systems seeds are neither preexisting nor externally imposed. Rather, self-organizing systems create *their own* seeds."[88] The majority of traffic patterns (and therefore delays) are simply caused by the pattern of the cars themselves: the density and arrangement of the parts within the whole. No external seed is needed to produce an emergent structure.

When envisioning the shift toward decentralization, we may also be guilty of looking for *the* catalyst, *the* domain that is sparking decentralization in all of the others. Are new decentralized scientific models influencing the way we design technologies, conceive of organizations, and envision art? Or are new technologies provoking us to view the natural world, ourselves, and our interactions with society in more decentralized ways? Or does the activity of art provoke us to feel emergence and decentralization in ways that affect how we live in and engage with the world around us? And if we believe this to be the case, which art form is provoking the others?

It seems better to view these domains and practices as a type of autocatalytic system in which the decentralization of each domain reinforces and catalyzes the decentralization of the others. The network structure of social, economic, artistic, and scientific organizations continually impacts how ideas circulate and which ideas are deemed valuable? Resnick writes: "Most likely, there is no single, ultimate cause. Each domain provides new models and new metaphors that influence the others, refining and accelerating the decentralization trend."[89] As we saw in the previous chapter, however, musicking can provide an especially powerful "consequence-free" space for playfully exploring new modes of interaction, organization, and understanding.

A Web Without a Spider

> In the new systems thinking, the metaphor of knowledge as a building is being replaced by that of a network. As we perceive reality as a network of relationships, our descriptions, too, form an interconnected network of concepts and models in which there are no foundations.[90]
>
> —Fritjof Capra

> For mathematicians and physicists, the biggest surprise is that complexity lurks within extremely simple systems. For biologists, it is the idea that natural selection is not the sole source of order in the biological world. As for the social sciences, I suggest that emergence—the idea that complex global patterns with new properties may emerge from local interactions—may someday have a comparable impact.[91]
>
> —Stephen Lansing

Because we tend to value individualism and innovation so highly in this culture, we have often fostered, directly and indirectly, the notion that individual musicians spin their own individual web from whole cloth as they create. But as we move our gaze into the social and historical realm, and we realize that all thought is in fact social, the notion that any one individual is controlling the unfolding web becomes rather untenable. Models that focus on the creativity of individuals are not wrong, but like Newtonian science, they may be inappropriate for trying to make sense of certain types of phenomena. What we need are new models operating at a different level. As much as we may be conditioned to imagine our selves and our leaders as in control, the complex and interconnected age we inhabit is making it increasingly clear that structure and organization can emerge both without lead and even without seed. What happens and how it happens depends on the nature of the network.

Music, as an inherently social practice, thrives on network organization. On perhaps the most tangible level, a musician's livelihood and creative opportunities frequently depend on the breadth and depth of one's network of social and professional contacts. But network dynamics shape the sounds, practices, and communities of music in decidedly more complex and subtle ways as well. Musicians are influenced by their years of training or apprenticeship, countless hours spent listening to music both publicly and privately, and perhaps most comprehensively (yet frequently least acknowledged) by the historical and cultural conventions of a given time and locale. The topics and techniques of music education also depend on these network-style dynamics, which inform the process of choosing canons and of exploring and imparting the intricacies of musical theory and musical aesthetics. Finally the music industry's far-reaching networks of production and distribution, and increasingly its consolidated and insular organizational practices, have the power to structure, to some degree or another, the networks of inspiration and possibility for nearly everyone who is deeply committed to music.

What implications does the study of networks have for musical scholarship and, more broadly, for our understandings of human creativity, history, and culture? Networks may organize not only the social world of musical performance (with whom you play) but also the ideascapes of musical creativity (by whom you are influenced and what you chose to create) and the realities of musical community (how historical, cultural, and economic factors often dictate which musicians and musical ideas gain notice and prestige). Well aware of these concerns, George Lewis writes in a recent essay reflecting on improvisation and the orchestra:

> Orchestra performers operate as part of a network comprised not only of musicians, composers and conductors, but also administrators, foundations, critics and the media, historians, educational institutions, and much more. Each of the nodes within this network, not just those directly making music, would need to become "improvisation-aware," as part of a process of resocialization and economic restructuring that could help bring about the transformation of the orchestra that so many have envisioned.[92]

Networks make communication and community possible, but they can also concentrate power and opportunities in the hands of a few. In this section I explore some recent insights from the emerging fields of network study in order to investigate some ways in which musical studies might productively grapple with the complex of factors that establish, maintain, expand, and even destroy musical communities.

Although networks have interested researchers for decades, until recently, each system tended to be treated in isolation, with little apparent reason or possible means to see if its organizational dynamics had anything in common with other networks. From molecules to microorganisms, plants to people, and genes to Gaia, networks play a crucial role in shaping our physical and biological worlds. On the social level, networks also organize the structure and activities of everything from families and friends to corporate boards and terrorist cells. Additionally, layers of technology continue to facilitate and, at times, impede these network dynamics. Electric power lines and transportation routes crisscross the country. Satellites relay signals to distant parts of the planet. And the World Wide Web is already linking ideas and information in ways that cannot be easily predicted nor understood. We are only now beginning to piece together some important qualities of, and approaches to, the study of complex dynamic networks on a broad scale. But Albert-László Barabási, one of the leading researchers in this still nascent field, optimistically predicts: "Network thinking is poised to invade all domains of human activity and most fields of human inquiry. It is more than another helpful perspective or tool. Networks are by their very nature the fabric of most complex systems, and nodes and links deeply infuse all strategies aimed at approaching our interlocked universe."[93]

The notion of networks may bring to mind rather bare-boned models of how things are connected. To some extent this is true, since simplifying detail on one level of a network can highlight organizational similarities on another that would otherwise go unnoticed. Perhaps the most compelling example of this is the way in which Lynn Margulis's research into symbiosis in microbiology, combined with James Lovelock's research into the self-regulating aspects of the Earth's atmosphere, has led to the notion that "Gaia is just symbiosis as seen from space": all organisms are coexisting symbiotically since they are all bathed in the same air and the same flowing water.[94]

Network models, however, are increasingly able to take account of some of the rich dynamics that occur when individual components are not only doing something—generating power, sending data, even making decisions—but also are affecting one another over time. Steven Shaviro writes in his book *Connected, Or What It Means to Live in the Network Society*:

As it seems to us now, a network is a self-generating, self-organizing, self-sustaining system. It works through multiple feedback loops. These loops allow the system to monitor and modulate its own performance continually and thereby maintain a state of homeostatic equilibrium. At the same time, these feedback loops induce effects of interference, amplifications, and resonance. And such effects permit the system to grow, both in size and in complexity. Beyond this, a network is always nested in a hierarchy. From the inside, it seems to be entirely self-contained, but from the outside, it turns out to be part of a still larger network.[95]

The notion of "six degrees of separation," based on an experiment by sociologist Stanley Milgram, has popularized "small-world" networks to many.[96] But despite this intriguing idea, that individuals are much more closely linked than might normally be imagined, we still know very little about how these network dynamics evolve. How can six billion people on the planet be linked so closely? And if this *is* the case, why are we usually unaware of this small-world property? Are there ways that we might more successfully navigate in a small-world, to take advantage of these close connections? Or are others already doing so in ways that make for an inherent power imbalance? What are the implications of small-world properties for other networks besides our network of friends? And how does the structure of networks change over time or reflect both internal and external dynamics? As Duncan Watts summarizes:

> Networks are dynamic objects not just because things happen in networked systems, but because the networks themselves are evolving and changing in time, driven by the activities or decisions of those very components. In the connected age, therefore, *what happens and how it happens depend on the network*. And the network depends on what has happened previously.[97]

Watts, along with Steve Strogatz, his advisor at Cornell University, started off working on the synchronized chirping of crickets. But Watts's research direction changed dramatically when his father asked him during a phone conversation if the notion of six degrees of separation might relate to his work on sync. Strogatz and Watts decided to see if they could shed some mathematical light on the subject. They gave themselves a semester, thinking either that the problem had most likely already been tackled, or that it might not lead anywhere productive.

The problem, simply stated, is if we imagine the six billion people on the planet as six billion dots, how can we connect them so that they will exhibit this small degree of separation. Our first instinct might be an orderly, linear approach. But to achieve six degrees of separation, each individual would need to be connected to approximately 250 million people. This is hardly a realistic model of our network of friends.

For graph problems that are more complex than linear approaches would allow, mathematicians have used random distributions as a working approximation.[98] If we, instead, connect each individual dot randomly to fifty friends (a more reasonable figure), at six degrees of separation we arrive at upwards of fifteen billion connections, enough to cover our global population and then some. But although a random model did produce the desired result, Watts and Strogatz were troubled by its inability to conform to common sense. Although fifty friends may sound like a reasonable figure for one individual, does each of our friends in turn have fifty distinct friends, who in turn have fifty more distinct friends? Even more troubling, is each new group of fifty friends connected randomly across the globe? This was a tough pill to swallow, even in our interconnected age. In short, random graphs pay no attention to physical proximity or similarity of habit. What Watts and Strogatz needed was a graph that is neither entirely ordered nor entirely random.

They found their answer in a 1973 paper by sociologist Mark Granovetter titled "The Strength of Weak Ties." By asking people about how they got referred to their current job, Granovetter found that 84% reported that the contact was through a friend or associate whom they only saw rarely. Only 16% got jobs through a close contact. Granovetter realized that these weaker ties linked together more distant parts of the social network. A rumor, fad, or fashion, for example, will spread much farther if it is not only shared with close friends, but also with a few more distant ones who are connected to other social groups as well.

Drawing on Granovetter's insight, Watts and Strogatz created a graph that linked close friends in an orderly manner, but also added a few random "weak ties" that could easily span large distances. Their "small-world" model exhibited the high degree of clustering we would expect in social situations, but also the low degree of separation that Milgram had first uncovered, which allows for unexpected surprises.[99] And their model even offered some insight into the way in which fireflies and crickets synchronize.

Our own brains appear to exploit small-world properties as well.[100] There are approximately six billion neurons in a marble-sized portion of our gray matter. And clustering plays an important role in localized processing centers. But long-distance axons can link different parts of the cerebral cortex in ways that appear to facilitate the integrated and instantaneous qualities of consciousness. These weak ties allow for speed, flexibility, efficiency, and resilience in cognitive functioning. Recent research on our working (or short-term) memory also points to a small-world dynamic, in which neurons participate in self-sustaining burst of electrical activity in order to store a memory temporarily.

Although only limited work has been done on music networks to date, one study that explored the relationships between jazz musicians from 1912 to 1940 found small-world properties. By using the Red Hot Jazz Archive database on the Internet, Pablo Gleiser and Leon Danon found that, on average, early jazz musicians were separated from one another by only 2.79 steps. Their model also captured the clustering of jazz musicians by geography, with New York and Chicago as the major hubs, and by race, due to the highly segregated nature of the music industry at the time. As in most human networks, a few individuals had very high degrees of connectivity. Guitarist Eddie Lang topped their list, with connections to 415 other musicians, while artists like Jack Teagarden, Joe Venuti, and Louis Armstrong were all in the top ten of most connected musicians. A similar study with more contemporary artists might uncover interesting properties of clustering and connectivity as well.

This notion of extremely well-connected hubs highlights some shortcomings of the Watts and Strogatz model that were illuminated by the work of Albert-Laszlo Barabási and his team working at Notre Dame University. Although Watts and Strogatz captured the high clustering and small degree of separation that is characteristic of small-world networks, their model was not dynamic. It did not take account of the evolution that is characteristic of all real-world networks, in which new nodes may be added all the time, and established nodes—those already with many connections—tend to attract even more.

Barabási and his team were interested in understanding the network organization of the Internet and the World Wide Web.[101] No one knows the exact structure of either. They have connected in exceedingly complex ways as an unavoidable consequence of their evolution, and they continue to do so. But by sending out "robots" to scour the Internet for connection information, Barabási was able to show that the Internet and the World Wide Web demonstrate small-world properties. It typically takes no more than four network connections to transmit an email from the United States to Hong Kong, and never more than ten. And with over one billion pages, the World Wide Web demonstrates only nineteen degrees of separation (nineteen clicks can get you from any page on the web to any other). Even with the expected thousand-fold increase in the next five years, that number should only increase to twenty-one.

The data that Barabási and his team uncovered, however, did not conform to the mathematics of Watts and Strogatz. Barabási found enormous hubs and an extreme disparity in the connectivity of various nodes that could not be explained through "weak ties" alone. Their data represented what we might intuitively expect about the World Wide Web, given the prominence of sites such as Yahoo, Amazon, or Google and the huge number of personal web pages that are often linked to very few others. The exact distribution that Barabási found is called "scale-free," and it can be described mathematically by a power law. Unlike the well-known bell curve, in which the majority of individuals fall in the middle of a given range (e.g., the average height of adults, or the average grades in a class), power laws imply that there is no expected or average size. When plotted on a logarithmic graph, the connectivity of the World Wide Web produces a descending straight line, which means that as the number of links increases, the number of web pages with that many links decreases exponentially. In other words, there are many poorly connected web pages and only a few with huge numbers of links.

We commonly think of this principle as "the rich get richer," and it was first identified by Vilfredo Pareto, who noted that 80% of the property in Italy was owned by 20% of the population. Often referred to simply as the 80/20 principle, this relationship offers a reasonable approximation for the wealth distribution on local, regional, national, and even international levels.[102] Recently, the 80/20 principle has been applied to a large variety of managerial situations, many of which are true, some of which are not.[103] Barabási describes this general principle as preferential attachment, and he offers a few network situations that approximate this 80/20 rule well: 80 percent of links on the web point to only 15 percent of web pages, 80 percent of citations go to only 38 percent of scientists, 80 percent of links in Hollywood are connected to 30 percent of actors.[104] Many natural systems demonstrate power laws with slightly different exponents, including the metabolic network within the cell, the network of inlets and outlets produced by river formation, the distribution of earthquakes due to tectonic shift, even the network organization behind the English language (Zipf's law).[105] But why do these diverse systems appear to share a similar design? What do power laws imply (other than nonlinearity)?

One clue is in their evolutionary history. Hubs tend to emerge in systems that are complex, operate without a designer, and take account of the compounding effects of historical development. For instance, visible web pages attract links, visible researchers attract citations and coauthors, and well-connected musicians attract both attention and imitation. Two qualities are essential for scale-free organization to emerge in a system: growth and preferential attachment. Growth offers a clear advantage to senior nodes, but preferential attachment can, in some instances, allow relative latecomers to quickly establish themselves as hubs.

Barabási's more detailed network models take account of both external growth—the new links that are formed as new nodes are continually added to a system—and internal growth, which may involve the disappearance or rewiring of existing nodes and links. In the social realm, these internal dynamics correlate to the fact that senior members of a community may begin to take in fewer new connections or may lose connections as they age or retire. In the business world, while early arrivals certainly prosper, established companies can lose their edge and rival companies with innovative ideas or products can attract their customer base and outpace them.

In the real world there are also limits to growth potential. These can take the form of control factors that are imposed on a system, or they may be due to the inherent costs associated with continual growth. Many explicitly designed systems display more uniform qualities than a scale-free network. For example, dictatorships aim to keep the power in the exclusive hands of the ruling class and to ensure that all others are kept in a roughly equal subordinate position. And networks such as the interstate highway system or the electrical power grid have been purposefully designed to have roughly the same number of connections between each node. The airline industry, however, is based on the idea that a few centralized hubs can, in turn, connect passengers to smaller flights and farther flung destinations. As these hubs grew, they tended to attract more and more business from different carriers looking to increase their own numbers and connections—a clear example of the scale-free properties of growth and preferential attachment. But airline hubs can also become overloaded, resulting in reduced efficiency and cancelled or delayed flights, potentially encouraging smaller carriers to find less-traveled markets in which to locate their business (e.g., the Southwest Airlines business model that has proven so successful). In the real world, unlike on the Internet, adding new links can carry with it considerable costs (financial, social, psychological, etc.). For many networks, there is a point at which adding new links becomes increasingly difficult or begins to have a negative impact, and this can place an upper limit on scale-free growth.

Barabási found that for his models to be more realistic he also needed to include an intrinsic property for each node, a fitness factor, that could account for the ability of newcomers to succeed in a rich-get-richer environment. For instance, Google has emerged as the undisputed hub of the search engine market even though it was preceded in the marketplace by several years by Yahoo! and AltaVista among others. Due to Google's superior technologies, its fitness factor outweighed the advantage of the earlier arrivals. Barabási calls this "beauty over age" or the "fit get rich" principle[106] Even in these more involved models of dynamic networks, as long as growth and preferential attachment are at work, a scale-free organization almost invariably follows, although the exact power law coefficient can vary considerably.

Scale-free organization tends to fail only when the competition or interconnectivity of a system is in some way jeopardized. For instance, Microsoft managed to create an environment in which healthy competition and a natural hierarchy are all but absent, producing the near-monopoly situation we see today in computer operating systems.[107] One of Barabási's students, Ginestra Bianconi, calculated that in terms of topology, all networks fall into one of only two possible categories: either the "fit get rich" behavior of competitive hierarchies or the "winner takes all" behavior of a system that has reached a tipping point.

With this critical juncture in mind, much of the research on network dynamics has been concerned with their robustness. How will the Internet fare if a given number of routers fail? How will a given disease spread based on its infection rate and the society's network dynamics? How will a given species extinction effect the global ecosystem? Or conversely, what is the best strategy for producing failure in a network of terrorist cells? Scale-free networks, it turns out, are remarkably resistant to random fluctuations—a very good reason for them to be favored in natural systems. Remove a

163

few links or nodes at random and a scale-free system will often reorganize and continue as if unaffected. But under focused attack, scale-free systems do not hold up so well. Removing a few central hubs can produce far greater damage, from which a system may not be able to recover. For instance, the quite common failures of routers on the Internet rarely create a significant problem, but if one were to target just a few main hubs and disable them completely, the entire system might fail. Similarly, the global ecosystem appears able to recover from random events and extinctions, but biologists are concerned that if a few keystone species are lost, the functioning of the entire system may be jeopardized.

Are there lessons in all of this network research for musical studies? One lesson of network thinking in the social domain is that the emergence of well-connected hubs cannot be attributed solely to the properties of individuals. To attribute the inequities of Pareto's principle strictly to the "talent" of individuals—whether we are discussing money or music—is to miss the point that emergent structure is also shaped in important ways by the dynamics of the system. Many of the first generation of free jazz innovators—Cecil Taylor, Ornette Coleman, Albert Ayler, and John Coltrane—had their work dismissed by critics and musicians alike. And for every artist that was eventually able to land a record deal, how many went unrecorded? The reemergence of players like Sonny Simmons, Charles Gayle, and most recently Henry Grimes attests to the fact that countless skilled and innovative musicians do not fare well in the network of the music industry. And even those who did—Miles Davis and Sonny Rollins among others—voluntarily dropped out for lengthy periods to reassess their creative direction. If the quality of their work simply spoke for itself, then why did it take so long for others to recognize it? This is not to deny the merits of any individual's work, only to acknowledge that countless other factors play a role both in how that work is accomplished and in how one's work is brought to the attention of others.

Network thinking demonstrates that, because power laws emerge in a network from the compounding effect of historical development, our standard explanations for the observed inequities in the world may not be correct. They may simply be describing what Jared Diamond calls proximate causes. In his important book titled *Guns, Germs, and Steel,* Diamond highlights how geographic differences, including climate and the availability of crops and animals for domestication, played a more fundamental role in producing the global inequities of the modern era than those proximate causes referenced in his title that are usually offered as explanation.[108]

But this should not be seen as providing an incontrovertible explanation for continuing inequities. Although scale-free networks imply a certain disparity—an increasing number of better-connected hubs—the range of this disparity can vary dramatically. To return to Pareto's principle of wealth distribution, although 80/20 is a decent approximation across various locales and scales, economies can veer closer to 90/10 or 70/30. In general, more spending across the board redistributes wealth, and taxation operates as a type of forced trade, but more unregulated investment can increase wealth disparity. If investment irregularities overwhelm the natural distribution of wealth via transactions, an economy may "tip" into an extreme range in which only a few hubs, the equivalent of Bill Gates's Microsoft, prosper. In Mexico, for instance, by some accounts the richest 40 people control 30% of the total wealth of the country. The Mexican economy may have already tipped into this extreme range. More exchange between people does not remove a power law, but it can make it less severe.

In music, the disparity of attention also seems to be regulated through the process of interaction. This can come in the direct form of collaboration between artists, but also in the indirect form of media attention, record sales, performance opportunities, and arts funding or sponsorship. While the improvised music world may seem insulated from the rapid fads and fashions of the music industry on the whole—in both desirable and undesirable ways—even here the logic of networks can be hard to dispute. Derek Bailey often adamantly denounces his title as one of the "grandfathers" of free improvisation, but his career and creative work is still shaped in dramatic ways by the network that has bequeathed him this "dubious" honor. And this is true no less for those who readily accept the acclaim that they are offered.[109]

As any musical tradition expands in scope and popularity, better-connected "hubs" will tend to emerge. In jazz, for example, the "hubs" of Armstrong, Ellington, Parker, Davis, and Coltrane are impossible to ignore. During their lifetimes they were well respected and well connected (although not always early in their careers and not by everyone) and their influence has only grown since. With the spread of jazz education and the increasing reliance of major labels on re-releasing canonical jazz recordings, the visibility and "connectedness" of these hubs may only continue to grow. In the last few years, Columbia, Atlantic, and Verve have all drastically reduced their roster of living artists in favor of re-releasing older material. Even the Marsalises, perhaps the most visible jazz performers today, no longer have a major record deal. David Hajdu perceptively writes in a recent *Atlantic Monthly* spread on Wynton: "Where the young lions saw role models and their critics saw idolatry, the record companies saw brand names—the ultimate prize of American marketing. For long established record companies with a vast archive of historic recordings, the economies were irresistible: it is far more profitable to wrap new covers around albums paid for generations ago than it is to find, record, and promote new artists."[110]

For an artistic tradition to remain dynamic and healthy, however, the scale-free dynamics that take note of history and provide hubs for a common language and style should not become too powerful. The hubs of the "great person" approach to jazz instruction ensure that the music is not in jeopardy of disappearing, since scale-free networks are inherently resilient to minor fluctuations. Pops, Duke, Bird, Miles, and Trane will continue to be remembered, esteemed, and emulated—as they should be. And as individual clubs, record labels, local scenes, and musicians come and go, there is no possibility of these established styles of jazz practice evaporating on the whole. But if the disparity between the hubs and the remainder becomes too great, there may be a "tipping point" beyond which communication and innovation in a tradition can suffer dramatically.[111] In the same *Atlantic Monthly* article, Jeff Levinson, the former Columbia Jazz executive, is quoted as saying: "The Frankenstein monster has turned on its creators. In paying homage to the greats, Wynton and his peers have gotten supplanted by them in the minds of the populace. They've gotten supplanted by dead people."[112]

Another lesson of network thinking is that power law dynamics happen on every scale through the process of growth and preferential attachment. When physicists find power laws, they often conclude that a system is poised at a critical state, on the border of disorder and order. Power laws, in fact, are at the heart of many of the discoveries of chaos theory, including fractals and phase transitions. Like fractals, power laws display a type of self-similarity, in which the properties of the system operate on all scales; they are "scale-free."[113] The discovery of power laws has allowed scientists to claim that there are universal principles behind many complex networks. But does this imply that all real networks that display scale-free dynamics are on the edge of randomness and chaos or en route from a random to an ordered state? Not necessarily. Barabási attributes this scale-free topology to the fact that organizing principles are acting at each stage of the network formation process. As the earlier chapters have argued, the process of nonlinear growth does appear to function across scales, from individuals to ensembles, and from communities to cultures.

While this topological insight on the nature of complex webs can be interesting, does network theory have anything to say about ways in which to navigate the web? While contemplating the Watts and Strogatz small-world model, Jon Kleinberg, a professor at Cornell, wondered how individuals in a network might actually find the shortest path. Milgram's original "six degrees" experiment had asked people in Nebraska to send a letter to a specific stockbroker in Boston by passing it on to a close friend that might be in a better position to know the target person. Kleinberg wondered how these folks might have arrived at their decision. He reasoned that they used contextual cues to pick an optimal person to whom to forward the letter. Geography may be the most obvious clue—think of someone near Boston who could help out—but the other cues were undoubtedly based on things like profession, class, race, income, education, religion, or personal interests: in short, all of the social cues that people use every day to identify themselves and others. These are technically called "affiliation networks," and the fact that Watts and Strogatz did not even consider these options to make their original model more realistic is a telling reminder that, while attempting to simplify situations and problems, scientists often ignore those characteristics that add complexities, challenges, and meaning to our daily lives.

Kleinberg realized that the random "weak ties" of the small-world model did not conform at all to the reality of how people make decisions. So he devised a variation in which the probability of a random link connecting two nodes decreases with their distance apart.[114] In other words, his model makes those connections that link together extremely distant parts of the network less likely, while more moderate "weak ties" occur more frequently. Mathematically, Kleinberg's model demonstrates that the "ideal" small-world network in terms of "searchability" would follow an inverse square law, implying that each person has the same number of friends in their neighborhood as in the rest of the region, the rest of the country, and the rest of the world. Although certainly an idealized situation, this may increasingly be the case for many individuals—and in particular musicians—who travel extensively and who rely on telecommunications technologies to maintain their network of contacts. Kleinberg found the perfect drawing to illustrate this principle: a 1976 *New Yorker* cartoon that shows 9th Avenue taking up roughly as much space as an entire city block, which in turn occupies the same space as the rest of Manhattan, the rest of the United States, and the rest of the world.[115]

Watts, inspired by Kleinberg's research, developed a more nuanced model that took account of a *homophily parameter*, named after the sociological tendency of like to associate with like. Watts's new model could now begin to take account of the fact that people, in order to maximize the efficiency of their small-world searches, take account of multiple social variables at the same time. The notion of "distance" from the original model no longer applied simply to geographical remove, but also to how one perceives themselves as more or less distant to others based on a variety of social factors.

People who share a profession, for instance, may regard themselves as close even if they live in different parts of the country or world. Watts reasoned that the multidimensional nature of individual social identity enables messages to be transmitted via a network even in the face of what might appear to be daunting social barriers.

The physicists and mathematicians whose work had propelled modern network theory into the spotlight finally had to take a dose of sociological reality. The field of sociology is intimately concerned with the relationship between individual agency and social and network structures. And some remarkable insights have emerged from analyses that take into account the dynamics of individuals, the role or position that they may take in social groups, and the ways in which social groups are related to the network structure of economic, political, and religious organizations. But sociologists have also been guilty of centralized conceptions of networks, searching for those key individuals or institutions that wield the most influence. Watts, who recently took a post as a professor of sociology at Columbia University, has a different view:

> But what if there just isn't any center? Or what if there are many "centers" that are not necessarily coordinated or even on the same side? What if the important innovations originate not in the core of a network but in its peripheries, where the chief information brokers are too busy to watch? . . . In such cases, the network centrality of individuals, or any centrality for that matter, would tell us little or nothing about the outcome, *because the center emerges only as a consequence of the event itself.*[116]

Actor-Network Theory (ANT), a sociological approach that has emerged out of science and technology studies, is geared toward embodying this very tension between the centered "actor" on the one hand and the decentered "network" on the other. As John Law, one of the field's leading researchers, remarks: "In one sense the word [actor network theory] is thus a way of performing both an elision and a difference between what Anglophones distinguish by calling 'agency' and 'structure.'"[117] In short, ANT does not accept the notion that there is a macrosocial system on the one hand, and bits and pieces of derivative microsocial detail on the other. According to Law:

> If we do this we close off most of the interesting questions about the origins of power and organization. Instead we should start with a clean slate. For instance, we might start with interaction and assume that interaction is all that there is. Then we might ask how some kinds of interactions more or less succeed in stabilising and reproducing themselves: how it is that they overcome resistance and seem to become "macrosocial"; how it is that they seem to generate the effects such as power, fame, size, scope or organisation with which we are all familiar. This, then, is the one of the core assumptions of actor-network theory: that Napoleons are no different in kind to small-time hustlers, and IBMs to whelk-stalls. And if they are larger, then we should be studying how this comes about—how, in other words, size, power or organisation are generated.[118]

In what is perhaps its most radical move, ANT attempts to take account of the heterogeneous networks that include not only social or human dimensions, but also the material dimensions that make human and social behaviors possible. ANT explores how these heterogeneous networks come to be patterned to generate effects like organizations, inequality, and power. Joseph Goguen explains:

> Actor-Network Theory can be seen as a systematic way to bring out the infrastructure that is usually left out of the "heroic" accounts of scientific and technological achievements. Newton did not really act alone in creating the theory of gravitation: he needed observational data from the Astronomer Royal, John Flamsteed, he needed publication support from the Royal Society and its members (most especially Edmund Halley), he needed the geometry of Euclid, the astronomy of Kepler, the mathematics of Galileo, the rooms, lab, food, etc. at Trinity College, an assistant to work in the lab, the mystical idea of action at a distance, and more, much more.[119]

As in a house of mirrors, the science of networks has seemingly led us to a place in which all of the details matter and, to some extent, none of them do. Since at least the work of Emile Durkheim we have known that large-scale social phenomenon—the predictable number of Parisians who commit suicide every year—can be independent of the particulars—which Parisians are actually led to kill themselves and why. And despite the enormous complexities of the Isaac Newton example described above, scientists in the modern era glean what they need to from Newton, usually without reading his original work, and they move on to more pressing concerns.

Yet the details and vagaries of a network system do seem to matter enormously. Although network theory often focuses on large-scale behaviors, these large-scale behaviors are fundamentally provoked by the ability of one individual to influence another and the notion that people can change their strategies depending on what other people are doing. Barabási acknowledges that, "We must move beyond structure and topology and start focusing on the dynamics that take place along the links. Networks are only the skeleton of complexity, the highways for the various processes that make our world hum. To describe society we must dress the links of the social network with actual dynamical interactions between people."[120]

The goals of network theory are gradually shifting from describing the topology of systems to understanding the mechanisms that shape network evolution. Network theory tells us that very different things can be connected through surprisingly short distances. Small effects can have large causes, while at other times large disturbances may be absorbed without much notice. Although the predictive power of network theory is still an open question, it may be enough that through these perspectives and approaches we can gain a better understanding of the structure of connected systems and the way that different sorts of influences propagate through them. Watts reminds us that, "Darwin's theory of natural selection, for instance, doesn't actually predict anything. Nevertheless, it gives us enormous power to make sense of the world we observe, and therefore (if we chose) to make intelligent decisions about our place in it."[121]

The musical community has a vested interest in understanding network dynamics, although individuals may vary considerably in their specific expectations. Network thinking can shed light on the cultural power inequities that produce imbalances in social and economic interactions. It may also tell us much about the spread of ideas in musical communities and marketplaces under diverse historical and cultural conditions. Creative musicians may hope to find in network dynamics glimpses of future directions for innovation or influence, strategies for how to avoid or disrupt network hubs and established practices in hopes of alternative community reorganization, or the means by which they might increase their own professional contacts and opportunities.

In our increasingly complex and interconnected age, both dimensions of network thinking—the historical and the future-oriented—seem to be taking on a greater importance. Through the proliferation of recorded music in the twentieth century, historical hubs are both better known and more influential than ever could have been imagined in previous eras. Historiographic research is consequently focusing on situating these icons, as well as lesser-known individuals, more fully in a historical and cultural context. The motivation is not to dethrone any individuals from canonical status as much as it is to make us fully aware of the rich context that affected the lives and work of all musicians, both those remembered and those forgotten.

Contemporary popular culture and the consumer-driven music industry have also seemingly sped up exponentially the rate at which new stars are made and forgotten. Individuals are faced at times with a disorienting array of options and opportunities, unable to decide on or to take advantage of any of them. While much jazz, improvised, and classical music may appear to exist outside of the machinations of the popular music industry, because the immediate networks for these musics are smaller does not mean that they are any less impacted by processes of growth and preferential attachment (as the scale-free property of networks suggests).

Moments in which humans come together to synchronize their ears, brains, and bodies may be more vital than ever. Through the wonders of technology we can connect to the farthest reaches of the globe in an instant, but in the age of iPods and web surfing we also experience the world in increasing isolation at the same time. Musical improvisation may even allow us to explore our own homophily parameter, as familiar and less familiar sounds and people join together to find a common ground, if only temporarily. Duncan Watts's current research shows that the most searchable networks involve individuals who are neither too unidimensional nor too scattered. As long as people have at least two dimensions along which they are able to judge their similarity to others, then small-world networks are possible—people can still find short paths to remote and unfamiliar areas.

7
Harnessing Complexity

Western educational systems have traditionally relied on a strong distinction between *knowing* and *doing*, tending to value the former over the latter. Knowing, in this dichotomous formulation, comprises static information structures within one's head, and doing refers to the straightforward process of executing a given operation based on these preexisting knowledge structures. This duality is also apparent in folk wisdom, which makes a distinction between "know what" and "know how," in this case often valuing the latter over the former.

But a small revolution is underway in fields related to psychology, education, and cognition (including things like robotics and artificial intelligence), involving a shift in perspective from knowledge as *stored artifact* to knowledge as *constructed capability-in-action*.[1] From a systems perspective, what people perceive, how they conceive of their activity, and what they physically do all develop together. In other words, knowing is a process co-constituted by the knower, the environment in which knowing occurs, and the activity in which the learner is participating. In contemporary lingo, it is both *situated* and *distributed*—situated in the general sense that all knowledge is in part a product of the activity, context, and culture in which it is developed, and distributed because knowledge as action rather than artifact exists not simply in the mind of the individual, but rather as something shared between individuals in a physical and social setting.

Learning, from this perspective, is not so much a matter of what one knows, but who one becomes. And education becomes less about the transmission of abstract knowledge and more about helping students to participate in a community of practice. In other words, learning is best thought of not as receiving a body of factual knowledge, but rather as a process that involves becoming a different person with respect to possibilities for interacting with other people and the environment.[2] Music, in particular, provides an especially fertile site for acknowledging and studying these situated and distributed aspects of learning. While improvisation, broadly conceived, becomes a critical component of both the learning and teaching process in general.

Yet improvisation in the contemporary music classroom has been, for the most part, neglected. Tom Nunn laments that, "It may be acknowledged—in a way akin to chicken soup as a cure for a cold (it can't hurt)—but it is not taken seriously. It may be presented in some extramusical way, such as notation, analysis, etc., but as an expression of composition, it goes unrecognized."[3] Even more pessimistically, Jonty Stockdale remarks: "The ability to improvise freely is a common skill applied whether in conversation, role-play, movement, dance, or the playing of games, and yet it is an ability that is seemingly suppressed through the conventions of music training."[4] In this chapter, I investigate and scrutinize methods for imparting the skills, and perhaps more important, the culture and even ethics, of improvisation. In addition to my own experiences performing with and coaching improvising ensembles, I draw on ethnographic interviews with celebrated musician/educators Anthony Davis, Mark Dresser, Lisle Ellis, and Bertram Turetzky.

The Map Is Not the Territory

> Abandon Knowledge About Knowledge All Ye Who Enter Here.[5]
>
> —Bruno Latour

> There are no wrong intervals if played in succession
> There are no wrong chords, only wrong progressions
> There are no wrong notes, only wrong connections
> There are no wrong tones, only wrong inflections[6]
>
> —Eddie Harris

> The score was never meant to imprison the performer's imagination.[7]
>
> —Larry Soloman

> It don't mean a thing if it ain't got that swing.
>
> —Duke Ellington

Referencing the well-known phrase by semiotician Alfred Korzybski, William Clancey writes in his tutorial on situated learning: "Knowledge is not a thing or set of descriptions or collection of facts and rules. We model knowledge by such descriptions. But the map is not the territory."[8] Our educational system in the West, however, has notoriously underappreciated the situated and distributed aspects of learning, often tacitly accepting that knowledge, or at least knowledge worth having, is primarily conceptual and hence can be abstracted from the situations in which it is learned and used. But by ignoring or downplaying these aspects of the learning experience, it is becoming increasingly clear that educators and educational institutions are often unable to provide usable, robust knowledge to students.

Improvisation instruction in the music academy, for instance, has frequently operated under the notion that conveying the map is all that music educators are able to offer. Although practice and performance may be emphasized, they are frequently separated out from the process of learning "what" and "how" to improvise: in other words, the process of "learning" is conceived of as distinct from the process of "doing."[9]

This often leads to an emphasis on product-oriented music making and instruction. Teachers highlight the "materials" of improvisation, usually relying heavily on standard European musical notation to do so, and they prescribe the "parameters" or "structures" on which to improvise, often employing "lead sheets" that highlight the melody, form, and chord changes of "standard" compositions. Although these can serve as useful mnemonics for improvisers, to use them as a starting point and as a continual centerpiece of the learning experience tends to devalue the visceral, embodied, and experiential qualities of improvisation and to underemphasize the importance of developing musical ears, memory, instincts, sensitivity, and creativity.

During a recent interview, Bertram Turetzky exclaimed: "The academics talk about scales and this and that strategy—and I've read all the books—but that is not the way the masters taught."[10] Turetzky favors a more embodied and experiential approach. When working with students, his goal is "to hook up the fingers to the ears." According to him, "You have to learn how to hear. You can listen, but you've got to hear. In other words, you have to process some of the stuff."

For one exercise, he asks students to sing a passage from a fixed starting point—at first simply a few notes—and then to reproduce the passage on their instrument. Turetzky finds that even many advanced players can't perform this exercise well at first. He remarks: "If you can't do it, you are depending on scales. It is not visceral. It is not integral to your being. It doesn't express anything except the tricks that you have learned."

Turetzky is referring to a disjuncture between inscribed and incorporated forms of knowledge. Many music schools, and jazz programs in particular, place undue emphasis on the normalized, abstract, and detached mode of inscription, rather than the more collective, visceral, and engaged qualities of incorporation. Turetzky's remarks are also confirmed by recent neurological findings that show that in order for our senses to be able to engage productively with the world, they must develop over time and in tandem with action and intention.[11] If one learns to play music through the predominant use of inscribed forms of knowledge, making the necessary connections between ear, mind, and hand to become a fluent improviser may always remain difficult.

Mark Dresser, a former student of Turetzky, comments, "You find in jazz schools there are some very skilled people, but the music ends up being variations on the same theme, because the notation ends up leading the way that everything is formed." Dresser is referring to the fact that Western notation, when used to convey aspects of jazz and improvised music, tends to place undue emphasis on notes, chords, and harmonic progressions because these are most easily represented. The rhythmic, timbral, expressive, and interactive dimensions of the music do not translate as easily to paper. To counterbalance this trend, Dresser stresses to his students the importance of "learning how to hear spectrally—the big implications of the overtone series." Yet notation has remained central to many programs that teach improvised music not only for its perceived convenience—it translates well to blackboards and textbooks and can facilitate complex, hierarchical performances easily—but also because it allows instructors to have an "objective" means with which to evaluate the progress and understanding of students.[12]

In a panel discussion on free jazz held at the 2000 International Association of Jazz Educators (IAJE) Convention—one of the few of its kind in the history of that organization—Ed Sarath, a flugelhorn player and head of Jazz and Contemporary Improvisation Studies at the University of Michigan, and Graham Collier, the former artistic director of the Jazz Course at the Royal Academy of Music in London, joined

Allan Chase, a saxophonist and Chair of the Jazz Studies and Improvisation Department at the New England Conservatory of Music, for a frank discussion of their experiences exploring freer forms of improvisation with students.[13]

Chase argued that educators tend to avoid engaging with freer forms of improvisation in a hands-on way because (a) they are unfamiliar with most of it (many had an initial negative experience with the avant-garde and have stayed away ever since); and (b) they are concerned with how to assess progress, how to measure results. The first concern is of course a self-fulfilling prophecy if freer forms of jazz and improvisation are not allowed a place in the academic classroom. Regarding the second concern, Chase pointed out that it is equally difficult to assess the progress of composition students, or to grade an abstract painting, or even to measure the quality of a bebop solo beyond the point where someone masters playing changes in the basic sense. In all of these situations, he asserted, "There are things you can teach, ways you can critique a piece of work. There are suggestions you can make and there is a dialog you can have with the students."

Even when teachers do introduce freer improvisation with their students, Chase finds that their own reservations affect how they present the music, how they frame the creative moment. He advises them not to be apologetic, not to say, "Hang in there with me, because it's going to be weird." Rather, Chase explained: "It's very important to center yourself and say, 'We're going to create a beautiful work of art. . . . Let's listen to each other and be sensitive and play like an ensemble and here's a new idea of how to do that.' Give a structure, a way to guide it, a way to end it so it doesn't go one for the rest of the day. Then talk about it a little bit and do it again. Just like rehearsing any other music."[14]

The English drummer John Stevens discusses in Derek Bailey's book how he would try to create a situation with students in which they did not rely on him to set the improvisation up. Everyone had to respect the playing space and upon arrival be prepared to immediately start playing with purpose and interacting with whomever was already present. Describing Stevens's instructional philosophy, Bailey writes: "The aim of teaching is usually to show people how to do something. What Stevens aims at, it seems to me, is to instill in the people he works with enough confidence to try and attempt what they want to do *before* they know how to do it."[15]

This implied shift in pedagogic approach does involve some fairly radical ideas for the educational establishment. Rather than insisting on a prescribed plan and a controlled environment for learning, instructors must focus on creative ways to facilitate learning in a dynamic context that is shaped and negotiated by all of the participants. Instead of creating a situation in which there is a predetermined outcome and the sum of the parts is already known, instructors must be comfortable presenting unpredictable situations and exploring open-ended possibilities. Rather than simply imparting problem-solving skills in the abstract, teachers must motivate and encourage students to develop problem-finding approaches by demonstrating when appropriate and by allowing time and creating the context for experiment, exploration, and discovery. The notion of teachers as "experts" and "gate keepers" must also give way to a more engaged and interactive role as mentors, facilitators, and negotiators.

In the community of jazz and improvised music, the notion that learning is embedded in, and shaped by, its social and physical context is not new. Jazz music instruction traditionally took place within the context of the family, formal and informal musical apprenticeships, and the local community and music scene—often focused on the well-known practice of "jam sessions." These highly competitive "cutting contests" played an important role in jazz's earlier eras, though they have diminished both in number and arguably in importance in recent decades.[16] Freer approaches to improvisation often require a more cooperative approach to learning, perhaps best exemplified by Chicago's Association for the Advancement of Creative Musicians (AACM) and the Creative Music Studio (CMS), founded by Karl Berger in Woodstock, New York.[17] The formal music academy, however, has been less successful at integrating the situated aspects of learning into the pedagogy of improvisation.

We have to be careful, though, since situated learning is not simply a recommendation that teaching be "relevant." It also does not refer to the obvious claim that learning always happens "in a location," or the common oversimplification that people learn best by "trying something out." Nor should the theory of situated cognition lead us to conclude necessarily that there are no concepts in mind, no internal representations of knowledge. Rather, it implies that learning occurs in all human activity, all the time.

Foundations for this new perspective can be found in the fields of sociology of knowledge (Marx, Durkheim, Manheim), functionalism (the anti-associationalism of Dewey and Bartlett), activity theory (Vygotsky, Leontiev, Luria, Cole, Wertsch), cybernetics and systems theory (Bateson, von Foerster), ethnomethodology (Garfinkel), and ecological psychology (Gibson, Jenkins, Bransford, Neisser, Barker). Although little known in the West at the time, Vygotsky's work, in particular, has posthumously provided a common theme that runs through much of the new educational paradigm. In a passage that resonates strongly with the title of my book and with John Stevens's instructional approach mentioned above, Vygotsky wrote:

> Just as you cannot learn how to swim by standing at the seashore . . . to learn how to swim you have to, out of necessity, plunge right into the water even though you still don't know how to swim, so the only way to learn something, say, how to acquire knowledge, is by doing so, in other words, by acquiring knowledge.[18]

Vygotsky proposed that activities of the mind, including creativity, cannot be separated from overt behavior, from the external materials being used, or from the social context in which the activities occur. For example, many young children are unable to name what they are drawing until the activity is completed. Their minds produce stimuli while they interact with the physical materials (e.g., crayon and paper), and they react to the resulting visual stimuli and to the responses of others, creating a cycle of action and reaction. Over time, these experiences can form the basis for more abstract planning and cognitive reasoning about art, but the art in the mind cannot exist without mediating tools and a foundation of lived, social experience.

Describing their working methods to me, both Bert Turetzky and Mark Dresser stressed the importance of disciplined and directed practice: focusing on specific techniques or ideas and exploring their implications fully, so that they begin to form a personal yet flexible vocabulary of musical creativity. Turetzky shared:

> I have file cards, three-by-five, and I write things down on the file cards. And when I practice, sometimes I pull them out and I say, "OK, let's work this for two

minutes." [Sings an intervallic passage combining the intervals of a third, fourth, and fifth.] How about contrary motion? How about inversion? My idea was to develop discipline and just do certain things. Now would I do this in an improvisation? Maybe not. But I was learning how to do two minutes with just scratching the strings, and doing this, and doing that. And all of a sudden I was enriching my vocabulary, enlarging my vocabulary, and learning how to not do everything all at once, the "young lover's syndrome."

Mark Dresser described his working process as a cycle of moving back and forth from improvising, either alone or in a group setting, while also recording—in order to capture what he intuitively does—to then stepping back and analyzing and codifying those moments that strike him as interesting or filled with potential. This allows him a process of "rigorously looking at one's instrumental sounds, one's vocabulary, in a way that you could make a lexicon out of it, try to measure it, much in the way you would look at parameters of electronic music."[19] Although this approach to resources may at first appear to emphasize musical properties in the abstract, Dresser stresses that it is the process of personal involvement, using one's analytical abilities to analyze one's intuition or one's hearing, that is most important.

He often asks his students to undergo a similar reflexive process: to create a personal lexicon of extended techniques, sounds, and approaches. At the beginning of his course called "Sound and Time," Dresser asks the students to make a short environmental transcription, say thirty seconds, of a recording of ambient sounds captured "in the field." He instructs them to create a time line and to locate and describe the sounds they are hearing. The point of the exercise, he explains, is almost "Cage-like": to investigate "how you listen and how you organize how you hear." Then the students are asked to use their transcriptions to make an arrangement for the specific instruments, and, more important, for the specific musicians in the class. The arrangements are to be designed as compositions that also use structured improvisation drawing on the personal vocabularies of the other class members. Gerry Hemingway, who took over Dresser's class at the New School in New York City, adopted this same strategy but also asks the students first to improvise in the style of their environmental recordings, both as individuals and in groups, before committing them to paper. Dresser now recommends this practice to his students as well. For him, "The bottom line is musicianship. The ability to perceive pitch and time can never be too fine. The more we teach our musicians to develop ears and skills, the better equipped they will be to work in an ever-changing situation."

There is an inherent danger, however, if we maintain a pedagogic focus on the individual as the primary locus for knowledge and learning, as has been the educational norm in the past. Only if ensemble music is conceived of as the simple addition of parts can skills be taught to individuals in isolation and summed together for performance. But if music is in fact a whole that is greater than the sum of its parts—as I have argued throughout—then the skills necessary to perform/improvise cannot be developed in isolation. During our conversation, Dresser reflected on the importance of performing in front of an audience: "I believe in the magic of performance to bring out people's best thing, best qualities. I've seen that happen time and time again. All of a sudden at the performance people transcend the rehearsal process because there is that dynamic with an audience."

Yet our educational institutions and curricula have maintained an unwavering and unquestioned focus on the individual and on her "acquisition" of knowledge. David Ake suggests that freer forms of improvisation do not conform to standard conservatory values or to the soloist-centered approach of much conventional university jazz education. "With lessons, assignments, and practice spaces geared towards the development of individual skills," Ake muses, "little if any time or space remains for the development of the very different musical tools necessary to improvise successful collective jazz."[20]

The new educational paradigm, by contrast, acknowledges that all learning is inherently a social activity. Rather than conceiving of education as the transmission of abstract information out of context, it stresses that learners and teachers are already involved in a community of practice, which embodies certain beliefs and behaviors to be acquired. The theories of situated and distributed learning, therefore, emphasize issues of participation, membership, and community, and the ways in which knowledge and identity are shaped by these and other factors.

To say that all learning is social, however, is not simply to say that all learning happens in the presence of other people. Rather, learning is situated because it is shaped by a person's understanding of his or her "place" in a social process. The world in which we live is full of material and symbolic objects that are culturally constructed, historical in origin, and social in context. Since all human actions, including acts of thought, involve the mediation of such objects, they are, on this score alone, social in essence. From this perspective, even individual music lessons or private study are thoroughly social activities when properly conceived. To arbitrarily separate individual musical skills from collective ones is to already subscribe to a dualistic mode of thought.

Again Vygotsky's work was well ahead of its time in this regard.[21] For instance, in contrast to the work of Piaget, whose theories of childhood development tacitly reflected the ideology of individualism, Vygotsky emphasized a sociocultural approach in which the intellectual development of children is seen as a function of communities.[22] His writings take for granted that the personal and the social are not self-contained but have a shared existence. For instance, children develop language alongside the need to communicate with others. Vygotsky also proposed that all of the higher mental processes, including problem solving and consciousness, are of social origin; they originate as relationships between individuals and are constructed through a subject's continuing interactions with a social and physical world. Our inner speech and self awareness that define thought and consciousness emerge after communication; they are the end product of socialization. According to Vygotsky, the interpersonal comes before the intrapersonal, and the latter cannot be fully illuminated without acknowledging the former.

According to this perspective, separating the learner, the material to be learned, and the context in which learning occurs is both impossible and irrelevant. As Barab and Plucker explain: "A learner's ultimate understanding of any object, issue, concept, process, or practice, as well as her ability to act competently with respect to using these, can be attributed to, and is distributed across, the physical, temporal, and spatial occurrences through which her competencies have emerged."[23] Far from a nebulous theory of holism, however, the new educational paradigm envisions all learning—

and by connection all "knowledge"—as an activity that involves the concrete particulars of the situation rather than abstracted symbolic representations in the mind.[24]

This seemingly radical orientation has also sparked a reconceptualization of our conventional notions of intelligence and talent. Often thought of as static qualities that are intrinsic to individuals, they are, in the new outlook, conceived of as dynamic and collective properties; they are "accomplished" or "engaged" through the use of tools and other artifacts, the development of internal and external modes of representation, and through collaboration with other individuals. In general, the theories of situated and distributed cognition seek to displace the conventional notion of causal influence from either environment or culture to individual with the more systemic view in which individuals, environments, and sociocultural relationships can all be transformed through "intelligent transactions." Barab and Plucker propose replacing our standard notion of talent as well with the idea of "talented transactions," which describe "a set of functional relations distributed across person and context, and through which the person-in-situation appears knowledgeably skillful." This move has a special resonance for music education, downplaying a notion of "talent" as a specialized endowment of a chosen few and replacing it with "talented transactions" that are within the reach of all learners.[25] According to Barab and Plucker, "Nobody has talent, yet everybody can engage talented transactions."[26] They conclude that educators must support the development of "smart contexts"—not simply smart individuals.

A related concept here is Gibson's notion of "environmental affordances," which describe the possibilities for action that the environment offers to individuals.[27] For a physical example first, consider the perceptual category of an object's heft. Unlike an object's mass, which is a property of the object, and its weight, which is a relation between the object and gravity, heft is the perceived resistance of an object in motion. For example, when we move a carton of milk up and down to determine how full it is, we are measuring its heft. Moving the carton in a certain manner affords us perceptual knowledge of how full the carton is. Heft, therefore, is measured relative to an organism's perception-action coordination; it is characteristic of an affordance relation.

Learning to play a musical instrument involves an affordance relation as well. On the physical level, we develop a relationship between our actions with the instrument and our perception of resulting sounds over time. But our perceptions and our actions are also shaped by a social matrix in which sounds may be deemed desirable or not, and actions may be encouraged or not, depending on cultural and personal factors. Playing with a group necessarily creates an affordance situation, since the sounds that one produces trigger reactions and perhaps responses when perceived by others. But all music settings, in fact, are group music settings from the perspective of these emerging theories. Other listeners are always either present, within earshot (as sounds leak through walls and rooms), or imagined, in the sense that our understandings of music and performance are already shaped in complex ways by social factors.

Affordances are best thought of as capacities for interactive behavior. Although it may be possible to talk about music outside of this dynamic and systemic orientation, it is analogous to talking about the mass and weight of an object. They can be measured and discussed in the abstract, but they are immediately supplanted by the perceptual frame of heft when a human being becomes involved in attempting to manipulate or make sense of something. This perspective reconciles the notion that musical improvisers are best left to develop entirely "on their own," with the notion that they are blank slates onto which must be poured the "knowledge" of theory and tradition. All musical development is social in its essence, yet individuals develop and learn based on their particular experiences and accumulated understandings.

Although we commonly talk about information and knowledge as things, they are in fact relationships. Both depend for their existence on being perceived by living creatures. In her book *How We Became Posthuman*, Katherine Hayles questions the emerging postmodern ideology in which the body's materiality has been subsumed, and at times replaced, by the logical or semiotic structures that it encodes; or put more simply, how information lost its body. She suggests that work in both the humanities and the physical sciences has reduced the body to its play of discourse systems on the one hand (e.g., Foucault) or to that which can be encoded into a computer on the other (Hans Moravec et al.). But Hayles reminds us that, "Even if one is successful in reducing some area of embodied knowledge to analytical categories and explicit procedures, one has in the process changed the kind of knowledge it is, for the fluid, contextual interconnections that define the open horizons of embodied interactions would have solidified into discrete entities and sequential instructions."[28]

One of Vygotsky's more influential concepts for the contemporary educational paradigm is the Zone of Proximal Development, which describes the difference between what a child can learn unaided and what he or she can learn when given appropriate support. While few would argue with the notion that learners can develop further with adult guidance or peer collaboration, many classroom learning activities still focus on knowledge that is presented as abstract and out of context.[29] In her often-cited work on situated learning, Jean Lave developed the related notion of Legitimate Peripheral Participation to describe the process through which novices or newcomers can move from the periphery of a community of practice to its center by becoming more active and engaged in the culture.[30] In the music-centered disciplines, ethnomusicology, with its emphasis on ethnographic studies that emphasize apprenticeship in order to reveal the indivisible character of learning and practice, has been a beacon for this type of approach for decades.[31] In these types of apprenticeship situations, often very little teaching may appear to be happening and yet a considerable amount of learning is taking place.

The jazz community has also traditionally stressed the importance of apprenticeship, but it has tended to play a much less central role as jazz and improvised musics have entered the music academy. Describing his educational philosophy, pianist and composer Anthony Davis stressed that, "You have to play with someone who is more experienced." His formative years were spent under the guidance of many jazz and improvising masters, including Waddada Leo Smith, Anthony Braxton, Jimmy Heath, Charles McPherson, Leroy Jenkins, David Murray, and Ed Blackwell. Carrying on this practice of mentoring younger musicians, Davis seems to be intuitively aware of their Zone of Proximal Distance: "Playing with them is very important. I try to drop bombs on them. See what they do with it; stuff that engages them and challenges them in an immediate way when you play. That's the best way to do it."

He shared three general methods he uses to engage with and to inspire developing improvisers. First, he pushes them to acknowledge and deal with the tradition. Without this, Davis believes, one cannot become a truly profound improviser. For example, he might ask students to play a blues in order to push them to find a relationship with the history of the music, even though at times this makes some of his students rather uncomfortable. As a second tactic, Davis uses a dialectical approach. While playing with the students, he likes to "find something that is in opposition to what they think is happening to see how they react to it, whether that moves them into different directions or other kinds of thoughts." He finds that in a group setting people naturally assume different roles, so he consciously tries to make the students reverse or change these roles: "Have someone play up front, and someone who is more aggressive, have them play a supporting role." For Davis, "Teaching improvisation *is* an improvisation. I try to respond to the group dynamic, the direction, what makes them comfortable, what makes them uncomfortable." Finally, he looks to build on what students already do well to assist them in finding ways to do it better, although he acknowledges that this can be a very subjective process. He pushes them to "see the bigger picture," to become aware of the formal aspects of the music as it unfolds. And he tries to make them aware of their own mannerisms, to "make them think beyond the limited vocabulary they may have developed."

In our interview, Bert Turetzky described an internal dialog that takes place between the hand and the mind when he plays that helps to offset the subtle dangers that habits can present for the creative improviser: "All of a sudden you see that there are certain things that you go to. I see I'm going somewhere, and I slap my hand—but it's invisible—and I say, 'Don't go there. Where else can you go? Surprise yourself.'" Recalling a particular instance of this, he continued, "I was listening to a record with [Wolfgang] Fuchs. I hit open strings. I do that too often. So I'm listening and shit, it's the sixth time in this thing. Stop it! And the next one, it's not there. . . . So I'm editing as I go."

The internal dialog that Turetzky describes, however, does not need to be viewed through the lens of traditional Cartesian dualism. The "mind" that keeps the "hand" in check does not exist on some isolated plane, but has been situated through action and intention over time in much the same way.[32] We need to recognize that our current pedagogical vocabulary and conceptualization has emerged out of the decidedly Western notion that knowledge is about external constructs that can be conveniently indexed, retrieved, and applied by individuals. As long as knowledge is conceived of in this dis-embodied and de-contextualized way, musicians and music teachers will be at the mercy of the presiding educational philosophy that values abstract intellectual concerns as the real determinant of educational worth. Wayne Bowman worries that:

In our determination to substantiate the educational value of music and the arts . . . we have accepted uncritically notions of "knowing" and "understanding" crafted in different domains. . . . As a result, we find ourselves advocating music study for reasons that fit with prevailing ideological assumptions about the nature of knowledge and the aims of schooling, but on which we are ill-equipped to deliver, and that neglect what may be most distinctive about music: its roots in experience and agency, the bodily and the social. Our most revered justifications of music education are built upon deeply flawed notions about mind, cognition, and intelligence.[33]

Even within the community of improvising musicians, however, very different approaches to education are commonplace. Lisle Ellis, a bassist who studied at the Creative Music Studios in Woodstock with Karl Berger and Cecil Taylor, contrasted their approaches for me. Berger, according to Ellis, worked to "demystify the music." He focused on the basic building blocks—rhythm and pitch perception—that can help musicians to engage with a whole world of music.[34] Taylor, on the other hand, "musicifies the mystery." In his book documenting the Creative Music Studios, Robert Sweet writes: "Music, according to Cecil, is not something that we should be trying to demystify or divide and conquer. Rather than breaking down music, separating its parts, we should be working on music as a process of unification."[35]

Playing with Taylor, Ellis discovered a way of exploring music through the music itself, without verbal discussion, or without stopping to "rehearse" in any conventional manner. Taylor is well known for his insistence on teaching his music to fellow musicians by ear, for always bringing something new for his musicians to learn, and equally for his penchant to disregard any of the music that was prepared ahead of time once the moment of performance arrives. As Ellis puts it: "You want to be an improviser? Let's improvise!" Referencing Duke Ellington, Ellis explained: "The music never stops, you just get onboard. . . . This is an old idea. Everyone says this is new music, but this is some kind of ancient thing going on."

Highlighting the important shift from teachers as "experts" to teachers as "facilitators," Ellis remarked: "A good teacher is always teaching a lesson that the teacher needs to learn. I work with students on things that I am interested in and I am trying to discover myself how to do. It keeps me from going into a rote thing. And also they can see me make mistakes. I think that is a really good thing to impart to young people: let them see you fail and let them see you deal with it. And no matter how many times you fail, you still get up and go back at it." Ellis also made references to the teacher-student relationship in many traditional African cultures and to the activities surrounding African festivals, remarking that art need not be viewed as separate from the rest of life.

Vygotsky's notion of a Zone of Proximal Development refers not only to the student's activities, but also to the teacher's. It is mutually constructed to maintain a correspondence between other- and self-regulated behavior. Learning occurs in the Zone of Proximal Development by recoordinating perception, talk, and other actions. The constraints, or better said, affordances, are mutual (bidirectional) and the result is codetermined by each person's conceptions and actions.

During the IAJE panel discussion, Ed Sarath described some of the particular challenges of exploring collective free improvisation in the academic setting in general, and in the large ensemble setting of his Creative Arts Orchestra in particular. At first, he tried to balance composed parts and sections featuring more traditional soloing with free "interludes" in order to frame the "riskier" parts of performance. But the students wanted to do more collective free improvising. After some soul searching, Sarath decided to program entire concerts of completely improvised performance as well:

> Where I used to sit in the audience and be just terrified as to what was going to happen, and making a list of who I hoped hadn't come to the concert, in recent years I've become a little bit more comfortable with this completely improvised

format. And at the December concert, it was just amazing what happened. It's almost like some external force overtakes the ensemble and guides the orchestration, creative decisions, formal sections, etc. But there's no middle ground to this kind of thing. . . . We can extend the boundaries of bad beyond belief! In the other direction I have to say that when it works it becomes one of the most profound things I have been involved in. Something takes over the group. We've all experienced this in smaller group situations but there are twenty-five people up there. No conductor. No format at all and you have to tune in to whatever that force is that is going to orchestrate the thing, deal with formal proportions, deal with transitions. It's an amazing thing and it's terrifying. It still is.

Seasoned musicians, in all styles and traditions, are intimately aware of the ways in which the cognitive demands of performance are distributed across the group.[36] Individuals cultivate specific instrumental skills and knowledge about specific musical roles, but in order to create an effective ensemble they must constantly listen to each other and synchronize their gestures, sounds, and sentiments in order to create a compelling performance. Qualities like ensemble timing, phrasing, blend, intonation, and groove are continually negotiated in a distributed fashion, but even the formal structures of the music can be spread across the minds of individual musicians in performance. In notated genres, this is literally the case, as each musician has only a portion of the entire music represented in front of them. But in all musics that involve oral and aural modes of transmission—in other words, in all music—players communicate, negotiate, and recoordinate during performance in very subtle ways.

For instance, in a standard jazz performance, if one or more musicians are executing a particularly risky improvised passage, another individual in the ensemble might choose to remain more grounded to the beat or to articulate clearly a key moment in the phrase to ensure that everyone is able to stay connected. Or individuals in the group might assist one another by articulating an important formal point in a composition (e.g., the reoccurrence of the bridge in an AABA song form) or a specific harmonic or rhythmic aspect of a song (e.g., a chord voicing, turnaround figure, or tag). At times, groups may even need to recover from moments in which the timing or phrasing of a performance got temporarily derailed, all without making it apparent to an audience.[37] In a more positive light, distributed cognition allows ensemble members to negotiate and impart a specific musical or emotional character to a given performance on different nights. And in the freest forms of improvised music, distributed aspects of cognition can shape the entire performance. Jared Burrows writes:

A group improvisation is a complex social phenomenon. During a performance, there is a subtle, web-like interplay of individual psychological needs and intentions, technical tasks and difficulties associated with playing musical instruments, awareness of the audience (if the performance is public) and, most centrally, conscious and unconscious reactions to sound stimuli. Cognitive distributions in this context occur between musician and instrument, between or among two or more musicians, and between dialectical relationships among mediational artifacts, stimulus, response, and action. . . . As each new element is added, it becomes subsumed in the overall tapestry of aural stimuli, and these stimuli form the basis for further thought and action. Because all members of the group both react and contribute to the same set of stimuli, their cognition is linked in a profound fashion. Once certain sound-actions have been brought into play, the players construct a kind of group meaning from those actions.[38]

While the freest forms of collective improvisation not only highlight but also clearly hinge on the distributed aspects of performance, these qualities can be found and should be emphasized in all forms of musicking. Graham Collier, during the IAJE panel discussion, advocated for a broad and integrated approach to improvisation: "How do we teach this in our schools? Not just by playing free. . . . We have to absorb free jazz into the whole education of the student." As a helpful illustration, Collier described three kinds of improvisation: (1) *soloing*, or the conventional approach to jazz improvisation where one musician provides a dominant voice; (2) *textural improvisation*, which occurs in freer improvisation but also in conventional jazz as the musicians explore and develop a variety of ways to frame a solo or the entire piece; and (3) *structural improvisation*, where the shape of the piece itself is improvised by the ensemble.[39] Conventional jazz pedagogy focuses on the first type, gives limited attention to the second, and almost completely ignores the third.

Jonty Stockdale also finds that it is difficult to encourage students to explore simultaneous approaches to improvisation. Using language common to jazz musicians, he finds that music programs rarely give equal treatment to playing "time over changes," "time no changes," and "no time no changes."[40] According to Stockdale, "A jazz musician should travel back and forth along the line between playing that which is predigested, through to re-territorisation, and on to new territory." With a hint of optimism, he writes: "By explaining ways of thinking and working within a improvised framework and using comparative studies from non-musical pursuits, it is possible to develop an understanding of why improvising freely can be beneficial to the overall development of any music student, and a jazz student in particular."[41]

To embrace this new perspective does not involve throwing out all of the methods and techniques that educators have found useful in the past. The theories of situated and distributed cognition acknowledge the value of descriptive models of knowledge, but insist that these models alone are incapable of capturing the full flexibility of how perception, action, and memory are related. Human conceptualization has properties relating to physical and social coordination that cannot be captured by decontextualized models. As William Clancey explains, "Knowledge is a capacity to behave adaptively within an environment; it cannot be reduced to (replaced by) representations of behavior or the environment."[42] These new theories represent a theoretical commitment to avoid the philosophical stance of dualism: to conceptualize knowing and doing, knower and known, mind and body, intelligence and skill, learned and acquired, content and context, and subjective and objective as inseparable. And they represent a pedagogical commitment to develop more useful learning environments.

A perspective on musical creativity that views it as inextricably embodied, situated, and distributed may help to overcome the dualistic mode of musical instruction and inquiry that separates musical "materials"—the tools and theory of music—from musical "behaviors"—the application of those materials in context. Improvisation can play a particularly powerful role in this regard, although it requires us to embrace complexity and uncertainty in ways that still make many uncomfortable. Learning to improvise, particularly in a freer setting, remains a rather frightening proposition for many musicians. Acknowledging these challenges faced by both younger as well as experienced players, Turetzky exclaimed:

It's a terrifying feeling. All of a sudden there is no net and no rules. What does one do? Well, my answer is you listen. And you just hope that you have an imagination. And you trust yourself to say, "I'm going to grab something. It's going to be an anchor. I'll hook up with somebody." And then you do, and you go from there.

Group Creativity

However much you try, in a group situation what comes out is group music and some of what comes out was not your idea, but your response to somebody else's idea. . . . The mechanism of what is provocation and what is response—the music is based on such fast interplay, such fast reactions that it is arbitrary to say, "Did you do that because I did that? Or did I do that because you did that?" And anyway the whole thing seems to be operating at a level that involves . . . certainly intuition, and maybe faculties of a more paranormal nature.[43]

—Evan Parker

I suspect that it makes more sense to see solo improvisation as a special case of collective improvisation than [the] other way around.[44]

—Nicholas Cook

The nature of creativity in the arts and sciences has been of a topic of enduring human interest. But the dominant scholarly approach to the subject, until recently, has proceeded from the assumption that creativity is primarily an individual psychological process, and that the best way to investigate it is through the thoughts, emotions, and motivations of those individuals who are already thought to be gifted or innovative. In the past several decades, however, creativity researchers have begun to focus more attention on the historical and social factors that shape and define creativity, and on its role in everyday activities and learning situations.

This shift is attributed in great part to the work of Mihaly Csikszentmihalyi, who has argued for a systems view of creativity.[45] His work introduced two influential notions into our understandings of creativity: *the domain* and *the field*. The domain describes that set of rules and conventions through which, or in relationship to which, creative work is produced and evaluated as such, while the field refers to those gatekeepers or senior individuals who in turn evaluate new work and decide which of it is valuable. In other words, these terms describe the environment in which the creative individual operates; the domain refers to its cultural or symbolic aspect, and the field to its social aspect. The work of sociologist Howard Becker has also been influential in this regard through his focus on the network qualities of art worlds and the informal or implicit rules of etiquette that can shape and define creative work.[46]

Yet despite this shift in the field toward systemic perspectives that take account of the social, cultural, and historical dimensions of creativity, the notion that creativity operates primarily on the level of *individuals* (albeit now situated within a rich and complex environment), or that creativity necessarily results in a creative *product,* has proved to be remarkably resilient. In his recent book titled *Group Creativity,* Keith Sawyer draws on empirical studies of jazz music and improvised theater in order to highlight the interactive and emergent dimensions of creativity that are frequently overlooked or ignored.[47]

Creativity research has tended to make a distinction between an ideation stage, in which the nonconscious brain produces novelty through divergent thinking, and an evaluation stage, in which the conscious mind decides which new ideas are coherent with the creative domain. Sawyer argues, however, that ideation and evaluation occur in a complex rather than a linear fashion. During collective improvisation, in both theater and music, they also become externalized into a group process. When one performer introduces an idea, the other performers may or may not decide to shift the performance in order to incorporate this new idea. Acknowledging the complexity of group performance, bassist Richard Davis remarked: "Sometimes you might put a idea in that you think is good and nobody takes to it. . . . And then sometimes you might put an idea in that your incentive or motivation is not to influence but it does influence."[48] The quote from Evan Parker at the beginning of the section also attests to the fact that, from a systems perspective, it is often impossible to separate provocation from response in group improvisation.

Csikszentmihalyi is equally well known for his notion of "flow," in which the skills of an individual are perfectly matched to the challenges of a task, and during which action and awareness become phenomenologically fused. Sawyer expands this concept to illuminate the process of entire groups performing at their peak. Group flow can inspire individuals to play things that they would not have been able to play alone, or would not have explored without the inspiration of the group. Yet as a collective and emergent property it can be difficult to study empirically. As Sawyer explains, "Group flow is an irreducible property of performing groups, and cannot be reduced to psychological studies of the mental states or the subjective experiences of the individual members of the group."[49]

Many improvising musicians and actors speak of the importance of group flow or of developing a "group mind" during performance.[50] This requires, at the very least, cultivating a sense of trust among group members. According to some, it also involves reaching a certain egoless state in which the actions of individuals and the group perfectly harmonize. Percussionist Adam Rudolph described his trio's approach this way: "We all participate in creating the musical statement of the moment. In the process of being free as a collective, you have to have selflessness to give yourself to the musical moment and not come from a place of ego."[51]

Facilitating group flow, however, can depend on the level of familiarity between the participants, and it requires musicians and actors to resolve aspects of conscious and nonconscious performance in order to achieve a balance appropriate to the moment. Describing his general approach to improvised performance, Bertram Turetzky remarked:

> One way when I play free music, I try not to think of anything. I respond or I initiate. And whatever my intuitions tell me, I go with them. . . . Other times in

free music, I play with people perhaps I don't know. And I say, well, the last one started soft and slow and got faster and then went back. . . . So all of a sudden I start banging things and doing all kinds of stuff. . . . For some people, I think you have to be very rational. And you perhaps have to have an idea of where you think it could go, and be the quarterback.

Perhaps an even better sports analogy than football for capturing the fluid and complex dynamics of an improvising group during group flow is basketball. George Lewis writes, "It is striking to note how an African-American perspective on improvisation reflects a similarity with recent thinking in the game of basketball, an area in which African-American players have continually presented revolutionary possibilities." While both a basketball team and an improvising ensemble must utilize each player's individual skills, Lewis finds that, "In both situations it is essential that each individual develop an intuitive feel for how their movements and those of everyone else on the floor are interconnected."[52]

Although group flow may be the most desirable state for improvised performance, Turetzky acknowledged that it can be a problem, "If someone has a big ego and wants to make everything compositional." When he perceives that the group is not easily establishing a rapport or a musical direction, he often adopts a third strategy: "If there are three of four people, maybe I'll stop a little bit and let them see what they want to do. If there is a mess, let them sort it out. Let them start something and maybe I can support them."

As we saw in the previous section, conventional approaches to teaching musical improvisation tend to stress individual facility through memorization and preplanning, leaving little room for collective experimentation. Dramatists, on the other hand, frequently argue that humans are too skilled in suppressing action. For instance, Keith Johnstone believes that, "All the improvisation teacher has to do is to reverse this skill and he creates very gifted improvisers. Bad improvisers block action, often with a high degree of skill. Good improvisers develop action."[53] Drawing a comparison between the training of actors and musicians, Jonty Stockdale writes:

> In the initial training of drama students, considerable emphasis is directed towards the development of self-confidence, the loss of inhibition, and the ability to role-play. This is achieved largely through improvisation workshops where individuals work individually and collectively. Surprisingly, improvisation in jazz studies programmes is infrequently developed through a collective process, with a preference for the development of soloing facility through the absorption and imitation of pre-existing language, usage, and style. Whilst this is regarded as important for the development of a young jazz musician, matters of self expression, individualism, and most importantly experimentation are often left to later stages, by which time exploration of free collective playing can appear unnecessary or even redundant.[54]

Sawyer makes an important distinction between a problem-solving and a problem-finding approach to art. Artists adopting problem-solving techniques begin with a relatively detailed plan and work to accomplish it successfully. Those employing a problem-finding approach, by contrast, search for interesting problems as the work unfolds in an improvisatory manner. Many beginning jazz improvisers are stuck in a problem-solving mode. As Anthony Davis expresses: "They have been taught right and wrong—these are the notes, these are the chords, these are the arpeggios that work on a given chord. This chord happens on the fifth bar [in a blues]." But through extended listening, practicing, and playing with musicians who are more experienced, Davis finds that jazz players can move from a "dependence on articulating the form" to "using the form, realizing that [the tune structure] is the beginning of something and you have to create something else. . . . They have to do more than just keep time, they have to articulate time. . . . They can make melodic choices that are at least as strong as the melody that was there before." Even as students become more proficient, however, Davis reminds them that, "You have to get beyond your mannerisms to really come up with a musical idea as opposed to a catalog of what you do."

Successful group improvisation demands a problem-finding approach, since it is often impossible to determine the meaning of an action until other performers have responded to it. The particular challenge of group improvisation is that each performer may have a rather different interpretation of what is going on and where the performance might be going. In other words, intersubjectivity is an inherent property of improvised performances. For Sawyer, however, "The key question about intersubjectivity in group creativity is not how performers come to share identical representations, but rather, how a coherent interaction can proceed even when they do not."[55] In part, this is possible because individuals shape a performance on both denotative and metapragmatic levels; they simultaneously enact the details of a performance and negotiate their interactions together. Even if a singular meaning to performance always remains elusive, participants can shape the ways in which their various interactions unfold. Listeners, too, must be able to make their own path through the music.[56]

One of the most common bits of advice to aspiring improvisational actors is known as the "yes, and . . ." rule, or, inversely, as the practice of "no denial."[57] Actors are taught that in every conversational turn they should do two things: accept the offer proposed in the prior turn, and add something new to the dramatic frame. In other words, instead of denying or rejecting what has previously been introduced, they should present complementary offers or revoice an existing offer. Through a similar form of incremental development, improvising musicians also build on and subtly shape those sounds that have come before. They must listen intently and acknowledge the gestures of others as a form of musical "offer."

Improvising actors are also taught not to ask direct questions or to propose specific actions that would limit the range of possible responses for others.[58] Rather, they are coached on ways in which they can support the ongoing development in a more open-ended fashion, or ways in which they can assign attributes to another performer's character without limiting the possibilities for narrative development. Often referred to as "endowing," this may correspond with the ways in which improvising musicians support or shape in subtle ways the gestures and ideas of others without circumscribing or overdirecting them.

Although these bits of advice can be helpful in encouraging students to focus on interactive strategies and the evolving group performance rather than on their own specific contributions, they remain somewhat general and difficult to evaluate precisely. For instance, Sawyer points out that, "The line between a subtle denial and a constructive revoicing is fuzzy and open to interpretation." Moments in which endowing is used to good effect also exist on a fuzzy continuum with moments in which overly specific musical gestures can stifle group creativity. For instance, if a musician initiates a pronounced idiomatic gesture in a freer improvised setting, perhaps something with a strong tonal or metric character to it, it can have the effect of limiting the options available to others.[59] Yet at times, or in groups that value a strong play of signifiers, this practice can be used to good effect to produce either a pronounced disjuncture in the music or a type of stylistic pastiche.

The advice to accept and build upon the "offers" of others also does not preclude the possibility of departing from a direction that is already underway. For instance, one common theatrical practice called "shelving" involves abruptly shifting the focus of the performance in ways that may make other immediate developments off limits for the time being, yet keeps them available for future moments of reference or expansion: it displaces rather than denies what has come before. Again, evaluating when this has been successful presents a tricky proposition.

Excessive or harsh denials, however, can result in one actor overcontrolling the direction of a scene. In improvised theater, this is often referred to as "driving" a scene, or "playwriting." It can occur when one actor is attempting to structure a collective performance too far in advance, anticipating what others will do rather than listening closely to their performance and responding in the moment. As we have seen, the notion of "driving" a performance through individual ego also pertains to group musical improvisations. With inexperienced improvisers, however, the opposite problem also occurs. Anthony Davis stresses that it is critical in musical improvisation that students learn the difference between listening and following: "In order to listen, you don't necessarily follow, you respond. You try to construct something that coexists or works well with something else—not necessarily this tail-wagging-the-dog thing where you just follow someone." For Davis, "Listening is knowing what someone is doing and using it in a constructive way, as opposed to mimicry, just trying to demonstrate that you are quote-unquote listening."

Davis's comments highlight the fact that, unlike most group theater, group musicking happens concurrently as well as consecutively. Aware of the limitations of analogies between theatrical and musical performance, Sawyer writes: "In musical groups, group flow requires a type of parallel processing; the musicians are playing nonstop, yet while they are playing they must simultaneously listen to their band members, hearing and immediately responding to what they are playing."[60] This notion that everything is heard and immediately responded to during complex moments of improvised music may, however, be too facile. George Lewis describes a type of "multidominance" in improvised music—an African-American aesthetic by which individuals articulate their own perspectives yet remain aware of the group dynamic, ensuring that others are able to do so as well.[61]

Another lesson for aspiring improvisational actors is to avoid "crossing the fourth wall" that separates the performers on stage from the audience. In other words, stepping out of the dramatic frame, either by speaking directly to the audience or by metacommunicating about the proceedings, can endanger the natural development of the group's performance. In theater, it is too easy to drive a scene by stepping out of the dramatic frame to narrate or direct the action. Although the polyphony and polysemy of music makes this explicit directing of the unfolding narrative a more complex affair, musicians can "cross the fourth wall" when they play to an audience's expectations rather than to the evolving group dynamic and musical moment. Although a well-timed instance of signifyin' or double-voiced discourse in both improvised music and improvised theater can evoke humor, recognition, or insider knowledge to both performers and listeners.

In certain instances, the performance spaces themselves lend credence to the idea of a shared aesthetic. Discussing Derek Bailey's annual Company Week gatherings of free improvisers, Ben Watson writes: "Bailey has always liked theatrical spaces. The acoustics favour the softest sounds, while the setting makes the musicians appear larger than life. In plays, actors entertain the conceit of talking to each other rather than addressing the audience point-blank, providing a workable model for public Free Improvisation."[62] One final aphorism for improvising actors may ring true for their musical counterparts as well: "Listen and Remember." Many of the pedagogic exercises adopted by both actors and musicians are designed to improve these two basic skills. For instance, the "Word at a Time Story," in which each actor offers only one word to the evolving narrative, is an exercise that focuses the attention of individuals on quick interactions and on the meaning of the emergent whole rather than on their own contributions. In certain ways, this exercise is rather similar to the *Click Piece* by John Stevens, discussed in the previous chapter, in which each musician plays only short sounds in order to focus on the group pattern and interaction. "Zip-Zap-Zowie," another improvised theater game, asks actors in a circle to improvise nonsense syllables and then point at the next participant. This, too, mirrors many musical improvisation games that highlight shifting solos or subgroups within a larger ensemble and are designed to increase the ability of individuals to make effective transitions between various sections and instrumental configurations. These exercises, in both theater and in music, can also motivate individuals to remember what has occurred, either to avoid duplication or to make long-term connections to previous events. As Sawyer explains, "Not everything is resolved and connected right away, so there will always be small bits and pieces of plot and frame, waiting to be picked up and connected to the current scene."[63]

John Zorn's *Cobra* may be the best-known "game piece" for improvising musicians, but others have also explored gamelike strategies for improvisation (e.g., Rova Saxophone Quartet's system, dubbed *Radar*).[64] Techniques for using a conductor to structure musical improvisation in larger ensembles have also been productively explored by Butch Morris (conduction) and Walter Thompson (soundpainting) among others. Taking suggestions from audience members, although less common in musical performances than in improvised theater, can also inspire new creative explorations and demonstrate that the specific content of a performance is not worked out elaborately beforehand. Making a distinction between his game pieces and conventional notions of composition, Zorn remarks:

> In my case, when you talk about my work, my scores exist for improvisers. There are no sounds written out. It doesn't exist on a time line where you move from one point to the next. My pieces are written as a series of roles, structures, relationships among players, different roles that the players can take to get different events in the music to happen. And my concern as a composer is only dealing in

the abstract with these roles like the roles of a sports game like football or basketball. You have the roles, then you pick the players to play the game and they do it. And the game is different according to who is playing, how well they are able to play.[65]

With their attentions already engaged in complex ways during performance, others worry that highly involved schemes for structuring improvisation can hinder rather than assist the natural development of the music. Tom Nunn writes:

When improvisation plans are complicated—no matter how clear or well explained they might be—the attention of the improviser is constantly divided between the plan and the musical moment, having to remember, or look at a score, a graphic, or even a conductor. What often happens is that both the plan and the music suffer from this divided attention. When plans, methods or scores are complicated, they are less immediate, requiring practice individually and rehearsal collectively. As long as there is sufficient time under the circumstances, such devices may work well.[66]

During our conversation, Mark Dresser acknowledged the challenges inherent in structuring pieces for improvisers: "Composition is often about control. You have to build [improvisation] in. I've built pieces that have been little prisons, too. You're looking at something really specific." But he added, "It's a trip to find the balance. You try to find combinations where you have real focus and condensation, and points of real expansion. For me, it is all about being a complete musician. All of those things are interesting. At different points in the evening I try to have all of those things. Its funny, though, when you get in the composer's head it's really hard to let go of trying to control it or to create this kind of balance."

Acknowledging a similar danger, Anthony Davis commented on the importance of maintaining an improviser's aesthetic when he composes:

For me, what is very important when I'm writing music is that sense of discovery that you have as an improviser: that moment when you get to a place that you've never been before. You don't know how you got there. You don't know what's happened. And you say, "Wow, it's wonderful! How did that happen?" It's that magical thing that allows you to discover something else, something new. . . . There's an improvised aesthetic that I bring to what I compose. As an improviser you realize that you can discover the form through the music itself. A lot of classical composers have lost that. They have to apply the form rather than discover it. . . . This objectification of music is a way of distancing from the immediate. [With improvisation] you end up with more anomalous things, more interesting things.

But he also reflected on the delicate balance between structuring music ahead of time and allowing room for creativity and spontaneity in performance. For an illustration, Davis recounted a particular performance of his music in San Francisco when the improvised section opened up and extended well beyond his original intentions for the piece. He described it as "a rubber band that had been stretched too far and it broke. The focus was lost, even though what happened in it was great."

Even compositional strategies that have the sole intent of facilitating group improvisation during performance can backfire. Dresser commented, "I've seen the conduction thing be a disaster with people who just don't like to be controlled." Without preconceived strategies, however, there is an ever-present danger that improvised music will fail on its own. This danger may also increase with the size of the group. Philip Alperson writes: "As the number of designing intelligences increases, the greater is the difficulty in coordinating all the parts; the twin dangers of cacophony and opacity lurk around the corner."[67]

This makes those moments when group improvisation is deemed successful all the more powerful. Lisle Ellis explained: "A lot of improvised music I don't think is very good music. But man, when it hits, it's extraordinary! That's what I've spent my life doing—waiting for those moments when it really lines up—to find a way to have some consistency in it. Some days I think I really know how to do that and other days I think I don't have a clue." In a telling aside that highlights this balancing act of harnessing creativity, Ellis remarked, "I've got to write more stuff down. I've got to write less stuff down."

When discussing improvisation and composition, it can be particularly challenging to avoid thinking in terms of simple dichotomies while at the same time remaining leery of equally facile truisms about the music. Only with dualistic thinking, which presents two things as opposed and forces one to choose between them, are preparing for something in advance and the leap of freedom into the unforeseen viewed as antithetical or incompatible. Dresser finds that, "Within control there are lots of possibilities for freedom." Discussing his time spent as young man in classes with Muhal Richard Abrams at the AACM school, George Lewis writes: "Improvisation and composition were discussed as two necessary and interacting parts of the total music-making experience, rather than essentialized as utterly different, diametrically opposed creative processes, or hierarchized with one discipline framed as being more important than the other."[68]

Ellis, however, has grown uncomfortable with the facile notion that "composers try to make it sound improvised while improvisers try to make its sound composed." Composition and improvisation are not mutually exclusive, but neither are they synonymous with one another; they are interwoven and implicated in one another. Mike Heffley argues that improvisation and composition are two similar and equal generative forces in the same one music, pushed to either complimentary or conflicting roles, according to personal and social dynamics.[69] And Dresser recounted a telling moment during his first tour with Anthony Braxton's quartet that resonates well with this issue: "The only time that Braxton criticized the quartet, he said, 'Well, you guys are playing the music correctly, but you're just playing it correctly.' The criticism was you are being too dutiful, you're not taking a chance. That was the day that the format of the music actually changed, from being a solo-based music to an ensemble music. All of a sudden, the nature of the music became different. That moment articulated when the group came into its own."

To return briefly to my own formative experiences with Surrealestate, when I first began playing with the group I remember struggling with the seemingly insurmountable challenge to always play something new, something fresh, or something innovative. Without the conventional song structures of jazz to organize my improvisational approach, the musical options often appeared to me to be unlimited and, therefore, unmanageable. I remember fondly, however, fellow saxophonists Robert Reigle sharing with me that, for him, the goal of improvisation is not to play something new at every moment, rather it is to play something that is entirely appropriate to the moment. All of a sudden, something that had seemed beyond me—both in terms of its difficulty and in the sense that music could exist as an abstraction outside of its real-time production—was transformed into something that was fully situated. I realized that how I behaved and the music that I made was both affected by and would affect how others behaved and the music they made. Being myself in the moment, then, meant acknowledging the interconnectedness of the individual, social, physical, and historical dimensions of experience.

The Shores of Multiplicity

> Of all the travels made by man since the voyages of Dante, this new exploration along the shores of Multiplicity and Complexity promised to be the longest.[70]
>
> —Henry Adams

> My feeling about artists is that we are metaphor explorers of some kind.[71]
>
> —Brian Eno

> Artists teach people how to live.[72]
>
> —Lester Bowie

Due to the proliferation of recordings in the previous century, and the gradual (and ongoing) shift from a colonial to a postcolonial world, contemporary music (and society more broadly) is just now arriving on the shores of multiplicity. Musical traditions, styles, and approaches coexist (and frequently intertwine) to a greater extent now than was ever possible. Yet far from simply expanding our choices at the local record store, this ongoing shift to multiplicity must engender a growing awareness of varied and diverse musical understandings and a deeper acknowledgment of one's own relationship within and to a given music culture.

The process of improvising music can teach us a way of being in the world that is particularly appropriate to this new exploration. Multiplicity refers to the state of being multiple or varied, but a less well-known definition of the word comes from physics, where it describes the number of energy levels of a molecule, atom, or nucleus that result from interactions between angular momentum.[73] In this light, multiplicity can describe the varied interactions that occur as performers and listeners navigate improvising music together. Additionally, improvising music has the power to provoke an internal condition of multiplicity in individuals, challenging us to move beyond simple binaries and dichotomies. With a playful hint of paradox, John Corbett describes improvisation as "making a decisive statement and at the same time giving oneself over to the situation."[74]

Here I wish to return to a bit of semantic play that I offered in the introductory chapter while describing the subtitle of my book. *Improvising music*—in lieu of the static construct "improvised music"—refers to the dynamic and indissoluble relationship between performances and people, between sounds and society, that is found in every culture and in every time. Conventional discourses on music have frequently reinforced distinctions between composition and improvisation, music and noise, sound and silence, and tradition and innovation that are, under close scrutiny, untenable. While improvising music, individuals balance comfort and caprice, groups enable structure and spontaneity, and traditions become articulated by and respond to both continuity and change. Improvising music is not simply an alternative approach to composition, but rather the ongoing process of internalizing alternative value systems through music.

Multiplicity, therefore, must mean more than simple pluralism. At its heart, the still nascent shift to multiplicity must involve acknowledging uncertainty while foregrounding complex visions of agency, identity, embodiment, community, and culture. By necessity, this involves a leap into unknown territory and uncharted waters—perhaps accompanied by the unsettling yet exhilarating feeling of "sync or swarm"—yet without abandoning a sense of individual, communal, and historical empowerment. Daniel Belgrad has identified a "culture of spontaneity" that emerged in post-World War II America articulated by the arts in general, and by modern jazz in particular. Bebop and free jazz have provided important symbols of spontaneity, liberation, and resistance to oppression for many in the intervening years, and they will undoubtedly continue to do so. But acknowledging a shift toward multiplicity will involve augmenting, arguing over, and perhaps even replacing many of the notions that have come to be strongly associated with these forms. George Lewis writes: "[T]he pluralist tendency to situate African-American music as the vehicle of orchestral transubstantiation, while well-grounded historically, risks becoming overly narrow in the new century, as improvisation traditions from around the world, influenced or not by African-American forms, become part of a landscape that could inform the classical music of the future."[75] Envisioning what a "new American classical music" might sound like in a postcolonial world, Lewis continues:

> Certainly, such a new music would need to draw upon the widest range of traditions, while not being tied to any one. Rather than quixotically asserting a "new common practice," perhaps such a music would exist, as theorist Jacques Attali put it, "in a multifaceted time in which rhythms, styles, and codes diverge, interdependencies become more burdensome, and rules dissolve"—in short, a "new noise."

Are there aspects of the emerging scientific understanding of complexity that might assist us in harnessing the complexities of improvising music? For a system to be truly complex, it must be an aggregation of simpler systems that both work and can work independently; a whole made up of wholes. Systems of this sort are able to take advantage of positive feedback, to cultivate increasing returns. They exploit errors or unexpected occurrences, assess strategies in light of their consequences, and produce self-changing rules that dynamically govern. Complex systems, however, must strike an uneasy and ever-changing balance between the exploration of new ideas or territories and the exploitation of strategies, devices, and practices that have already been integrated into the system. In other words, complex systems seek persistent disequilibrium; they avoid constancy but also restless change. Because of this uneasy balance, complex systems are not necessarily optimized for a specific goal; rather, they pursue multiple goals at all times. Although they cannot be explicitly controlled, they can respond to guiding rules of thumb and are susceptible to leverage points of intervention.

It is interesting to note that two of the hottest current topics for organizational design are the sciences of complexity and jazz music. Both domains emphasize adaptation, perpetual novelty, the value of variety and experimentation, and the potential of decentralized and overlapping authority in ways that are increasingly being viewed as beneficial for economic and political discourse. Robert Axelrod and Michael Cohen see in the move from the industrial revolution to the information revolution a powerful shift from emphasizing discipline in organizations to emphasizing their flexible, adaptive, and dispersed nature. They write, "Just as the clock and the steam engine provided powerful images for the metaphor of society as a machine, distributed information technologies can provide a powerful image for the metaphor of society as a Complex Adaptive System."[76] And Karl Weick, in a special issue of the journal *Organization Science* devoted to an exploration of "the jazz metaphor," finds that the music's emphasis on pitting acquired skills and precomposed materials against unanticipated ideas or unprogrammed opportunities, options, or hazards can offset conventional organizational tendencies toward control, formalization, and routine.[77] In a response to the heavy reliance by journal contributors on swing and bebop as the source of their jazz metaphors, Michael Zack outlined ways in which free jazz might propel discourse even further into the realm of emergent, spontaneous, and mutually constructed organizational structures.[78]

Are there lessons from improvising music that can help us to understand, or at least to cope with, the complexity of our world? Improvising music makes us aware of the power of bottom-up design, of self-organization. It operates in a network fashion, engaging all of the participants while distributing responsibility and empowerment among them. Networks facilitate reciprocal interactions between members, fostering trust and cooperation, but they also can concentrate power in the hands of a few (as we saw in the previous chapter). Under the best circumstances, improvising music encourages social activities that support the growth and spread of valued criteria through the network. For instance, improvisers tend to value diversity, equality, and spontaneity and often view their musical interactions as a model for appropriate social interactions. Tom Nunn writes:

> Free improvisers are important to the society in bringing to light some fundamental values and ideas, for example: how to get along; how to be flexible; how to be creative; how to be supportive; how to be angry; how to make do. So there is a social and political "content" in their music that seems appropriate today, though it may not usually be overt.[79]

As we continue to explore ways of improvising music, we should look for ways to assist would-be cooperators in interacting more easily and more frequently. The robustness and equity of a network system is a direct result of the range and number of interactions. We should also look to maximize participation from the fringes, rather than the core. In complex systems, a healthy fringe speeds adaptation, increases resilience, and is almost always the source of innovations. For instance, nearly every new style of American popular music has emerged from the periphery—from a localized, and often disadvantaged, community—to capture the attention of national and international audiences (at which time much of the music's original meaning may of course have been sacrificed).

Fostering improvising music has the potential to overcome the inherent problems of a slow-moving traditional hierarchy, providing an effective way to handle unstructured problems, to share knowledge outside of traditional structures, and to inject local knowledge into the system. Improvising music also ensures that the cognitive models and metaphors we live by remain flexible, while it reminds us that our flexibility to learn and adapt are grounded in the bodily and the social. Without cultivating this embodied, situated, and distributed approach to music making, and without maintaining a healthy reverence for uncertainty, we can build complicated music systems, but not complex ones.

Perhaps in a way similar to democracy, which has been another powerful symbol of liberation and resistance to oppression, improvising music teaches us to value not only cooperation, but also compromise and change. In politics, as in music, a notion of the "common good" is bound to mean different things to different individuals and groups, such that the democratic experience is one of not getting everything you want. In a similar way, the value of improvising music lies not in the outcome of a single performance, but rather it emerges over time through continued musical and social interactions. Improvising music together does not necessarily produce optimal outcomes, but the decision to improvise music together does.

NOTES

Preface

1. Waldrop (1992).
2. Waldrop (1992:12).

Chapter One

1. For an example of this "third culture" see *The Edge* (www.edge.org).
2. For modern treatments of the subject, see Rothstein (1995) and Fauvel et al. (2003).
3. For more on the decline of improvisation in the Western musical tradition, see Sancho-Velazquez (2001).
4. Hayles (1990:4).
5. Taylor (2003:3).
6. Kellert (1993:85).
7. Small (1998).
8. Mandelbrot (1982).
9. Roberts (1977–78:39).
10. Bouchard (1998:n.p.).
11. Surrealestate *Contrafactum* (Acoustic Levitation AL-1004). Robert Reigle also used the name Surrealestate for his 1978 LP, *Bob Reigle with Surrealestate* (Lincoln, NE: Aardwoof Records).
12. A more complete list of individuals who participated in Surrealestate sessions from 1995–2000 would also include: Cristian Amigo (electric guitar), Roman Cho (percussion, pedal steel guitar), Andy Connell (saxes and clarinet), Tonya Culley (dramatic readings), Dave DiMatteo (double bass), Joe DiStefano (alto sax), Dan Froot (soprano sax), Kaye Lubach (tabla drums), Brian McFadin (saxes, carinets, trumpet), Brana Mijatovic (drum set, piano, vocals), and Christian Molstrom (electric guitar).
13. The live performance of "The Marriage of Heaven and Earth" from the concert at the Armand Hammer, as well as a rehearsal version of the improvisation with Koenig's "Ants Eating Through Brick," can both be heard on Robert Reigle's compact disc titled *The Marriage of Heaven and Earth* (1999, Acoustic Levitation AL-1002), which also features Reigle's original recording of the title piece.
14. Satie's composition involves a single, short melody and two subsequent variations on that melody designed to be played 840 times! Although a complete performance of the piece lasts roughly twenty-eight hours, we contented ourselves with having the music continuously loop in the background during our hour-long set.

15. In addition to the "Surrealism in Music" concert described at the outset of this section, Surrealestate gave several other notable performances during my time with them, including an interpretation of Ornette Coleman's seminal 1960 *Free Jazz* recording, a soliloquy to Charles Ives entitled "ImprovIves," a live interaction with painters at UCLA called "Spontaneous Combustion of Music and Art," and a set at the Big Sur Experimental Music Festival. Most recently the group has "reunited" in newly expanded form for a performance at the SoundWalk festival, an evening of sound installations and performances in the downtown corridor of Long Beach, California, and for a special recital at El Camino College near Los Angeles.

16. In Borgo (2002) I discuss a particular episode when a new member, after sitting in with us at a rehearsal, joined our group with little discussion and began to play with us regularly. Although he was a skilled musician, because of personality conflicts and certain actions on his part that were viewed by many as transgressions, there was some danger that our group would cease to exist. After much discussion, we collectively made the difficult decision to inform this person that he would not be able to continue attending our sessions. For many of us, this episode highlighted the delicate ways in which freer improvisation relies on shared social codes and a strong bond of trust and conviviality. The process of recording our group CD also brought to the surface several aesthetic and technical disagreements that unfortunately led to a few members voluntarily ending their participation.

17. Guitarist and composer Jonathon Grasse was especially prolific in offering new work to the group and finding inspiration in a wide range of sources. And Robert Reigle's pieces and ideas for the group provided much grist for the improvising mill. One particularly sly reference that I remember was his composition inspired by the Japanese mouth organ used in the court music *gagaku* called *shô*. Reigle's piece was named "Shô Tune."

18. For instance, for our compact disc release we recorded a version of Charles Ives's "Charlie Rutledge," already a rather humorous piece based on an American frontier ballad, on which we riffed and signified in ways perhaps more akin to Sonny Rollins's version of "I'm an Old Cowhand."

19. Difference tones describe the process whereby two tones are played together at sufficient volume until the ear hears a fictitious difference frequency. For a tribute to composer Toshio Hosokawa, we did an extended group improvisation referencing his notion of "vertical time."

20. This is a common technique used in educational clinics on free improvisation to help students better hear what is happening and to focus more responsibility on how they are contributing to the ensemble.

21. The term "contrafact" has also been applied to much bebop-era jazz when a newly composed (and often through composed) melody was based on an extant set of chord changes, such as "I Got Rhythm" or the 12-bar blues.

22. Lewis is currently the Edwin H. Case Professor of Music at Columbia.

23. See Lewis (2000a).

24. One of the particular challenges of writing this book has been finding a way to present what are essentially nonlinear relationships in the linear format of a book without doing too much harm to them. See Laszlo (1996) for a very readable introduction to systems theory.

25. Hayles (1999:21).

26. Kellert (1993:xiii–xiv).

27. In other words, just as the bones in the forearm of a dog, elephant, seal, bat, and human share a fundamental pattern, certain human beliefs, artifacts, or practices—including musical and scientific practices—can share similarites despite their seeming temporal, geographic, or social distance.

Chapter Two

1. Corbett (1995:237).
2. Williams (1984:32).
3. Cope (1976:147).
4. Bailey (1992:ix).
5. See Ferrand (1961) for work on improvisation in the European classical tradition and Nettl (1998) for a survey of ethnomusicological work on the subject.
6. Quoted in Taylor (1993:48).
7. See Eric Lott (1995) for an excellent treatment of the politics of style associated with bebop music.
8. See Saul (2003) for an excellent treatment of notions of freedom in hard bop jazz with a focus on the music of Charles Mingus and John Coltrane. The earliest recorded ensemble improvisations without preconceived harmony or form are "Intuition" and "Digression," recorded by a group under Lennie Tristano's leadership in the year 1949. Charles Mingus also pioneered the use of open-ended and pyramid-style forms as evidenced on "Love Chant" and "Pithecanthropus Erectus," both recorded in 1956. However, few of these pre-free experimentalists accepted the subsequent challenges of the new jazz. Tristano never again recorded in this fashion and Mingus, who inspired many free bassists, often expressed his discontent with the musical practice: "I used to play avant-garde bass when nobody else did. Now I play 4/4 because none of the other bassists do" (Litweiler 1984:29).
9. *Gramophone Explorations* volume 3 (1998:85), no author cited. Even from the European perspective, this historical development is not entirely clear. Evan Parker remarked of his experiences at the famed Little Theater Club in Englang, "We started by playing tunes and stuff and ended by playing free. I don't know how that happened." Quoted in Beresford (1998:90).
10. See Ake (2002b) for a detailed discussion of Coleman's arrival in New York and a general discussion of the debate surrounding the role of avant-garde jazz in the music conservatory.
11. Litweiler (1984:39).
12. Corbett (1994b:50).
13. Litweiler (1984:200).
14. In his discussion of Taylor's cover of Monk's composition "Bemsha Swing" from *Jazz Advance*, Steven Block (1998:226–27) illuminates Taylor's "radical constructionist" approach to improvisation as well as his deep connection with the jazz tradition. He writes: "Taylor bases his improvisation on the structural implications of Monk's composition while avoiding the more overt, observable references which would be expected of the Hard Bop style (variations based on the chord changes, returning to the tune) which dominated new jazz works of the period. . . . Taylor's improvisation is still firmly rooted in Monk's theme, but Taylor chooses to vary elements [texture, chromatic pitch class transformations] which had previously been largely ignored in jazz improvisation."
15. Litweiler (1984:208–9).
16. Durant (1989:257). For more on the decline of improvisation in the Western musical tradition, see Sancho-Velazquez (2001).
17. Durant (1989:260).
18. George Lewis (2003) highlights the ways in which terms such as "interactivity," "indeterminacy," "intuition," and even "happening" or "action," have frequently been employed to mask the importance of improvisation in the arts.
19. Composers who have experimented with improvisation include Ugo Amendola, Larry Austin, Klarenz Barlow, Richard Barrett, John Cage, Cornelius Cardew, Alvin Curran, John Eaton, Robert Erickson, José Evangelista, Lukas Foss, Sofia Gubaidulina, Barry Guy, Jonathan Harvey, Charles Ives, Luigi Nono, Per Nørgärd, Pauline Oliveros, Harry Partch, Terry

NOTES

Riley, Frederic Rzewski, Giacinto Scelsi, Stefano Scodanibbio, Karheinz Stockhausen, Morton Subotnik, and Frances-Marie Uitti, as well as the groups FLUXUS, Il Gruppo di Improvisazione da Nuova Consonanza (GINC), KIVA (at University of California, San Diego), Musica Electronica Viva, New Music Ensemble (at University of California, Davis), and the Scratch Orchestra. Pioneering work by composers in the American "third stream," such as Gunther Schuller, George Russell, Bob Graettinger, John Lewis, and others, could be mentioned here as well.

20. Cope (1976:10).
21. Cardew (1976:250).
22. One treatment of the problems associated with categorizing such diverse musical approaches under a single, often misleading heading is found in Such (1993, 15–29).
23. Quoted in Belgrad (1997:2).
24. Heffley (2005:279–280).
25. Bailey (1992:85).
26. Stanyek (1999:47).
27. For example, Dean (1992), Jost (1994), and Westendorf (1994).
28. For example, Jones (1963), Kofsky (1970), Wilmer (1977), and Hester (1997). For a contemporary, impassioned look at the dreams of freedom in the black radical imagination, see Kelly (2002).
29. For example, Prévost (1995) and Attali (1985).
30. See Monson (1996, 200–206) for a related discussion of "colorblind" interpretations of jazz. See also Harris (2000) for discussion of issues surrounding the globalization of jazz. And Atton (1988–89) offers the results of a survey raising important issues of national and cultural identity in improvised music.
31. Litweiler (1984:257).
32. *Gramophone Explorations* volume 3 (1998:85), no author cited. For more on the cultural aspects of this European "emancipation" from American jazz, see Lewis (2002 and 2004a) and Heffley (2005).
33. Day (1998:4).
34. Couldry (1995:7).
35. Nunn (1998:13).
36. Berio (1985:81,85).
37. From conversations collected as *Musicage*, quoted in Toop (2002:243).
38. Toop (2002:244).
39. See Boulez (1976:115) for a similarly critical stance toward improvisation.
40. Quoted in Spellman (1966:70–71).
41. Quoted in Porter (2002:265).
42. Lewis (2002:128).
43. See Heble (2000, 2004), Tucker (2004), Smith (2004).
44. Quoted in Porter (2002:284).
45. Lewis (1996).
46. Jones (1963:188).
47. Lewis (1996:94).
48. Bailey (1992:83).
49. Quoted in Bailey (1992:115).
50. Quoted in Lock (1991:30).
51. Carr (1973:70–71).
52. Quoted in Taylor (1993:112).
53. Quoted in Day (1998:35).
54. See, for example, Hou (1995, 1985–88). Tracy McMullen (2003) offers a cogent critique of the Afrological/Eurological dyad presented by Lewis (1996).

55. Lewis (2002:126).
56. Quoted in Porter (2002:247).
57. Important festivals that feature improvisation and new music include Le Festival International de Musique Actuelle de Victoriaville in Québec, The Vision Festival in New York City, The Guelph Jazz Festival near Toronto, and several in Europe, including Saalfelden (Austria), Willisau (Switzerland), La Batie (Geneva, Switzerland) and Vilshofen, and the Total Music Meeting (Germany).
58. The annual Company Week, organized by Derek Bailey since the 1970s, is an event that encourages first-time meetings and unusual groupings of well-known improvisers.
59. Nunn (1998:58).
60. Improvisation seminar held at the "(Re)soundings" festival in Atlanta, Georgia, July, 1998.
61. Personal communication with the author, April 2002. The instruction to play one note is of course not limited to improvisation pedagogy. Long-tones, a staple of much conventional instrumental teaching, are perhaps examples of this, as are pedagogic practices found in jazz, pan-European classical music, and Indian classical traditions, among others.
62. Personal communication with the author, February 2003.
63. Nunn (1998:70).
64. See Borgo (2003).
65. Quoted in Gershon (2001:15).
66. See Borgo (1997).
67. Quoted in Such (1993:131).
68. See Lewis (forthcoming) and Looker (2004). Important artist-run collectives in the United States have included the Association for the Advancement of Creative Musicians (AACM) in Chicago (which has continued to the present date), The Jazz Composers Guild (organized by Bill Dixon shortly after his famed October Revolution in Jazz in 1964) and Collective Black Artists (CBA) in New York City, the Black Artists Group (BAG) in St. Louis (the birthplace of the World Saxophone Quartet), and the Underground Musicians Association (UGMA) in Los Angeles (formed by Horace Tapscott). Notable European collectives have included the Spontaneous Music Ensemble (SME), the Music Improvisation Company (MIC), the Association of Meta-Musicians (AMM), the London Jazz Composers Orchestra (LJCO), the South African-influenced Brotherhood of Breath, The Jazz Center Society, The Musician's Co-operative, the Musician's Action Group, and the London Musicians Collective, all in England, as well as the Instant Composers Pool in Holland, the Globe Unity Orchestra and the Berlin Contemporary Jazz Orchestra in Germany, and the Instabile Orchestra in Italy.
69. Lewis (2002:121).
70. See Lewis (2002:121–123) for many additional issues regarding the various "downtown" improvising scenes and the discriminatory arts funding policy regarding "new music."
71. See Sarath (1996) and Borgo (2002, 2004).
72. Nunn (1998:93).
73. Bailey (1992:44).
74. Day (1998:143). Freeman (2001) presents a more limited view of this music from the perspective of a rock music journalist who writes primarily as a recently converted fan.
75. Watson (2004:160).
76. Stockdale (2004:102).
77. Stockdale (2004:102).
78. Stockdale (2004:104).
79. Barthes (1991:245–7).
80. Ray Cole in an email response to the author, September 27, 2004.
81. Truax (1986).
82. Bradlyn (1991:15).

83. Bradlyn (1991:18).
84. Bradlyn (1991:15).
85. Stanyek (1999:47).
86. Stanyek (1999:44).
87. Stanyek (1999:47).
88. Stanyek (1999:45).
89. Bailey (1992:102).
90. Watson (2004:251).
91. Watson (2004:229).
92. See, for instance, Bailey (1992:103–104).
93. Nunn (1998:154).
94. Cardew (1971:xvii).
95. Roberts (1977–1978:39).
96. Davidson (1984:23).
97. See Nunn (1998:252–6) for a variety of opinions.
98. Bailey (1992:104).
99. See, for instance, Sidran (1981).
100. Rose (1994:86).
101. Belgrad (1997:193).
102. Smith (1973).
103. The legal battle over the use of an improvised flute passage by James Newton in the Beastie Boys song "Pass the Mic" brought additional attention to this issue. The Beastie Boys paid the proper licensing fees from Newton's record label for the rights to use the recording, but did not obtain rights for the composition from Newton. A panel of judges recently ruled in favor of the Beastie Boys, arguing that the passage was not long enough to merit the necessity of obtaining a compositional license. Newton argued, however, that the short passage formed the framework for the entire Beastie Boys song and that its distinctive timbral qualities (a pronounced multiphonic on the flute) represented a significant compositional achievement. Timbre is a musical dimension that is little served by the current copyright law, as evidence by the fact that the court only considered Newton's compositional materials in terms of number of notes.
104. Quoted in Porter (2002:251).
105. Porter (2002:253).
106. Lewis (2002:124).
107. See Lewis (2002:129).
108. Journals and magazines that provide coverage of this music include *Avant, Bananafish, Cadence, Coda, Contact, Downbeat, Gramophone Explorations, Hurly Burly, Improjazz, The Improvisor, Musicworks, Opprobrium, Resonance, Rubberneck, Signal to Noise,* and *The Wire.*
109. Barry (1985:173).
110. Lake (1977).
111. See Couldry (1995).
112. See Borgo (2003).
113. Johnson (1989:461).
114. Quoted in Porter (2002:251).
115. Porter (2002:283).
116. Lewis (2002:129–130).
117. Porter (2002:207).
118. Heble (2000:8).
119. Gennari (1991:449).
120. Lipsitz (1997:178).
121. Harris (2000:122).
122. Harris (2000:124).

Chapter Three

1. Quoted in Lock (1991:64).
2. Quoted in Carr (1973:76).
3. Quoted in McCrae (1985:10).
4. Quoted in Lock (1991:33).
5. In an email with the author (June 7, 2005), Parker recounted that during his time at University he heard Peter Geach lecture, saw Elizabeth Anscombe carrying their baby around campus in a shopping bag, heard Alex Comfort speak to the Anarchist group, shook hands with Malcolm X when Malcolm gave a talk at the Student's Union, and played the national anthem in quarter tones for the Queen's visit. He described the early termination of his studies as "somewhere between a drop-out and an ejectee."
6. Quoted in Lock (1991:33).
7. See Martinelli (1994).
8. Quoted in Henkin (2003:n.p.).
9. Parker (1992).
10. Quoted in Tisue (1995:n.p.).
11. Parker (1992,n.p.).
12. Quoted in Corbett (1994:204).
13. Quoted in Corbett (1994:206–7).
14. Cardew (1971:xviii,xx).
15. A considerable amount of music analysis and criticism in the past has proceeded under similar epistemological assumptions. Not only are performances and scores often dissected into their component parts with little concern for their overall temporal effect or their situational context, but the supposedly "rational" and "intellectual" aspects of music have often been heralded above all others. In musical improvisation, however, the connection between intention and act may be strengthened until the performer achieves a phenomenological condition that feels neither purely mental nor purely physical. The popular and scholarly literature that expresses related views on this subject is considerable. For example, see Berendt (1983,1985), Boyd (1992), Hamel (1986), Khan (1983), Nachmanovitch (1990), Sarath (1996), Sawyer (1997), Sudo (1997), Sudnow (1978), and the special issue of *The Journal of Aesthetics and Art Criticism* 58/2 (Spring 2000).
16. See Hayles (1998) for an excellent overview of the cybernetics revolution and related issues of embodiment.
17. Bowman (2004:36).
18. See also Varela (1979) and the work of Maturana (1975), the founder of autopoetic theory. For excellent introductory work see Maturana and Varela (1988) and (1980), Winograd and Flores (1986), and Whitaker (1996).
19. Capra (1996:68).
20. Maturana et al. (1959).
21. In an interview with Anthony Korner (1996), Brian Eno makes this point while describing his early interest in minimalist music.
22. See Hayles (1999), chapter six.
23. Varela et al. (1991:9).
24. Varela et al. (1991:149).
25. Bowman (2004:36).
26. Iyer (2002:389).
27. Bowman (2004:36).
28. Bateson (1972).
29. Bach y Rita (1962), reported in Varela, et al. (1991:175).
30. Reported in Varela et al. (1991:175).
31. Held and Hein (1963).

NOTES

32. Varela et al. (1991:175). Also cited by Iyer (2002:390).
33. Varela et al. (1991:172). For early representative work, see Maturana, et al. (1959).
34. See Varela, et al. (1991) and Hutchins (1995).
35. Bowman (2004:47).
36. For examples of work with this orientation see Gioia (1988), Johnson-Laird (1988), Sloboda (1985), and Pressing (1998). Important work on jazz with an ethnomusicological perspective can be found in Berliner (1994) and Monson (1996).
37. Quoted in Lock (1991:32–33). See also Lewis (1996).
38. Johnson (1987). See also Lakoff and Johnson (1980).
39. See Such (1993) for a detailed discussion of the spatial metaphor of "outside" and its use in avant-garde jazz.
40. Turner (1996) asserts that simple stories are basic to human communication and cognition. And Damasio (1999) offers considerable empirical evidence and neurophysiological detail to support the idea that "simple stories" are fundamental not only to human communication and cognition, but also to consciousness itself.
41. Lakoff and Johnson (1980).
42. Zbikowski (1998:n.p.).
43. In an email posted on the Society for Ethnomusicology listserv on December 8, 2004, Andrew McGraw mentioned that these designations are used to discuss vocal music in general, and are used by some string players as well.
44. Several other musical traditions base their pedagogic vocabulary on the direction of motion required to produce an instrumental pitch rather than on its perceived direction in pitch space: for instance, Japanese shamisen and the Dominican button accordion.
45. Email posted on the Society for Ethnomusicology listserv by Julie Strand on December 8, 2004. Strand points out that the more cosmopolitan musicians among the Bamana-Jula acknowledge that the Western world conceives of pitches differently.
46. One embodied way in which pitches do appear to be higher or lower comes from the feeling in our vocal chords as we sing, and this may in fact have provided the initial impetus to map pitches vertically on staff paper.
47. Zbikowski (2002:72).
48. Walser (1991:120).
49. Maquet (1994:18).
50. Walser (1991:122). I agree that timbre and its cultural and psychological impact have been understudied, possibly due to the fact that its various structures and manipulations are least amenable to standard notational presentation. It should however be mentioned that musical timbre, or spectral envelope, has been a major subject area for acoustics and music perception researchers, although their goals differ considerably from music scholars interested in context-sensitive and culturally configured meanings. For an intriguing article that attempts to bridge this scholarly gap see Fales (2002).
51. Cardew (1971:xviii.).
52. Bowden (2004:43), italics added.
53. Fauconnier and Turner (2002).
54. See also Grady, Oakley, and Coulson (1999).
55. For one example see Borgo (2004).
56. Cusick (1994:16).
57. Cusick (1994:20).
58. Hayles (1999:206).
59. Grosz (1994:19).
60. Cusick (1994:16).
61. McClary and Walser (1994:76).
62. Quoted in Lock (1991:30). In addition to jazz influences, Parker is an avid listener to traditional musics the world over. He contributes the occasional record review or brief article on

world music to *Resonance* magazine and is an advocate for the field of ethnomusicology in general. According to Peter Riley (1979:3), Parker's favorites include "Scottish bagpipe music, aboriginal music from Australia, Korean music, music from Southeast Asia generally, Japanese music, [and] African music."

63. Quoted in the liner notes to *Towards the Margins*, ECM 1612 (1997).

64. For theoretical discussion on the notion of "noise" in contemporary music see Attali (1985) and Cox and Warner (2004).

65. Racy (1994:50).

66. See Iyer (2002:392–3).

67. Several musicians, including Rudresh Mahanthappa (*Mother Tongue*), Jason Moran (*The Bandwagon*), and Greg Burk (*Carpe Momentum*), have recently made this connection explicit by composing music for improvisers based on recorded speech patterns.

68. Iyer (2002:392).

69. Bowman (2004:39).

70. After reading a draft of this chapter, Evan Parker provided one possible answer to this question to me via email: "I thought of Ornette's 'Dancing in Your Head.' — I have spoken of a move to dance music for the nervous system too." (June 7, 2005).

71. Quoted in Lock (1991:33).

72. Quoted in Corbett (1994:204–205).

73. Quoted in Lock (1991:32).

74. In the late 1990s Parker started his own record label (with the assistance of Martin Davidson) and called it Psi to reference not only the associations with irrational numbers and golden ratios, but also the psi phenomena, which he believes are at the heart of improvised music making.

75. Quoted in Carr (1973:69).

76. Quoted in Corbett (1994:205).

77. Johnson (1989:461).

78. From the liner notes to the CD reissue of Evan Parker's album *Monoceros* (Chronoscope CPE2204–2).

79. Watson (2004:159).

80. Watson (2004:145). Other authors have commented on an apparent stylistic/aesthetic split between the various European national traditions. Nick Couldry relays the standard generalization this way: the English are severe, the Dutch are funny, and the Germans are aggressive. But improvisers, while acknowledging the importance of local and formative influences on their own playing, are often reluctant to give credence to this way of thinking, and the transnational nature of much contemporary free improvisation can render these generalziations somewhat flat and meaningless. Christopher Atton (1988–89) compiled views by various British musicians on the question, "Does British improvised music have a discernible national identity?" Nearly all of the respondents, while aware of certain trends and stylistic qualities related to social, economic, political, and national concerns, preferred to focus on the global or transnational relevance of the music.

81. From the liner notes to the CD reissue of Evan Parker's album *Monoceros* (Chronoscope CPE2204–2).

82. Quoted in Lock (1991:32).

83. Watson (2004:149). Although the music and musicians Watson is referencing are different, the tone of his comments is not too dissimilar from those of Mark D. Miller, who, in 1958, argued that jazz produces pleasure by satisfying repressed impulses (reprinted in Walser 1999:234–8).

84. Watson (2004:150).

85. Watson (2004:166).

86. As a quick illustration, Derek Bailey was married several times and appears to have had an "extremely complicated" personal life by his own account, but in a biography verging on

450 pages, Watson includes less than a handful of sentences that reference any of this, most of which were supplied by Bailey's current partner from a taped interview in which she asks Bailey to elaborate a bit on some of his earlier relationships (pp.36–38). Bailey responds with such telling remarks as: "Single, yes, free as a bird. I think my main sexual activity was masturbation" (36); "I married this woman because at the time it seemed the easier thing to do than not marrying her" (37); and "I met a woman there who I lived with. We had a very successful—the only successful arrangement with a female I've ever had other than my present one." (38).

87. Lock (1999).

88. From the liner notes to the CD reissue of Evan Parker's album *Monoceros* (Chronoscope CPE2204-2).

89. In an interview with the *Monastery Bulletin*, Parker has many interesting things to say about the life of a professional musician in free improvisation and his own personal perspective on the spiritual dimension of music (http://www.monastery.nl/bulletin/parker/parker.html).

90. Prior to the twentieth century few individuals traveled more than a handful of miles from their birthplace during their lifetimes.

91. Hofstadter (1979).

92. von Forester (1981).

93. Hayles (1999:8).

94. Kelly (1994:72).

95. There is an analog here to the fact that we often perceive things that are in flux as relatively permanent and vise versa. For instance, items that appear to be solid in our environment are in fact composed of atoms and subatomic particles that are in constant motion, while dynamical processes such as rivers and waterfalls are often spoken about and perceived as relatively fixed phenomena. We also have no trouble thinking of ourselves as comprising relatively stable bodies and personalities despite the fact that our cells completely replenish themselves every seven years or so.

96. Quoted in Toop (2004:243). In a communication with the author, Parker also recommended Muses (1985) for his perspective on the interactive connectedness of time called chronotopology.

97. Quoted in Henkin (2003:n.p.). In an email to the author (June 7, 2005), Parker commented, "Even 'notation' and 'improvisation' as if they are somehow opposed categories is not supported by musical practice. Memorised material can be and often is written down is some sort of *aide memoire* form."

98. Paul Berliner (1993:127–135) discusses a similar relationship between player and instrument.

99. Quoted in Lock (1991:64). This quote may remind some readers of Norbert Weiner's idea that "We are but whirlpools in a river of ever flowing water. We are not stuff that abides, but patterns that perpetuate themselves." (Quoted in Capra 1996:52). One of Evan Parker's earliest recordings was a collective effort released under the name *Cybernetic Serendipity Music*.

100. Quoted in Svirchev (1993:7).

101. Parker (1992:n.p.).

Chapter Four

1. Liner notes to the album *Concept* (RivBea RB50101).

2. Quoted in Turner (1982:4).

3. In an interview, Rivers stated: "The idea of a non-harmonic approach had occurred to me, but I just didn't know how to put this situation together. Cecil Taylor and Ornette Coleman

provided me the key that opened the door, and I walked right in along with them" (Turner 1982:4). Although Cecil Taylor, Ornette Coleman, Albert Ayler, and others had certainly made an earlier impact with freer forms of improvising, even they tended to rely on structuring devices or short melodies that were learned ahead of time to organize their ensembles. Sam Rivers's earliest professional experiences improvising in a freer manner were with a group of classically trained musicians at a Boston art gallery (McGaughan 1998:12). Saxophonist Steve Lacy reckons that his album titled *The Forest and the Zoo* (1966) may in fact be "the first completely free lp" (Watson 2004:182).

4. Quoted in Turner (1982:5).

5. To be precise, a more exact notion is that "the whole is *different* from the sum of its parts." In certain cases, emergent properties can arise by focusing on some of the parts at the expense of others, in which cases the whole may in fact by *smaller* than its parts. I have chosen to maintain the better-known phrase "the whole is *greater* than the sum of its parts" for its poetic ability to challenge the reductionist thinking that has dominated Western science for centuries.

6. See Borgo and Goguen (2005).

7. The field of consciousness studies is increasingly filled with decentralized models of the self and mind. In place of a "stream of consciousness," many researchers are proposing something more akin to "rivers of consciousness." In the "Society of Mind" model, for instance, Marvin Minsky (1987) envisions societies of mental agents that work together and compete with one another to do things that no agent could do on its own. And Daniel Dennett (1991) proposes a "multiple drafts" model of consciousness, arguing that multiple narratives are simultaneously created and edited in different parts of the brain.

8. Toop (2002:247).

9. Mead (1932:2). Quoted in Sawyer (2003:12).

10. Gleick (1987:23).

11. Kellert (1993:119–158). Kellert is only one of many philosophers of science who are currently seeking to tease out the cultural biases that often profoundly affect notions within the scientific community about what makes for interesting and worthwhile science. See also the work of Evelyn Fox Keller (1985,1996), Donna Haraway (2004), David Hess (1997), and Scott Gilbert (2000).

12. See Nettl (1998) for work that addresses and helps to correct this deficiency.

13. Bailey (1992:ix).

14. There is, however, a large body of scholarship on improvising music, in the Middle East for instance, dating back many centuries that would seem to negate this claim.

15. Regardless of the level of detail of the notation, a score, just like a book, can be read and interpreted in many ways by different individuals. See Gabrielsson (1988) and Palmer (1996) for a compelling argument that performance is a better starting point than a musical score for understanding musical experience and musical expression.

16. See Sancho-Velasquez (2001).

17. In fact, music scholarship on the whole has been surprisingly slow in adopting formats that could allow for sound to accompany written text. Most of the journals that have adopted new technologies and practices are done on the graduate student level (e.g., *The Pacific Review of Ethnomusicology* and *Echo: A Music Centered Journal*).

18. That no recordings exist of the earliest jazz formulations (Buddy Bolden, etc.) is a fact much lamented by historians of early jazz.

19. See Lewis (2000a).

20. For instance, the proliferation of so-called "real books," both illegal and legal, has standardized the performance practice and repertoire of "gigging musicians" at jazz "jam sessions" to the point that the notational errors and transcription mistakes that exist in the books have become common practice.

21. Briggs and Peat (1989:29).
22. Although we use the word "chunks" here, our approach is very different from the classic text by Miller (1956) on the short-term memory limit of 7 + or − 2 meaningful units.
23. For more discussion of technical topics in this section, see Goguen (2004). These concepts were explored and presented in a concert/lecture titled "Improvisation, Situatedness and Emotion in Music" by Joseph and Ryoko Goguen at Keio University, Faculty of Literature, Tokyo, December 9, 2003, and also appear in the Keio University Yearbook. See Joseph's Qualia Project Homepage for more information (http://www-cse.ucsd.edu/users/goguen/projs/qualia.html).
24. Saliency should be thought of as a technical concept that will have to be determined empirically. It is related to protention, but since it also involves expectations over periods that can greatly exceed ten seconds, it has much in common with the notion of *anticipation* found in Meyer (1956).
25. Csikszentmihalyi (1991).
26. For related work on the phenomenology of music and improvisation in particular see also Benson (2003).
27. Damasio (1999).
28. For a more technical discussion of these issues see Borgo and Goguen (2005).
29. To demonstrate how this system can be mathematically modeled, let n be the number of musicians involved, and let i vary from 1 to n, denoting these musicians. Let $m_i(t)$ denote the *sound* produced by musician i from time t to time $t+1$, where t is an integer indicating the number of time units elapsed. This unit is somewhat arbitrary, and might for example be the reaction time of the musicians, or 1/8 of a beat, or 1/10 of a second. The total musical sound is a superposition of the sounds of the individual musicians, defined by $m(t) = m_1(t) + m_2(t) + \ldots + m_n(t)$. Now let $x_i(t)$ denote the *state* of musician i at time t; this should include retention, protention, short-term memory, and long-term memory, as well as all currently salient qualia with their saliency levels. Note that the long-term memory component of $x_i(t)$ will include cultural patterns and predispositions for musician i as well.

   Let f_i be the *sound transition function* for musician i; it tells what sound $m_i(t+1)$ that musician i will produce at time $t+1$, given the musician's state $x_i(t)$ at time t and any influences on performance at time $t+1$, whether provided by a score in its broadest sense, denoted $s_i(t)$, or through more subtle contextual factors. And let g_i be the *state transition function* for musician i describing that musician's next state $x_i(t+1)$, given the current state $x_i(t)$ and the just prior total musical sound $m(t)$. Then the following is the complete set of dynamical equations for the music making of n musicians, according to the theory sketched above:

   $$m_i(t+1) = f_i(s_i(t+1), x_i(t)) \text{ for } i = 1, \ldots, n$$
   $$m(t) = m_1(t) + m_2(t) + \ldots + m_n(t)$$
   $$x_i(t+1) = g_i(m(t), x_i(t)) \text{ for } i = 1, \ldots, n$$

   The first equation is a formal statement of the definition of *music*; what musician i does next depends on what the score, if any, says and on that musician's current state, including the understanding of what has gone before, and the anticipation of what might be next. The second equation says that the total sound is a superposition of the sounds of the individual musicians. And the third equation provides a formal statement of the definition of *listening* previously given: the next state of musician i depends on the sound heard and the present state. Thus, for n musicians, the system has $2n+1$ equations. The first and third sets of n equations each form a discrete time dynamical system in the usual sense of formal dynamical systems theory, where the first argument of the transition function is a control parameter and the second is the state. The fact that the state of each system acts as the control of the other says that these two systems are "tightly coupled," since each involves feedback from the other. This feedback, along with the sheer complexity of factors involved, can produce nonlinearity in the system.

30. See Goguen (1977) and (2004).

31. The efficacy of these transformations is, of course, tied to the enculturated and embodied expectations of specific listeners.

32. See Goguen (1977) and (2004).

33. This is called the E (for emotion) Hypothesis in Goguen (2004), which also suggests that this explanation for emotion applies quite generally to all qualia, just as the Qualia Hypothesis seems to apply to all experience. We are also aware that under certain social, cultural, and historical circumstance, music listening may not be or have been entirely safe.

34. Cardew (1971:xvii).

35. We must be careful not to assume any ontological status for the abstractions involved in modeling, no matter their complexity. Models are always constructed by human beings for some particular purpose and should not be viewed as definitive descriptions of reality. We believe that models of music should always be grounded in the realities of human experience, social as well as bodily.

36. Although the bibliography of works discussing free jazz is lengthy (see Gray 1991), only a few authors have offered detailed analytical work (see Block 1990 and 1997, Jost 1994, and Westendorf 1994). See also Bailey (1991) for his notion of nonidiomatic improvisation, which for him and others involves a more complete departure from the traditions of American jazz.

37. Technically speaking, the pendulum in a vacuum would need to be mechanically boosted in order to produce an exact limit cycle. See Briggs and Peat (1989:37).

38. In Russia as early as the 1950s, A.N. Kolmogorov, Vladimir Arnold, and J. Moser followed up on Poincarés ideas by investigating the mathematical aspects pertaining to the stability of the solar system.

39. Like the term "chaos," some researchers have bitterly complained that "strange attractors" evokes inexact connotations that do not correlate well with mathematical reality, but the term has stuck to describe these fascinating, fractal figures in phase space.

40. For more discussion of these examples, see Lorenz (1996). Remember, also, that even though chaos demands nonlinearity, nonlinearity does not ensure chaos. In the ski-slope-with-moguls example, the system is certainly nonlinear, but if the height of the moguls above the adjacent pits is relatively small, the board may, after weaving back and forth at the top of the hill, gain enough velocity to maintain a constant direction over the moguls. A second board released very near the first, may diverge rapidly at the top, but further down the hill converge on the constant directional path of the first board. The qualitative behavior of a system can often change when the intensity of some disturbing influence passes a critical level.

41. The word "cybernetics" is derived from the Greek word for piloting a boat.

42. Resnick (1994:135).

43. This is referred to as "reification of concepts": the belief that our models of experience fully capture it and can replace it. We wrongly make the assumption that the "categories" or cognitive "chunks" that we construct in order to make sense of continuous, information-heavy stimuli are "natural." What is natural is the human need to "chunk" and to "categorize." What these will be and will mean is culture-dependent (among other things).

44. Briggs and Peat (1989:175).

45. Bifurcations (or multifurcations) technically occur in state space, whereas "transitions" occur in the phase space used to describe that state space.

46. Cohen and Stewart (1994: 206–7).

47. Rivers, Sam. 1998 [1973]. *Trio Live*. GRP CD 278.

48. See Nunn (1998:52–54). Nunn's terminology, while useful, relies on a linear conception of musical flow and cannot easily accommodate moments in which the collective phase space

becomes rather dense and tangled. He does, however, acknowledge that oftentimes several of these transitional approaches may be in play at once.

49. We would like to thank Ryoko Goguen for her helpful observations about these transitional catalysts.

50. The harmonic relationship here also points to a strong V-I feeling as the trill is on concert D, the modal section uses concert A as a root, and the final climax is to concert D.

51. There are also some strong similarities and connections between the sections marked *I2* and *L2* in Tabe 1 with their bowed bass passages and flute modality.

52. Henry Louis Gates (1988) offers perhaps the most comprehensive treatment of the subject.

53. For important work on signifyin(g) in jazz studies see Borgo (2004), Murphy (1990), Monson (1996), Tomlinson (1991), and Walser (1995), as well as Zbikowski (2002), who also incorporates insight from music theory and cognitive linguistics.

54. Quoted in Day (2000:108).

55. Quoted in McGaughan (1998:12).

56. Of course the performance of a sonata or an improvised treatment based on a 32-bar song form can exhibit an organic quality that is not bounded by the syntax of the form.

Chapter Five

1. Of course chaos can still mean extreme disorder to some musicians as well. See *Lords of Chaos: The Bloody Rise of the Satanic Metal Underground* by Michael Moynihan and Didrik Soderlind.

2. Thom (1989).

3. Briggs and Peat (1989). Their notion of a turbulent mirror is borrowed from an ancient Chinese myth, in which the Yellow Emperor imprisoned the forces of chaos in mirrors and cast a spell compelling them to repeat the actions and appearances of men, until one day they began to escape again.

4. In particular, their notion of a turbulent mirror is based on the Chinese legend of the Yellow Emperor who cast a spell to imprison the forces of chaos in mirrors, though the legend also predicted that the spell would not last and the world of chaos would come bubbling back into our own. In one Chinese creation story, the forces of yin and yang interact to create the 10,000 things (in other words, everything). And similar cosmological theories in Ancient Greece and Babylonia speak of the necessary interaction between the forces of chaos and order.

5. Briggs and Peat (1989:21).

6. Philosopher of science Steven Kellert (1991:81) uses a witty turn-of-phrase to illuminate this distinction: "chaos theory allows us to understand how unpredictable behavior appears in simple systems." The phrase can be read in two ways: first, in the sense of "how does it come to be that simple systems display such complicated behavior," and second, in the less obvious way of "how unpredictable behavior *appears*" or "what does this behavior look like?" How do intelligible patterns persist or emerge from this seemingly chaotic milieu?

7. Modern dynamical systems theory now speaks of four classes of behavior. Class I behavior describes a system whose dynamics will either disappear with time or settle into a fixed, homogeneous state. Class II behavior is found in systems whose dynamic pattern evolves to a fixed and finite size, forming structures or patterns that repeat indefinitely. Class III behavior represents highly irregular states in which structures never repeat. This represents chaos in its most disorderly and dramatic form. Class IV behavior, however, is perhaps the most mysterious, because it can produce complex patterns that grow and contract irregularly. Although it is usually given its own designation, this type of behavior has been mathematically shown to exist somewhere between periodic (Class II) and chaotic (Class III) behaviors and has been described, somewhat poetically, as the "edge of chaos."

8. One of the first great discoveries of chaos theory, the Feigenbaum number, demonstrates how a simple period-doubling cascade—for instance, a dripping faucet with a regular increase in water—reaches a particular point at which the period has doubled infinitely often, resulting in turbulence or chaos. Period-doubling cascades are one of the most common routes to chaos and are now describable in a very orderly way through Mitchell Feigenbaum's discovery. Benoit Mandelbrot's well-known fractal image also contains the Feigenbaum number and provides another example of the "new simplicities" and "natural laws" in the realm of chaos that are of primary interest to order-within-chaos researchers.

9. Ralph Abraham (1994:2).

10. Quoted in Steinitz (1996a:14).

11. Quoted in Lehrer (2004:n.p.).

12. Bradlyn (1988–89) and Pignon (1998) are the only work I have found that specifically deals with the relationship between chaos theory and musical free improvisation.

13. Hayles (1991:7). She credits the term to Ihab Hassan, but three European scholars, George Anderla, Anthony Dunning, and Simon Forge, also coined the term, perhaps independently.

14. See Bidlack (1990), for example.

15. See Madden (1999:xii), Bader (2002a, 2002b), Little (1995), and Steinitz (1996).

16. Lochhead (2001:211). Similarly, little work has been devoted on the "perceptibility" of such mathematical structures expressed in music.

17. Lochhead (2001:216).

18. Boulez (1975:56–57); Gleick (1987:22); Quoted in Lochhead (219–220).

19. By including derogatory quotes about improvisation from Carter and Xenakis without any rebuttal, Lochhead appears to agree tacitly with the notion that improvisation can involve nothing more than conditioned habit, and that it is somehow an inappropriate way to explore the dynamics and intricacies of chaos (its *ontological* and *denotative* qualities), or at the very least that it is an inferior way of doing so.

20. Lochhead (2001:235).

21. Lochhead (2001:239).

22. In her brief discussion of Hendrix and the Grateful Dead, Lochhead points out that the 1960s generation of guitarists were experimenting with new sonic developments resulting from the electrification of their instruments, including distortion, feedback, and reverberation. She argues that "noise in this context was not a term describing any sound that presented annoying sonic surfaces but rather a means of sonically charting the multidimensionality of *chaos*." Although she mentions the sonorous and performance-practice goals of improvisation, she cannot refrain from describing the work of both Hendrix and the Grateful Dead in terms of "a Cageian aesthetic of creative chaos," glossing over some important processual and cultural differences in the ways in which these "noisy" sounds were articulated.

23. See Lewis (2000a:35).

24. This story is recounted in Watson (2004:167–170).

25. Lochhead (2001:232). Lochhead's formulation of the category *chaos as creative potential* also focuses on the ways in which "Asian conceptions of chaos as a *creative force* provided the conceptual basis for the compositional use of procedures which allowed this potential to emerge within a Western tradition of musical expressivity." But here again she only references Cage's work (217). She makes no mention of how similar Asian-inspired influences also made their way into the realm of jazz and improvised music in the 1960s, John Coltrane's work being only the most obvious example. In Europe, the work of Joe Harriott and John McGlaughlin also highlights this emerging Asian influence in jazz. Nor does she acknowledge the ways in which Coltrane's music in particular influenced early minimalist composers such as LaMonte Young and Terry Riley.

26. Lochhead (2001:243).

27. Attali (1985).
28. Lochhead (2001:240).
29. Lewis (2003).
30. Lewis (2003:3).
31. Quoted in Lochhead (2001:233).
32. Even if Cage was successful at removing personal ego from the act of composing many of his works, his ego frequently resurfaced as he edited his final work and as he presented that work to audiences. Joseph Goguen recently recounted to me the details surrounding a particular Cage concert in the 1960s at the Naropa Institute in Boulder, Colorado, when his ideas were highly criticized by the veteran Buddhist monks in attendance.
33. Steinitz (1996:17). Steinitz's use of the word "composers" instead of "musicians" emphasizes the fact the nearly all of the interpretive and analytical work on the relationship between the new sciences of chaos and complexity and music has been on so-called "New Music" composers.
34. Briggs and Peat (1989:43).
35. Melchior (n.d.).
36. Quoted in Sardar and Abrams (1999:34).
37. The recent horrendous tsunami in the Indian Ocean also reminds us that coastlines are constantly being reshaped and reformed by natural processes.
38. Briggs and Peat (1989:95).
39. Beresford (1998:92).
40. http://www.monastery.nl/bulletin/parker/parker.html.
41. Parker (1992). In an email communication with the author, Parker added more context to the original occasion when he first made correlations between his musical processes and fractal patterns. He was giving a solo concert at the Slade School of Art at which Michael Parsons, a co-founder of the Scratch Orchestra (along with Cornelius Cardew and Howard Skempton), was in attendance. On this occasion, Parker felt some pressure to elaborate on the ways in which he works on audible processes in improvised music, so he drew parallels with Mandelbrot figures.
42. Reich (1974).
43. Email communication with the author, June 7, 2005. Parker's formal response appears in the first issue of an obscure publication titled *Microphone*.
44. Taylor et al. (2000).
45. Nicolis and Nicolis (1984).
46. See Bader (2002a, 2002b).
47. Technically, the pseudo-phase space must involve $2n + 1$ dimensions, where n is the maximum fractal number finally calculated.
48. For a technical explanation of this process, see Argyris et al. (1994).
49. Of course, one can use intersections to get an even more detailed version, i.e. using 50ms sections starting from time points in a series of 10ms resulting in 100 values per second. But as the calculations take much time, for large pieces this makes little sense since we have to use mean values to display the data in a useful form.
50. Argyris et al. (1994).
51. In this light, I welcome any feedback from readers on their experiences following the various plots while listening to the musical recordings.
52. See Keefe and Laden (1991) for a technical discussion of the correlation dimension of woodwing multiphonics.
53. In an email, Parker described this technique to me and admitted that he "stole" it from Steve Lacy and developed it further during his time with Music Improvisation Company.
54. Quoted in Corbett (1994:205).
55. Parker's comments also relate to the well-known "inverted U" curve of Wilhelm Wundt. Wundt's curve indicates the relationship between complexity and preference/interest relative to a listener. Very simple stimuli contain little information and are therefore boring,

while extremely complex stimuli are so informative as to be difficult to comprehend and appreciate. Listeners tend to prefer an intermediate level of complexity that is both comprehensible and challenging. In other words, their interest level will peak slightly in front of their preference level. Parker's use of the term "information" also highlights the fact that two conflicting interpretations (Shannon's and Brillouin's) have circulated for this common term. For related discussion, see Hayles (1990, chapter two).

56. Quoted in Corbett (1994:206).
57. Quoted in Lock (1991:33).
58. This performance is also available on the 2-CD set compiled by David Toop titled *Not Necessarily English Music*.
59. *Cadence* magazine, September 1997.
60. After recently listening to this recording on headphones, and then removing them, my entire office space seemed to be humming with this drone for minutes. The only explanation I could find was that the music left in my head had augmented the natural hum of the fan on my laptop, but even that explanation did not seem to account for the phenomena.
61. The phenomenological analysis from chapter four was completed well before I undertook the computer analysis with Rolf Bader, and I left it unaltered to provide the most accurate point of comparison.
62. See Meyer (1956) for more on expectations.
63. Jenkins (2004:xxxi).
64. Briggs and Peat (1989:70) make an interesting point about the "chaos" found even in Euclidian geometry: "It seems ironic that pi, the number used to calculate the circumference of what many consider to be the most perfect and ordered object of our imagination—the circle—can never be calculated exactly. Even in the Euclidian world, order and chaos go hand in hand." (70)
65. Briggs and Peat (1989:91).
66. The qualities most associated with Western notation—tempered and chromatic pitch, metered rhythms, functional harmony, etc.—have also undoubtedly imfluenced the way in which diverse non-Western musics are often grouped together under the meaningless yet marginalized category of "world music"; what some have referred to as the "West and the Rest" syndrome.
67. Briggs and Peat (1989:91).
68. Briggs and Peat (1989:110).
69. Some current research also shows that our heart follows a subtle chaotic rhythm so that no individual cells or group of cells are unduly stressed by performing the exact same function at the exact same pace.
70. Kauffman (1995:20–21).
71. Briggs and Peat (1989:139–40).
72. Prigogine (1981).
73. Briggs and Peat (1989:139).
74. Quoted in Bailey (1992:141). Also recounted in Rzewski (2002).
75. Quoted in Watson (2004:183). Lacy was perhaps the first to record a completely free album, one with no preconceived themes or structures (*The Forest and the Zoo* in 1966).
76. Quoted in Bailey (1992:128).
77. Quoted in Lochhead (2001:228).
78. Bailey (1992:127). Evan Parker responded directly to the quote by Eliott Carter in an interview with John Corbett: "Improvisation is played to keep the player from playing what the composer already knew" (Corbett 1995:223).
79. Montuori and Purser (1997:10).
80. Axelrod and Cohen (2000:16).
81. Axelrod and Cohen (2000:7).

82. Kelly (1994:22–23).
83. Kelly (1994:24).
84. It is interesting to note that, for a music predicated on what can be a very risky endeavor—to improvise collectively in a group setting—accounts of failure can be very difficult to locate in both the academic and trade coverage of the music.
85. I was unable to attend the festival in 2004, but I did have the opportunity to talk with two of our graduate students who attended the concert in question and I was able to view a video that an audience member had made of the entire event. Several articles appeared in connection with the festival and a vibrant Internet debate continued for weeks after the event. Much of the relevant Internet commentary can be found at http://www.zoilus.com/documents/live_notes/2004/000208.shtml under the heading "Guelphgate."
86. For a helpful introduction to Namtchylak, see Corbett (1994:160–2).
87. "Singer wails up a storm," *The Globe and Mail* (Toronto), Monday, September 13, 2004.
88. Ms. Namtchylak seemed disturbed that a major sponsor of the evening's concert whose ad appeared in a prominent place in the program was a therapy organization and she had, in fact, only recently recovered from a vicious personal attack. She also let the audience know that she had not been picked up at the airport or hotel and, in general, was not in her opinion treated professionally. Several audience members attributed this shoddy treatment to the fact that she was a non-Western woman, one proclaiming, "If they'd been dealing with Cecil Taylor or Anthony Braxton, you know they'd make damn sure that nothing like that got screwed up." Other comments by Ms. Namtchylak were less easy to decipher and some seemed to lash out at the audience, so that those in attendance appeared at turns sympathetic and confused. The growing unrest was surprisingly quelled when William Parker began to rub the sides of a Buddhist meditation bowl, prompting the crowd and Ms. Namtchylak to quiet their conversations and the musicians to begin performing anew.
89. Luke Bowden, the volunteer who was directly responsible for handling the artists' needs during the festival, and in particular those of Ms. Namtchylak, provided some additional context on the behind-the-scenes deliberations in a lengthy email post. Twenty-or-so minutes into her rather stoic performance, Ajay Heble, the Guelph festival organizer, reportedly was frantically soliciting opinions offstage on how to handle the situation. The sponsors had stormed out by that point exacerbating the situation, according to Bowden. Initially, and following Bowden's suggestion, the festival staff told the soundman to remove her from the in-house mix, but this change was not even noticed by most in attendance as her voice still projected well and was picked up in the microphones set for the other musicians. One audience member after the fact rather pointedly described this decision by the organizers as a "passive-aggressive approach" by "Canadian wimp-ass pissants." Eventually the emcee for the evening was instructed to "give her the hook," as many of the Internet contributors later described it. The official press release from the festival apologizing for the event described this as "a very difficult decision . . . made in consultation with numerous Festival organizers, the artistic director, audience members, volunteers, artists performing at the Festival, and other experienced arts presenters."
90. Day (1998:129–30).
91. Heble (2000:225).
92. springgardenmusic.com.
93. Steve Lacy, *The Wire* 1 (Summer 1982:6–7). Quoted in Cox and Warner (2004:249).
94. Quoted in Sardar and Abrams (1999:169).
95. Peckham (1965:xi).
96. Peckham (1965:79).
97. Peckham (1965:220).
98. Cross (2003:51). The notion of music as a "consequence-free" activity is somewhat problematic, but it is used here in the biological sense that music, in most all cases, does not by

itself do physical harm to humans. Since social interactions play an important role in our cognitive development (a topic we will look into in greater detail in chapter seven), it should also be clear that these two properties cannot be easily divorced from one another.

99. For instance, the Hindu concept of *lila* is often translated as the divine play of creation, destruction, and re-creation (Nachmanovitch 1990:1). And the Yoruban concept of *ere* can signify both a sense of play and improvisation (Drewal 1992:12).

100. Quoted to me in an interview with Adam Rudolph, a percussionist and former collaborator with Cherry.

101. Gadamer (1993:102).

102. Yet even a scientist such as Richard Dawkins, whose famous work *The Selfish Gene* has often been read (and misread) as reductionist, can state unequivocally: "Science proceeds by having hunches, by making guesses, by having hypotheses, sometimes inspired by poetic thoughts, by aesthetic thoughts even, and then science goes about trying to demonstrate it experimentally or observationally. And that's the beauty of science, that it has this imaginative stage but then it goes on to the proving stage, the demonstrating stage." (Quoted in the online journal *The Edge* 153 (2005), www.edge.org).

103. Mechling (1991:267). Mechling envisions play not as nonsense, but rather as "uncommon sense."

104. Hall (1992:224).

105. Hall (1992:233). I am less fond of Hall's distinction between high and low context communication and acquired and learned aspects of culture. Although they may be helpful in articulating the poles of learning continuum, maintaining this dualistic conception runs counter to much current thinking in education, as we will see more in chapter seven.

106. Cross (2003:51).

107. Hess (1997:133–4).

108. Some recent studies show that a healthy human brain maintains a low-level chaos that self-organizes into simpler order when presented with a familiar stimulus.

Chapter Six

1. Strogatz (2003:14).

2. Strogatz (2003:2).

3. Carroll-Phelan and Hampson (1996:554).

4. Benson's position here draws heavily on the research of Nils Wallin (1992).

5. Quoted in Strogatz (2003:274).

6. Strogatz (2003:274).

7. Strogatz (2003:72).

8. See Martha McClintock's classic article titled "Menstrual Synchrony and Suppression" (*Nature* vol. 229, pp. 244–5, 1971).

9. Condon (1986). Cited in Benzon (2001:26).

10. Benzon (2001:27–8).

11. Perper (1985:75–111). Cited in Benzon (2001:28).

12. Benson (2001:28).

13. See Wallin (1992) for an introduction to the field of biomusicology. See also Deutsch (1999) for related research.

14. Clayton et al. (2004:21).

15. See Keil and Feld (1994).

16. Clayton, Sager, and Will (2004:20).

17. Berliner (1994:217).

18. Sudnow (1978:152).

19. Johnson (2002:104). Quoted in Cook (2004:8).

20. Clayton et al. (2005:21). For related work see Schutz (1964) and Weeks (1996).

21. Cook (2004:16).
22. Rusch (1979:11).
23. Evan Parker has named the record label he recently started *Psi* to reference these types of parapsychological phenomena.
24. Interview with the author, Feb 1, 2005.
25. Strogatz (2003:2).
26. Strogatz (2003:2).
27. Quoted in Strogatz (2003:11–12).
28. See Strogatz (2003) chapter two.
29. Strogatz (2003:52–3).
30. Strogatz (2003:13).
31. Toop (2002:247).
32. Corbett (1995:237).
33. Lewis (2000b:38).
34. Kelly (1994:6).
35. Quoted in Kelly (1994:7). Maeterlink's book is available online at http://www.eldritchpress.org/mm/b.html#toc.
36. Quoted in Kelly (1994:7).
37. For a compelling discussion of why the notion of humanity as a superorganism or a global brain is a "non-crazy" question see Wright (2000:302–9), particularly his lengthy footnotes. Also Peter Russell (1983) and Howard Bloom (2000) have both written intelligently on the notion of an emerging global brain. And Pierre Teilhard de Chardin may be best known for his notion of a noosphere that represents an emerging planetary consciousness, similar to the biosphere that describers the combined effects of life on the planet. If the reader still thinks that these notions are truly crazy, it may be beneficial to ponder our own consciousness: not simply how we think or why we are self-aware, but more broadly, and as Thomas Nagel expressed, "Why is it *like something* to be alive?"
38. Stevens titled the reverse strategy "Sustained Piece."
39. Toop (2004:242–3).
40. Bonabeau and Théraulaz (2000). Although this field is often presented as evolving in only the past few years, examples drawn from the world of social insects can be found in early cybernetics theory (Weiner 1961:156–7) and in dissipative structures as well (Prigogine and Stengers 1984:181–6).
41. Bonabeau and Théraulaz (2000:79).
42. Bonabeau et al. (1999:9–11).
43. Here we might want to envision the creative process of each individual as a type of swarm dynamic, drawing on Marvin Minsky's notion of a "Society of Mind."
44. Lansing (2003:194).
45. Similar pedagogical strategies abound in the world of free improvisation. For instance, Jack Wright and Bob Marsh presented a version of this same idea at a clinic at UCSD in late 2004. Instead of asking participants to use instruments, however, they asked us to recline on the floor and to shout out individual words (eventually moving to short phrases) that were not meant to relate to one another. Although a valuable lesson on the emergent possibilities of group improvisation was imparted, with only limited interaction possibilities and without an intended semantic dimension (many of course chose to ignore that particular instruction), the exercise seemed to languish a bit. But clearly pedagogical approaches like this one that aim to control certain parameters can instill a sensitivity in performers that makes the more open and adaptive approaches to improvisation possible. These ideas are taken up in the final chapter as well.
46. See Bonabeau et al. (1999:14–17).
47. Surowiecki (2004) chapter 9.

48. Bonabeau and Théraulaz (2000:79).
49. Kelly (1994:12).
50. Bonabeau et al. (1999:22).
51. Resnick (1994:120).
52. Mainzer (1994:271).
53. Nunn (1998:157).
54. Keller (1985). Also recounted in Resnick (1994:122).
55. For other research offering a feminist critique of science see Keller (1985), Keller and Longino (1996), Haraway (2004), and Gilbert (2000).
56. Resnick (1994:123–129). The StarLogo program has been supplanted by more recent multi-agent modeling systems including NetLogo and Swarm, the latter developed at the Santa Fe Institute.
57. As one of my astute readers pointed out, one may be compelled to ask: Could our "invention" (for some) of God be proven to be as much an assumption/presumption error?
58. Resnick (1994:129).
59. Resnick (1994:131).
60. Johnson (2001:20–21).
61. The Institute for Complex Studies at the University of Michigan is also supporting similar innovative work.
62. Waterman (1990).
63. Quoted in Toop (2004:242).
64. The main criticisms of a view of evolution focused exclusively on random mutations include an insufficient or inconclusive fossil record regarding intermediary species in the evolutionary timeline leading to the emergence of new species, insufficient time for random mutations to create many of the remarkably complex features of biological species (like the mammalian eye), and a general difficulty in understanding how gradual mutations can explain certain behaviors that seem to arise without continuous selective pressures (like insect mimicry) or that lead to both older and newer forms of a given species inhabiting the same geographic area or ecological niche.
65. Capra (1996:227–28).
66. Margulis (1998:5).
67. Quoted in Joseph (1990:39).
68. Margulis and Sagan (1986:15).
69. Margulis (1998:33).
70. Margulis (1998:6).
71. Toop (2004:244).
72. Toop (2004:244).
73. http://www.shef.ac.uk/misc/rec/ps/efi/.
74. "New Research Opens a Window on the Mind of Plants." http://www.csmonitor.com/2005/0303/p01s03-usgn.htm.
75. http://www.miyamasaoka.com/interdisciplinary/.
76. Quoted in Toop (2004:245). See Rothenberg (1995 and 2002).
77. Most people envisioned computers in their infancy as offering little more than simple number crunching or bookkeeping assistance. And since the earliest models filled entire rooms and were off limits except to a privileged few, many initially viewed computers as representative of a centralized mindset. Computers do still function as excellent bookkeepers and electronic typewriters, and they are still out of reach of many, but increasingly computational tools and networking technologies are playing a role in the spread of decentralized ideas.
78. Eno (1996).
79. Helmreich (1998:95). Quoted in Lansing (2003:200).

80. Quoted in Toop (2004:245).
81. Eno (1996).
82. Quoted in Henkin (2003:n.p.).
83. For one example of future directions, the Brooklyn-based group of artists and technologists LEMUR (League of Electronic Musical Urban Robots) is developing robotic musical instruments that "play themselves" and can interact with human performers as well.
84. Resnick (1994:133).
85. Although this blurring may be artistically encouraging, we still need to be aware of cultural assumptions that accompany our notions of musicking. Eddie Prévost, in his book *Minute Particulars*, recounts an AMM performance after which a woman came up to the musicians and remarked how moved she had been by the music. Once she learned that the group had been improvising rather than playing from a memorized score, she not only doubted their artistic and intellectual integrity, but she was forced to question her own powers of discrimination. "How had it been possible for her to enjoy and admire such work when its practice had been so . . . primitive."
86. I am indebted to Pantelis Vassilakis for this intriguing comment. See also Russell (1983) and Bloom (2000).
87. For another example, in an economic downturn or upturn, people often struggle to identify *the* cause for celebration or dismay. Was it the rise in oil prices, or the drop in consumer confidence? Is the Federal Chairman responsible for this?
88. Resnick (1994:137).
89. Resnick (1994:8).
90. Capra (1996:39).
91. Lansing (2003:192).
92. Lewis (2004b).
93. Barabási (2002:222).
94. Margulis (1998:2).
95. Shaviro (2003:10).
96. Six Degrees of Separation gained popularity through John Guare's play of the same name and more recently in the Oracle of Kevin Bacon game on the Internet.
97. Watts (2003:28), italics in original.
98. Like all of these emerging sciences, the contemporary study of networks did not emerge from whole cloth. Graph theory in mathematics dates to at least the early eighteenth century when Leonhard Euler solved the problem of taking a stroll across all seven bridges in the Prussian city of Königsberg without crossing the same bridge twice by constructing an elaborate graph. The methods that were developed in the following years, however, were exclusively linear. Paul Erdós and Albert Rényi were first to introduce the notion of random graphs. Since Erdós was such a prolific scholar, coauthoring hundred of papers, he is also well known for the notion of an Erdós number that calculates how many degrees of separation lie between any given mathematician and the master. Most have no more than three or four degrees separation and no mathematician who has coauthored a paper has more than seventeen as their Erdós number.
99. Barabási (2002:39) makes the point that six degrees is a product of our modern society in which people are insistent about keeping in touch and they have the opportunity to do so. And Watts (2003:132–5) explains many of the shortcomings of Milgrams's original experiment and the difficulty of establishing the notion of "six degrees of separation" empirically and unequivocally so that it could be considered any sort of "universal."
100. Scientists have studied extensively the connections in the brain of the nematode worm since the map of its 282 neurons is well understood.
101. See Barabási (2002).
102. Economist now believe that Parteo's law only holds for the richest people in a society. The majority of others may follow a distribution closer to gas laws. See Hogan (2005).

103. For example, in many instances it may be accurate to say the 20% of the workers produce 80% of the profit for the compoany, but it is not accurate to say the 20% of the workers do 80% of the work.

104. Barabási (2002:66).

105. For a very readable introduction to power laws and the related study of self-organized criticality, see Bak (1996).

106. Barabási (2002:97, 103).

107. Barabási's team was able to show that the Microsoft example follows the quantum laws of a Bose-Einstein condensate. See Barabási (2002:105–6).

108. Diamond (1997).

109. So that this does not read like Bailey bashing, a particularly astute Amazon.com reviewer noted recently that Evan Parker has drastically reduced the rate at which he is releasing new CDs: "Perhaps Parker is trying to answer the increasing jadedness of music critics & fans who feel that he has released too many discs in recent years while treading water as a player."

110. Hajdu (2003:54).

111. For a recent example of how powerful these hubs have become, the San Francisco Jazz Spring 2005 series of concerts features no less than seven tributes to the music of John Coltrane within a month's time, including versions of his music from the albums *A Love Supreme, Ascension, Africa Brass, Crescent,* and *Interstellar Space.* There is also a concert by the Mingus Big Band and a tribute to the music of Rashaan Roland Kirk planned as well.

112. Hajdu (2003:54).

113. For a rather technical discussion of this topic see Song et al. (2005).

114. Kleinberg (2000). See also Watts (2003:139–146).

115. The cartoon conveniently summarizes the attitude of many American jazz musicians as well, that New York City is the "center of the musical universe."

116. Watts (2003:53).

117. Law (1999:5). For other important work in ANT see the publications of Geoffrey C. Bowker and Susan Leigh Star.

118. http://www.comp.lancs.ac.uk/sociology/soc054jl.html.

119. http://carbon.cudenver.edu/~mryder/itc_data/ant_dff.html. Goguen is referencing the work of Michael White, *Isaac Newton: The Last Sorcerer* (Perseus Books, 1999).

120. Barabási (2002:225).

121. Watts (2003:302–3).

Chapter Seven

1. William Clancey (1997:4). See also Clark (1997) for a very readable introduction to this perspective.

2. Lave (1988) studied adults of various backgrounds using arithmetic while grocery shopping. In making purchase decisions, they employed a flexible real-time arithmetic in order to select better prices per unit weight, continually taking into account the constraints imposed by the layout of the stores, the capacities of their home refrigerators, and the dietary requirements of their family members. These skills with situated arithmetic, however, were rarely reflected in their performance on grade-school math problems.

3. Nunn (1998:179).

4. Stockdale (2004:112).

5. Latour (1987:7).

6. From the book by Eddie Harris, *Jazz Astrology, Nemerology, and Information.* Quoted in liner notes to his album *There was a Time — Echo of Harlem* (Alfa/Enja R2 79663).

7. Quoted in Nunn (1998:180).

8. William Clancey (1995:49). See also Korzybski (1948: 58).

9. Despite this and subsequent generalizations, I am aware that there are many music educators who have developed innovative pedagogical strategies, usually in isolation. They tend to be, however, the exception that proves the rule. Brown, Collins, and Duguid (1989) write: "Though there are many innovative teachers, schools, and programs that act otherwise, prevalent school practices assume, more often than not, that knowledge is individual and self-structured, that schools are neutral with respect to what is learned, that concepts are abstract, relatively fixed, and unaffected by the activity through which they are acquired and used, and the 'just plain folks' behavior should be discouraged."

10. This and all subsequent quotes from Turetzky, Dresser, Davis, and Ellis stem from interviews with the author in January and February of 2005.

11. For an intriguing example of this, consider the case of Mike May. May is one of only a handful of individuals who, blind from early childhood, were able to regain their sight. After cornea- and stem cell-implant surgery in 2000, sight was restored to May's right eye. But vision is more than just eye function, just as "good ears" means much more to a musician than having properly functioning ears. Although May can interpret many objects, often through the perception of simple shapes and colors, and he can perceive objects in motion (a process that may in fact be hardwired into the brain), three-dimensional perception and the ability to recognize complex objects such as the faces of his family and friends remain severely impaired. His optical hardware is in perfect order, but May's brain has not learned to process the visual information it receives. Vision, like language and hearing, appears to be a skill that is developed and honed through experience.

12. For more on this issue and the many important curricular questions it raises see Ake (2002a).

13. Chase et al. (2000).

14. Although the notion of repeating an improvisation exactly runs counter to its very practice, I have found that recording student improvisations not only helps to center everyone's creative energies during performance, but it has the additional benefit of providing the possibility for listening back as a group and critiquing, in constructive ways, what occurred and how the ensemble might work together to improve on things for the next time.

15. Bailey (1992:121).

16. See Lewis (2000a) and Ake (2002b) for related discussion.

17. See Lewis (2000a and In Press) and Sweet (1996).

18. Vygotsky (1997:324).

19. For more technical detail see Dresser (2000).

20. Ake (2002a:268).

21. For an excellent introduction to the work of Vygotsky and its impact on current thinking, see Daniels (2001).

22. See Vygotsky (1978). For a dynamical systems perspective on developmental psychology, see Thelen (2003).

23. Barab and Plucker (2002:170).

24. Much of the important work on distributed cognition has been completed aboard vessels at sea. Thomas Gladwin detailed how traditional Micronesian sailors use the local conditions of the sea, including waves and winds, combined with a final objective rather than a formal plan to navigate long distances successfully. And Edwin Hutchins (1995) worked aboard a Navy ship investigating the ways in which the cognitive demands of successful navigation are distributed among the various crewmembers and the tools and physical layout of the ship's bridge. See Bereiter (1997) for a cogent critique of a strong reading of situated cognition.

25. For a related ethnomusicological study on the social dimensions of competence and talent, see Brinner (1995) on Central Javanese gamelan.

26. Barab and Plucker (2002:179).

27. Gibson (1977).
28. Hayles (1999:13,202).
29. The educational activities that surround the notion of a Zone of Proximal Development are often referred to as "scaffolding," although the term originated not from Vygotsky but from his later commentators.
30. Music is clearly an ideal area for this type of participatory learning, but Lave's work with Etienne Wenger (1991) demonstrated that in settings as diverse as Yucatec midwives, Vai and Gola tailors, US Navy quartermasters, meat-cutters, and nondrinking alcoholics in Alcoholics Anonymous, individuals gradually acquire knowledge and skills from experts in the context of everyday activities.
31. See Davidson and Torff (1992) for related discussion.
32. See Sudnow (1978) for a related treatment of this subject.
33. Bowman (2004:33). Although the widely influential theory of Howard Gardner (1983) categorizes multiple types of intelligences, including a "musical" one, it still treats the notion of intelligence as the exclusive provenance of an individual. And while Gardner acknowledges the role that the environment and context can play in the application of intelligence, he does not highlight the ways in which they can shape its ontological existence.
34. Berger's system called "gamala taki" helps musicians to break down complicated rhythms into patterns of threes ("ga-ma-la") and two's ("ta-ki").
35. Sweet (1996:108–9).
36. For a technical study of the distributed and emergent aspects of song performance in a rock cover band see Flor and Maglio (1997).
37. See Monson (1996) for examples in jazz and Sawyer (2003:176–8) for discussion of related work on interactional synchrony in orchestral performance.
38. Burrows (2004:n.p.)
39. For more, see Collier (1996).
40. Stockdale (2004). In other language, Stockdale's three broad categories might be described as bebop, freebop, and free.
41. Stockdale (2004:112).
42. Clancey (1997).
43. Quoted in Corbett (1994:203).
44. Cook (2004:14).
45. See Csikszentmihalyi and Rich (1997).
46. Becker (1982).
47. Sawyer (2003). Much of his work with jazz draws on ethnographic work by Paul Berliner (1994) and Ingrid Monson (1996).
48. Quoted in Monson (1996:88).
49. Sawyer (2003:46).
50. Sawyer (2004:195).
51. Borgo (1996:80).
52. Lewis (2000b:37–8). John Corbett (1995:233) also points out that sports analogies describe well the constant transgression and reestablishment of codes that takes place in the process of improvising music.
53. Johnstone (1979:95). For a related treatment regarding jazz improvisation, see Werner (1996).
54. Stockdale (2004:109).
55. Sawyer (2003:9).
56. This sentiment comes from Wadada Leo Smith and was quoted to me by Ralph "Buzzy" Jones.
57. Sawyer (2003,2004).
58. Sawyer (2004) uses this and other examples of the actor's craft to suggest ways in which classroom teachers might be more effective in encouraging collaborative discussion.

59. See Borgo (2002) for one example.
60. Sawyer (2003:44).
61. See Lewis (2000b).
62. Watson (2004:263). Peter Brook, in his classic theater text *The Empty Space* (1968:9), draws attention, however, to the inextricable relationship theater has with an audience: "I can take any empty space and call it a bare stage. A man walks across the empty space whilst someone else is watching him, and this is all that is needed for an act of theater to be engaged."
63. Sawyer (2004:198).
64. See Larry Och's essay on RADAR (http://www.rova.org/foodforthought/radar.html) or his essay in Zorn (2000). Ensemble strategies or role playing may also be used in less explicit ways or they may intentionally be hidden from the awareness of audiences.
65. Solothurnmann (1985:32). Quoted in Corbett (1995:233).
66. Nunn (1998:162).
67. Alperson (1984:22).
68. Lewis (2000a:86).
69. Heffley (2005:292).
70. From the first sentence of chapter XXXI in *The Education of Henry Adams* (1918).
71. Eno (1996:n.p.).
72. Quoted in Sweet (1996:47).
73. From Microsoft Word dictionary.
74. Corbett (1995:225–6).
75. Lewis (2004b:n.p.). See Attali (1985:147) for the complete quote in context.
76. Axelrod and Cohen (2000:30).
77. Weick (1998).
78. Zack (2000). Other authors, including Kamoche (2003), worry that there are inherent dangers in relying on the jazz metaphor to the exclusion of others and to the exclusion of grounded and empirical research.
79. Nunn (1998:133).

REFERENCES

Abraham, Ralph. 1994. *Chaos, Gaia, and Eros*. Harper San Francsico.

Ake, David. 2002a. "Learning Jazz, Teaching Jazz." In *The Cambridge Companion to Jazz*, ed. by Mervyn Cooke and David Horn. Cambridge University Press.

Ake, David. 2002b. *Jazz Cultures*. University of California Press.

Alperson, Philip. 1984. "On Musical Improvisation." *Journal of Aesthetics and Art Criticism* 43(1):17–29.

Argyris, John, Gunter Faust, Maria Haase. 1994. *An Exploration of Chaos*. North-Holland.

Attali, Jacques. 1985. *Noise: The Political Economy of Music*. University of Minnesota Press.

Atton, Christopher. 1988–89. "Some Answers to Some Questions about Improvised Music." *The Improvisor* 8:32–40 (also published in *Contact* 1988, no. 33).

Axelrod, Robert, and Michael D. Cohen. 2000. *Harnesing Complexity: Organizational Implications of a Scientific Frontier*. Basic Books.

Bach y Rita, P. 1962. *Brain Mechanisms in Sensory Substitution*. Academic Press.

Bader, Rolf. 2002a. "Fractal Correlation Dimension and Discrete-Pseudo-Phase Plots of Percussion Instruments in Relation to Cultural World View." *Ingenierias* V(17):1–11.

Bader, Rolf. 2002b. "Fraktale Dimensionen, Infomationsstrukturen und Mikrorhythmik der Einschwingvorgänge von Musikinstrumenten." Ph.D Dissertation, University of Hamburg.

Bailey, Derek. 1992. *Improvisation: Its Nature and Practice in Music*. Da Capo.

Bak, Per. 1996. *How Nature Works; The Science of Self-Organized Criticality*. Copernicus.

Bakhtin, Mikail. 1984. *Problems of Dostoevsky's Poetics*, translated by Caryl Emerson. University of Minnesota Press.

Balliett, Whitney. 1959. *The Sound of Surprise*. Dutton.

Barab, Sasha, and Jonathan Plucker. 2002. "Smart People of Smart Contexts? Cognition, Ability, and Talent Development in an Age of Situated Approaches to Knowing and Learning." *Educational Psychologist* 37(3):165–182.

Barabási, Albert-László. 2002. *Linked: The New Science of Networks*. Perseus.

Barry, Malcolm. 1985. "Improvisation: The State of the Art." *British Journal of Music Education* 2(2):171–175.

Barthes, Roland. 1991. *The Responsibility of Forms: Critical Essays on Music, Art, and Representation*. University of California Press.

Bateson, Gregory. 1972. *Steps to an Ecology of Mind*. Ballantine Books.

Becker, Howard. 1982. *Art Worlds*. University of California Press.

Belgrad, Daniel. 1997. *The Culture of Spontaneity: Improvisation and the Arts in Postwar America*. University of Chicago Press.

221

REFERENCES

Benson, Bruce Ellis. 2003. *Improvisation of Musical Dialog: A Phenomenology of Music Making*. Cambridge University Press.

Benzon, William. 2001. *Beethoven's Anvil*. Basic Books.

Bereiter, Carl. 1997. "Situated Cognition and How to Overcome It." In *Situated Cognition: Social, Semiotic, and Psychological Perspectives*, ed. by D. Kirshner and J.A. Whitson, pp. 281–300. Erlbaum Publishers.

Berendt, Joachim-Ernst. 1983. *The World Is Sound: Nada Brahma*. Destiny Books.

Berendt, Joachim-Ernst. 1985. *The Third Ear: On Listening to the World*. Henry Holt and Co.

Beresford, Steve. 1998. "Process and Reality: Up and Down the City Road. Evan Parker in Conversation with Steve Beresford." *Gramophone Explorations* vol 3:86–92.

Berio, Luciano. 1985. *Two Interviews*. Marion Boyars.

Berliner, Paul. 1993. *The Soul of the Mbira* (rev. ed.). University of California Press.

Berliner, Paul. 1994. *Thinking in Jazz: The Infinite Art of Improvisation*. University of Chicago Press.

Bidlack, Rick. 1990. "Music from Chaos: Nonlinear Dynamical Systems as Generators of Musical Materials." UCSD Dissertation.

Block, Steven. 1997. "'Bemsha Swing': The Transformation of a Bebop Classic to Free Jazz." *Music Theory Spectrum* 19(2):206–231.

Bloom, Howard. 2000. *Global Brain: The Evolution of Mass Mind from the Big Bang to the 21st Century*. John Wiley & Sons.

Bonabaue, Eric, Marco Dorgio, and Guy Théraulaz. 1999. *Swarm Intelligence: From Natural to Artificial Systems*. Oxford University Press.

Bonabeau, Eric, and Guy Théraulaz. 2000. "Swarm Smarts." *Scientific American* (March):72–79.

Bordiue, Pierre. 1977. *Outline of a Theory of Practice*, translated by Richard Nice. Cambridge University Press.

Borgo, David. 1996. "The Dialogics of Free Jazz: Musical Interaction in Collectively Improvised Performance." M.A. thesis, UCLA.

Borgo, David. 1997. "Emergent Qualities of Collectively Improvised Performance: A Study of an Egalitarian Intercultural Improvising Trio. *Pacific Review of Ethnomusicology* 8:23–40.

Borgo, David. 1999. "Reverence for Uncertainty: Order, Chaos, and the Dynamics of Musical Free Improvistion." Ph.D. Dissertation, UCLA.

Borgo, David. 2002. "Synergy and Surrealestate: The Orderly-Disorder of Free Improvisation." *Pacific Review of Ethnomusicology* 10:1–24.

Borgo, David. 2002. "Negotiating Freedom: Values and Practices in Contemporary Improvised Music." *Black Music Research Journal* 22(2):165–188.

Borgo, David. 2003. "Between Worlds: The Embodied and Ecstatic Sounds of Jazz." *The Open Space* 5.

Borgo, David. 2004. "The Meaning of Play and the Play of Meaning in Jazz." *Journal of Consciousness Studies* 11(3/4):174–190.

Borgo, David, and Joseph Goguen. 2005. "Rivers of Consciousness: The Nonlinear Dynamics of Free Jazz." *Jazz Research Proceedings Yearbook* vol. 25.

Borgo, David. In press. "The Chaotic Self, Or the Embodiment of Evan Parker," In *Playing Changes: New Jazz Studies*, ed. by Robert Walser. Duke University Press.

Bouchard, Fred. 1998. Liner notes to the CD *Chaos* by Paul Bley, Furio Di Castri, and Tony Oxley. Soul Note Records.

Boulez, Pierre. 1975. *Conversations with Célestien Deliege*. Eulenberg Books.

Bourdieu, Pierre. 1977. *Outline of a Theory of Practice*. Cambridge University Press.

Bowman, Wayne. 2004. "Cognition and the Body: Perspectives from Music Education." In *Knowing Bodies, Moving Minds: Towards Embodied Teaching and Learning*, ed. by Liora Bresler. Kluwer Academic Publishers.

Boyd, Jenny. 1992. *Musicians in Tune: Seventy-Five Contemporary Musicians Discuss the Creative Process*. Simon and Schuster.

Bradlyn, Mark. 1991. "Figure, Ground and Field, Gesture and Texture: A Gestalt Strategy for Group Improvisation." *The Improvisor* 9:23–26.

Bradlyn, Mark. 1988–89. "Chaos Theory and Group Improvisation." *The Improvisor* 8:15–18.

Briggs, John, and F. David Peat. 1989. *The Turbulent Mirror*. Harper & Row.

Brinner, Benjamin. 1995. *Knowing Music, Making Music: Javanese Gamelan and the Theory of Musical Competence and Interaction*. University of Chicago Press.

Brook, Peter. 1968. *The Empty Space*. MacGibbon & Kee.

Brown, John Seely, Allan Collins, and Paul Duguid. 1989. "Situated Cognition and the Culture of Learning." *Educational Researcher* 18(1):32–42.

Burrows, Jared. 2004. "Musical Archetypes and Collective Consciousness: Cognitive Distribution and Free Improvisation." *Critical Studies in Improvisation* 1.

Capra, Fritjof. 1996. *The Web of Life*. Doubleday.

Cardew, Cornelius. 1971. "Towards an Ethic of Improvisation." In *Treatise Handbook*. Peters Press.

Carr, Ian. 1973. *Music Outside: Contemporary Jazz in Britain*. Latimer New Dimensions.

Carroll-Phelan, B., and P.J. Hampson. 1996. "Multiple Components of the Perception of Musical Sequences: A Cognitive Neuroscience Analysis and Some Implications for Auditory Imagery." *Music Perception* 13(4).

Casti, John L. 1994. *Complexification: Explaining a Paradoxical World Through the Science of Surprise*. Harper Collins.

Chase, Allan, Graham Collier, and Ed Sarath. 2000. "The Shape of Jazz to Come?" Transcription of a panel discussion at the International Association of Jazz Educators Convention. http://www.jazzcontinuum.com/jc_rtcl1.html.

Clancey, William J. 1995. "A Tutorial on Situated Learning." In *Proceedings of the International Conference on Computers and Education* (Taiwan), ed. by J. Self. Charlottesville, VA: AACE, 49–70.

Clancey, William J. 1997. *Situated Cognition: On Human Knowledge and Computer Representations*. Cambridge University Press.

Clark, Andy. 1997. *Being There: Putting Brain, Body, and World Together Again*. MIT Press.

Clayton, Martin, Rebecca Sager, and Udo Will. 2004. "In Time with the Music: The Concept of Entrainment and Its Significance for Ethnomusicology. *ESEM Counterpoint*, vol. 1.

Collier, Graham. 1996. *Interaction: Opening Up the Jazz Ensemble*. Advance Music.

Condon, William. 1986. "Communication: Rhythm and Structure." In *Rhythm in Psychological, Linguistic and Musical Processes*, ed. by J.R. Evans and M. Clynes, pp. 55–78. Charles E. Thomas Publishers.

Cope, David. 1976. *New Directions in Music*, 2nd ed. Miami University.

Corbett, John. 1994. *Extended Play: Sounding Off from John Cage to Dr. Funkenstein*. Duke University Press.

Corbett, John. 1995. "Ephemera Underscored: Writing Around Free Improvisation." In *Jazz Among the Discourses*, ed. by Krin Gabbard, 217–40. Duke University Press.

Couldry, Nick. 1995. "Turning the Musical Table: Improvisation in Britain 1965–1990." *Rubberneck* 19:1–38.

Cox, Christopher, and Daniel Warner, eds. 2004. *Audio Culture: Readings in Modern Music*. Continuum.

Cross, Ian. 2003. "Music, Cognition, Culture, and Evolution." In *The Cognitive Neuroscience of Music*, ed. by Isabelle Peretz and Robert J. Zatorre, 42–56. Oxford University Press.

Csikzentmihalyi, Mihaly. 1991. *Flow: The Psychology of Optimal Experience*. Dimensions.

Csikzentmihalyi, Mihaly, and Grant Jewell Rich. 1997. "Musical Improvisation: A Systems Approach." In *Creativity in Performance*, ed. by R. Keith Sawyer, pp. 43–66. Ablex Publishing Corporation.

Damasio, Antonio. 1999. *The Feeling of What Happens: Body, Emotion, and the Meaning of Consciousness*. Harcourt.

Daniels, Harry. 2001. *Vygotsky and Pedagogy*. Routledge.

REFERENCES

Davidson, Lyle, and Bruce Torff. 1992. "Situated Cognition in Music." *The World of Music* 34(3): 120–139.

Davidson, Martin. 1984. "On Recording Improvisation." *The Wire* 9 (November), 23.

Day, Steve. 1998. *Two Full Ears: Listening to Improvised Music*. Soundworld.

Day, William. 2000. "Knowing as Instancing: Jazz Improvisation and Moral Perfectionism." *Journal of Aesthetics and Art Criticism*, 58(2):99–111.

Dean, Roger. 1992. *New Structures in Jazz and Improvised Music Since 1960*. Open University Press.

Deutsch, Diana. 1999. *The Psychology of Music*. Academic Press.

Diamond, Jared. 1997. *Guns, Germs, and Steel: The Fates of Human Societies*. W.W. Norton.

Dresser, Mark. 2000. "A Personal Pedagogy." In *Arcana: Musicians on Music*, ed. by John Zorn. Granary Books.

Drewal, M. T. 1992. *Yoruba Ritual: Performers, Play, Agency*. Indiana University Press.

Durant, Alan. 1989. "Improvisation in the Political Economy of Music." In *Music and the Politics of Culture*, ed. by Christopher Norris, pp. 252–282. Lawrence and Wishart.

Eno, Brian. 1996. "Generative Music." *In Motion Magazine*. //www.inmotionmagazine.com/eno1 .html.

Fales, Cornelia. 2002. "The Paradox of Timbre." *Ethnomusicology* 46(1):56–95.

Fauconnier, Gilles, and Mark Turner. 2002. *The Way We Think: Conceptual Blending and the Mind's Hidden Complexities*. Basic Books.

Fauvel, John, Raymond Flood, and Robin Wilson. 2003. *Music and Mathematics: From Pythagorus to Fractals*. Oxford University Press.

Ferand, Ernest T. 1961. *Improvisation in Nine Centuries of Music*. A. Volk Verlag.

Flor, Nick, and Paul Maglio. 1997. "Emergent Global Cueing of Local Activity: Covering in Music." *Computer Supported Collaborative Learning Conference Proceedings*.

Freeman, Phil. 2001. *New York Is Now!: The New Wave of Free Jazz*. The Telegraph Company.

Gabrielsson, Alf. 1988. "Timing in Music Performance and Its Relations to Music Experience." In *Generative Processes in Music*, ed. by John Sloboda. Clarendon Press.

Gadamer, Hans Georg. 1993. *Truth and Method*. Continuum.

Gardner, Howard. 1983. *Frames of Mind: The Theory of Multiple Intelligences*. Basic Books.

Gates, Henry Louis, Jr. 1988. *The Signifying Monkey: A Theory of Afro-American Literary Criticism*. New York: Oxford University Press.

Gennari, John. 1991. "Jazz criticism: Its development and ideologies." *Black American Literature Forum* 25 (Fall):449–523.

Gershon, Pete. 2001. "Jameel Moondoc: Organically Grown." *Signal to Noise* 15.

Gibson, J.J. 1977. "The Theory of Affordances." In *Perceiving, Acting, and Knowling: Toward an Ecological Psychology*, ed. by R.E. Shaw and J. Bransford. Lawrence Erlbaum Associates.

Gilbert, Scott F. 2000. "Mainstreaming Feminist Critques into the Biology Curriculum." In *Doing Sciene + Culture*, ed. by Roddey Reid and Sharon Traweek. Routledge.

Gioia, Ted. 1988. *The Imperfect Art: Reflections of Jazz and Modern Culture*. Oxford University Press.

Gladwin, Thomas. 1964. "Cuulture and Logical Process." In *Explorations in Cultural Anthropology: Essays Presented to George Peter Murdock*, ed. by W. Goodenough. McGraw-Hill.

Gleick, James. 1987. *Chaos: The Making of a New Science*. Penguin.

Gleiser, Pablo, and Leon Danon. 2003. "Community Structure in Jazz. *Advances in Complex Systems* 6(4):565–573.

Goguen, Joseph. 1977. "Complexity of Hierarchically Organized Systems and the Structure of Musical Experiences." *International Journal of General Systems* 3, 233–251.

Goguen, Joseph. 2004. "Musical Qualia, Context, Time, and Emotion." *Journal of Consciousness Studies* 11(3/4):117–147.

Grady, Joseph E., Todd Oakley, and Seana Coulson. 1999. "Blending and Metaphor." In *Metaphor in Cognitive Linguistics*, ed. by G. Steen and R. Gibbs. John Benjamins.

Gray, John. 1991. *Fire Music: A Bibliography of the New Jazz, 1959–1990*. Greenwood Press.

Grosz, Elizabeth. 1994. *Volatile Bodies: Toward a Corporeal Feminism.* Indiana University Press.

Hajdu, David. 2003. "Wynton's Blues." *The Atlantic Monthly* (March).

Hall, Edward T. 1992. "Improvisation as an Acquired, Multilevel Process." *Ethnomusicology* 36(2): 223–235.

Hamel, Peter Michael. 1986. *Through Music to The Self.* Element Books.

Haraway, Donna. 2004. *The Haraway Reader.* Routledge.

Harris, Jerome. 2000. "Jazz on the Global Stage." In *The African Diaspora: A Musical Perspective,* ed. by Ingrid Monson. Garland Publishing.

Hayles, N. Katherine. 1990. *Chaos Bound: Orderly Disorder in Contemporary Literature and Science.* Cornell University Press.

Hayles, N. Katherine. 1999. *How We Became Posthuman: Virtual Bodies in Cybernetics, Literature, and Informatics.* University of Chicago Press.

Heble, Ajay. 2000. *Landing on the Wrong Note: Jazz, Dissonance, and Cultural Practice.* Routledge.

Heble, Ajay, and Daniel Fischlin, eds. 2004. *The Other Side of Nowhere: Jazz, Improvisation, and Communities in Dialog.* Wesleyan University Press.

Heffley, Mike. 2005. *Northern Sun, Southern Moon: Europe's Reinvention of Jazz.* Yale University Press.

Held, Richard, and Alan Hein. 1963. "Movement-Produced Stimulation in the Development of Visually Guided Behavior." *Journal of Comparative and Physiological Psychology* 56(Oct):872–6.

Henkin, Andrey. 2003. "Artist Profiles: Evan Parker Solo." http://www.allaboutjazz.com. (posted February 17).

Hess, David. 1997. *Science Studies: An Advanced Introduction.* New York University Press.

Hester, Karlton E. 1997. *The Melodic and Polyrhythmic Development of John Coltrane's Spontaneous Composition in a Racist Society.* Edwin Mellen.

Hofstadter, Douglas. 1979. *Gödel, Escher, Bach: An Eternal Golden Braid.* Basic Books.

Hogan, Jenny. 2005. "Why It Is Hard to Share the Wealth." *New Scientist* (March).

Horgan, John. 1995. "From Complexity to Perplexity." *Scientific American* 272(6):104–10.

Houn, Fred Wei-Han. 1985–88. "Asian American Music and Empowerment." *Views on Black American Music* 3:27–32.

Houn, Fred Wei-Han. 1995. "'Jazz,' Kreolization and Revolutionary Music for the 21st Century." In *Sounding Off!: Music as Subversion/Resistance/Revolution,* ed. by Ron Sakolsky and Fred Wei-han Ho. Autonomedia.

Husserl, Edmond. 1964. *Phenomenology of Internal Time-Consciousness.* Indiana University Press.

Hutchins, Edwin. 1995. *Cognition in the Wild.* MIT Press.

Iyer, Vijay. 2002. "Embodied Mind, Situated Cognition, and Expressive Microtiming in African-American Music." *Music Perception* 19(3):387–414.

Jenkins, Todd S. 2004. *Free Jazz and Free Improvisation Encyclopedia.* Greenwood Press.

Johnson, Mark. 1987. *The Body in the Mind: The Bodily Basis of Meaning, Imagination, and Reason.* University of Chicago Press.

Johnson, Stephen. 2001. *Emergence: The Connected Lives of Ants, Brains, Cities, and Software.* Scribner.

Johnson, Tom. 1989. *The Voice of the New Music (New York City 1972–1982): A Collection of Articles Originally Published in the Village Voice.* Het Appollohuis.

Johnson-Laird, Philip N. 1988. "Freedom and Constraint in Creativity." In *The Nature of Creativity: Contemporary Psychological Perspectives,* ed. by Robert J. Sternberg, 202–19. Cambridge University Press.

Johnstone, Keith. 1979. *Impro: Improvisation and the Theater.* Faber and Faber.

Jones, LeRoi. 1963. *Blues People: Negro Music in White America.* William Morrow.

Joseph, Lawrence. 1990. *Gaia: The Growth of an Idea.* St. Martin's Press.

Jost, Ekkehard. 1994 [1975]. *Free Jazz.* Da Capo Press.

Kamoche, Ken. 2003. "Towards a Theory of Organizational Improvisation: Looking Beyond the Jazz Metaphor." *Journal of Management Studies* 40(8).

Kauffman, Stuart. 1995. *At Home in the Universe: The Search for Laws of Self-Organization and Complexity.* Oxford University Press.

REFERENCES

Keefe, Douglas H., and Bernice Laden. 1991. "Correlation Dimension of Woodwind Multiphonic Tones." *Journal of the Acoustic Society of America* 90(4):1754–65.

Keil, Charles, and Steven Feld. 1994. *Music Grooves*. University of Chicago Press.

Keller, Evelyn Fox. 1985. *Reflections on Gender and Science*. Yale University Press.

Keller, Evelyn Fox, and Helen E. Longino. 1996. *Feminism and Science*. Oxford University Press.

Kellert, Steven. 1993. *In the Wake of Chaos*. University of Chicago Press.

Kelly, Kevin. 1994. *Out of Control: The New Biology of Machines, Social Systems, and the Economic World*. Addison-Wesley Publishing Company.

Kelly, Robin. 2002. *Freedom Dreams: The Black Radical Imagination*. Beacon Press.

Khan, Hazrat Inayat. 1983. *The Music of Life*. Omega Publications.

Kleinberg, Jon. 2000. "Navigation in Small Worlds." *Nature* 406, 845.

Kofsky, Frank. 1970. *Black Nationalism and the Revolution in Music*. Pathfinder.

Korner, Anthony. 1996. "Aurora Musicalis." *Artforum* (Summer).

Korzybski, Alfred. 1948. *Science and Sanity*. International Non-Aristotelian Library.

Lake, Steve. 1977. "Steve Beresford Talks to Steve Lake," *Musics* 14 (October), 15.

Lakoff, George, and Mark Johnson. 1980. *Metaphors We Live By*. University of Chicago Press.

Lansing, J. Stephen. 2003. "Complex Adaptive Systems." *Annual Review of Anthropology* 32:183–204.

Laszlo, Ervin. 1996. *The System View of the World: A Holistic Vision for Our Time*. Hampton Press.

Latour, Bruno. 1987. *Science in Action*. Harvard University Press.

Law, John, and John Hassard. 1999. *Actor Network Theory and After*. Blackwell.

Lehrer, Jonah. 2004. "Disorder Is Good for You." Seed Magazine Online. http://www.seedmagazine.com/?p = article&id = 100000030&cp = 0.

Lewis, George. 1996. "Improvised Music After 1950: Afro- and Eurological Perspectives." *Black Music Research Journal* 16(1):91–122.

Lewis, George. 2000a. "Teaching Improvised Music: An Ethnographic Memoir." In *Arcana: Musicians on Music*, ed. by John Zorn. Granary Books.

Lewis, George. 2000b. "Too Many Notes: Computers, Complexity and Culture in Voyager." *Leonardo Music Journal* 10:33–39.

Lewis, George. 2002. "Experimental Music in Black and White: The AACM in New York, 1970–1985." *Current Musicology* 71–73, 100–157.

Lewis, George. 2003. "The Secret Love between Interactivity and Improvisation, or—Missing in Interaction: A Prehistory of Computer Interactivity." Unpublished lecture delivered at UCSD, February.

Lewis, George. 2004a. "Getting to Know Y'all: Improvised Music, Interculturalism, and the Racial Imagination." *Critical Studies in Improvisation* 1.

Lewis, George. 2004b. "Improvisation and the Orchestra: A Composer Reflects." Essay to accompany a performance by the American Composers Orchestra at the Improvise! Festival, April 28.

Lewis, George. In press. *Power Stronger than Itself: The Association for the Advancement of Creative Musicians*. University of Chicago Press.

Lipsitz, George. 1997. *Dangerous Crossroads: Popular Music, Postmodernism and the Poetics of Place*. Verso.

Little, David Clark. 1995. "Composing with Chaos: Applications of a New Science for Music." http://www.fortunecity.com/victorian/holbein/113/musicchaos.html.

Litweiler, John. 1984. *The Freedom Principle: Jazz after 1958*. William Morrow.

Lochhead, Judy. 2001. "Hearing Chaos." *American Music* 19(2):210–246.

Lock, Graham. 1991. "After the New: Evan Parker, Speaking of the Essence." *Wire* 85:30–33,64.

Lock, Graham. 1999. *Blutopia*. Duke University Press.

Looker, Benjamin. 2004. *BAG: The Black Artist's Group of St. Louis*. University of Missouri Press.

Lorenz, Edward. 1996. *The Essence of Chaos*. University of Washington Press.

Lott, Eric. 1995. "Double V, Double Time: Bebop and the Politics of Style." In *Jazz Among the Discourses*, ed. by Krin Gabbard. Duke University Press.

Mainzer, Klaus. 1994. *Thinking in Complexity: The Complex Dynamics of Matter, Mind, and Mankind.* Springer-Verlag.

Mandelbrot, Benoit. 1982. *The Fractal Geometry of Nature.* W.H. Freeman.

Maquet, Jacques. 1994. "L.A.: One Society, One Culture, Many Options." *Selected Reports in Ethnomusicology* 10:15–21.

Martinelli, Francesco. 1994. *Evan Parker Discography.* Pisa: Bandecchi & Vivaldi Editore.

Maturana, Humberto, and Francisco Varela. 1980. "Autopoiesis and Cognition: The Realization of the Living," In *Boston Studies in the Philosophy of Science,* ed. by Robert S. Cohen and Marx W. Wartofsky, vol. 42. D. Reidel Publishing Co.

Maturana, Humberto, and Francisco Varela. 1988. *The Tree of Knowledge: The Biological Roots of Human Understanding.* Shambhala/New Science Press.

Maturana, Humberto, Warren McCulloch, Walter Pitts, and Jerry Lettvin. 1959. "What the Frog's Eye Tells the Frog's Brain." *Proceedings of the Institute for Radio Engineers* 47:1940–51.

Maturana, Humberto. 1975. "The Organization of the Living: A Theory of the Living Organization." *International Journal of Man-Machine Studies* 7, 313–332.

McClary, Susan, and Robert Walser. 1994. "Theorizing the Body in African-American Music." *Black Music Research Journal* 14(1):75–84.

McDonough, John. 1992. "30 Years of Free." *Down Beat* (January):29–31.

McGaughan, Mac. 1998. "Sam Rivers." *Tuba Frenzy* 4:11–18.

McRae, Barry. 1985. "Evan Parker: Moving Forward with Tradition." *Jazz Journal International* 38(1):10–11.

Mead, G.H. 1932. *The Philosopy of the Present.* University of Chicago Press.

Mechling, Jay. 1991. "*Homo Ludens* Subs. *Scientificus.*" *Play and Culture* 4(3):258–71.

Melchior, Chris. n.d. "Ambient Music, Beginnings and Implications." http://music.hyperreal.org/epsilon/info/melchior.html.

Meyer Leonard. 1956. *Emotion and Meaning in Music.* University of Chicago Press.

Miller, George A.1956. "The Magical Number Seven, Plus or Minus Two: Some Limits on our Capacity for Processing Information." *Psychological Review* 63:81–97.

Monson, Ingrid. 1996. *Sayin' Something: Jazz Improvisation and Interaction.* University of Chicago Press.

Monturi, Alfonso, and Ronald Purser. 1997. "Social Creativity: The Challenge of Complexity." http://www.ciis.edu/faculty/montuori.html.

Murphy, John. 1990. "Jazz Improvisation: The Joy of Influence," *The Black Perspective in Music* 18(1/2):7–19.

Muses, Charles. 1985. *Destiny and Control in Human Systems.* Kluwer Academic Publishers.

Nachmanovitch, Stephen. 1990. *Free Play: The Power of Improvisation in Life and the Arts.* G.P. Putnam and Son.

Nettl, Bruno, ed. 1998. *In the Course of Performance: Studies in the World of Musical Improvisation.* University of Chicago Press.

Nicolis, C. and Nicolis, G. 1984. "Is There a Climatic Attractor?" *Nature* 311, 529–532.

Nunn, Tom. 1998. *Wisdom of the Impulse: On the Nature of Musical Free Improvisation.* Self Published (tomnunn@sirius.com).

Palmer, Caroline. 1996. "Anatomy of a Performance: Sources of Musical Expression." *Music Perception* 13(3):433–453.

Parker, Evan. 1992. "Man & Machine 1992: 'De Motu' for Bushi Niebergall." http://www.shef.ac.uk/misc/rec/ps/efi/fulltext/demotu.html.

Peckham, Morse. 1965. *Man's Rage for Chaos.* Chilton Books.

Perper, Timothy. 1985. *Sex Signals: The Biology of Love.* ISI Press.

Pignon, Paul. 1998. "Far From Equilibrium." *Unfiled: Music Under New Technology,* n.p.

Pressing, Jeff. 1990. "Pitch-Class Transformation in Free Jazz." *Music Theory Spectrum* 12/2: 181–202.

REFERENCES

Pressing, Jeff. 1998. "Psychological Contraints on Improvisational Expertise and Communication." In *In the Course of Performance*, ed. by Bruno Nettl, 47–69. University of Chicago Press.

Prévost, Edwin. 1982. "The Aesthetic Priority of Improvisation: A Lecture." *Contact* 25:32–37.

Prévost, Edwin. 1995. *No Sound Is Innocent*. Matchless.

Prévost, Edwin. 2004. *Minute Particulars*. Matchless.

Prigogine, Ilya. 1980. *From Being to Becoming*. W. H. Freeman and Co.

Prigogine, Ilya, and Isabelle Stengers. 1984. *Order Out of Chaos*. Bantam Books.

Racy, Ali Jihad. 1994. "A Dialectical Perspective on Musical Instruments: The East-Mediterranean Mijwiz." *Ethnomusicology* 38(1):37–57.

Reich, Steve. 1974(1968). "Music as a Gradual Process." In *Writings about Music*. New York Universtiy Press. http://www.artsci.wustl.edu/~abauer/MusicasProcess.htm.

Resnick, Mitchel. 1994. *Turtles, Termites, and Traffic Jams*. MIT Press.

Riley, Peter. 1979. "Incus Records." *Coda* 167:3–8.

Roberts, David. 1977–78. "Record Reviews." *Contact* 18:39–40.

Rose, Tricia. 1994. *Black Noise: Rap Music and Black Culture in Contemporary America*. University Press of New England.

Rothenberg, David. 1995. *Hand's End: Technology and the Limits of Nature*. University of California Press.

Rothenberg, David. 2002. *Sudden Music: Improvisation, Sound, Nature*. University of Georgia Press.

Rothstein, Edward. 1995. *Emblems of Mind: The Inner Life of Music and Mathematics*. Avon Books.

Rusch, Bob. 1979. Interview with Evan Parker. *Cadence* 5(4):8–11.

Russell, Peter. 1983. *The Global Brain: Speculations on the Evolutionary Leap to Planetary Consciousness*. J.P. Tarcher, Inc.

Rzewski, Frederic. 2002. "Little Bangs: A Nihilist Theory of Improvisation." *Current Musicology* 67/68.

Sancho-Velazquez, Angeles. 2001. "The Legacy of Genius: Improvisation, Romantic Imagination, and the Western Musical Canon." Ph.D. Dissertation, UCLA.

Sarath, Ed. 1996. "A New Look at Improvisation." *Journal of Music Theory* 40(1):1–38.

Sardar, Ziauddin, and Iwona Abrams. 1999. *Introducing Chaos*. Icon Books.

Saul, Scott. 2003. *Freedom Is, Freedom Ain't: Jazz and the Making of the Sixties*. Harvard University Press.

Sawyer, R. Keith, ed. 1997. *Creativity in Performance*. Ablex Publishing Corp.

Sawyer, R. Keith. 2003. *Group Creativity: Music, Theater, Collaboration*. Lawrence Erlbaum Associates.

Sawyer, R. Keith. 2004. "Improvised Lessons: Collaborative Discussion in the Constructivist Classroom." *Teaching Education* 15(2):189–201.

Shaviro, Steven. 2003. *Connnected, Or What It Means to Live in the Network Society*. University of Minnesota Press.

Schutz, Alfred. 1964. "Making Music Together: A Study in Social Relationships." In *Collected Papers, Volume 2: Studies in Social Theory*, ed. by A. Brodessen. Martinus Nijhoff.

Sidran, Ben. 1981 [1971]. *Black Talk*. Da Capo.

Sloboda, John. 1985. *The Musical Mind: The Cognitive Psychology of Music*. Oxford University Press.

Small, Christopher. 1998. *Musiking: The Meanings of Performance and Listening*. Wesleyan University Press.

Smith, Julie Dawn. (2004) "Playing Like a Girl: The Queer Laughter of the Feminist Improvising Group." In *The Other Side of Nowhere: Jazz, Improvisation, and Communities in Dialog*, ed. by Daniel Fischlin and Ajay Heble. Wesleyan University Press.

Smith, Leo. 1973. *Notes (8 Pieces) Source a New World Music: Creative Music*. self published.

Snow, C.P. 1993. *The Two Cultures*. Cambridge University Press.

Solothurnmann, Jürg. 1985. Interview with John Zorn. *Cadence* 5(4):8–11.

Song, Chaoming, Shlomo Havlin, and Hernan A. Makse. 2005. "Self-similarity of Complex Networks." *Nature* 433:392–395.

Spellman, A.B. 1966. *Black Music: Four Lives*. Shocken Books.

Stanyek, Jason. 1999. "Articulating Intercultural Improvisation." *Resonance* 7/2.

Steinitz, Richard. 1996. "Music, Maths, & Chaos." *The Musical Times* (March):14–20.

Stockdale, Jonty. 2004. "Reading Around Free Improvisation." *The Source: Challenging Jazz Criticism* 1:101–114.

Strogatz, Steve. 2003: *Sync: The Emerging Science of Spontaneous Order*. Hyperion.

Such, David. 1993. *Avant-Garde Musicians Performing 'Out There.'* University of Iowa Press.

Sudnow, David. 1978. *Ways of the Hand: The Organization of Improvised Conduct*. Harvard University Press.

Sudo, Philip Toshio. 1997. *Zen Guitar*. Simon and Schuster.

Sweet, Robert E. 1996. *Music Universe, Music Mind: Revisiting the Creative Music Studio, Woodstock, New York*. Arborville Publishing.

Surowiecki, James. 2004. *The Wisdom of Crowds*. Doubleday.

Svirchez, Laurence M. 1993. "Evan Parker: An Intensity of Purpose." *Coda* 250:4–7.

Taylor, Arthur. 1993 [1977]. *Notes and Tones: Musician-to-Musician Interviews*. Da Capo.

Taylor, Mark C. 2003. *The Moment of Complexity*. University of Chicago Press.

Taylor, R.P., A.P. Micoloch, and D. Jonas. 2000. "Investigating Jackson Pollock's Drip Paintings." *Journal of Consciousness Studies* 7(8/9):137–150.

Thelen, Esther. 2003. "Grounded in the World: Developmental Origins of the Embodied Mind." In *The Dynamical Systems Approach to Cognition,* ed. by Wolfgang Tschacher and Jean-Pierre Dauwalder. *Studies in Nonlinear Phenomena in Life Sciences* 10 (World Scientific Press).

Thom, René. 1989. *Structural Stability and Morphogenesis: An Outline of a Genereal Theory of Models*. Addison-Wesley.

Tisue, Seth. 1995. Transcription of a radio interview with Evan Parker, WNUR Chicago, 14 November. www.shef.ac.uk/misc/rec/ps/efi/ehome.

Tomlinson, Gary. 1991. "Cultural Dialogics and Jazz: A White Historian Signifies," *Black Music Research Journal* 11(2):229–264.

Toop, David. 2002. "Frame of Freedom: Improvisation, Otherness and the Limits of Spontaneity." In *Undercurrents: The Hidden Wiring of Modern Music*. Continuum.

Truax, Barry. 1986. "The Listener." *Musicworks* 35:13–16.

Tucker, Sherrie. 2003. "Big Ears: Listening for Gender in Jazz Studies." *Current Musicology* 71–73, 375–408.

Tucker, Sherrie. 2004. "Bordering on Community: Improvising Women Improvising Women-in-Jazz." In *The Other Side of Nowhere: Jazz, Improvisation, and Communities in Dialog*, ed. by Daniel Fischlin and Ajay Heble. Wesleyan University Press.

Turner, Marcus. 1982. "Sam Rivers." *Coda* 185:4–6.

Turner, Mark. 1996. *The Literary Mind*. Oxford University Press.

Tynan, John. 1961. "Take Five." *Downbeat* (November 23):40.

Varela, Francisco J. 1979. *Principles of Biological Autonomy*. Elsevier (North Holland).

Varela, Francisco J., Evan Thompson, and Eleanor Rosch. 1991. *The Embodied Mind: Cognitive Science and Human Experience*. MIT Press.

Von Forester, Heinz. 1981. *Observing Systems*, 2nd ed.. Intersystems Publications.

Vygotsky, Lev. 1978. *Mind in Society*. Harvard University Press.

Vygotsky, Lev. 1997. *Educational Psychology*. St. Lucie Press.

Waldrop, Michael M. 1992. *Complexity: The Emerging Science at the Edge of Order and Chaos*. Simon and Schuster.

Wallin, Nils. 1992. *Biomusicology*. Pendragon.

Walser, Robert. 1991. "The Body in the Music." *College Music Symposium* 31:117–25.

Walser, Robert. 1995 "'Out of Notes': Signification, Interpretation, and the Problem of Miles Davis," In *Jazz Among the Discourses*, ed. by Krin Gabbard. Duke University Press.

Walser, Robert. 1999. *Keeping Time: Readings in Jazz History*. Oxford University Press.

REFERENCES

Waterman, Christopher. 1990. *Juju: A Social History and Ethnography of African Popular Music*. University of Chicago Press.

Watson, Ben. 2004. *Derek Bailey and the Story of Free Improvisation*. Verso.

Watts, Duncan. 2003. *Six Degrees: The Science of a Connected Age*. W.W. Norton & Co.

Weeks, Peter. 1996. "Synchrony Lost, Synchrony Regained: The Achievement of Musical Coordination." *Human Studies* 19:199–228.

Welding, Pete, and John Tynan. 1962. "Double View of a Double Quartet." *Downbeat* (January 18):28.

Weick, Karl. 1998. "Improvisation as a Mindset for Organizational Analysis." *Organization Science* 9(5):543–555.

Weiner, Norbert. 1961. *Cybernetics*. MIT Press.

Werner. Kenny. 1996. *Effortless Mastery: Liberating the Master Musician Within*. Jamey Aebersold.

Westendorf, Lynette. 1994. "Analyzing Free Jazz." D.M.A. Diss., University of Washington.

Whitaker, Randall. 1996. "Introductory Tutorial: Autopoiesis & Enaction." www.informatik.umu .se/~rwhit/AT.

Williams, Davey. 1984. "Towards a Philosophy of Improvisation." *The Improvisor* 4:32–34.

Wilmer, Valerie. 1977. *As Serious as Your Life: The Story of the New Jazz*. Allison and Busby.

Winograd, Terry, and Fernando Flores. 1986. "Cognition as a Biological Phenomenon." In *Understanding Computers and Cognition: A New Foundation for Design*. Addison-Wesley Publishing Co., Inc.

Wright, Robert. 2001. *Nonzero: The Logic of Human Destiny*. Vintage Books.

Zack, Michael. 2000. "Jazz Improvisation and Organizing: Once More from the Top." *Organization Science* 11(2):227–234.

Zbikowski, Lawrence. 1998. "Metaphor and Music Theory: Perspectives from Cognitive Science," *Music Theory Online* 4/1.

Zbikowski, Lawrence. 2002. *Conceptualizing Music: Cognitive Structure, Theory, and Analysis*. Oxford University Press.

Zorn, John, ed. 2000. *Arcana: Musicians on Music*. Granary Books.

INDEX